# PSYCHOANALYSIS AND PERFORMANCE

The field of literar⸺ ⸺lysis as a method for lookin⸺ ⸺between psychoanalysis an⸺ ⸺ysing the nature of perform⸺ ⸺ormance-related activities.

In this volume ⸺ ⸺nake this exciting new conn⸺ ⸺of topics, including:

- hypnotism an⸺
- ventriloquism⸺
- dance and sub⸺
- the unconscio⸺
- melancholia a⸺
- cloning and th⸺
- censorship an⸺
- theatre and s⸺

The arguments ad⸺ ⸺oanalysis can provide a pro⸺ ⸺ormance, and that performa⸺ ⸺ity.

Contributors: Lisa⸺ ⸺nor, Elin Diamond, Ernst⸺ ⸺Timothy Murray, Ann Pell⸺ ⸺regory L. Ulmer.

**Patrick Campbell** is Academic Chair of Performing Arts at Middlesex University.

**Adrian Kear** is Senior Lecturer in Drama and Theatre Studies at the University of Surrey Roehampton.

# PSYCHOANALYSIS AND PERFORMANCE

Edited by
*Patrick Campbell and Adrian Kear*

London and New York

First published 2001
by Routledge
11 New Fetter Lane, London EC4P 4EE

Simultaneously published in the USA and Canada
by Routledge
29 West 35th Street, New York, NY 10001

*Routledge is an imprint of the Taylor & Francis Group*

Typeset in Baskerville by
BOOK NOW Ltd
Printed and bound in Great Britain by
Biddles Ltd, Guildford and King's Lynn

*British Library Cataloguing in Publication Data*
A catalogue record for this book is available from the British Library

*Library of Congress Cataloging-in-Publication Data*
Psychoanalysis and performance / [edited by] Patrick Campbell and Adrian Kear.
p. cm.
Includes bibliographical references and index.
1. Performing arts–Psychological aspects. I. Campbell, Patrick, 1935– II. Kear,
Adrian, 1970–
PN1590.P76 P77 2001
791'.01'9–dc21      00-054289

ISBN 0 415 21204 9 (hbk)
ISBN 0 415 21205 7 (pbk)

# CONTENTS

# ILLUSTRATIONS

# CONTRIBUTORS

**Lisa Baraitser** and **Simon Bayly** co-direct the London-based company, Theatre PUR. Their work has been staged at a number of British venues, including The Young Vic Studio and The Tramway, Glasgow. Lisa is also a practising psychotherapist and Simon combines his theatre work with academic research.

**Herbert Blau** is Byron and Alice Lockwood Professor in the Humanities at the University of Washington, Seattle. He has also had a distinguished career in the professional theatre, as co-founder and co-director of The Actor's Workshop of San Francisco, then co-director of the Repertory Theater of Lincoln Center in New York, and as artistic director of the experimental group KRAKEN, the groundwork for which was prepared at California Institute of the Arts, where he was founding Provost, and Dean of the School of Theater and Dance. Among his books are *The Audience* (Johns Hopkins University Press, 1990), *To All Appearances: Ideology and Performance* (Routledge, 1992) and, most recently, *Nothing in Itself: Complexions of Fashion* (Indiana University Press, 1999). He has also completed the forthcoming *Sails of the Herring Fleet: Essays on Beckett*.

**Patrick Campbell** runs the MA in Performing Arts at Middlesex University and has been Visiting Professor at the Universities of British Columbia and Colorado. His books include *Wordsworth and Coleridge: Lyrical Ballads* (Macmillan, 1991), *Siegfried Sassoon: A Study of the War Poetry* (McFarland, 1999) and the edited collections of commissioned essays *Analysing Performance* (Manchester University Press, 1996) and *The Body in Performance* (Harwood, 2000).

**Steven Connor** is Professor of Modern Literature and Theory at Birkbeck College, London. He has published books on Dickens, Beckett, Joyce and the postwar novel, as well as *Postmodernist Culture: An Introduction to Theories of the Contemporary* (Blackwell, 1989, 1996), *Theory and Cultural Value* (Blackwell, 1992) and *Dumbstruck: A Cultural History of Ventriloquism* (Oxford University Press, 2000).

**Elin Diamond** is Professor of English at Rutgers University. She is the author of *Unmaking Mimesis: Essays on Feminism and Theater* (Routledge, 1997) and *Pinter's Comic Play* (Bucknell, 1985), and editor of *Performance and Cultural Politics* (Routledge, 1996). Her essays on performance and feminist theory have appeared in

*Theatre Journal, ELH, Discourse, TDR, Modern Drama, Kenyon Review, Cahiers Renaud-Barrault, Art and Cinema, Maska*, and in numerous anthologies in the USA, Europe and India.

**Ernst Fischer** is a performance artist living and working in London. He has won recognition as a queer performer and in particular for his creation of 'Living-room Theatre'. Ernst holds degrees from Middlesex University and the University of London and is completing a Ph.D. at the University of Surrey Roehampton. He currently teaches at the universities of North London and Middlesex.

**Adrian Kear** lectures in Drama and Theatre Studies at the University of Surrey Roehampton. He is the author of several articles investigating the relationship between critical theory, cultural politics, performance and ethics. He is the co-editor, with Deborah Lynn Steinberg, of *Mourning Diana: Nation, Culture, and the Performance of Grief* (Routledge, 1999) and a contributor to the academic journals *Contemporary Theatre Review, Performance Research* and *JPCS: Journal for the Psycho-analysis of Culture and Society*. He is currently working on a book entitled *Making Time: Theatre, Temporality and the Ethics of Performance*.

**Joe Kelleher** lectures in Drama and Theatre Studies at the University of Surrey Roehampton. He is the author of a monograph, *Tony Harrison* (Northcote House, 1997), and recent essays on children in film, and on writing, rhetoric and con-temporary performance. His texts for the theatre include *The Wolfman, Mrs Freud and Mrs Jung* and *The Clouded Eye*. He is a member of the London-based company, Theatre PUR.

**Anthony Kubiak** is Associate Professor of English at the University of South Florida in Tampa. He is the author of *Stages of Terror: Terrorism, Ideology, and Coercion as Theatre History* (Indiana University Press, 1991). His articles have appeared in *TDR, Theatre Journal, Modern Drama, Journal of Dramatic Theory and Criticism, Comparative Drama*, and in the series *Psychiatry and the Humanities*.

**Timothy Murray** is Professor of English and Director of Graduate Studies in Film and Video at Cornell University. His books include *Theatrical Legitimation: Allegories of Genius in Seventeenth-Century England and France* (Oxford, 1987), *Like a Film: Ideological Fantasy on Screen, Camera, and Canvas* (Routledge, 1993) and *Drama Trauma: Specters of Race and Sexuality in Performance, Video, and Art* (Routledge, 1997). He has also edited *Mimesis, Masochism, and Mime: The Politics of Theatricality in Contemporary French Thought* (Michigan University Press, 1997) and has curated an international exhibition, *Contact Zones: The Art of CD-Rom*, which can be accessed at http://contactzones.cit.cornell.edu. His book, *Baroque Interface: Electronic Art, Utopic Vision, and Cultural Memory*, is forthcoming from Minnesota University Press.

**Ann Pellegrini** is Associate Professor of Women's Studies at Barnard College, Columbia University. She is the author of *Performance Anxieties: Staging Psycho-analysis, Staging Race* (Routledge, 1997). With Janet Jakobsen she is co-author of a forthcoming book on religion and sexual regulation in American public life.

**Alan Read** is Professor and Chair of Drama and Theatre Studies at the University of Surrey Roehampton, and was formerly Director of Talks at the ICA in London. His books include *Theatre and Everyday Life: An Ethics of Performance* (Routledge, 1993) and the collections *The Fact of Blackness: Frantz Fanon and Visual Representation* (Bay Press, 1996) and *Architecturally Speaking: Practices of Art, Architecture and the Everyday* (Routledge, 2000). He is a contributing editor to the journal *Performance Research*, recently compiling a special issue 'On Animals', and is currently working on a book entitled, *A Natural History of Performance: Actors, Animals and Other Anomalies*.

**Rebecca Schneider** is Assistant Professor of Theater and Performance Studies with Cornell University's Department of Theater, Film and Dance. She is the author of *The Explicit Body in Performance* (Routledge, 1997) and is working on a second book titled *Playing Remains*. She is also co-editing an anthology forthcoming from Routledge, entitled *Directing Reconsidered: Essays on Twentieth Century Theatre*. Schneider has published essays in several anthologies, including *Acting Out: Feminist Performances* and *Performance and Cultural Politics*. She has essays forthcoming in *Embodied Pedagogy* and *TDR*, to which she is contributing editor.

**Diana Taylor** is Professor and Chair of Performance Studies at NYU. She is the author of *Theatre of Crisis: Drama and Politics in Latin America* (University Press of Kentucky, 1991), and of *Disappearing Acts: Spectacles of Gender and Nationalism in Argentina's 'Dirty War'* (Duke University Press, 1997). She is the co-editor of *Negotiating Performance in Latin/o America: Gender, Sexuality and Theatricality* (Duke University Press, 1994) and *The Politics of Motherhood: Activists from Left to Right* (University Press of New England, 1996). Professor Taylor has also edited three volumes of critical essays on Latin American, Latino and Spanish playwrights. Her work on Latin American and Latino performance have appeared in *TDR*, *Performing Arts Journal, Latin American Theatre Review, Estreno, Gestos* and other scholarly journals. She has also participated in staging Latin American and Latino theatre in Mexico and the United States.

**Gregory L. Ulmer**, Professor of English and Media Studies at the University of Florida, is the author of *Heuretics: The Logic of Invention* (Johns Hopkins University Press, 1994); *Teletheory: Grammatology in the Age of Video* (Routledge, 1989); *Applied Grammatology: Post(e)-Pedagogy from Jacques Derrida to Joseph Beuys* (Johns Hopkins University Press, 1985). In addition to two other monographs and a textbook for writing about literature, Ulmer has authored some 50 articles and chapters exploring the shift in the apparatus of language from literacy to electracy. His current projects include two book-length studies: *Choragraphy: from Literacy to Electracy*, and *Miami/Miautre: An Experiment in Choragraphy* (co-authored with the Florida Research Ensemble).

# ACKNOWLEDGEMENTS

The editors would like to record their indebtedness to a number of people who have given generously of their time and expertise during the production of this book. First and foremost, we would like to pay tribute to the contributors to this collection, without whose hard work, thoughtfulness, patience and good humour it would not have come to fruition. We also want to acknowledge the palpable if unseen influence of those colleagues and students who enthusiastically endorsed the idea for a book about the links between psychoanalysis and performance. In this connection, especial thanks are due to Helen Spackman and Joe Kelleher, who were amongst the first to identify the need for a collection of essays of this topic; to Talia Rodgers and Rosie Waters at Routledge for having faith in the project; and to Nancy Jenkins, and the extended family of friends who supported our endeavours throughout. Finally, we would like to express our gratitude to our respective institutions, Middlesex University and the University of Surrey Roehampton, for their support.

# PREFACE

## The returns of psychoanalysis, and performance

*Adrian Kear*

> I am working on the assumption that our psychic mechanism has come into being by a process of stratification: the material present in the form of memory traces being subjected from time to time to a *rearrangement* in accordance with fresh circumstances – to a *retranscription*. Thus what is essentially new about my theory is the thesis that memory is not present once but several times over, that it is laid down in various kinds of indications.
>
> Freud, Letter to Fliess, 6 December 1896[1]

In his book, *The Return of the Real* (1996), Hal Foster draws attention to the critical possibilities made available by positing the psychic processes of 'rearrangement' and 'retranscription' as material social practices. By insisting on the productivity of linking '*turns* in critical models' with '*returns* of historical practices', Foster attempts to demonstrate how 'a reconnection with a past practice' might 'support a disconnection from a present practice and/or a development of a new one'.[2] For example, he locates in Lacan's famous 'return to Freud' the desire to perform a rigorous rereading of the foundational texts of psychoanalysis that not only seeks to 'restore the radical integrity of the discourse but to challenge its status in the present, the received ideas that deform its structure and restrict its efficacy'. This, he argues, is a 'contingent strategy' which '*re*connect[s] with a lost practice in order to *dis*connect from a present way of working felt to be outmoded, misguided, or otherwise oppressive'.[3] In this respect, the key to Lacan's endeavour is the identification of an implicit connection between Freudian theory and structural linguistics, a connection unavailable to Freud but crucial to the renewal of psychoanalysis as a paradigm. By introducing one field of critical inquiry to another, by explicitly staging the implicit dialogue between them, Lacan is able to effect a 'retranscription' of psychoanalytic discourse.

The more modest project of this book is to deploy a similarly contingent strategy in exploring a range of connections between psychoanalysis and performance, both as concrete historical practices and as conceptual modes of enquiry. Its aim is both to bear witness to their generative interpenetration and to open up new spaces of exchange between them. Hence, the book is not primarily concerned with the psychoanalytical study of performance; rather, it seeks to situate performance and psychoanalysis within a dialogical framework that speaks to the affiliations and correspondences between the two fields. The methodological moves it makes to bring about this encounter are multiple: from returning performance to its proper place within the psychoanalytic scene, to tracing the psychodynamics of the rehearsal process, to foregrounding the political and ethical imperatives embedded within psychic and social performatives. In the process, it offers 'various kinds of indications' as to the current and future configuration of the historical palimpsest that constitutes these relations. As such, *Psychoanalysis and Performance* is not intended to be the definitive statement on its subject; rather, it seeks to provide the occasion and opportunity for its contributors to outline the 'complex relay of anticipated futures and reconstructed pasts'[4] that performance studies can currently envision in the discourse of psychoanalysis.

The book comprises a series of original, commissioned essays by authors with some of the most distinctive critical voices in the discipline. Each one attempts to articulate and address problematics and thematics made available by linking together psychoanalysis and performance, and each author stages their own points of departure and arrival accordingly. They are, of course, in dialogue with one another; but, taken together, they can be seen to chart a course – however hazardous – that is flagged by the section headings. These suggest the essays take the reader from thinking through psychoanalysis's relationship with rehearsal process and theatre practice, to considering its social and political connection to parallel modes of performance, to investigating the insights into the effects of historical trauma produced by remotivating psychoanalysis in the service of materialist cultural critique. That this route is contested and contradictory virtually goes without saying; but it is none-theless important to locate the concerns of this collection firmly in the explication of the ideological and affective bonds through which performance and psychoanalysis speak.

Although *Psychoanalysis and Performance* advances no presumptuously 'curative interpretations',[5] it nonetheless marks a terminal moment for an otherwise interminable analysis. It is our hope that in drawing a line under certain topics of discussion, this volume will prove to be productive of a variety of new ones. By simultaneously reconnecting and disconnecting the terms in the title, by effecting their 'rearrangement', so to speak, we trust that *Psychoanalysis and Performance* will contribute to the current renewal and future development of performance studies as a critical practice.

## Notes

1 Sigmund Freud, *The Origins of Psycho-Analysis: Letters to Wilhelm Fliess, Drafts and Notes 1887–1902*, ed. Marie Bonaparte, Anna Freud and Ernst Kris, trans. E. Mosbacher and J. Strachey, New York: Basic Books, 1954: 173.

2  Hal Foster, *The Return of the Real: The Avant-Garde at the End of the Century*, Cambridge, MA: MIT Press, 1996: x.
3  Foster, *The Return of the Real*, 2–3.
4  Foster, *The Return of the Real*, 29.
5  Peggy Phelan, 'Introduction: The Ends of Performance', in Peggy Phelan and Jill Lane, eds, *The Ends of Performance*, New York: New York University Press, 1998: 7.

# INTRODUCTION

*Patrick Campbell*

## Umbilical connections

When Susan Sontag delivered her broadside *Against Interpretation*, she singled out for opprobrium what she called the 'most celebrated and influential modern doctrines, those of Marx and Freud', adding that they 'actually amount to elaborate systems of hermeneutics, aggressive and impious theories of interpretation'.[1] While her fire was primarily directed against such tyrannical and tunnel-visioned strategies, 'a philistine refusal to leave the work of art alone',[2] it has to be said that psychoanalytic approaches, judiciously applied, had already begun to expand the parameter of art criticism in fruitful directions: the belief in a 'latent' content which reveals the workings of a textual or authorial unconscious; the attention to personal motives and drives, especially sexual ones, whether of author, character or recipient; the identification of a psychic as well as a social content for the art work; the artistic implication of neurotic, fetishistic impulses or the process of sublimation; the mechanisms of the Oedipal economy of desire and its impact on textuality; the centrality of dream and its attendant processes of symbolisation.

But if these now seem to map out well-reconnoitred territory, the connections between psychoanalysis and *performance* have rarely been considered in a systematic way, either in terms of analysing the nature of performance itself, or in terms of making sense of specific performance-related activities. Indeed, the two fields seem to possess a particular affiliation that goes beyond the strict application of a hermeneutic theory. Rather than simply providing further grist to the mill of psychoanalytic interpretation, performance constitutes an activity that both resembles and resists its procedures. As Shoshana Felman has observed of the relationship between literature and psychoanalysis, the two fields appear to imply and mutually depend upon one another for their analytic coherence.[3] After all, if performing is a process in which individuals, physically present on stage, think, speak and interact in front of other individuals, then that very activity must throw into relief crucial questions about human behaviour. In making the hidden visible, the latent manifest, in laying bare the interior landscape of the mind and its fears and desires through a range of signifying practices, psychoanalytic processes are endemic to the performing arts. Similarly, the logic of performance infuses psychoanalytic thinking, from the 'acting out' of hysteria to the 'family romance' of desire.

1

Many of these connections had been duly noted by Freud in his essay 'Psycho-pathic Characters on the Stage'[4] (1905–6), in which he considers spectatorial reaction to a range of traditional theatrical experiences. The dramatist's avowed function in what Freud calls 'religious' or 'social' drama is to allow the spectator 'to take the side of the rebel'; to enter into a collusive pact, along with the playwright, with the character(s) on stage. So too with 'psychological drama', the drama of 'character', where we can identify with the struggle 'between different impulses in the hero's mind' that inevitably lead to the suppression of one of these impulses in an act of renunciation. But, as Freud counsels us, 'the series of possibilities grows wider' when the impulses involved are both conscious and repressed. In this kind of theatrical encounter the spectator needs to be neurotic in order to enjoy it: someone able to derive pleasure rather than aversion from the revelatory nature of the repressed material.[5] According to Freud, if this staged struggle is too threatening, the average spectator's defences will inhibit the play of empathy and the generation of cathartic feelings linked to unconscious desire. So it is incumbent on the dramatist artfully to lower the spectators' resistance to the repressed material by 'diverting' them and thus enabling them to enter into the neurosis of the stage figure. The dramatist thereby creates a neurotic space where the spectators may 'live out their conflicts and even gain "masochistic" satisfaction in identifying with the hero's defeat'.[6] Such 'psychopathological drama' (again Freud's own term) reveals, in embryo, a spectator theory that would be articulated by post-structuralism.

Amongst the most significant contributions to the development of this theory is André Green's formulation of the dynamics of 'the tragic effect'. Whilst cautioning against both a reductive conflation of author and artwork and an over-generalisation of psychoanalytic interpretative strategies, Green 'recognizes in all the products of mankind [sic] the traces of the conflicts of the unconscious'.[7] He specifically charac-terises performance as occupying a 'transitional position' in mediating between the individual and the social, making possible the 'displacements of sublimation' that commute neurosis into theatrical pleasure. The 'sentient, corporeal space' of performance constitutes a world of objects 'that both are and are not what they represent' for the spectator, setting into play 'the inevitable disguising and indirect unveiling' that the fantasy structure of the work undertakes. Rather than simply 'exposing the unconscious in all its starkness', tragic performance, Green argues, breaks the action of repression by a parallel set of substitutions, allowing an 'inhibited and displaced *jouissance*' to emerge through this metonymy.[8] For Green, as for Freud, performance contributes to the 'assuaging of unsatisfied or unsatisfiable desires' by providing a 'yield of pleasure' from 'deeper psychical sources' – a 'partial discharge' emanating from the commerce between revelation and the threat of further repression.[9]

In so-called extreme art, where this threat is not diverted – and here one recalls a transgressive performance tradition embracing work as diverse as Viennese Aktionism and the contemporary 'body art' of Stelarc, Ron Athey or Franko B. – the process is an altogether more unsettling one. In formulaic Freudian terms, the bloody rituals and visceral events of Hermann Nitsch's work, for instance, may be construed as an attempt to unsettle the psyche, to break down the divide between super-ego and id, between socially and culturally imposed patterns of behaviour and the drives of the libido. But as Gunther Berghaus reminds us, 'unveiling the psychic condition of the human race' in this way often has wider ramifications: in the case of the Aktionists, it led to 'permanent conflict with the representatives of state power'.[10] Lest this be seen as an isolated example, one should remember, as Ann Pellegrini's essay in this volume exhorts us to do, that 1998 witnessed an outburst of hegemonic repression against American 'transgressors' which showed the extent of conservative resistance to the performance of identities outside the male heterosexual mainstream, and a court ruling which resulted in Karen Finley's, Tim Miller's, John Fleck's and Holly Hughes' spirited but ultimately losing battle against the United States judiciary.

It is to Freud that we owe the elucidation of these mechanisms of displacement, substitution and repression – mechanisms that monitor subjectivity in accordance with the mechanisms of socio-political restraint. In *Totem and Taboo* (1912–13), he argued that such prohibition must be thought of as the result of 'an emotional ambivalence': whenever there is prohibition, it must have been motivated by an unconfessed, unconscious desire or longing.[11] Following Freud's logic, if the function of art, and especially dramatic art is to express what is hidden behind the wall, then it is hardly a matter for surprise that prohibition, in the form of censorship, has dogged the pratfalls of exorbitant performers throughout the recent history of Western civilisation. Freud's essay on *The Ego and the Id* (1923) also has implications, albeit couched in very different terms, for censor-mongering of a peculiarly vindictive kind: 'From the point of view of instinctual control, of morality, it may be said of the id that it is totally non-moral, of the ego that it strives to be moral, and of the super-ego that it can be super-moral, and then becomes cruel as only the id can be'.[12]

Of course, staged activities not only provide a link with quotidian life, but also with the cloistered environment of the consulting room. As Alan Read's essay reminds us, the psychoanalytic cure was at first based on Aristotelian catharsis whereby the revelations of the analysand's past might prompt the therapeutic release of buried feeling and discharge of emotion known as abreaction, just as a spectator's experience of tragic drama might generate emotions of pity and fear. Subsequently, Freud replaced this procedure with the concept of transference. No longer seeing it as a phenomenon of dubious worth, Freud concluded that finally every conflict has to be fought out in the sphere of transference: 'Transference, which seems ordained to be the greatest obstacle to psychoanalysis, becomes its most powerful ally, if its presence can be detected each time and explained to the patient'.[13] Thus, in the talking cure, the consulting room becomes a theatre in which the patient may be given the opportunity to revisit past conflicts, 'transferring' those repressed feelings for parent or sibling on to the supposedly detached figure of the analyst. In this process the notion of 'playing' or 'acting out' becomes crucial, since the analyst is required to assume a role and to 'play it badly so that the patient may be freed from the compulsion to repeat the script of childhood'.[14] As Freud put it: 'the patient does not *remember* anything of what he has forgotten or repressed, but *acts* it out . . . He *repeats* it, without . . . knowing he is repeating it'.[15] Such an idea is given a specifically performance-related resonance by Lisa Baraitser and Simon Bayly who see, in the disclosures of the rehearsal process, a nexus with the play of psychotherapy.

It is a truism that the interpretation of dreams was a cornerstone both of Freud's clinical practice and psychoanalytic theorising, providing the so-called 'royal road to the unconscious'. In this regard, Jacques Lacan was at one with his distinguished predecessor in not only reaffirming that dreams and their symptoms employ the figurative tropes of condensation and displacement, but that these processes correspond to metaphoric selection and metonymic combination (identified by Roman Jacobson as the twin axes of poetic language). Such concepts are helpful in understanding any artistic activity – including text-based theatre – that involves the deployment of words in the act of creation. Indeed, in 'Creative Writers and Day-Dreaming' (1907–8), Freud likened the imaginative artist to a daydreamer, maintaining that 'the writer softens the character of his egoistic day-dreams by altering or disguising it and bribes us by the purely formal – that is aesthetic – yield of pleasure which he offers us in the presentation of his fantasies'.[16] Freud also held the belief that not only can dreams be likened to drama, but that dramatisation is in fact the primary activity in dreaming. It follows then that if dreams resemble drama, drama too can partake of the stuff of dreams. While the theatre may mirror the world of external appearances, it may also, in Maud Ellman's words 'give external form to the internal dramaturgy of the mind, where anything may be involved and brought to life'. By this definition of theatre, the spectatorial process is one both of decoding, however haltingly, what is being staged, but also of reaching down into the unknown, of getting involved in the interpretive business of 'dreamwork'. If the techniques of dramatisation are 'designed to hide us from ourselves', then the role of the watcher is to 'discern the words encoded in the pictographic script of dreams'.[17]

Not that it is always that simple or straightforward. Dreams, as we know, operate by yoking together apparently disparate images in order to create a new reality: what the Comte de Lautréamont famously described as 'the possibility of a sewing-machine and an umbrella meeting on a dissecting table'.[18] But while such dreams, like most traditional drama, exist in what Michael Kirby has called a matrix (an information structure), much of the creativeness of avant-garde work – for example 'many Dada, Surrealist, and Expressionist plays' (and similarly Absurd plays and Happenings) – stems from the fact that the work partakes of the distortions, the irrationality, the associative nature of dream. It becomes difficult to understand precisely at that point where, like the umbilical 'knot' in the 'meshwork' of the dream's structure (Freud's famous 'navel'), it resists interpretation as it 'reaches down into the unknown'.[19]

André Green has suggested that in such instances of 'unreadability', psycho-analytic criticism should endeavour

> to show the double articulation of the theatrical fantasy: that of the scene, which takes place on the stage, and is given ostensible significance for the

4

spectator; and that of the other scene that takes place – although everything is said aloud and intelligibly and takes place in full view – unknown to the spectator, by means of this chain-like mode of unconscious logic.[20]

For Green, as for Freud, the fantasy structure that performance or, more particularly, *tragic* performance, articulates, is the foundational fantasy of the Oedipus complex. Everything stems from and returns to here, effectively confirming Deleuze and Guattari's insistence that 'Oedipus is always and solely an aggregate of destination fabricated to meet the requirements of an aggregate of departure constituted by a social formation'.[21]

Freud famously ushered in his theory in *The Interpretation of Dreams* with his analysis of Sophocles' play, adding that King Oedipus's destiny is so crucial 'only because it might have been ours – because the oracle laid the same curse upon us before our birth as upon him. It is the fate of all of us, perhaps, to direct our first sexual impulse towards our mother and our first hatred and our first murderous wish against our father. Our dreams convince us that this is so.'[22] Freud believed, moreover, that the revelatory action of *Oedipus Rex* – a causal process of inexorable revelation, with cunning delays and ever-mounting excitement – was a process that could 'be likened to the work of psychoanalysis'.[23] Its narrative seems to follow the same trajectory as that of psychoanalytic interpretation, such that 'Oedipus's desire is the desire to know the last word on desire'.[24]

Jacques Lacan has also written influentially on *Oedipus* as well as on *Hamlet* and *Antigone*. In his discussion of *Oedipus*, Lacan opens up, as one would expect, an avowedly linguistic perspective, by arguing that complicity between the laws of kinship and laws of language accounts for the hero's fall. That incest rather than murder is what torments Oedipus is a consequence of sinning against the symbolic, against the name – the name of brother (to his children); of love (to his mother), of father (to his siblings). But at least Oedipus atones by acting; for Hamlet, the sins of the father visited upon the son so haunt him that he lacks any defining sense of self. Hamlet's drama, for Lacan, is 'the drama of Hamlet as the man who has lost the way of his desire'.[25]

Herbert Blau, a distinguished presence in this book, talks elsewhere about 'our Oedipal Drama'[26] – a phrase which powerfully iterates a point, already adumbrated here, namely that theatre, like life, is involved in the Freudian notions of identity, repression and familial bonding, notions given fuller articulation in the Lacanian concepts of misrecognition and desire. The specifically ideological aspects of this 'Oedipal Drama' are explored by Gilles Deleuze and Felix Guattari who see us as products of political forces such as capitalism and the authoritarian state, structures to which theatre, and especially commercial theatre, is inevitably wedded. Thus theatrical discourse is the language of the master, the dramatist an authority figure who supervises operations after the manner of a super-ego. The protagonists – and here one recalls Augusto Boal's jaundiced vision of a 'classist' Greek tragedy where the ordinary people have merely choric roles – duplicate societal hierarchies in their decision-making and their control over the lesser characters or the voiceless Others.

## Beyond blind Oedipus

*Psychoanalysis and Performance* seeks to further the investigation of these links and connections and to offer new – often unexpected – ones, examining not only the relationship between the terms in its title but their extension into the social, political and ideological domain. For, as post-structuralist or feminist psychoanalytic theory is keen to tell us, things have moved on since Freud. In raising our consciousness in terms of artistic and critical practice, recent theory has challenged the very nature of performance and created an uneasy bedfellow – performativity. In focusing on the body, it has, in the wake of Brecht and Artaud, created a notion of performance which has problematised the author's voice, the authority of the text, the charisma of the star actor and 'of both the illusion of reality and the Brechtian challenge to that illusion'. From the Tantztheater of Pina Bausch to the explicit displays of 'live art', the performing body 'is no longer fitted into characterological representation as "intended" by the author'. 'Abandoning all notions of the individual', this kind of performance 'shows the theatricalised subject working through a variety of fantasies, with the spectator called upon to scatter her/his own identification from among a variety of subject positions'.[27]

In these debates, the single voice of Lacan and the collective voice of feminism(s) have dominated discussion. We have already seen that in asserting that symbolisation was central to dreams, Lacan both reiterated and enlarged on Freudian principles. In considering the unconscious, he went further. Not only structured like a language, it was also part of a subject identified by a chain of signifiers, a subject created by language who engages both with the self and the external world by operating first in the Imaginary and then in the Symbolic mode. Lacan's Imaginary is initially a blissful world inhabited by mother and child, only disrupted when the father intervenes. This 'Law of the Father' discourages child–mother incest, threatens castration in the Oedipal drama of the family, and ushers in the symbolic order, an order predicated not only on language, but on its avowal of separateness. For language has its roots in absence: 'the symbol manifests itself first of all in the murder of the thing and this death constitutes in the subject the eternalization of desire'.[28] Lacan sees in this 'melancholy awareness of separateness and lack' (and his name does not resist the play on words), the price that we pay for our sense of self. Such an idea is given a peculiarly dramatic resonance by Josette Féral who distinguishes between theatre – a linear, narrative and representational medium that inscribes the subject in the Symbolic, in 'theatrical codes' – and performance, which subverts these codes and competencies, allowing the subject's flows of desire to speak. In this kind of performance, the actor neither 'plays' in role nor 'represents' himself but is a source of 'production and displacement'.[29]

In connection with this issue, Julia Kristeva, a linguist turned practising psychoanalyst, conceived the subject very much in terms of a post-structuralist reworking of Bakhtin, Marx and Nietzsche as well as Freud. The subject, is, for her, both semiotic *and* symbolic: the symbolic, in line with Lacan, is the paternal order associated with rationality, fixity and closure; the semiotic is the rhythmic, energetic flow of forces linked to the pre-linguistic mother/child dyad. Kristeva suggested, *contra* Lacan, that the symbolic need not be dominant and that the semiotic drive was capable of disrupting the 'status quo', allowing the feminine to re-enter discourse through its very exorbitance, its transgressing of the phallogocentric signifying process. This overflowing of symbolic boundaries via semiotic emotions is, for Kristeva, given artistic expression in certain avant-garde texts – dramatic, musical, visual or auditory – which allow a more direct expression of the semiotic than is likely with conventionally structured art works. Kristeva's views also offer insights into subjectivity and performance, insights that have surfaced in many feminist projects of the last decade.

Many of these post-Freudian ideas have proved fecundating for a new wave of transgressive performers anxious to challenge empathetic responses, to disrupt the collusive bond between actor/character and spectator, and to stimulate dynamic interrelationships between watcher and watched. But they have also appealed to marginalised groups who have seen in the notion of the heterogeneous 'Other' – that part of the subject alienated from itself – a fruitful principle for exploration in performance. Feminists, post-colonialists, proponents of gay, lesbian and disabled politics have all recognised an identity which is 'Other' than that inscribed in hegemonic discourse – that is to say white, male, bourgeois, Western, heterosexual and dominant.

Perhaps unsurprisingly, Freud's own theories have, however, been less than passionately embraced by feminists, especially his contention that femininity has an essential connection with passivity, masochism and hysteria, and that penis envy – with its recognition of the phallus 'as the superior counterpart of their own small and inconspicuous organ'[30] – is a 'given' in the female psyche. Feminist psychoanalysts and critics have not been slow to highlight this phallocentricity – witness Hélène Cixous' dramatic adaptation of Freud's incomplete case-study, 'Dora', in which, by highlighting Freud's capacity for counter-transference, she consistently takes issue with what she sees as male authorial bias in the analyst's account. Similarly, feminist theatre criticism has asserted that the hegemony of 'realist theatre' has invariably produced a realism linked inexorably to a phallogocentric culture. The decentring of the subject – conventionally masculine – and the recognition that the feminine is not only 'Other' but objectified and gazed upon, is an area that has been explored elsewhere by a number of feminist theatre scholars, but is also a key problematic investigated further in *Psychoanalysis and Performance*.

Kristeva's related theory of the Abject has also proved instructive in reading the work of extreme body artists such as Orlan, Franko B. and Ron Athey. For to abject is to expel: such leakages of blood, faeces, urine, saliva and the rest not only confuse the 'inner' and 'outer' bodies but 'confound our sense of identify, system, order'. Furthermore they are a constant reminder of our own mortality. 'These body fluids, this defilement, this shit, are what life withstands . . . with difficulty on the part of death. There I am at the border of my condition as a living being. Such wastes drop so that I might live.' Only at the end is it 'no longer I who expel, "I" is expelled'.[31]

Such liminal blurrings of the distinction between art and life, now so much a feature of experimental performance, characterised the work of Antonin Artaud who argued with prescience that words were not only inadequate to capture the interior life, but that they conspired, along with the trappings of Western society to repress – and here the links with psychoanalytic theory are clear – what he saw as the real cruelty of existence. In fact, Artaud adopts a psychoanalytical stance in suggesting that if we confront our libidinous impulses, we can, if not be released from them, at least use them creatively. Such thinking underpins a number of essays in *Psychoanalysis and Performance*. But while Artaud sought to relegate mimesis from its established place in performance, recent debates have tended to concentrate not only on the nature and role of mimesis, but also on the question of *what* it actually imitates. Elin Diamond has observed: 'For feminist historians, philosophers and literary critics . . . Truth and the sameness that supports it cannot be understood as a neutral, omnipotent, changeless essence, embedded in eternal Nature, revealed by mimesis', adding, 'in all cases, the . . . universal standard for determining the true is the masculine, a metaphoric stand-in for God the Father'.[32]

Lacan, an implied presence here, also fuelled arguments about representation and subjectivity. For the staged subject is also 'Other' and not to be confused either with the actor's, author's or spectator's self. True, we may empathise and identify with these staged representations; we may experience catharsis. But to do so is to deny the benefits of distanciation, to deny what some recent commentators have remarked as a kind of double consciousness, a tension between the mimetic and the originary. Such discussions inevitably impinge on the Freudian notion of the 'uncanny', 'something which ought to have remained hidden but which recurs', for example, in 'apparent death and the re-animation of the dead'.[33] Such a concept underpins Ernst Fischer's reflections in *Psychoanalysis and Performance*, and finds further resonance within Rebecca Schneider's essay on the double in and out of the theatre. On the other hand, Richard Schechner, for example, has developed a different concept of double negativity: while the performer in a production is not her/himself because of the imperative to act, equally s/he is not not her/himself because personality and consciousness of self intrude, despite attempts to suppress the signals. Similarly, the spectator's psyche operates in a world of potential double consciousness, a world in which – to use Arthur Miller's phrase – there is a 'mobile concurrency' of our empathising and reflective selves. Michael Quinn makes a related point in suggesting that knowledge of an actor's actual life may further undermine the mimetic process by triggering associations between actor and spectator that have nothing to do with her/his dramatis persona.[34]

Peggy Phelan has given such discussions of the duality of acting and performance a markedly psychoanalytic inflection by invoking Lacan's distinction between metaphor and metonymy to assist in the analysis of what takes place during performance. In her well-rehearsed reading of 'the ontology of performance', she argues that 'performance uses the performer's body to pose a question about the inability to secure the relation between subjectivity and the body *per se*', adding that by 'employing the body metonymically, performance is capable of resisting the reproduction of metaphor' – and 'the metaphor of gender' in particular. By offering an alternative dramaturgy of misrecognition, displacement, loss and pain, the performance spectacle (and the spectacle of performance art especially), functions for the spectator as 'a projection of the scenario in which her desire takes place'. In the harshest of instances, those of 'hardship' or 'ordeal' art, the body of the performer is situated 'as a metonymy for the apparently nonreciprocal experience of pain' which invites the audience 'to do the impossible' and witness the intrusion of death into the presence of the 'live'.[35]

Herbert Blau's essay in *Psychoanalysis and Performance*, 'Rehearsing the impossible: the insane root', is similarly a disquisition upon the dynamics of performance and especially upon performance at its limits: 'just this side that loss of control' which Banquo fears has overtaken Macbeth and himself on encountering the witches. In what the author calls 'impossible theatre' – he offers provocative examples of American footballers, of Stelarc's extreme body art, of Philippe Petit aloft on his nocturnal tight-rope, and of Artaud's body released from 'logocentric repression into its complete, sonorous, streaming, naked realisation' – Blau argues that such brinkmanship can become an obsessional neurosis, 'perilous, self-punishing . . . as it may be in psychoanalysis, where the accretions of the subject's symptoms may push things to the limit.'

Drawing on his experience as a director (of the avant-garde group *Kraken*), he singles out the rehearsal process (as do Baraitser and Bayly in their essay) as a process which can tap this interior energy, even to that point, as Banquo fears, of its getting out of hand. Indeed if the performance itself does not interrogate such fears, it is unlikely to be much of a performance. And the root is not just 'insane' but 'insatiable' – when violence is staged, we, the spectators want more. Meaningful theatre, *pace* Blau, demands a certain way of thinking – provisional and experimental – but such indeterminacy does exert an inexorable pressure towards forming and performing, a demand for enactment on stage. The greatest drama can embody experience 'in extremis' so painful that one is tempted, like a doctor unable to confront cancer, to turn away. But then not only could it not be performed, it would fail to produce the experience of that generative loss of control which only happens when you are operating at the limit.

Again using Artaud's pronouncements, this time about cinema ('made to express matters of thought, the interior of consciousness'), Timothy Murray's punningly entitled 'Scanning sublimation: the digital Pôles of performance and psychoanalysis' takes issue with Freud's account of sublimation – that of 'the energetic passage from the sexual instincts to non-sexual activities'. Recent commentators such as Laplanche have reconfigured Freud's thinking, seeing sublimation less as a precise mathematical and transformational process than as a new energy, emanating perhaps from 'the sublimated activity itself; through this new trauma comes new energy'. Murray sees in such revisions a prescient relation with the suspended time of much digital performance and its energised means of production.

In a detailed and fully documented analysis of *Pôles*, a digital dance piece performed by two male dancers of PPS, Montreal, Murray explores these ideas – in particular the capability of mainstream critics to idealise the piece's vision, to desexualise its erotic exhibition and thereby enshroud it in the Freudian language of sublimation. For Murray such a reductive reading fails to take account of the psychic energy emanating from the dance's choreography – 'a confrontation of the body and its many attached affects'. This process occurs on two interrelated levels – 'the holographic form of the spectacle, and the affect of the dancer's interaction with the spectral other'. In returning to his subliminal theme and Artaudian reflections on interiority, Murray concludes that in realising what Artaud foresaw as the psychic promise of technology's 'virtual force', 'the holographic doublings of *Pôles* render in performance the energetic trauma of sublimation thought anew'.

'Violence, ventriloquism and the vocalic body' deals with an aspect of performance that has, unlike digital performance, a long-established provenance. Steven Connor provides a context for his discussion of the art of ventriloquism by considering the voice's primal function in infancy and the child's fantasy of 'sonorous omnipotence' (akin to Freud's 'magical thinking'). But the voice is both good and bad in that it provides both a sense of 'sadistic mastery' and an expression of suffering and need: it confers shape upon the body and is thereby 'involved in the process whereby the body itself accomplishes, or shapes its world'. Different voices reflect different kinds of relationship with the body; we are surrounded by a 'sonorous envelope'. While modern technology, for example, has given reality to the voice of power separated from the source of its enunciation, playback has confirmed it as a source of repeatable pleasure.

The principle of the 'vocalic body' of the title is that, while these voices are generated by bodies they can also themselves produce bodies – the business of ventriloquism. Oddly, the art as we understand it has been largely visual, utilising conservative bodies of dummies – usually boys or men with puerile faces. That these dummies were traditionally male meant that they could be treated more roughly than girls, a celebration of violence that recalled the angry voice of the child and might even, in a kind of vocalic uncanny, allow an inversion of roles. Boys, it seems, were expected to identify with both dummy and ventriloquist.

The mediatisation of contemporary culture might be expected to render anachronistic this performance of ventriloquism but, Connor points out, the disembodied voice of technology bespeaks a loss, a severance not just from our voices but from the pain of that severance. Certainly earlier distinctions between 'good' and 'bad' voices have become irrelevant, as technology – in the shape of Laurie Anderson's 'vocoder' or musical compositions which disarticulate the voice – ensures that the human instrument, despite some vocal performers' attempts to reclaim it, becomes one more 'allotrope of the mobile, multimediary intersensorium' which we inhabit.

Rebecca Schneider's musical refrain – 'Hello Dolly Well Hello Dolly' – in her essay's title ironically highlights Western culture's preoccupation with cloning and its anxiety about repetitive processes. Our fear of mimesis is, she argues, a fear of indiscreet origins, a concern that the copy will come to be recognised – perhaps like undetected plagiarism – as author, father, first. Such fears are compounded in a postmodern culture that consistently elides distinctions between representation and reality. Theatre has always relied on repetition – 'different bodies on the same stage' – and in this and its fears about reproductive rights it shares some 'uncanny' connections with biological cloning. In both activities Schneider suggests, we might be forced to acknowledge that the original becomes repetition, just as repetition becomes the original. The fear of the double is not just that it renders the original as secondary but that, *pace* Freud, it relates to our regressive wish to return to a state before birth.

In the theatre, mimesis, which we associate with the mother's capacity to reproduce, does not remain. Live theatre inevitably disappears without palpable trace, while the archive, the mummified remains of the dead author, stays intact. Quoting Derrida, Schneider notes that 'the culture of the copy that threatens is also the culture of the archive that redeems'. This archival drive is, according to Freud, in essence both patriarchal and parricidic. Paradoxically Barthes' *The Death of the Author* is therefore 'in a long line of attempts to keep the prerogatives of the author resolutely alive'.

Freud's notion of the 'uncanny' is explored from a different perspective in Ernst Fischer's 'Writing home: postmodern melancholia and the uncanny space of living-room theatre'. In charting his growing awareness of otherness, the writer recalls his own self-conscious parading of his emergent homosexuality and links it to his subsequent feelings – as a German living in London in a post-modern age of fragmentation – of disorientation and, above all, of melancholia. This condition, according to Freud, results from an 'inability to mourn an unidentified or insufficiently identified loss', a condition that can, as Fischer's adolescent behaviour did, assume a manic dimension.

The author sees a link here with 'the uncanny' which itself seems to operate as a space of disorder between the public and private spheres. Living-room theatre, Fischer's own homely performance environment, occupies this hinterland where the theatrical vies for attention with the domestic, where the dramatic and the quotidian overlap to create a third 'uncanny' space. Living-room theatre offers a safe environment for 'intimate encounters with the ambiguous . . . while simultaneously exposing the familiar to the play of the imagination'. In linking this house/theatre to a space of transgressive sexuality and desire, Fischer argues, via a number of architectural analogies, that the project of a queer living-room theatre 'is to facilitate and house the return of the abject with all its connotations of death, disease, desire and the unclean body'.

Joe Kelleher's 'The writer's block: performance, play and the responsibilities of analysis' offers to raise 'questions about what we might term analytic proxemics'. Since proxemics deals with relationships in space, it is not surprising that the essay should seek to address notions of distance 'across which analyses and performances may face each other', to explore the tension between an analytic procedure that both seeks to 'embrace its object and . . . maintain a proper distance'. He argues that analysis must be tempered with responsibility, 'for if analytic writing reifies the performance immanent in a play, the play – even as it passes – remains resistant to such certainties'. Which is why the analyst must, as Freud counsels, respect that which incapacitates interpretation.

The focus for Kelleher's discussion is a production, by Out of Joint, of Caryl Churchill's double bill *Blue Heart*. Aware of the dangers of analysing the theatrical experience in purely psychoanalytical terms, the writer believes that analysis must needs sustain 'an ethics of performance' aware of responsibilities towards its object as well as drawing the performance into the penumbra of self-understanding. In this regard Churchill's plays are particularly interesting: concerned with the responsibilities of analysis, they demonstrate a commitment to both theatrical representation and to sub-textual subversions and repressions that question the manifest content of the work. In considering *Blue Heart*, Kelleher finds Freud's 'Mourning and Melancholia' (1915), a seminal text. If Freud's preconditions of melancholia are 'loss of the object, ambivalence and regression of the libido into the ego', then *Blue Heart* seems to invite a mapping of such a schema. Melancholia is a process of interpretation that in aiming to address something beyond self 'produces instead a performance of self-consciousness'.

While Kelleher is exercised by the critical and analytical process whereby a spectator interprets a performance and thus reifies it, perhaps against the grain of its own sub-texts, Alan Read, like Lisa Baraitser and Simon Bayly, is keen to explore links between the procedures of performance and psychoanalysis. In 'The placebo of performance: psychoanalysis in its place', Read argues that both activities are offshoots of a placebo effect that seeks to please. After all, Freud's talking cure is, in terms of its performative origins, its confessional apparatus, its concern with possession and exorcism, a theatrical activity. Asking how this coalescence has occurred, particularly in relation to avant-garde performance, Read looks to Freud's own practice, his early convictions about hypnotism and the very public procedures of Charcot and their apparent capacity to override the autonomous power of the patient's mind.

Only later did Freud discover the drawbacks of a procedure that might elevate mind over body – 'the placebo effect' – and which, in cases of hysteria, could highlight the tension between simulation and sincerity, between malingering and authentic illness. This disavowal of hypnosis, of its screening of repressed impulses and their conversion into symptoms, led to Freud's rejection of the term 'catharsis' and its replacement by 'psycho-analysis'. It also, to some extent, weakened the perceived nexus between psychoanalysis and performance. The visibility of practice, most evident in *Une leçon du docteur Charcot à la Salpêtrière*, becomes, in the talking cure, the absence of seeing in favour of a concentration on acts of memory and remembering. What does remain is this compulsion to repeat – a process at the heart of both mimetic behaviour and staged performance – a compulsion played out in the very setting in which the cure was performed – Freud's consulting rooms in Hampstead.

Such comparisons between the consulting room and the stage, between analyst and spectator are pursued elsewhere in this enterprise. As Elizabeth Wright has noted, both are, in Lyotard's phrase, 'disreal spaces' where 'representations are tried and the question arises of what is "real" outside representation'; in both 'there recur the crises that bespeak underlying conflicts of interpretation'.[36] Baraitser and Bayly's essay 'Now and then: psychotherapy and the rehearsal process' pursues this analogy by examining the overlap between the process of psychotherapy and the process of rehearsal, both probing encounters between individuals in small spaces. While rehearsal has often been played down, a mere vestige of the performance to come, it does, like psychotherapy, offer a temporal and spatial environment in which emotions can be laid bare and dissected. In establishing a psychoanalytic link with Winnicott's notion of transitional objects – inanimate things with which the child develops a special relationship in his/her progress to self-hood – the authors suggest that this is the kind of space that rehearsal seeks to occupy. While transitional phenomena gradually lose significance during childhood, their traces may be fruitfully rediscovered in rehearsal. Here identities and meanings can remain fluid; here relationships can be developed with fragments of cultural artefacts, with transitional objects. This is an indeterminate, ongoing process that goes against the grain of healed person/finished play.

Citing recent performance examples – the ongoing work of their own theatre group PUR, the Wooster Group's *LSD* and Forced Entertainment's *Hidden J* – the authors maintain that such work bears witness to something prior: those risk-taking moments in rehearsal that are effaced in performance. Paradoxically, it is these moments, when the process of transformation/cure is being experienced that spectators want more of, just as clients entering therapy do so by rehearsing anxieties and fears in the hope that it will 'bring on that significant moment of self-awareness'.

Similarly, Anthony Kubiak avers that theatre is both more crucial to and consonant with psychoanalysis and consciousness theory than many current rubrics of performance and the performative. The 'Cartesian stage' of the essay's title posited the idea that one organ in the brain produces consciousness rather after the manner of a single black box theatre in which the mind's organisation is presented. Kubiak notes that much recent theoretical work – he cites Dennett, Damasio and others – while rejecting such a theatrical metaphor to describe consciousness, nonetheless relies on theatrical ontologies when formulating an approach to the world of the mind. Thus he is able to argue that Dennett's approach to consciousness reflects Strindberg's theatrical structuring of it, namely that in the theatre what we see 'is always and only what we thought we saw; the "real" play is "split", multiple and non-unified, a cacophony of voices, impulses and perceptions, each crying out for attention'.

Stanislavski, we are reminded, argues that theatre was never simply mimetic, but more 'a refiguration of the present through the refracting lens of emotion/memory'. 'Seemingness', which Laplanche calls the 'as if' mode, is integral to the appearance of the self; it requires an imaginary being, present only as absence, always existing in another scene. Using incidents from Strindberg's *Miss Julie*, some of which are enacted off stage, the author argues that theatre is 'the modus operandi' of the unconscious, that the suggestion in the play of play's endless and cruel regressions, its myriad of remembered and misremembered parts, words, stagings and script-ings, is akin to what Herbert Blau might call 'ghostings'.

In exploring the topic of 'bodily madness' (the poet Marinetti's *fisicofollia*), Elin Diamond's essay reveals connections between Freud, Futurism and the English suffragette movement (the link with the figure 'Polly Dick' in her enigmatic title). The dynamic violation of bodily integrity promoted by technophilic Futurists found an echo in Freud's metapsychological papers, which posited a turbulent body pulsing with transgressive drives, a theory rife with spatial types akin to the 'plasticity', 'dynamism' and 'simultaneity' championed in Futurist manifestos. Umberto Boccioni, for example, saw the human body as perpetually disarticulated into unstable retinal sensations – a 'mad body' indeed.

This 'mad body', which hammered a nail in the coffin of rationality, is particularly relevant to the discourse of/on the militant suffragettes (branded by the contemporary press 'hysterics') who turned this tortured, disarticulated body into public performance. Thus Mary Richardson's (aka Polly Dick's) frenzied axe attack on Velasquez' *Rokeby Venus* was an assault upon patriarchal representation as well as on the traditional and static museum culture that Futurism had denounced. Diamond concludes that while Richardson transformed her body into 'an efficient instrumental body in the service of politics', the source of such impulses 'remain as unknowable in a political woman as it is in the most influential of medical myth-makers, or in an avant-garde movement soon to be associated with Fascism'.

Diana Taylor reopens the issue of collective trauma in 'Staging social memory' by posing the question: 'How can genocidal violence and political atrocity be remembered and restaged without witnesses or a written record?' In its quest to create a theatrical identity that could re-live their pasts, the 'embodied knowledge of exploited Andean communities', Peru's leading theatre collective, Yuyachkani, faced up to this problem. It was a problem exacerbated by an establishment that privileged the urban over the rural, the national over the ethnic, literacy over orality.

In making visible the survival struggles of these 'other' communities, Yuyachkani had to avoid the predictable charge of cultural appropriation, while eschewing the simplistic solution of an anti-capitalist, anti-imperialist theatre. In re-educating themselves in what Taylor calls 'the complexity of the Andean spirit', the troupe assimilated indigenous and mestizo performance idioms and restaged their folk-tales and struggles. Thus was rendered visible a history of cumulative oppression, a performative recall of memories about colonial dismemberment. By partaking actively in workshop or street events, spectators could enter into dialogue with a history of trauma. The witness, like Boal's spect-actor, was able to accept the dangers and responsibilities 'of seeing and of acting on what one has seen'. In this way, such performances continue to reaffirm to these communities the value of collective subjectivity and communal memory.

The imperatives of a very different establishment underpin Ann Pellegrini's 'Laughter'. Citing Althusser's theory of interpellation – the insidious process whereby we are drawn into subjection by the apparatus of the state – and drawing on Freud's *Jokes and their Relation to the Unconscious* (1905), the author focuses on a recent case of artistic repression. In 1998, in a celebrated action – the NEA versus Karen Finley *et al.* – the Supreme Court upheld 'a decency and respect clause regulating government funding for the arts'. The context for this case was highly politicised controversies over the 'pornographic' work of Robert Mapplethorpe and Andres

Serrano and the withdrawal of funding for Finley and three homosexual performers: Holly Hughes, Tim Miller and John Fleck. In essence, as Pellegrini reminds us, the debate concerned the difference between 'saying and meaning'; it was about keeping such 'diversity' safely within bounds while asserting that it was doing so in the interests of free speech and the diverse values of the American people. Such a case ironically reveals that if individuals need to be called back into line, then interpellation, in the Althusserian sense, is not functioning properly.

Holly Hughes' 'Preaching to the Perverted' was a witty and iconoclastic response to this traumatic encounter with establishment power. The performance involved a restaging of the arguments produced in court and a renaming of the injuries wrought by homophobia, racism and sexism that she and the other live artists had endured. In making the whole experience into a parodic performance – the Supreme Court becomes 'The Supremes', its command 'Silence in Court' broken by an audience laughing at Hughes' responses – spectators are brought into collective 'disidentification'. By thus resituating this personal trauma within a national frame, Hughes exposes its political dimensions. And the 'perverted' become, in a nice irony, not so much Hughes and friends, but the nine Supreme Court justices with their perverted sense of justice and humanity. 'Laughter' may be a different response to that of Yuyachkani's spect-actors, but in both cases audiences are made actively aware of the repressive power of state institutions.

The connection between the social performances of the state apparatus and the ideological performativity of psychic processes is also pursued in Adrian Kear's contribution to the book. In the context of a discussion of the politics of 'race' and nation in contemporary Britain, Kear suggests that 'the historical conjunction of colonial relations of power and psychoanalysis's theorisation of unconscious desire invests the latter with particular importance in the analysis of psychic and social identifications'. In particular, he argues that psychoanalysis articulates the fantasy structures of a racially constituted subjectivity, a 'regime of representation' which, in concert with Fanon's conception of its 'epidermal schema', might be productively spoken of as 'whiteness'.

Kear points out that the temporalising and historicising of these structures can be detected in their eruption through the discourse of 'alterity' in post-colonial society. For example, a significant shift could be detected in the public performances surrounding the public inquiry into the murder in London of the young black teenager Stephen Lawrence, a case which put the politics of 'race' and nation in Britain on trial on a global stage. By remotivating Walter Benjamin's historical conception of tragedy to demonstrate the significance of 'the word' which Stephen Lawrence's death might have 'endowed' British society, Kear argues that 'whiteness' is implicated in the psychoanalytic subject's political psyche.

As further evidence of a shifting pattern of intersubjectivity, Forced Entertainment's acts of 'performing responsibility' are investigated. The 1999 revival of *Speak Bitterness* is invoked as testimony to a dialogical structure of feeling in which 'non-representational performances have sought to enjoin' audience to performers, 'to entrust us with the responsibility for events', to make us 'witnesses' rather than mere 'spectators'. The litany of confessions that form the texture of the show come to take the form of a collective 'We', implicating and interpellating performers and audience alike into the acknowledgement of an intersubjective 'responsibility' for the 'crimes, banalities and failings of the twentieth century'.

Greg Ulmer's essay, 'The Upsilon Project: a post-tragic testimonial', approaches the idea of communal responsibility from a very different perspective by describing the genesis of 'The emerAgency', a virtual consultancy, and one of its performative initiatives – the creation of an electronic monument. While the Vietnam wall already commemorates the sacrifice of lives in a public and collective cause, Ulmer argues the case for a new type of me-morial which might, for example, electronically record traffic deaths as they occur, in a reconsideration (as the AIDS quilt project high-lighted the shift from waste to atonement) of the idea of sacrifice and monumentality.

Such an initiative finds an analogy in ancient Greece; what tragedy was to an Athenian culture, guiding it from an oral to a literary tradition, the electronic memorial is to post-modern America, taking the nation a stage further along the road from literacy to 'electracy'. If Greek tragedy focused public attention on disaster and especially on how the 'protagonist's loss of control has catastrophic consequences for society', we now need a new recording mechanism which both reflects our electronic culture and illuminates the myopia of contemporary society. In proposing a me-morial for abused children, Ulmer draws attention to the case of 'Bradley McGee', an example of individual abuse that reveals a community's failure to recognise such death as sacrificial. In short, he argues, we need a new cartography, a tracing of the paths joining blindness and calamity. In advocating a peripheral for abused children connected to – say – the astronauts' memorial – a link between Bradley McGee and sacrificial hero Gus Grissom could be forged.

As can be seen, *Psychoanalysis and Performance* is a wide-ranging and provocative collection of essays that imaginatively explores the multiple affiliations between the disciplines of psychoanalysis and performance studies. Its authors adopt a range of innovative strategies designed to investigate the connections and correspondences between these fields, opening up original perspectives and new insights into the interdisciplinarity of cultural practices. Their essays subject current debates to sustained scrutiny and suggest emergent areas of academic concern. From rehearsal process to consciousness theory, from digital performance to collective social trauma, the arguments advanced in this book are predicated on the dual principle that psychoanalysis can assist our understanding of performance and related activities, and that performance, in its protean forms, can help to illuminate the workings of psychic and social processes.

## Notes

1 Susan Sontag, 'Against Interpretation', in *A Susan Sontag Reader*, Harmondsworth: Penguin, 1983: 98.
2 Sontag, 'Against Interpretation': 99.
3 See Shoshana Felman, 'To Open the Question', in *Literature and Psychoanalysis: The Question of Reading: Otherwise*, ed. S. Felman, Baltimore: Johns Hopkins University Press, 1982: 5–10.

4 Sigmund Freud, 'Psychopathic Characters on the Stage', in *The Pelican Freud Library*, vol. XIV: *Art and Literature*, Harmondsworth: Penguin, 1985: 121–7.

5 Freud, 'Psychopathic Characters on the Stage': 125.

6 Elizabeth Wright, 'Psychoanalysis and the Theatrical: Analysing Performance', in *Analysing Performance*, ed. P. Campbell, Manchester: Manchester University Press, 1996: 176.

7 André Green, *The Tragic Effect: The Oedipus Complex in Tragedy*, trans. A. Sheridan, Cambridge: Cambridge University Press, 1979: 22.

8 Green, *The Tragic Effect*: 23.

9 Green, *The Tragic Effect*: 26.

10 Gunter Berghaus, 'Happenings in Europe: Trends, Events and Leading Figures', in *Happenings and Other Acts*, ed. M. Sandford, London and New York: Routledge, 1995: 367.

11 See Sigmund Freud, *Totem and Taboo*, in *The Freud Reader*, ed. P. Gay, London and New York: Vintage Books, 1995.

12 Sigmund Freud, *The Ego and the Id*, in *The Freud Reader*: 655.

13 Freud in *The Freud Reader*: 236.

14 Maud Ellman, ed., *Psychoanalytic Literary Criticism*, London: Longman, 1994: 8.

15 Sigmund Freud, *The Standard Edition of the Complete Psychological Works of Sigmund Freud*, ed. and trans. J. Strachey, vol. X, London: Hogarth Press and the Institute for Psychoanalysis, 1955: 150.

16 Sigmund Freud, 'Creative Writers and Day-dreaming', in *The Pelican Freud Library*, vol. XIV: 443.

17 Ellman, *Psychoanalytic Literary Criticism*: 6–7.

18 Michael Kirby, 'Happenings: An Introduction', in *Happenings and Other Acts*: 24.

19 See Jacques Derrida, *Resistances of Psychoanalysis*, trans. P. Kamuf, P.-A. Brault and M. Naas, Stanford, CA: Stanford University Press, 1996: 14.

20 Green, *The Tragic Effect*: 28–9.

21 Gilles Deleuze and Felix Guattari, *Anti-Oedipus: Capitalism and Schizophrenia*, trans. R. Hurley, M. Seem and H. Lance, London: Athlone Press, 1984: 101.

22 Sigmund Freud, *The Interpretation of Dreams: The Pelican Freud Library*, vol. IV: 365.

23 Freud, *The Interpretation of Dreams*: 365.

24 Jacques Lacan, *The Ethics of Psychoanalysis: The Seminar of Jacques Lacan*, book XII, ed. J.-A. Miller, trans. D. Porter, London: Routledge, 1992: 309.

25 Jacques Lacan, 'Desire and the Interpretation of Desire in *Hamlet*', trans. J. Hulbert, in *Literature and Psychoanalysis: The Question of Reading: Otherwise*: 12.

26 See Herbert Blau, 'Ideology and Performance', *Theatre Journal*, 35(4), 1983: 441.

27 Wright, 'Psychoanalysis and the Theatrical': 178.

28 Jacques Lacan, *Ecrits: A Selection*, trans. A. Sheridan, London: Tavistock, 1977: 104.

29 Josette Féral, 'Performance and Theatricality', *Modern Drama*, 25, 1982, quoted in Marvin Carlson, *Theories of the Theatre*, Ithaca and London: Cornell University Press, 1984: 517.

30 Freud, 'Fragment of an Analysis of a Case of Hysteria ('Dora'), in *The Freud Reader*: 673.

31 Julia Kristeva, *Powers of Horror: An Essay in Abjection*, trans. L. Roudiez, New York: Columbia University Press, 1982: 3–4.

32 Elin Diamond, *Unmaking Mimesis: Essays on Feminism and Theater*, London and New York: Routledge, 1997: iv.

33 Freud, 'The Uncanny', in *The Pelican Freud Library*, vol. XIV: 364.

34 Michael Quinn, 'Celebrity and the Semiotics of Acting', in *New Theatre Quarterly*, 22, 1990: 155.

35 Peggy Phelan, 'The Ontology of Performance: Representation Without Reproduction', in *Unmarked: The Politics of Performance*, London and New York: Routledge, 1993: 150–2.

36 Wright, 'Psychoanalysis and the Theatrical': 175.

# Section A

# THINKING THROUGH THEATRE

# 1

# REHEARSING
# THE IMPOSSIBLE

## The insane root

*Herbert Blau*

A few prefatory remarks, theoretical, personal, before we get to the root, or at least the root of the title. What I want to reflect upon eventually are the limits of performance, to the degree that approaching those limits seems to resemble an obsessional neurosis, in theater as in sports or any activity exceeding itself, its very discipline not only demanding but threatening, perilous, self-punishing in extremis – as it may be in psychoanalysis, where the accretions of the subject's symptoms may push things to the limit. It is there, as Lacan remarks in his thesis on aggressivity as '*intended aggression*,' that 'the analytic experience allows us to feel the pressure of intention,' while the symptoms – hesitations, evasions, parapraxes, the improvised or calculated deceits, sullen breakings off, remorse, returns, excesses of renewed commitment, and then again the vacillations, the turning off or against, 'recriminations, reproaches, phantasmic fears, emotional reactions of anger, attempts at intimidation'[1] – might constitute a repertoire familiar in the course of rehearsal, especially to the director whose own pressures of intention may be arduous to the point of cruelty. I like to believe that Freud was right, however, when he observed

> that the instinct for knowledge can actually take the place of sadism in the mechanism of obsessional neurosis. Indeed it is at bottom a sublimated off-shoot of the instinct for mastery exalted into something intellectual, and its repudiation in the form of doubt plays a large part in the picture of obsessional neurosis.[2]

It is the instinct for knowledge to which I'll also return, and to theater as heuristic, interrogative, a function of thought. But when I first began working with actors, the American theater was profoundly thoughtless. The repudiation of the intellectual, next to no doubt at all, accounted in part for my own obsessions – all of which were registered in *The Impossible Theater: A Manifesto*, which I wrote in the early 1960s,[3] anticipating the dissidence about to break out. Before that happened, however, psychological realism possessed the stage and, while there were multiple versions of it – not quite as polyvalent as performance is today (or, in 'performativity,' the bodies that presumably matter[4]) – the Method was dominant, with its subtexts and 'emotional memory' and, as a legacy from Stanislavski, ratified by Freud, the activating assumption of an 'inner life.' Since then, with equivocal views of authenticity during the countercultural sixties, performance has passed through a period in which notions of interiority – like the Freudian unconscious itself or, as Lacan would have it, 'the level of symbolic overdetermination that we call the subject's unconscious'[5] – have been something more than suspect. As depth acceded to surface in an age of the antiaesthetic, a developing jaundice about the inner life had its correlative of suspicion in the outer world of appearance, which, if not always what it appears to be, or only a shadow of it, was fetishized in the Oedipal drama because of the shadow's shadow. To be sure, a renewed historical materialism would soon be monitoring that, with the zeal of demystification; and after the emergence of deconstruction, exposing everywhere you looked the sediments of metaphysics, it seemed as if there were nothing but nostalgia assuring the future of illusion.

But then, to all appearances, things seemed at the end of the real, if not perpetuating illusion, 'proving theater by anti-theater.'[6] Or so it was if we hearkened to Baudrillard, who described the immanence of visual culture as an obscenity of images, but warned those still vigilant over the deceits of representation that 'it is dangerous to unmask images, since they dissimulate the fact that there is nothing behind them.'[7] Which is another way of describing the vanity of psychoanalysis. Whatever it is that appears in the *mise-en-scène* of the unconscious can be produced, says Baudrillard, like 'any other symptom in classical medicine,' or as 'dreams already are,'[8] with the metaphysical sediments in the scenography of regression. As for the interpretation of dreams, that has been seriously threatened by 'the liquidation of all referentials'[9] and, in the revolving causality of a vertiginous scene, the 'dead and circular replies to a dead and circular interrogation.'[10] So much, then, for what Christopher Bollas calls 'a kind of *countertransference dreaming*' or 'unconscious communications'[11] in the site of the talking cure. At the dialogical impasse of 'the negative transference . . ., the initial knot of the analytic drama,'[12] psychoanalysis itself is a factitious performance, of which Baudrillard asks, what can it do 'with the reduplication of the discourse of the unconscious in a discourse of simulation that can never be unmasked, since it isn't false either?'[13] It might very well be, as we passed through the Lacanian mirror into the precession of simulacra, that the ancient idea was consummated and that, finally, all the world *is* a stage, but who would have thought that, as Prospero's insubstantial pageant faded, leaving not a wrack behind, it would be a stage on which 'illusion is no longer possible, because the real is no longer possible?'[14] As Baudrillard sees it, the pageant no longer moves through an ontology of disappearance, nor – as all of human knowledge is miniaturized and mediatized, tipped into the hyperreal – with assent to that other talismanic proposition about the Theater of the World, the tenuous notion that life is a dream.

Yet sometimes, stubbornly or involuntarily, we incline to think it is. If dreams are wish-fulfillment, so are, it also seems, the waking correlatives of dreams, or facsimiles, like accident or coincidence, which occur at times as if we wished them into being, as Solness seems to do with the appearance of Hilda Wangel in Ibsen's *The Master Builder*, a drama which seems to occur out of some weird and un-fathomable debt at some limit of exceeding itself. 'This all must have been in my thought,' Solness says to Hilda, through the mirage of a mutual gaze. 'I must have willed it. Wished it. Desired it. And so – doesn't that make sense?'[15] Maybe so, maybe not. Lacan might have described the scene as a 'transaudition of the uncon-scious by the unconscious.'[16]

What I'm saying was occasioned, however, by a letter I received not long ago, just as I was reading again, for a seminar, *The Interpretation of Dreams*. It was written by a former student who became the production manager of my KRAKEN group, a nerve-racking job to which he brought, though he looked like an adolescent, extraordinary poise and sensitivity. Mature as he was even then, I still think of him as a young man, as I mostly think of myself as younger than I am, though as the body that knows the difference insists on what it is – neither cultural construct nor 'incorporated space,'[17] some effect of the signifier on the subject – I make a point of accepting, in the inarguable debit of age, the down-to-earth performative being that, since the gravedigger put on the forceps, in the Beckettian view of birth (unalleviated by Bion or Jung), is a lot less long for this world.

The letter began with – and was apparently prompted by – a dream about my dying, and refusing to delay the end. It seemed remarkable in that it arrived while I was thinking particularly of those dreams in which Freud is concerned with his professional life and achievement, linked immediately after to absurd dreams about dead fathers. 'Nor is it by any means a matter of chance,' Freud writes, 'that our first examples of absurdity in dreams relate to a dead father.'[18] Now, why did I *want* such a letter? I suppose it was because I had been questioning myself recently about why – after nearly forty years of it, the last stretch of which was the richest, most con-ceptually audacious work I'd ever done – I am not still doing theater. When that work ceased on the supposition that we might begin again, I started a book called *Take Up the Bodies: Theater at the Vanishing Point*, the vanishing point also marking the fact that, at the dying end of financial reasons, I wouldn't let it resume, though it was painful to leave it at that. Perhaps there was a lingering desire for assurance about the validity of that work, to which the letter – coming, as it said, out of the possibility of a mid-life crisis, his present turmoil reaching back to mine – made the warmest testament; in short, the dream of my dying and refusing to delay the end, given the nature of the work, its manic obsession with disappearance ('doesn't that make sense?'), was somehow a confirmation.

What the work of KRAKEN also confirmed, at least as I remember it (or want to remember it), is that the theater, carnal, tactile, occurring in space and time, is nevertheless at ground zero a function of thought – which, according to Freud, is also true of dream, inhabiting as it does an autoscopical space in a diffusion of time. 'We appear not to *think* but to *experience*,' he writes in *The Interpretation of Dreams*; 'that is to say, we attach complete belief to the hallucinations. Not until we wake up does the critical comment arise that we have not experienced anything but have merely been thinking in a peculiar way, or in other words dreaming.'[19] In his essay on 'Two Principles of Mental Functioning,' Freud speaks of thinking, which permitted the psychic apparatus to tolerate increasing stimulus without premature discharge, as 'essentially an experimental form of acting.'[20] It is probable, he adds, that thinking was unconscious in the beginning, while the unconscious itself, as Freud conceives it, is our oldest mental faculty. Which is how, over the years, I have come to think of theater, particularly at its incipience, the precipitation of theater from whatever it is *not*, as if mere thought ('but thinking makes it so'), had brought it into being. There are also the times when something happens in rehearsal, so stunningly that you wonder where it came from, whether by method or madness, for it seems to be other than theater, out of some pressure of intention before it was even thought, which is – as with the ghosting in *Hamlet*, which gave us a method in KRAKEN[21] – precisely what keeps us thinking. This occurs with the liability that, at the filamenting nerve-ends of thought, where intention warps under pressure, there may be a loss of control – the experimental form of acting, *thinking*, no less impelled by that.

But let me move the issue to another level, working to the extremities or limits of performance, by changing the scene entirely, more or less bracketing the psycho-analysis (or letting that be implicit) but not the aggressivity, nor – as if the mirror stage were mirrored to the size of a football field – the images of 'castration, mutilation, dismemberment, dislocation, evisceration, devouring, bursting open of the body, in short, the *imagos*' grouped together by Lacan 'under the apparently structural term of *imagos of the fragmented body.*'[22]

'When you think about it, it is a strange thing that we do,' said the New York Giants linebacker, Jessie Armstead, a couple of years ago, when the NFL was, as it still is, going through a reassessment of degrees of violence in the game: crack-back blocks, leg-whips, face masks twisted, kicks in the groin, or other vulnerable parts, thumbs in the nostrils, fingers bent and bitten, gouged eyes, head butts, or after a smashing tackle, gratuitous elbows in the massive piling on. Not every player, coached to perform 'like a bunch of crazed dogs,' as Lawrence Taylor once put it, can do so with the marauding grace of his lethal instincts, but there is among the league's statistics a ferocious inventory of serious damage, surreptitious or flagrant, intended and unintended, from repeated quarterback concussions to shredded tendons, snapped clavicles, ripped ligaments in the line. 'During a game we want to kill each other,' Armstead remarked. 'Then we're told to shake hands and drive home safely. Then a week later we try to kill each other again.' This is not to mention the subtler brutalities of psychological dominance which may erupt, too, in physical violence, or the physical violence that goes the other way, as when, before Bill Parcells brought them together as teammates, the Bears' linebacker Bryan Cox, stunned and upended by the Jets' 300-pound tackle, Jumbo Elliott, went down punching him in the ribs. As they grappled then on the ground, the simple question was this, posed by Elliott with his hands on Cox's throat: 'Do you know who's in control of this situation?'[23]

It would seem that acting in the theater is a somewhat tamer game, but at the extremities of performance – where, when you think about it, a strange thing is being done, and in certain modes of performance, outside the precincts of theatre (e.g. body art, from Viennese Aktionism to Chris Burden's crucifixion to Orlan's cosmetic surgeries), even stranger yet – the same question may be asked: 'Do you know who's in control of this situation?' And indeed, if the performance doesn't rise to the level of that question – as it must, too, in the knot, the negative transference – it's not likely to be very much of a performance. Which is to say that, if we're really talking of limits, it must include the kind of performance that occurs in dubious peril just this side of a loss of control – not only strange but wondrous when the peril is only a seeming. If this is not quite the case with a wide receiver who, going up for the ball, risks being sliced in mid-air, it may be so with the actor who, in a kind of hallucination, like the blinded Gloucester in *King Lear*, jumps from the cliffs of Dover – the 'crows and choughs [winging] the midway air' – or, in conceiving a role like Macbeth, rehearses the impossible as if, as Banquo puts it after the witches vanish, having 'eaten on the insane root.'

I may have been eating on that root many years ago, back in the early sixties, when I wrote – with a determined psychic violence and potential loss of control, feeling 'like the lunatic Lear on the heath, wanting to "kill, kill, kill, kill, kill!"' – the first paragraphs of *The Impossible Theater*, in which I said that 'if politics is the art of the possible, theater is the art of the impossible. "Seeming, seeming" is what it's made of,' as if there were no future but the future of illusion, as Nietzsche believed and Freud had to concede, given the ineliminability of civilization's discontents. What I had in mind, more immediately, was the instrumentality of illusion and the demands upon intelligence at the perceptual limits of the form. But given at the time, amidst the insanities of the Cold War, the woeful condition of our theater – institutionally, aesthetically, in every conceivable way, from the consensual humiliations of actors to the vacuity of most productions to the absence of continuity making for teamwork in performance – I added 'that among the meanings of the word *impossible* I have in mind is the one you get when you say it raging with your teeth clenched.'[24] I won't rehearse what has happened to the theater since, except to say that, as always, the impossible takes a little time, while the insanities persist, some of them undreamed of during the Cold War.

But let's stay at the limit of performance where doing the impossible, or nearly so, remains a constant dream, though what I have in mind at the moment is, if insanely rooted, also up in the air, and, as it turns out, if not without illusion, somewhere beyond seeming – as if performance were occurring somehow in phantasmic figures on the other side of the dream. For it's even higher up in the air than the body artist Stelarc, who thinks the body obsolete, and on that forbidding premise did a series of events – beautiful at a distance, at sites around the world: over the waves in Japan, above a street on the lower East Side of Manhattan, and way above the Royal Theatre in Stockholm – in which his body was suspended by fishhooks through the flesh. This transpired, no doubt, in 'the dimension of a vital dehiscence' that might have sent the spectator, who happened to be on the scene, into an 'organic disarray.'[25] For Stelarc, however, 'the stretched skin' was a kind of 'gravitational landscape,' in which he was setting up 'a biofeedback situation' to compensate for the incapacities of the worn-out body, which can no longer process the information it's required to take in. The hooks might have seemed nightmarish, conjuring up, as in Freud's description of mutilations in the unconscious, 'dead carcasses and all that,' but for Stelarc, who wished people would get over the 'emotional obsession with hooks,' they were merely incidental to the sculptured analytic of his suspended body.[26] Difficult as that was to take close up (you'd even wince looking at the pictures), the event I want to turn to was really out of sight, and somewhere beyond the kinds of performance that, now and then still persisting, grew out of 'the participation mystique' of the sixties, where anyone could perform, even the audience, regardless of talent or training, or any criteria of 'accomplishment' – to use the meaning of the word Noh in the most classical Japanese theater, its ideographic slow motion resembling a dream, but in a performance that is generically (*per-form*) an act of perfection.

Speaking of which, then: some years ago, with astonishing will and impeccable control, the equilibrist Philippe Petit walked a line way, way up between the twin towers of the World Trade Center in New York, doubly endangered by the awesome drafts between them, outdoing in that imperiled image even the slam-dunk exploits of an insuperable Air Jordan, as if, indeed, the dreamer were the body of the dream, but at some literalized empyrean of the unconscious. With a superb athleticism and the highest theatricality, it's as if it were negotiating in that crossing the ultimate logic of late capitalism, and I have invoked it before as the limit condition of the most consummate performance, where the imagination's audacity, impelled by the finest discipline, couldn't survive without it. If this clandestine event – the rope was stretched in the middle of the night, and the performance occurred with virtually no audience but the stars – is also the apotheosis of solo performance, it lifts to its meridian the notion of 'public solitude,' the condition sought for the actor, out of the inner life, by the Stanislavski Method, with that solitude, paradoxically, as the emptying out of distraction into a fully reflective consciousness, being the responsive basis or datum of the ensemble effect. At the same time, it is also the perfected image of Brechtian alienation, 'the self-observing distance of a body so adept it hardly seemed carnal, no less commodified, more like an ideograph of the mind aloft at its extremity.'[27]

In this regard, it suggests those figures crossing an abyss, 'like Ideas in Plato's cave,' in the van den Leyden painting admired by Artaud, in his essay on 'Metaphysics and the Mise en Scène,' because it suggests 'what the theatre should be, if it knew how to speak the language that belongs to it.'[28] It is a language, of course, which must be for Artaud material, tactile, 'affecting the brain directly, like a physical agent,'[29] yet as a 'poetry of the senses,'[30] nothing less than transcendent, though what he is describing, it seems, is the pictographic language in the dramaturgy of the unconscious. So with his notion of the actor, like a victim 'burnt at the stake, signaling through the flames,'[31] at that limit of performance never quite realized, nor maybe realizable, not by Artaud himself, nor by those of us, stirred by his enraptured vision, who weren't quite up to that suicidal idea, but who tried to remember in all the psychophysical exercises of a generation ago – pushing the narcissistic body beyond limits to some sensation of a *déchirement*, the originary splitting contained by thought – that actors in the West had forgotten how to scream. He didn't mean the indulgent noise that characterized some performance in the sixties but rather, in the 'essential theatre,' what released the body that matters from logocentric repression into its 'complete, sonorous, streaming naked realization,' which is also, as in the dreamscape of the Eleusinian mysteries, a 'transfusion of matter by mind.'[32] Unachievable as it may be, Artaud's conception of a Theater of Cruelty – mystical, alchemical, where all the 'perverse possibilities of the mind,'[33] are localized and exalted, opening up the 'gigantic abscess,'[34] of repression and deceit – nevertheless ups the ante on the crucial question of control, which in the more familiar regions of theater is part of the psychopathology of the rehearsal process that must shake off, in time, 'the asphyxiating inertia of matter which invades even the clearest testimony of the senses.'[35] It's as if in the deepest sense, as in the protocols of the death wish beyond the pleasure principle, the organism doesn't want to act, or with the illusion of commitment – as to a predictable plot or image – acts by a kind of default.

As for the Nietzschean 'true illusion,' that requires from the actor, according to Artaud, an inescapable commitment to 'the truthful precipitates of dreams, in which his taste for crime, his erotic obsessions, his savagery, his chimeras, his utopian sense of life and matter, even his cannibalism, pour out, on a level not counterfeit and illusory, but interior.'[36] As there are conventional forms of theater that hardly dream this way, and theories of theater that, from Brechtian alienation to the queerer deconstruction, distrust the energy of an 'interior,' or think of it as a fiction, there are evasive practices of rehearsal that try to defer it or ward it off, as there must be with working it up in practice on a football field, or for that matter, in the associational process of the analytical session. But when push comes to shove, that's where the action is, and the best of actors know it, to the point of obsessive compulsion that can make a rehearsal endless, and thrilling to the degree that it's always on the edge. Or to return to the image after Macbeth's encounter with the witches, close to the insane root, where it's sometimes impossible to ascertain who exactly is in control or, as we trammel up the consequence, 'smother'd in surmise, and nothing is/But what is not,' not who, but *what*.

Of course, to begin with, like the coach with firing power, head tricks, and playbook or, more subtly, the analyst introjecting the patient's idiom – presumably a 'shadow ego,'[37] but, in the countertransference, something more than that – the director may be in control; or in the commodified theater of Broadway, the producer who puts up the money; or moving from stage to screen, with Miramax, Disney, or Dreamworks, the source of megabucks. That may even produce, as it did recently, in *Saving Private Ryan* or *The Thin Red Line*, powerful images of fear and courage at the excruciating limits of performance, where teamwork exists at the edge of the imbecilic. If the harrowing realism of it depends on a prior teamwork of actors, crew, editors, stunt men, and wizards of special effects, what's achieved by camera and cutting is unavailable to the theater, whose teamwork always returns to the susceptible thing itself, the unaccommodated body that at any performative moment may really lose control, as in something so elemental as a case of stage fright. It should be apparent, though it's not, that while it may be superbly sublimated, stage fright is the latency of any performance, as it is there in the batter's box or down in the sprinter's crouch, or even in the supposed privacy of the analytic encounter, where the patient forgets the dream or stutters through made-up experience or, in a seizure of dislocation, is made speechless by the uncanny. Harrowing as it may be, the symptoms of stage fright, like the blanking out on lines, still occur in a situation that you can't shoot over again. Laurence Olivier was quite aware of that when, at the height of his career, having made his film of *Hamlet* and played triumphantly as Othello, he was directing the National Theatre and about to perform in *The Master Builder*. It was then, after some vague 'feelings of misgiving' at an afternoon dress rehearsal, that he experienced 'a much-dreaded terror,' which he thought of as the punishment his pride always deserved, but 'which was, in fact,' as he wrote of it in his autobiography, 'nothing other than a merciless attack of stage fright with all its usual shattering symptoms.'[38] For which, and other reasons, he had entered into analysis.

Meanwhile, the vicissitudes of control are endemic to the art of acting, and in the exacerbation of rehearsal – with its associational process – a director may work on that, escalating a certain danger that, in the reciprocity of actors, may really get out of hand, not only in scenes of violence but, as lyrical or tender as it may be, in a love scene as well: more of that, yes, it's splendid (so the director thinks, sometimes saying it, sometimes not) but if the sensuosity increases, whatever the text says, text or no text, the bodies becoming the book, when do you stop? and why? since the actors are into it now, and then again, if one of them is not, how do you get them to take it a little further? one controlling the situation, one ever so slightly resisting, and if the truth were known, you not sure that it isn't too much already. 'Do it again,' you say, but the demoralizing thing in rehearsal – what the French call *répétition* – is not really knowing what *it* is, 'it all, it all,' as Beckett says, the intangible referent that always escapes you, not that, *this*, not this, *that*, nor do you really want to repeat it, not that merely, because it wouldn't be the same if it were only the same, it would be nothing but a repetition, not as right as it was, spontaneous, as when it happened for the first time, because the actors were, as they say, 'living the moment,' not what was, but what *is*, while the desire to get at it, whatever *it* (again) is, drives the rehearsal even more, sometimes driving it crazy. Which suggests that, at some limit, you're dealing with the impossible, arousing an interior violence, which is the mythic source of theater, if we can believe the canonical drama (which moved into psychoanalysis), back through Oedipus to Dionysus, the root not only insane but insatiable as well. And when there is, indeed, physical violence on a stage (which can neither be achieved, escalated, cut away from as on film) – a swordfight, a murder, a rape, Othello smothering Desdemona – you always want more, more, but how far do you go, you wonder, before somebody does get hurt, emotionally or physically – you're not always sure which is worse.

That may become an incessant question when there *is* a sustained history among the actors, with mixed feelings of attraction and aversion, or along with devotion, inflexions of animosity, intensified by dependence, with the director as shadow ego (or, as with the analyst drawn into the 'emotional constellation,' a kind of 'somatic double,'[39] caught up in the displacements and condensations that eventually shadow them all, as intrinsic to what they do as the atmosphere they breathe. What they come to know about each other could naturally be an asset, drawn upon in performance, but it could also be a burden, cutting off surprise. That was certainly our experience at The Actor's Workshop of San Francisco, as it developed from a studio with eight actors to a company of about 150, at a time in the American theater, through the early fifties into the sixties, when (as I've said) there were no examples of continuity, and almost nothing like a company concept. As a performative proposition, the mixed feelings were addressed, even more intimately, in my work with the KRAKEN group (young people whom I trained, some of them famous now), where no matter what we did, whatever the theme or surface appearance, it was always at some level about relations among the performers and – whether on the brainstruck ramparts of *Elsinore,* a work derived from *Hamlet,* or forced to cannibalism in the Sierras in *The Donner Party, Its Crossing* – the psychic condition of the group, with none of the easy escape routes of therapeutic consciousness-raising.

So it was only to be expected when, at the exhausting limit of one improvisation, which was part of an exhaustive interrogation (some of these went on for hours) of materials resembling *Othello* that, when one of the men in the group started to smother one of the women, there was nothing like the accustomed Desdemona about her, certainly nothing submissive, as she threw him off in a rage, and shouted ceaseless obscenities, every scurrilous word of it meant, what they felt about each other being not merely a subtext, but rather the compulsively abrasive substance of the event. 'You bastard, you shit, don't you ever do that again!' she cried, as he backed away, 'you always do that, always!' – *what* wasn't entirely clear – 'don't you ever put your filthy hands on me again!' Whereupon he looked at her and said simply, 'But I can't help it, it's written,' and started moving toward her, big and powerful, overwhelmingly so, in a muted rage of his own, and I let him go until he touched her, because I really *wanted to see it,* you always want to *see* it, and then had all I could do to stop it – she there flailing, scratching, cursing when he grabbed her – because they were no longer simply acting and he was almost ready to kill her, and if I hadn't interfered it would have been something more than a fiction or mimicry of abuse. And it was something more than that, too, when it was reflected upon, debated, worked through in other sessions, then displaced to another context (over the months of analysis) and, in another imagistic form, dispersed among the actors, entered into the structure of a developing work, charged as it might not have been if the outbreak had never happened or, since I saw it all coming, if I wasn't entirely sure – in letting it go the limit, and wanting it to go beyond – that I hadn't, almost, lost control of the situation.

When you think about it, it's a strange thing that we were doing, but it may seem even stranger when I say that we were doing it, methodologically, *in order to think,* as if

29

thought were insufficient unless impassioned, imperiled, out there on the edge, caught in the awesome drafts of inconclusion. When I say, however, that something was debated, that might be verbally but also ideogrammatically, because the actors had the capacities of gymnasts or acrobats, and could act, literally, standing on their heads, which was only appropriate because at some limit, however emotionally charged, the work was intensely cerebral, as in a novel of Dostoyevsky, passionately so, to the point of brain fever or phobia, the vital dehiscence such that – mirror upon mirror mirrored all the show – it seemed that the mirror had shattered into 'the concrete problematic of the realization of the subject.'[40]

But I also mean this, as a reflection on limits, in a particular way. There is a certain kind of thinking that I associate with the thought of theater, not only when we think *about* the theater but when we think *as the theater thinks*, in its incipience, that is, coming into being, as if crossing whatever limit kept it (before) from *being performance*, not as the word is used today in almost every aspect of experience, or mere charade or drag or masquerade, or as embraced in identity politics or, through the play of signifying absences, confused with performativity, the '*stylized repetition of acts*'[41] that is not to be thought of as theater. Which, to be precise, is something else again. I mean, rather, the kind of thought which is deliberately, even relentlessly, subjunctive and provisional, putting out interrogative feelers, often thinking out loud what it doesn't quite (yet, if ever) understand, self-reflexive, yes, parenthetical, no doubt elusive, or allusive, trying out an idea, taking it back again, saying it another way, not saying it at all, but finding a gesture for it, putting it up for grabs in the exhaustive play of perception that, at some limit approaching meaning, always seems to escape, thus keeping meaning alive. And let me not be misleading, there is nothing loose about it, no slack in the void, there being in all the indeterminacy a pressure toward form, *per*-form, what insists in the end on *being thought*, now you see it now you don't, but even in the slippage nevertheless embodied, obdurately so, inarguably, as I wrote in *Take Up the Bodies*, creating 'the terms by which it is perceived, when it becomes its own system of value, when there is nothing *behind* what it is saying, when it certifies and substantiates itself as the sole species of its own genre.'[42] That, to me, is the ultimate limit.

If what happens, then, in the theater materializes in the flesh, any way you look at it, the theater is a play of mind, 'an abstraction blooded, as a man by thought,' as Wallace Stevens wrote in his *Notes toward a Supreme Fiction*. That's what I tried to suggest in the supreme image of Philippe Petit aloft at night between the towers, luminously there like a Platonic Idea. And while it comes with the ecstatic dance of a ritual plenitude, it was a similar sort of abstraction that Artaud defined when – describing the perpetual motion of Balinese drama, the dance of 'animated manikins' and 'robot squeakings,' the flights of elytra and sudden cries, the 'strange games of flying hands, like insects in the green air of evening,' an ensemble of 'explosions, flights, secret streams, detours in every direction of . . . *gestures made to last*' – he spoke of it as 'an inexhaustible *mental* ratiocination, like a mind ceaselessly taking its bearings in the maze of the unconscious.'[43]

To be sure, this is not everybody's notion of theater, and the mind needs to take its bearings, too, in the maze of history as it thinks through the politics of the unconscious, which is what we were trying to do, just before my work with KRAKEN stopped, in an extended project called *The Cell*, which moved from the molecular cell to the Maoist cell through various kinds of ideological formation, at that limit of perception where history looks like theater or, like theater, may be defined as 'blooded thought.'[44] The investigations for this work included a series of exercises that, on the edge of drawing blood, moved the question of limits into the theater of medicine, though that was unexpected. The exercises entailed a fastidious study of the body and selected body parts, from kneecaps and genitals to finger nails, eardrums, eyelids, skin, in an avid repertoire of torture, repellent at first, but eventually performed, as the actors got into it – wanting to see more, more – as a sort of dance, dreamlike, nightmarish, but with such exploratory and ingenious cruelty, each act refined and carried to such an extreme, then various acts together in an appalling ensemble of the utterly perverse, that were you to have come upon a rehearsal you'd have found it, if fascinating, wanting to see more, rather hard to take.

It was precisely because of that, however, that when we did a public demonstration – we were in residence at the time at the University of Maryland in Baltimore – I was approached by the chief psychiatrist at the medical school, who was in charge of a new program there in the humanities. He wondered whether we'd be interested in developing a workshop for medical students and interns. (When we met to talk about it, I actually had with me a friend of mine, a philosopher, who was then editor of the *Journal of Aesthetics and Art Criticism*, and the discussions did lead to a series of workshops that my group conducted while we were there.) What he wanted us to to deal with, by similar exercises (don't think of anything like psychodrama) was not so much the politics of the unconscious but the issue of pain, which at the unbearable limit of medical practice – and somewhere in the genetics of the unconscious, and probably untreatable by psychoanalysis – remains a problem, apparently, for many doctors, unable to work in cancer wards or burn clinics, or do an amputation, because they can't take the pain.

There's more I could say of that, but if we think of pain in the theater, there is an appalling limit, too, defined by the greatest drama – say, *Oedipus* or *King Lear* – which may test the power of acting by its capacity to deal with it, an experience so unbearable you're tempted to turn away. Maybe in fact you should, but then you couldn't perform it, and even then, when you think of it – 'Is this the promised end?' 'Or image of that horror?' – if you didn't lose control, it's probably not enough. 'Never, never, never, never, never.' All other limits are subordinate to that, which Freud in his final wisdom seemed to know.

## Notes

1 Jacques Lacan, 'Aggressivity in Psychoanalysis,' in *Ecrits: A Selection*, trans. A. Sheridan, New York: Norton, 1977: 10.
2 Sigmund Freud, 'The Disposition to Obsessional Neurosis,' in *The Standard Edition of the Complete Psychological Works of Sigmund Freud*, ed. and trans. James Strachey, 24 vols.,

London: Hogarth and Institute of Psycho-analysis, 1953–74, vol. XII: 324; hereafter references will be to this edition, with customary abbreviation *SE*.

3 Herbert Blau, *The Impossible Theater: A Manifesto*, New York: Macmillan, 1964. The book, which opens with a relentless assault on the state of the art, was started after ten years of trying to create a company with another attitude at The Actor's Workshop of San Francisco. That theater was still a work-in-progress when, shortly after the book was published, I left to become co-director (with Jules Irving) of the Repertory Theatre of Lincoln Center in New York.

4 See Judith Butler, *Bodies That Matter: On the Discursive Limits of 'Sex'*, New York and London: Routledge, 1993.

5 Lacan, 'Aggressivity in Psychoanalysis': 14.

6 Jean Baudrillard, *Simulations*, trans. P. Foss, P. Patton, and P. Beitchman, New York: Semiotext(e), 1983: 36.

7 Baudrillard, *Simulations*: 9.

8 Baudrillard, *Simulations*: 6.

9 Baudrillard, *Simulations*: 4.

10 Baudrillard, *Simulations*: 17.

11 Christopher Bollas, *Cracking Up: The Work of Unconscious Experience*, New York: Hill and Wang, 1995: 12.

12 Lacan, 'Aggressivity in Psychoanalysis': 14.

13 Baudrillard, *Simulations*: 6–7.

14 Baudrillard, *Simulations*: 38.

15 Henrik Ibsen, *The Master Builder*, Act 1, in *Four Plays*, vol. 1, trans. and fwd. Rolf Fjelde, New York: Signet, 1990: 331.

16 Lacan, 'The Function and Field of Speech and Language in Psychoanalysis,' in *Ecrits*: 45.

17 Judith Butler, *Gender Trouble: Feminism and the Subversion of Identity*, London: Routledge, 1989: 67.

18 Freud, *SE*, vol. V: 435.

19 Freud, *SE*, vol. IV: 50.

20 Freud, *SE*, vol. XII: 221.

21 See the chapter entitled 'Ghostings,' in Herbert Blau, *Take Up the Bodies: Theater at the Vanishing Point*, Urbana: University of Illinois Press, 1982: 195–247.

22 Lacan, 'Aggressivity in Psychoanalysis': 11.

23 Quotations from Mike Freeman, 'A Cycle of Violence, On the Field and Off,' *The New York Times*, 6 September 1998: 27, 34.

24 Herbert Blau, *The Impossible Theater: A Manifesto*, New York: Macmillan, 1964: 1, 5.

25 Lacan, 'Aggressivity in Psychoanalysis': 21.

26 'An Interview with Stelarc,' in *Obsolete Body/Suspensions/Stelarc*, ed. D. Paffrath with Stelarc, Davis, CA: JP Publications, 1984: 16–17.

27 Herbert Blau, *The Audience*, Baltimore: Johns Hopkins University Press, 1992: 334.

28 Antonin Artaud, *The Theater and its Double*, trans. M. C. Richards, New York: Grove Press, 1958: 36–7.

29 Artaud, *The Theater and its Double*: 35.

30 Artaud, *The Theater and its Double*: 37.

31 Artaud, *The Theater and its Double*: 13.

32 Artaud, *The Theater and its Double*: 52.

33 Artaud, *The Theater and its Double*: 30.

34 Artaud, *The Theater and its Double*: 31.

35 Artaud, *The Theater and its Double*: 32.

36 Artaud, *The Theater and its Double*: 92.

37 Bollas, *Cracking Up*: 39.

38 Laurence Olivier, *Confessions of an Actor: An Autobiography*, New York: Simon and Schuster, 1982: 261.

39  Bollas, *Cracking Up*: 12.

40  Lacan, 'Aggressivity in Psychoanalysis': 15.

41  Butler, *Gender Trouble*: 140.

42  Blau, *Take Up the Bodies*: xii.

43  Artaud, *The Theater and its Double*: 63 (emphasis mine).

44  This was how I defined it in a book with that title, *Blooded Thought: Occasions of Theater*, New York: PAJ Publications, 1982, written like *Take Up the Bodies* in a kind of theoretical fallout from the work of the KRAKEN group.

# 2

# AS IF

## Blocking the Cartesian Stage

*Anthony Kubiak*

In an essay published in 1998 entitled 'Cartesian Subject versus Cartesian Theater,' Slavoj Žižek sets himself the task of locating, against the grain of Hegelian thought, the beginnings of a history of the decentered subject.[1] Far from the recent phenomenon it purports to be, Žižek says, the struggle with the decentered subject is already emerging in the work of such German Idealist writers as Holderlin, Novalis, and Schelling. Rather than wrestle with prototypical precursors of decenteredness or their rationalist antagonists, however, Žižek chooses to interpellate more recent theorists of the decentered self: consciousness theorists like Daniel Dennett.[2] But while Žižek's argument has points of similarity to my own – that studies such as Dennett's develop a theory of consciousness that denies its unconscious element, and that this denial amounts to a kind of repression that, ironically, constructs a theory of the unconscious within the very work itself – he does not, as do I, locate this torsion primarily within the conceptual frame of the theatrical, a frame that I believe essential to the understanding of identity's stagings.

I am, then, suggesting in this essay that the many discourses of consciousness that have recently appeared are haunted by the unconscious specifically through the appearance and disappearances of the theatrical within those discourses. I do not intend to show here that theories of consciousness are somehow inevitably imbued with a performative unconscious (although they may very well be) but will instead suggest the nuance of *mise-en-scène* in the warp and woof of consciousness theory, and thus underscore the performative subtleties of psychoanalysis as an approach to the understanding of consciousness. Finally, I will suggest that theater as both concept and theoretical category is both crucial to and far more consonant with the movements of psychoanalysis and consciousness than many of the current rubrics of 'performance' and the performative.

## Patchworks and crazy guilts

Jean: I've never seen anything like it. She's crazy!
Kristine: She always has been, but never as bad as the last two weeks since her engagement was broken off.

Jean: . . . I wonder what the real story was there.

August Strindberg, *Miss Julie*[3]

When Jean speaks his line to Kristine early in the action, wondering aloud about Miss Julie's row and breakup with her own intended, he adumbrates another key event at the center of the play: an Ur-scene stuck like a mis-matched patch covering the theatrical lapse, the well-known ballet scene, a Lacanian plumb waiting to be sounded. In this scene, the two main characters, in a concealed 'ballet' of sexual tension and gamesmanship, sneak off stage and consummate the latent theater of class-conflict, patriarchal, and, in recent productions, racial struggle, through something that, in the Imaginary, takes on the lineaments of an off-off Broadway sex-show: 'None of my kind is ever as coarse as you,' Jean tells Miss Julie after the private show, loving every minute of it, and leaving us to wonder in salacious fury just what it was that happened off stage, especially in light of Miss Julie's earlier role as dominatrix, training her fiancé to jump over her riding crop 'the way you'd teach a dog to jump,' or Jean's boyhood stint as voyeur *par excellence*, hidden in the muck of Julie's latrine. Indeed, it seems that what 'doesn't' happen in this scene is so crucial to the action that one imagines serious production time might be spent deciding what, exactly, 'hasn't' happened, the ithyphallic moment brought to being elsewhere, out of ear and eyeshot, quartered in the imagination of the director directing the sex scene just as Miss Julie directs the scene with her fiancé, eliciting the illicit ('Do you think one of your maids would throw herself at a man the way you did?') from the actors playing their parts: the very substance of the ob-scene.

But while all of this off-scene stuff is presumably 'not' happening, other peasants arrive and perform the 'real' ballet, a kind of lurid fertility dance or Satyr-play of bawdy and intoxicated Dionysian ecstasy representing or rather displacing the other Imaginary action, the metaphoric and metonymic scene covering up the scene that never appears, a replay of sexual gaming, domination, and deceit occurring else-where, an elsewhere forever deferred, never realized – theater as as-if. We are, in that aphanic scene, in a fractal hall of mirrors, a *mise-en-abîme*, another scene endlessly re-encoded within the scene we seem to see, an endless re-framing of the central action of the play, the slide-show side-show between Jean and Miss Julie, porno-graphic in its intimations of excess, manipulation, and crass mis-representation.

As a dramatic moment, the scene of displacement certainly seems the turning point, the fulcrum upon which all else balances: the power shifts, the seemingly lightening-quick transferences of desire, domination, and violence that characterize the play. But this brief analysis is not designed to suggest mere censoring, or repression: that, in a psychologizing of the play that a later Strindberg would have hated, the sexual scene is always a scene of dislocated, displaced desire. Rather, what is of interest here is the sense in which the theater represented in this scene is a theater which, in its most important manifestations, *always occurs elsewhere*.[4] Any useful analysis of the play seems to depend on this something that really, but never 'really' happens. This something merely foregrounds the paradox of theater's unique ontology – none of it ever 'really' happens, even when, or especially when, it really does. If we were to rewrite the scene so that it does, like the sex show, 'really happen' right in front of the viewer's nose, the question of what it is that is really happening does not go away. The question in fact becomes endlessly exacerbated in the striations of consciousness, coming finally to the problem of consciousness itself: what is it, finally, that we are seeing? What, in the end, are we conscious of? Apart from the question of what consciousness is or might be, what is its substance? What is the relationship, if any, between the substance or contents of mind, and the world upon which that mind and its content reflects?

The theater, then, in its long tradition of the off-stage, the play-within-the-play, the *mise-en-abîme*, has, in the retrogressive vision of modernism, if not exactly post-structuralism, taken as its central concern the problem of consciousness and identity. From the classical Greek stage and its conventions of off-stage violence, through the Shakespearean traditions of plays played within the frame of the play itself, up to the modern and postmodern rendering of theater as a prison-house of mind in the work of Strindberg or Beckett, the endless obsession seems, in the end, a fixation on 'this globe here,' the mind/brain, the wet, auricled three-and-half pound universe, Golgotha rendered as play-house. This concern is, however, something more than the notion of a Lambian 'theater of consciousness,' the predisposition to see in mind an idealization of the theatrical performance, or even a sense that things are staged in mind in such a way that mind represents and is represented by theater, a stage on which theater becomes mere metaphor for 'the way we seem to think.' For it is in the *seeming* way we think that the real stuff lies hidden. Thus the emphasis here is less that consciousness is like a theater, than that consciousness is *like* a theater. It is not in the theatrical metaphor *per se*, but in the mind's likenesses, and thus its unlikeness to itself, very like the writing I am here presenting, that we see the issue.[5] In the mind's likeness to theater, and in its likeness its self-difference, lies an important under-standing of what consciousness is – or rather, not what it is, but that it must always, in the seeming, seem to be, and seem to be other than what it is – as-if . . .

## Medley and pastiche

Daniel Dennett, in his book *Consciousness Explained*, and again in his more recent *Kinds of Minds*,[6] describes a conceptual error among those attempting to understand conscious states, an error he calls the 'Cartesian Theater,' the persistent (according to Dennett) misperception that consciousness is brought together in a single place in the mind/brain.[7] The term 'Cartesian Theater' comes out of a passage in Descartes in which he apparently[8] suggests that there exists some organ in the brain that produces consciousness, an organ that represents a kind of black box/theater in which the organization of mind comes together and is presented, much like a theatrical play might be – something of an organic counterpart to the Freudian *Vorstellung*. Dennett roundly and repeatedly rejects this notion in favor of a model of consciousness that is fragmentary and multivalent, a 'multiple drafts' model in which several versions of consciousness are occurring at the same time. In this model information of various kinds is registered in the brain multifariously, but is never 'revised' into final form within a single locus, a 'theater of consciousness' which the self then perceives. Rather, the various sensory inputs are in some sense 'stored' in the brain, ready to be accessed along different possible pathways, each pathway subsequently either eliminated or weighted, by virtue of other stored information, until something 'rather like a narrative'[9] is generated that only *seems* to pull together the various strands of information that have been registered. Against this semichaotic production of meaning the experience of consciousness as a theater is false.[10] Where we seem to experience the play (in mind) we are in fact experiencing an illusion – in other words, what we experience as consciousness is not a theater of mind but rather an illusion of a theater of mind. What the tantalizing difference between theater and the illusion of theater might be is ignored, however. Instead, Dennett directs our attention to the 'real' play of consciousness beneath the seeming appearance of the theatrical: 'Once we take a serious look backstage, we discover that we didn't actually see what we thought we saw on stage.'[11]

But in the theater what we see is always and only what we thought we saw, and, moreover, as in Strindberg's scenes of displacement, what we 'really see' is very often not the real scene at all. Indeed, at this point we might begin to sense the foldover between Dennett's approach to consciousness and Strindberg's structuring of it: in either case the 'real' play is something other than what it seems to be; it is split, multiple, and non-unified, a cacophony of voices, impulses, and perceptions, each crying out for attention – a situation David Chalmers, another theorist of consciousness, calls the 'pandemonium model,' and what Lacan saw as the fragmented appearance of the post-Cartesian subject.[12]

At one point Dennett rather blithely introduces language as the culprit through which the illusion of the Cartesian self is created – thus his reference to narrative creation, but in a larger sense something like the poststructural, specifically Lacanian apotheosis of language as the determining condition of identity. The problem is, as it is in many of the theories of consciousness, that the duplicities and doublings of language are never addressed in Dennett's work. This is not merely a matter of overlooking a linguistic problem, it is to ignore the substance of language itself: its operation – like the operations of the consciousness that it constructs – as alterity, displacement, as-if. Dennett subsequently misses this crucial operation of language in the literary text when he likens the construction of reality in consciousness with the reading of a fictional work; within the realm of the fictional as fiction, Dennett assures us, interpretation is not a problem,[13] thereby casting aside a great chunk of literary and psychoanalytic theory of the past century. But, more importantly, this misplaced confidence in interpretability masks another, related issue which deeply concerned Lacan: the operation of agency in the decentered subject.

Indeed, although he might agree with Lacan on the split and fragmentary nature of the self, Dennett's approach, eschewing as it does any psychoanalytic stance, begs some rather important questions: if it is true that one voice 'yells louder than the rest,' who or what notices? Who or what decides which perceptions are more relevant, which worthy of belief or notice? And how exactly is that 'rather like a narrative' constructed? Indeed, just as the problem of agency still exists within the poststructural insistence on a decentered identity, the mind/brain of consciousness theory still *seems* to censor and select a final version of events that most closely resembles perception, though Dennett claims it does not. Exactly how this selection/censoring takes place, what or who the agent might be that enacts this Mengelian process, is never fully explained, leading one to think that Dennett is in fact ignoring or finessing the most obdurate issue in consciousness studies: is the agency of consciousness – the agency of thought that selects, that decides, that represses – the agency I call me. Am I the one that selects, or does a concealed mind select me? Am I the object or subject of my own desire? Or is agency perhaps 'outside' of me, in the shifting registers of language itself, or as Lacan himself asks, 'Once the structure of language has been recognized in the unconscious, what sort of subject can we conceive for it?' We are up against something like the old Lacanian *manqué à être* here, *in which consciousness simply cannot be conceived of within the self because the unconscious, the social space of the subject's history, surpasses it.* The invocation to language as one source of the problem in understanding consciousness, and the subsequent deflection of the discussion of language into an oddly positivist notion of the transparency of language (fiction), is precisely the *manqué à être* in Dennett's own discourse.

At one point, in an oversimplification of fragmentary consciousness, Dennett addresses the multiplicity of self within the fragmentary by veering off into a discussion of Multi-Personality Disorder as a kind of model for the multiple self, forgetting all the while that the multiple self of MPD may be as much an illusion as the unified, 'Cartesian' self itself.[14] Dennett, in fact, spends the greater part of his study trying to convince us of the illusory nature of the Cartesian actor/self, without spending much time considering the nature of illusion itself beyond its narrow connotations within psychological experiment.[15]

Indeed, in perhaps his most interestingly devious chapter, Dennett reveals what is most salient in my discussion of him: correlative to his comparison of consciousness to the reading of a novel, he introduces an interesting and quite dramatic literary device – an imaginary conversation with 'Otto' who quizzes him on the seeming/reality of phenomenological consciousness/self. By way of opening the discussion to the notion of this seeming, Dennett refers to an optical illusion on the dust-jacket of his book, an illusion in which a pink, donut-like apparition emerges from a grid of black lines:

> There seems to be a pinkish glowing ring on the dust jacket.
> > There sure does.
> But there isn't any pinkish glowing ring. Not really.
> > Right. But there sure seems to be!
> Right.
> > So where is it then?
> Where's what?
> > The pinkish glowing ring.
> There isn't any: I thought you'd just acknowledged that . . . There is no such thing as a pinkish ring that merely seems to be.[16]

Dennet underscores his point by claiming that there is 'no such phenomenon as really seeming.' But then where does that leave theater? Or, indeed, seeming itself? Is the seeming of theater the same seeming as the seeming of politics? Or the seeming of memory? Might we not think of theater as precisely 'really seeming,' admittedly seeming, as opposed to the seeming of political life which is a seeming that tries to appear not to be? Isn't theater precisely the space within which this seeming is problematized, within which we see the unconscious of the Socius refracted *through* the seeming?

Dennett ends the chapter by explaining that, like the work of fiction, Cartesian consciousness operates in the as-if, as as-if. He seems, finally, to think that the problem of consciousness will dissipate if we just understand and reject the seemingly as-if for some more real as-if. In a strange and thrilling way, Dennett seems to be peering through the flames of consciousness at the gesturing face of Antonin Artaud, who demanded in the work of theater precisely what Theater seemed not be: reality. Artaud wished, through the flame of thought, to strip away the seeming theater in order to expose a Theater of the Real. An impossibility.

Finally, then, Dennett's theory *seems* to miss the point that the very seemingness of consciousness – that it seems like a theater but (perhaps) is not – is its most salient aspect. To suggest that mind 'really' is different from what it seems to be is to miss the point that seemingness, self-difference, is, arguably, what most characterizes consciousness and the very torsions of its knowledge; consciousness, echoing the ballet of derangement in Strindberg's play, is defined by the very seemingness Dennett attempts to dispel. It is, he seems to be saying, as if there were an as-if causing all the problems. The issue here certainly seems bound to language and the presentation of self as language, a point that Dennett himself seems to make.

## Poetry in emotion

Julie: [To Jean, who has chopped off the head of Julie's songbird] (Approaching the chopping block, as if drawn against her will) No, I don't want to go yet. I can't . . . until I see . . . Shh! I hear a carriage – (She listens but her eyes never leave the cleaver and the chopping block) Do you think I can't stand the sight of blood? You think I'm so weak . . . Oh – I'd like to see your blood and brains on a chopping block – I'd like to see your whole sex swimming in a sea of blood, like my little bird . . . I think I could drink from your skull![17]

Although speaking from a different theater of intensities, Antonio Damasio agrees in substance, if not in discipline, with Dennett. A neurologist by training (Dennett is a psychologically oriented philosopher), Damasio also thinks that the notion of a Cartesian Theater is little more than wishful thinking – a latent desire to ratify a unified and stable self that doesn't exist, or at least doesn't exist in quite the way we think it does. In his book, *Descartes' Error*,[18] he goes to great lengths to resituate the issue of consciousness back into material being, away from Descartes' 'cogito' and towards a reassessment of the mind/body (mind/emotion) interrelationship. In doing so, Damasio does something quite remarkable: he elucidates in a compelling way, through two separate and harrowing narratives, the rational necessity of emotion.[19] Citing these case-studies, Damasio speaks of emotion as a kind of economic investment of the self in thought – whereas it is possible to make 'rational' decisions devoid of emotion, those decisions will seem oddly irrational within the context of experience. Hence, a patient of Damasio's who has undergone frontal lobe brain surgery is run through a battery of tests, all of which show him to be in full control of mental faculties and eminently rational in his associations and decision-making capabilities. But while he knows rationally what the correct decision 'would' be in theoretical contexts, he is in life incapable of making those decisions because he simply doesn't care: his emotional detachment, precipitated by the surgery which has damaged the emotion-controlling pre-frontal lobe, forbids him from assessing the impact of his action on his own well-being. He knows he ought not give money away to shady associates, but he doesn't care enough about his well-being or the well-being of others to make sufficient judgments about such impulses. He thus acts 'rationally,' but recklessly. Emotion, then, seen as antagonistic to rational thought at least since the Enlightenment, is, in Damasio's study, a crucial component of it. Moreover, it seems in its economic function, its push to meet the emotion of the Other, akin to the Freudian drive, or perhaps even more apt, to Lacanian desire.

Emotion/desire is so central, in fact, that Damasio, following William James, speaks of the body as 'emotion's theater,' the site within which emotion/desire is enacted. Of particular interest here, however, is the sort of acting/performance theory that his metaphor implies; setting the stage, as it were, for the discussion of the body as emotional theater, Damasio posits two 'sources' or enactments of emotion. The first is part of what he calls the body/brain feedback loop – the sense in which emotional states come from 'a "read-out" of . . . body changes.'[20] Although he is careful not to split emotion into mind/body dichotomies – he sees emotions produced in the body (which includes the brain) as a necessary part of consciousness and rationality, after all – he does distinguish between this kind of emotional experience and what he calls the 'as-if' loop, in which emotional recall (he does not use that Stanislavskian term) produces something like a 'fainter image of an emotional bodystate.'[21] New emotional states are in some sense always played out before (in front of, within the context of) these 'fainter images,' what Herbert Blau might call ghostings – precipitations of other times, other performances, playing over body/mind in a myriad of remembered and misremembered parts, words, stagings and scriptings: the ghostings that in Blau's work distinguish theater from 'mere' performance. Damasio, in fact, makes something like this distinction between a bad performance (theatrical or otherwise) and a fully realized Stanislavskian theater, couched all the while in the terms of neurophilosophy:

> Moreover, the brain is not likely to predict how all the commands – neural and chemical, but especially the latter – will play out in the body, because

the play-out and the resulting states depend on local biological contexts and on numerous variables within the body itself which are not fully represented neurally. What is played out in the body is constructed anew, moment by moment, and is not an exact replica of anything that happened before.[22]

In its interplay of newly constructed experience refracted through the as-if of previous emotional memory, this passage accords in a kind of inverse way with Stanislavki's notion of 'emotion memory,' the actor's use of previous emotional experience to clarify and vitalize the theatrical act. Throughout this portion of his work, Stanislavski exhorts his actors again and again to 'draw from the memory of your life' instead of taking material from 'the theatrical archives of your mind.'[23] Great theater, he suggests, is never simply mimetic, but requires an infusion of something more than the as-if of emotion recollected as mere performative repetition. It requires, in Stanislavski's technique, an invocation of the Real, something like the hallucinated return of memory as presence, something much closer to Artaud's desire to obliterate theater and put life on stage – a stranger affinity between Artaud and Stanislavski than we might at first surmise. Indeed, when one of his students reminds him that 'the great poets and artists draw [copy] from nature,' Stanislavski responds affirmatively, 'Agreed. But they do not photograph her. Their product passes through their own personalities and what she gives them is supplemented by living material taken from the store of emotion memory.'[24] Acting, then, is a refiguration of the present through the refracting lens of emotion/memory. In the above quoted scene in Strindberg's play, the emotional content and play-out is fantastically indeterminate: how the actor playing Julie plays the scene – whether as dissociated and dispassionate appraisal of Jean's cruel and callous action, or in the high emotion of rage and revenge – radically changes our entire sense of Miss Julie's mind and unconscious drives; whether her emotion is played-out or simply played out emblematizes both aspects of Damasio's models: rage as newly felt but embodied within the frame of remembered outrage, or rage simply enacted in a fatigued and dissociative state – mere shadow and replay of what has gone before, desire or its extinction, echoing the twin poles of the Freudian Eros and Thanatos.

Damasio seems to ratify both possibilities in his descriptions of 'played-out' emotional life. While previously acknowledging the 'as-if' as context for experience – that what is occurring resonates with other, previously recorded occurrences – he also insists on the vital, literally embodied originality of this re-presentation, otherwise

emotions and feelings would be limited, time after time, to a fixed repertoire of emotion/feeling patterns, which would not be modulated by the real-time, real-life conditions of the organism at any one moment. These patterns might be helpful [to survival] if that were all we had to go on, but they would still be 'rebroadcasts' rather than 'live performances.'[25]

The as-if, then, is not, in Damasio's work, the problematic phenomenological condition of consciousness, but rather a kind of unseen frame, an invisible proscenium within which emotion is experienced and given form, something very much like the 'fictional form' that Dennett invokes, and what, in the writings of Lacan, is signified by the structuring principle of the unconscious. As Žižek writes:

> the problem that Dennett does not resolve is that of the very *form* of narrative . . . which, in a way, *must already be here*. One is tempted to say that this silently presupposed form is Dennett's unconscious, an invisible structure he is unaware of, operative in the phenomena he describes.[26]

Similarly, in the emotion theater of Damasio, the body, while experiencing emotion as real and 'new,' none the less receives and enacts emotion only within the as-if, the ghostly outlines of past lives only partly remembered. But, as I have suggested, there is in the interplay between Damasio's and Stanislavski's words an inversion of seems. Whereas Damasio sees emotion as an immediate experience that wants the as-if of context and history, Stanislavski sees the history of the as-if – theater – as the immediate experience that needs a mediated emotion/memory for its expression. Blau, in a discussion of ghostings that itself invokes the ghost of Kant, fixes his gaze somewhere at the midpoint between these oscillating visions and recollections, again, at something very like the unconscious:

> I mean now something 'beyond' or 'prior to' structure *in* the structure, as if between word and breath, the knowledge that can't be discredited because it's there, you know it's there, in and out of performance – the felt actuality of it so intense it keeps returning like a compulsion dream, the scene repeated and repeated as if the replaying will dispel it (but it won't).[27]

And the hauntingly similar observation in Žižek,

> At this point, it is crucial to take into account one of the fundamental lessons of psychoanalytic theory: a form that precedes content is always an index of some traumatic 'primordially repressed' content.[28]

Or what I have called elsewhere a theater of terror: the line of fracture within which the emotional intensity of desiring consciousness both re-enacts and conceals the lines of the as-if, the lines and lies of history – theater, and not merely the formal re-enactments of a disengaged (from theatrical history) performative, and certainly not the imagined contours of a seemingly liberatory performance (art or otherwise).

In the end, the central implication of the as-if, whether as phenomenological set-scene, hidden theatrical context, or the shimmering disapparition of the ghost, is the question of (the question in) the unconscious. It is here that the psychoanalytic project and the sciences of consciousness collide and threaten to obliterate each other. It is at the point of the as-if, in fact, that Jean Laplanche articulates the torsions between scientific method and psychoanalysis in their respective approaches to mind:

> Criticisms of . . . Freudian or Kleinian psychoanalysis are based upon an ideal of constructing a scientific rather than a magical psychology . . . The obvious objection is . . . that Freud speaks in the mode of the 'as if', whereas the ideal of science is to find a language which does not have to use that mode. The only way to parry that objection is to ask whether human beings might not be constructed in an 'as if' mode. What if 'as if' were not merely a stylistic device to be used at the level of interpretation . . . what if human beings really were constructed in the 'as if' mode? What if all personalities, and not only 'as if' personalities were constructed in that mode?[29]

Certainly in the work of Damasio and Dennett, and, I would suggest, the work of any theorist of consciousness who tackles the 'hard problem,' the appearance of consciousness almost inevitably frames itself in terms of the 'as-if.' Seemingly, the only way out of this theater of mind is to deny, as other, more positivist theoreticians of consciousness do, some essential component of experience: my desire, the desire that constructs me, and out of this the contours of what it seems like to be me. As the philosopher of consciousness Colin McGinn puts it:

> The Janus-faced character of conscious content . . . involves presence to the subject, and hence a subjective point of view. Remove the inward-looking face and you remove something integral – what the world *seems* like to the subject.[30]

Thus the crucial element of consciousness is its seeming. But what does that seeming itself imply? It implies, for one thing, the existence of seeming itself, and thus an other, Imaginary space of *being*: the be that is finale of seem, to paraphrase Wallace Stevens. The seemingness that is seemingly so integral to the appearance of the self, requires a being, an Imaginary presence, but a presence that is in essence empty: not non-existent or meaningless, but present only as absence, the *mise-en-abîme* again, a series of framings reinscribed, one within another to nothingness. That is the meaning of the theatricality of mind: consciousness constructed always elsewhere and other, self-existing only in an other scene, what Žižek identifies as the unconscious:

> the form of thought whose ontological status is not that of thought, that is to say, the form of thought external to the thought itself – in short, some Other Scene external to the thought whereby the form of the thought is already articulated in advance.[31]

And what of that other aspect of the as-if, the as-if of theater? If consciousness is structured in the as-if, in the mode of the theatrical, what might it mean to say that theater is structured like consciousness? What, following Žižek, are we to read in theater as a symptom of mind, mind as symptom of the theatrical? Perhaps this: the 'revealed' seeming of the theatrical space, the articulation of that space as 'always already' doubled, divided within and against itself marks out a symptomology of mind: an engrailing of mind in a structure that seemingly precedes structure; or to paraphrase Blau, theater as the *modus operandi* of the unconscious; the revelation in the illusion of illusion's movements; the suggestion in the *play* of play's endless and cruel regressions; the fading iconographies of power, pain, and terror that seemingly beckon from theater's pasts, and indicate its future − performance and its performative, in other words, embedded in history.

Such a history and lineage of cruelty is certainly suggested in the final scene of Strindberg's play: 'pretend you're he, and I'm you,' pleads Julie, asking Jean to command her suicide from the site of power, to become, through the theatrical, the Father. But in the next line, she immediately inverts and redoubles the power hierarchy, again through the medium of the theater: 'You gave such a good performance before when you knelt at my feet − you were a real nobleman.' Then enacting the reversal again: 'Or − have you ever seen a hypnotist in the theater? (Jean nods) He says to his subject: "Take a broom," and he takes it. He says "Sweep," and he sweeps.'[32] Here we have in a short series of lines the recapitulation of labor's violent struggles in theater/history mediated in the gendered reversals of power and desire; but the oscillations of power and submission, the taking on of performative nuance *in* performance, even and especially the nuance of 'performing oneself' in becoming conscious of self, owe their embodiments to theater, to history *as* theater, and the silent invisible hand of power that moves it: 'Don't think, Don't think!' Jean counsels Julie, then falls to his own terror at the Pavlovian bell that will summon him into his master's presence: 'What was that? I thought the bell moved . . . To be so afraid of a bell! − But it isn't just a bell − There's someone behind it − a hand sets it in motion.'[33] The invisible hand of theater/history, the 'palm at the end of the mind,' the unconscious that beckons and subsumes the dream of performance.

## Notes

1 In *Cogito and the Unconscious*, ed. Slavoj Žižek, Durham: Duke University Press, 1998.
2 I had actually nearly completed work on this piece before stumbling across Žižek's essay in a collection entitled *Cogito and the Unconscious*. At first dismayed that he may have beaten me to the punch, I was then buoyed by Žižek's essential agreement with important aspects of my position. In what follows I will differentiate that position from Žižek's own.
3 I am using Harry Carlson's excellent translation of *Miss Julie* in *The Bedford Introduction to Drama*, third edition, ed. Lee A. Jacobus, Boston: Bedford Books, 1997: 735.
4 Anecdotally, and by example, when I teach this play in class, the interest inevitably shifts to what 'really' happens between Jean and Miss Julie.
5 This is a crucial difference between the present work and works such as the recent *In the Theater of Consciousness* by Bernard J. Baars (Oxford and New York: Oxford University Press, 1997), a very interesting book that tries to demonstrate through dramatic quote and current consciousness theory the metaphorical likeness of the mind's operation to the theatrical enterprise. Baars even discusses what this likeness might mean socially, hence

politically. But he never approaches the inverse and crucial question: what does it mean that theater is structured like consciousness? What, following Slavoj Žižek, are we to read in theater as a symptom of mind, mind as symptom of the theatrical?

6  Daniel Dennett, *Consciousness Explained*, Boston: Little, Brown and Company, 1991. *Kinds of Minds: Toward and Understanding of Consciousness*, New York: Basic Books, 1996, see especially chapter 3, 'The Body and its Minds.'

7  The caesura here is a recreation of Dennett's own and represents the fact that he never adequately distinguishes the precise nature of Descartes' error: is there no place in brain or in mind in which consciousness 'happens'? This is a crucial smearing: I have no argument with the organic side of the equation, but certainly reject the psychic side.

8  In an interesting instance of theatrical subterfuge none of the authors who discuss this aspect of Descartes' work cite the passage, and I am unable to find it or to comment on it in more detail.

9  Dennett, *Consciousness Explained*, 1991: 113.

10  It is interesting to note here that the experience of this multiplicity is precisely what Žižek understands as the theatrical: 'the construct of a "continuous stream of consciousness," a theatre, a screen in our mind in which the mind directly perceives itself.' Žižek, *Cogito and the Unconscious*: 267.

11  Dennett, *Consciousness Explained*: 434.

12  Chalmers, in fact, sums up the present field of consciousness studies as rather severely deficient. Most of the theorists, he insists, deal with the 'easy' problems of mind – visual perception, organic functions, and so forth – and ignore the hard problem: the nature of consciousness itself. Among the 'easy' theorists of mind I would cite the work of Patricia and Paul Churchland, Francis Crick, J. Allan Hobson, Stephen Kosslyn and Olivier Koenig, Robert Ornstein, and John Eccles. While hardly easy in terms of rigor and power, this body of work often represents the hard toil of experimental research, and as such garners my profound respect for the advances it has made in, for example, the treatment of neurological disease. My objection, like Chalmers', is that when theorists such as these do engage the 'hard' problem of consciousness, they more often than not bracket off the most powerful features of our experience of consciousness as irrelevant or inessential.

13  Dennett, *Consciousness Explained*: 78.

14  See Anthony Kubiak, 'Splitting the Difference: Performance and its Double in American Culture,' *TDR*, 42 (4), (T160), winter 1998: 91–114.

15  This seems to be a problem endemic to psychological testing throughout: unlike controlled experiments in fields like economics, for example, group testing in psychology very often relies on deceptive tactics to deflect attention away from the actual subject of the test in order to obtain a more objective result. See, for example, Bruce Bower's article 'Psychology's Tangled Web', in *Science News*, 20 June 1998: 394–5.

16  Dennett, *Consciousness Explained*: 363.

17  Strindberg, *Miss Julie*: 748.

18  Antonio Damasio, *Descartes' Error: Emotion, Reason and the Human Brain*, New York: G. P. Putnam and Sons, 1994.

19  Damasio's work has been cited in other studies of consciousness since his book appeared. *The Emotional Brain*, by Joseph LeDoux (New York: Simon and Schuster, 1998), for example, traces in more detail the evolutionary biology of chemical/brain states. Damasio also, unfortunately, opened a space for other, less interesting ideas: the rather tired, New Agey notion of 'emotional intelligence', for example, and the myriad self-help books that have followed from it.

20  Damasio, *Descartes' Error*: 157.

21  Damasio, *Descartes' Error*: 155.

22  Damasio, *Descartes' Error*: 158.

23 Constantin Stanislavski, *An Actor Prepares*, trans. Elizabeth Reynolds Hapgood, New York: Theater Arts Books, 1983: 156.

24 Stanislavski, *An Actor Prepares*: 163.

25 Damasio, *Descartes' Error*: 158.

26 Žižek, 'Cartesian Subject', in *Cogito and the Unconscious*: 255.

27 Herbert Blau, *Take up the Bodies: Theater at the Vanishing Point*, Urbana: University of Illinois Press, 1982: 197.

28 Žižek, 'Cartesian Subject': 256.

29 Jean Laplanche, *New Foundations for Psychoanalysis*, trans. David Macey, Oxford: Blackwell, 1989: 46–7.

30 Colin McGinn, *The Problem of Consciousness*, Oxford: Blackwell, 1991: 34.

31 Slavoj Žižek, *The Sublime Object of Ideology*, New York: Verso, 1989: 19.

32 Strindberg, *Miss Julie*: 750.

33 Strindberg, *Miss Julie*: 750.

# 3

# SCANNING
# SUBLIMATION

## The digital *Pôles* of
## performance and psychoanalysis

*Timothy Murray*

Grounded in electronics and informatics, the new technologies must
be considered, always in the same light, as material extensions of our
capacity to remember . . . taking into account the role played by
symbolic language as the supreme 'condenser' of the split between
matter and mind, at least in its reactive functions, which I call
performers.

Jean-François Lyotard[1]

At the dawn of a new era of technological artistry, cinema, Antonin Artaud dreamed
of extending the mechanical capabilities of performance to enact a violent
performance of affect. Fascinated by the 'virtual force' and movement of film,
he wrote compellingly about the cultural transformations promised by cinema's
'new atmosphere of vision.'[2] To this prophet of contemporary performance, film
provided the means for a welcome 'deformation of the visual apparatus.' Rather
than ground theatrical affect in the development of realism and the narrative of the
family drama, he situated performance at the abstract interface of modernist
developments in technology. The technological artifice of light and sound provided
Artaud with the promised break from the numbing effects of mimetic realism and its
attendant social passivity. What remains particularly haunting about Artaud's
assessment of the cinematic transformation, whose cruelty he soon adapted to the
extravagance of early multimedia performance, is his characteristically French
emphasis on the contribution made by new artistic technology to interiority: 'The
cinema seems to me to have been made to express matters of thought, the interior of
consciousness.'

It was around the same moment, when the allure of technology was capturing the
imagination of early twentieth-century culture, that Freud too was taken by the
affective pull of technology and its metaphors, the big difference being, of course,
that Freud was fascinated by the interiority of the unconscious and was drawn more

to the aural apparatus of the telephone than to the visual machinery of the silent cinema. Speaking of the role of the analyst, he recommended this technological analogy: 'he must turn his own unconscious like a receptive organ towards the transmitting unconscious of the patient. He must adjust himself to the patient as a telephone receiver is adjusted to the transmitting microphone . . . so the doctor's unconscious is able, from the derivates of the unconscious which are communicated to him, to reconstruct that unconscious, which has determined the patient's free associations.'[3] In adopting a telephonic metaphor for the practice of psychoanalysis, Freud rearticulates the structures of reception he had previously established for the study of dramatic character types through which the derivatives of a character's unconscious continue to transmit to twentieth-century audiences. His readings of the poetic hallucinations, paranoias, and repressions of Shakespearean tragedy inform both his understanding of the form of psychic life and how modern viewers respond telephonically to the symbolic traumas of the Oedipal drama.[4]

Curiously, however, it was around the time that Artaud saw in technology the promise of a performance of affect that Freud broke from his former fixation on the symbolic role of dramatic narrative to reflect more freely on the affects of the drives and the linkages of incorporation, masochism, and sublimation. French work on Freud's later writings, by analysts such as Jean Laplanche, André Green, Guy Rosolato, and J.-B. Pontalis, has revealed that his undeveloped thoughts on the super ego and the enigmatic link between incorporation, sublimation, and the drives opened the door to a challenge not merely of the causal dominance of the Oedipal structure but also to a questioning of the telephonic passivity of the sublimated analyst who too finds himself troubled by the charged currents of counter-transference and its vicissitudes. At the heart of all of this interference, so the post-Lacanian analysts maintain, lies a deformation of the visual apparatus and its linkage to sublimation.

## Subjective scansion

I frequently find myself wondering what might have happened had Freud paid more attention to the early discourse on cinema and its relation to performance, had he been able to profit from Artaud's prescient dream of a technologically aided performance of affect that was meant to impinge on the psychosocial comforts of the ideology of dramatic realism. Perhaps Freud and Artaud could have collaborated on something like *A Spurt of Blood*. Such a collaboration might have profited from the material representations of performance to better theorize or imagine the workings of incorporation and the death drive and their enigmatic relation to the visual scene. While such a missed encounter might be understood as a mere curiosity of history, it could just as easily be attributed to a gap in sensibility that continues to exist between psychoanalytic and artistic practice. Whereas psychoanalysis promotes the curative value of 'creativity' and champions the fine arts for its display of artistic sublimation, it frequently does so at the expense of contemporary art forms and practices that promise to complicate the fundamental premise of Freudian sublimation: that of 'the energetic passage from the sexual instincts to non-sexual activities,'[5] which Freud attributes to successful intellectual symbolization and procedures (ideologies) of normative homosocial binding. Even the sophisticated approaches to sublimation by Laplanche, Rosolato, and Green remain overdetermined by authoritative references to Renaissance and modern representational painting,[6] to such an extent that they fail to capitalize on the artistic nuances of their own metaphors.

I refer less to their general reliance on analogies of painting, such as Pontalis's foundational thesis, in *Perdre de vue*, that 'the painting and the dream teach that one must unlearn the conventions of sight so that the horizon and background of things can display themselves in their immediacy,'[7] than to their prescient references in their revisionary texts on sublimation to the burgeoning digital scene. Rosolato reminds his readers, for example, of the psychoanalytic distinction between primary imaging and the 'signifiants digitaux' that efface the prestige of images by opening the subject to linguistic abstraction.[8] Conversely, he turns to the metaphor of 'scanning' to describe the activity of reading through vision whose 'exploration demands patience and time' at the expense of visual representation.[9] Just as Freud called upon the apparatus of the mystic writing pad to understand the process of screen memory, Rosolato now could cite the digital scanner as precisely such a machine whose patiently close entry of data recognizes the object only in relation to the software's internalized recombination of form that easily can skew the representation and abstract thought of the source document. It is in this process of scanning, moreover, that Rosolato identifies a convergence in psychic space around what he calls 'the object of perspective' that grounds psychic life.

> We thus recognize the chiasm between the verbally digital and visually representational analogy which is centered around the aporia. This results in a double manifestation: that of the relation of the unknown in the aporia and that of the object of perspective that recovers the aporia as a topological object. So it goes that this object of perspective lends itself to the signifier of loss.[10]

Loss here is organized around the phenomenological procedures of scansion, not primarily around sexual differences or Oedipal triangularity. These are the social forms of representation through which the subject gives content to form. As a result of this doubled logic of scansion, through which the form or metaphorization of the scanned object may be recognized but not necessarily in terms of its content or what it represents, the status of 'representations themselves can be relegated only to that of the phantasm, whereas the visible, maintained at a distance, can only be a protection against more direct contacts, following other perceptions, other sensations, or inversely against abstract thought.'[11] Readers of these 1987 remarks on 'The Object of Perspective in its Visual Foundations,' may even recognize scanned repetitions of Laplanche's earlier seminar on sublimation. There Laplanche turns to a similar metaphor to emphasize the importance of the process of symbolization, over and against a symbol's content: 'here also we encounter the problem of time as subjective scansion with its heterogeneous moments particularly of "disqualification," symbolic loss, and anxiety.'[12] At the heart of subjective scansion for Laplanche lies his revised thinking about the energy of sublimation through which the subject remains motivated by the traumatic enigmas of subjective scansion as they circulate energetically in relation to the enigmatic uncertainty of content (what he calls elsewhere 'the enigmatic signifier'). 'So you have to think of sublimation,' insists Laplanche,

> in a less transformational and so-called mathematical way than Freud thought of it, which is of inhibited and desexualized drives and so on. We must try to think of sublimation as a new sexuality; it is something new, maybe coming from the message, from the work itself. It is a kind of new excitation, new trauma coming from the sublimated activity itself, and through this new trauma comes new energy.[13]

Taking the lead from such reflections on sublimation which were penned in the nascent stages of digital culture and teleportic communication, I would like to reflect on their prescient relation to the suspended time of much digital performance and its 'energetic' means of production. By introducing the uncanny intersection between recent digital experiments in performance and psychoanalytic discussions of the visual and its relation to the aesthetic activity of sublimation, I wish to suggest that recent developments in digital technology once again offer a promising deformation of the visual apparatus in a way that refigures and reenergizes performance while providing materialized metaphors for a better understanding of the vicissitudes of artistic affect. Both digital performance and recent French rereadings of sublimation thus prompt their audiences 'to unlearn the conventions of sight' so that the horizon or affect of the visual itself might destabilize psychoanalytical and philosophical assumptions about intersubjective and social relations. Whereas these assumptions pertain to the primacy of the live body on the scene of performance, they pertain to assumptions about the homosocial (read 'heterosexual') necessity of desexualized sublimation on the scene of psychoanalysis. The challenge posed by digital media to conventions of sublimation are not necessarily new but can be said to be forcefully technological, in the sense suggested by Lyotard, as 'une tache technologique . . . de passer outre au rappel de ce qui a été oublié . . . de se rappeler ce qui n'a pas pu être oublié parce que ça n'a pas été inscrit.'[14]

## *Pôles* of sublimation

Just such a passage from old paradigms of forgetfulness to new visions of what never have been registered is played out in the digital dance performance, *Pôles* (1996–9), by PPS Danse of Montreal. Dancers Pierre-Paul Savoie and Jeff Hall perform an enigmatic rivalry among dazzling back projections and stunning holograms that blur the difference between actual performer and virtual image while altering the spectators' perceptions of time, distance, and space. The dance begins with Pierre-

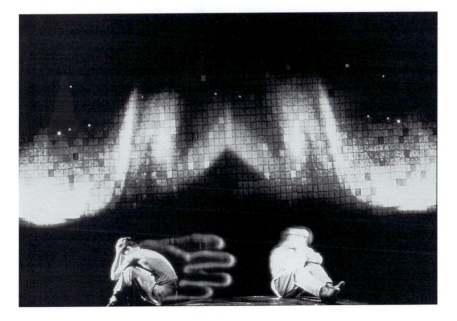

Paul Savoie seemingly falling from a sky full of colliding meteorites, as if crashing in an extraterrestrial vehicle or as a falling star itself. The display of his uncertainty with his newly discovered terrain surrounded by electronic sounds and multimedia shapes and colors is enhanced by the subsequent projectile of Jeff Hall from below the stage through a steamy, volcanic aperture at the center of the set. This second dancer embodies something of a more primitive, earthy existence in contrast to Savoie's ethereal demeanor. As the dancers interact cautiously around the steep incline of a revolving conic set, they exhibit signs of mistrust, competition, seduction, and togetherness. When the celestial being introduces the savage other to the delights of Beethoven's seventh symphony, the distrust dissipates in the haze of musical seduction. Later, the savage follows and saves the celestial figure who falls through the aperture of the rotating mound into a watery world represented through a combined spectacle of hologram and slide and light show. This is the endgame, as Savoie and Hall write in their directorial endnotes, of 'two exiles on their journey to a universe tangible yet surreal, an enticing and supernatural realm where cooperation and kindness ultimately supersede conflict and turmoil within humanity.'[15] In essence, it could be said that this is the endgame of homosocial sublimation, 'in accordance with the general estimate,' writes Freud, 'that places social aims higher than the sexual ones, which are at bottom self-interested.'[16]

Such an alignment of *Pôles* with the social tranquility of sublimation is certainly the utopic message sent out by the company and registered by its mass media reviewers. 'Based on a simple concept of harmony through cooperation,' asserts Susan Hickman in the *Ottawa Citizen*, '*Pôles* is, nevertheless, thought-provoking and suggestive of the dawning of a new age.'[17] 'While technology is king in *Pôles*,' writes Linde

Howe-Beck in Montreal's *The Gazette*, 'soul is a main ingredient in the hour-long piece, sending the message that humanity can't survive without compassion.'[18] Finally, Elissa Barnard, in a review for Halifax's *The Chronicle-Herald*, echoes Artaud's earlier dreams of a merger between technology and performance: 'This is no domestic drama. The story is epic and mythic.'[19] Such an almost predictable rallying of the popular press around the directors/performers' upbeat spin of 'an imaginary odyssey where body, soul, mind, image and motion memorably recount adventure in unison' attributes to this complex performance piece the seemingly simple business of recovering social harmony, of remembering the humanistic quietude which either late twentieth-century culture seems to have forgotten or which never existed to be forgotten in the first place.

By so diminishing the many tensions of this male-to-male dance and by desexualizing its erotic exhibition, critics and directors have enshrouded it in nothing short of the language of sublimation. For they seem to align it precisely with the work which André Green attributes to conventional understandings of sublimation: 'What is sublimated is related to an ideal object. Desexualization means dematerialization, and dematerialization is synonymous with idealization. The incorporeal, the spiritual, and the ideal are primarily at issue here. Idealization presupposes spiritualization and these become the model of an ideal.'[20] Perhaps the piece's appeal to such a non-specific ideal is why William Littler of *The Toronto Star* concludes that 'anyone who looked in *Pôles* for anything more narratively sophisticated than a variation on Saint-Exupéry's *The Little Prince* may similarly have found reason for loud complaint.'[21] Of course were the *Pôles* to be limited to responses to its narrative framework, its sophisticated technological achievements could be relegated to the cutting-room

floor along with other benign fragments of audiovisual experimentation. Where my complaint lies, however, is not with any juvenile appeal of *Pôles* but with its critics' passive acceptance of the company's publicity campaign that envelops this frightfully enigmatic spectacle of technology and movement in the bleakest of narrative simplicities: 'a daring duo filled with humanity transcends movement to conquer space and triumph over time.'[22] Put otherwise, such packaging fits directly into Guy Rosolato's cynical equation of the sublimational ideal with the technological destitution of the contemporary media: 'perhaps these ideals realize their imagery in the "clips" of a dominant audiovisual universe which, through its commercial nepotism, is propaganda for a certain happiness.'[23]

I do not mean, however, to dismiss out of hand the anchoring weight of time and infantile narrative in psychic life and its artistic expression. PPS Danse is correct to insist, alongside its journalistic critics, that the temporality and the infantile pull of this production are of consequence. But on what level and to what extent? Although the narrative impulse leads naturally to an equation of *Pôles* with a children's parable like *The Little Prince*, such focus on child's play leads us astray from the resonant psychic force of a production as powerful as *Pôles*. For it distracts us from contemplating the resonance in *Pôles* of those very traces of infantile life which, as Pontalis understands them, 'are not images or memories but figured retroactively in plastic and visual form.' At issue here is the status of what Pontalis calls 'le visuel,' through which sublimation signifies not so well through narrative but more through 'the overaccentuation of visual *elements*.'[24] The challenge open to the viewer of *Pôles* is how to translate these elements of the visual, of the formal, that may yet to have been scanned in the codes of narration. Pontalis poses the question, in this context, whether translation 'is an alteration of language, code, and register, or rather, an alteration of state, of regime, violent mutation, metamorphosis, exile in another place'. It should be no surprise that he recommends adoption of the second hypothesis.

Something like a change of register may be required to appreciate the mastery of time in *Pôles*. Perhaps the most misdirected slogan in the PPS press packet is the idealistic conception of the show's 'triumph over time.' Almost the opposite is true of *Pôles* in which the slow movement of time triumphs over the ideals of its narrative. Throughout this seventy-minute spectacle, time mimics the deliberate pace of the dancers' movements to envelop the viewers in a spectacle of prolonged duration and subjective scansions. As one reviewer ambivalently explains, 'the pace is often painfully slow.' Instead of putting effort into development of the dance, *Pôles* emphasizes the fusion of dance with technology.[25] Enveloped by the creative verve and technological precision of designer Michel Lemieux's holograms, the dancers seem at times to become one with the psychic projections emanating from their bodies and, at others, to be dwarfed and overwhelmed by the 'virtual force' of the holograms and projections whose colossal apparitions seem to haunt their every move. As the dance progresses and the performers interact more fluidly with the holographic specters accompanying them, the performance abandons the representation of corporeal performance and all its virtuosity for the display of the slow passing of time and light and the virtuality they simulate. This viewer was fascinated by the impression that the dancers themselves began to adapt their movements to the rhythm of the holograms to such an extent that their live performances became fused with the slow virtual time of scansion itself. The staging of *Pôles*, then, is less a triumph over time than 'une tache technologique' for which time is the matter.

Just how time matters is the subject of a detailed discussion by Rosolato of the change of psychic register required by 'a "reading," a glance, a "scanning," an exploration that demands patience and time.'[26] Not so much the fleeting of time, or any triumph over it, but the pause of time's passage constitutes for Rosolato the sensorial field of the 'horizon' of vision through which quality visual gathering opens up the limit between the visible and the invisible through which the known and the unknown enter into dialogue. Without a precise object, without a certain narrative, without an exact representation, time's pause liberates the spectators, in Rosolato's words, 'from the transcendental relation' to 'the way towards this object of perspective as triumph over representation and exposure to the unknown.'[27] A visual waiting, a digital pause, a triumph in time. This is scansion's precious gift of exile in an Other register that it offers to the audience of *Pôles*.

The radicality of *Pôles*'s contribution to a revisionary notion of sublimation might become even more apparent if positioned momentarily in relation to experiments with digital representation by other recent digital dance projects. Perhaps the most obvious example would be the celebrated collaborations of the digital artists Paul Kaiser and Shelley Eshkar with dancers Merce Cunningham and Bill T. Jones. In 1989, Cunningham began using LifeForms software to sketch his choreography on the computer prior to working with dancers in the studio. Kaiser and Eshkar then

worked with both Cunningham and Jones to extend the digital platform from its use as a design tool to an interactive device in performance itself. For Cunningham's *Hand-Drawn Spaces* (1998) and Jones's *Ghostcatching* (1999), the choreographers supplemented and added depth to their compositional line drawings on the touch pad with input of the heterogeneous rotations and positions of the dancer's body, data which had been captured in motion by sensors attached to the bodies of dancers from the two companies. These 'captured phrases' then provided the core material for the choreographers' subsequent development of the dance as they developed and combined individual movements, figures, and vocabularies. The resulting choreography is then performed on the computer screen by stunningly translucent three-dimensional drawings which are then projected in large-scale format on multiple screens that surround the viewer in the gallery space. While evacuating the body of the performer, these captivating performances display the traces and folds of human motion and movement in a way often obscured by the unscanned body.[28] The work of digital scansion in these pieces has gone so far as to eradicate the performing body by replacing it with ghostly figures representative of what could not have been inscribed in performance prior to the new technological moment.

This eradication and choreographic scansion is enough to align the virtual performance with the affect of trauma, at least, trauma insofar as these pieces pronounce the absent body that constitutes the very core of performance. Heidi Gilpin explains the dynamic this way: 'Performance presupposes (or at the very least anticipates) the absent body in the very moment of its presence. This absence can frequently be perceived as a site of trauma.'[29]

Of course, trauma in this context must be understood in relation to the disruption of the display and seduction attached to bodily presence. Yet the reconfiguration of this break between matter and spirit by the interiorized mechanics of scansion could also be understood to lend itself, as Laplanche would say, to 'a kind of new excitation, new trauma coming from the sublimated activity itself, and through this new trauma comes new energy.'[30] An ever greater resurgence of the energy of sublimation is what, I want to suggest, typifies the psychic energy of the holographic choreography of PPS Danse. When the performer's body in *Pôles* interacts with the holographic avatars of scansion, the excitation of performance can be said to cast a new light on the meaning of sublimation. Something like a confrontation of the body and its many attached affects is propelled by the visions of *Pôles*. This occurs on two interrelated levels: the holographic form of the spectacle and the affect of the dancers' interaction with the spectral other.

Of note is how readily the enigmatic form of this spectacle is translated by the critics into recognizable parables of art and technology without dwelling on the specificity, say, of the hologram. It is true that this tendency could find justification in theoretical discussions of the hologram. In a 1981 essay, 'Hologrammes,' Jean Baudrillard took the critical lead by lamenting the diminished charm of the virtual that results from its materialization in holograms:

> We dream of being able to go through ourselves and find ourselves on the other side: the day when your holographic double will be there, spatially, moving and speaking, then you will have achieved that miracle. Of course, this will no longer be a dream, the charm will have been lost.'[31]

As Baudrillard sees it, the hologram here mimes the verisimilar projection of Narcissus, the dream of interacting with one's exact double. The hologram, that is, stands in for its well-known narrative double of Narcissus (the original Little Prince?) looking to fulfill self-affirmation. But as I learned while researching the holographic work of the Australian artist, Paula Dawson, what is probably lost by the arrival of the hologram, *pace* Baudrillard, is not so much the charm of a dream but the loss of the narrative of verisimilitude itself in the enigmatic wake of holographic experiments with 'time, memory, and space.'[32] In keeping with the conceptual emphasis of Dawson's experiments with the uncanny valence of holograms set in everyday environments, I have been suggesting that the hologram in *Pôles* translates 'le visuel' onto a different register, not as the quaint charm of verisimilitude but as the energetic errancy of affect in time and space through which the hologram serves as the tertiary screen for the montage of 'traumatophilia.' In *Pôles*, the fragments of shape and visage on which the dancers are propped come not so much from without, in the sense of symbols to be deciphered or images to be recognized, but from within, as enigmatic and traumatic specters to be encountered as a result of sublimational trauma. So it goes that, in imaging the kind of radical heterogeneity that unbinds or disorganizes the fusion of sublimation, Laplanche argues similarly that the paradigm of sublimation needs to be shifted away from that of verisimilitude, of 'identity of

identity and non-identity', to leave room for energetic unbinding on the level of sublimation that remains indifferent to the certainties of identification.

I would like to suggest, far too rapidly in conclusion, that nowhere is the artistic display of such unbinding more apparent in *Pôles* than when Savoie and Hall are seated, as described by the insightful critic, Paula Citron, 'with their backs to each other, as holographic images are projected from their bodies that reveal their churning inner emotions.'[33] Related to the holographic errancy of affect, moreover, is the highly eroticized interaction of the dancers themselves. In addition to the primal residue of seduction (which Laplanche considers to be the core material of sublimational trauma) provided by the dancers' hesitant desire for contact, for touch, comes a direct refutation of Freud's most troubling assumption about sublimation: the detachment of homoeroticism from the sublimated scene of social production. For there are few crucial moments in this performance when the male dancers' proximity is not energetically doubled by the art of special effects, from the charged tension of corporeal distance to the electric energy of embrace. Very much undervalued by the company and most of its enthusiastic critics, who so readily translate the special effects of embrace into the normative ideal of unity, remains the imprint of desire and affect, the stuff of the sexual instincts, that lingers on stage from the very first hesitant encounter of these two highly erotic performers, almost as if a display of the unstable psychic work of sublimation.

In his essay on 'Matter and Time,' Lyotard echoes the subliminal theme of Laplanche by calling for sensitivity to the performative energetics of new technology. As if responding to the narrative impulses of PPS Danse and its critics, Lyotard cautions that 'in the actual state of the sciences and techniques, the tendency to resort to the entity "Life" to camouflage what I call, for lack of a better term, desire . . . disempowers bit by bit the objects of seduction.'[34] Experienced by the spectators of *Pôles* is precisely such an empowering of desire through the conjoined psychic and material procedures of scanning. Realizing what Artaud foresaw as the psychic promise of the new technology's 'virtual force,' the holographic doublings of PPS Danse render in performance the energetic trauma of sublimation thought anew.

## Notes

The illustrations in this chapter are scenes from *Pôles*, PPS Danse, Montreal.
1 Jean-François Lyotard, 'Matière et temps,' in *L'inhumain: causeries sur le temps*, Paris: Galilée, 1998: 52.
2 Antonin Artaud, 'Sorcellerie et cinéma,' in *Oeuvres complètes*, vol. III, Paris: Gallimard, 1970: 83.
3 Sigmund Freud, 'Recommendations on Analytic Techniques,' in *The Standard Edition of the Complete Psychological Works of Sigmund Freud*, vol. XII, ed. and trans. James Strachey, London: The Hogarth Press and the Institute for Psychoanalysis, 1958: 115–16.
4 For more on the Oedipal trajectory of Shakespeare tragedy, see Timothy Murray, ed., *Mimesis, Masochism, and Mime: The Politics of Theatricality in Contemporary French Thought*, Ann Arbor: University of Michigan Press, 1997, and Timothy Murray and Alan K. Smith, eds, *Repossessions: Psychoanalysis and the Phantasms of Early Modern Culture*, Minneapolis: University of Minnesota Press, 1998.
5 Jean Laplanche, *Problématiques III: la sublimation*, Paris: Presses Universitaires de France, 1983: 95.
6 Jean-François Lyotard argued against this habit as early as 'Freud selon Cézanne,' *Des dispositifs pulsionnels*, Paris: 10/18, 1973: 71–94.
7 J.-B. Pontalis, *Perdre de vue*, Paris: Gallimard, 1988: 282.
8 Guy Rosolato, 'L'objet de perspective dans ses assises visuelles,' *Pour une psychanalyse exploratrice dans la culture*, Paris: Presses Universitaires de France, 1993: 44.
9 Rosolato, 'L'objet de perspective dans ses assises visuelles': 34.
10 Rosolato, 'L'objet de perspective dans ses assises visuelles': 44.
11 Rosolato, 'L'objet de perspective dans ses assises visuelles': 32.
12 Laplanche, *Problématiques III: la sublimation*: 13.
13 Jean Laplanche, 'The Kent Seminar,' in John Fletcher and Martin Stanton, eds, *Jean Laplanche: Seduction, Translation, Drives*, London: Institute of Contemporary Arts, 1992: 32.
14 Jean-François Lyotard, *L'inhumain: causeries sur le temps*, Paris: Galilée, 1998: 65.
15 PPS Danse press packet.
16 Sigmund Freud, *Introductory Lectures on Psychoanalysis*, trans. J. Strachey, New York: Norton, 1966: 345.

17  Susan Hickman, 'Props, Special Effects Enhance Surreal Quality of Poles,' *Ottawa Citizen*, 19 January 1998.
18  Linde Howe-Beck, '*Pôles* Fuses Dance and Technology,' *The Gazette, Montreal*, 30 November 1996.
19  Elissa Barnard, '*Pôles* Dance Project like being in a Planetarium,' *The Chronicle-Herald*, Halifax, Nova Scotia, 17 September 1997.
20  André Green, *Le travail du négatif*, Paris: Seuil, 1993: 311.
21  William Littler, '*Pôles*' Holograms Push Dance One Step Further,' *The Toronto Star*, 19 September 1996.
22  PPS Danse press packet.
23  Rosolato, 'L'objet de perspective dans ses assises visuelles': 52.
24  Pontalis, *Perdre de vue*: 291.
25  Howe-Beck, '*Pôles* Fuses Dance and Technology.'
26  Rosolato, 'L'objet de perspective dans ses assises visuelles': 35.
27  Rosolato, 'L'objet de perspective dans ses assises visuelles': 38.
28  For descriptions and quicktime images of *Ghostcatching*, consult the web page maintained by Kaiser and Eshkar, www.riverbed.com. Documentation of Cunningham's piece, *Hand-Drawn Species*, can be found in Sarah J. Rogers, *Body Mécanique: Artistic Explorations of Digital Realms*, Columbus, Ohio: Wexner Center for the Arts, 1998.
29  Heidi Gilpin, 'Cybertrauma and the Disorders of Testimony,' in Rogers, *Body Mécanique*: 72.
30  I elaborate on the aesthetic import of Laplanche's theories of sublimation in *Drama Trauma: Specters of Race and Sexuality in Performance, Video, and Art*, London and New York: Routledge, 1997, and *Like a Film: Ideological Fantasy on Screen, Camera, and Canvas*, London and New York: Routledge, 1993.
31  Jean Baudrillard, 'Hologrammes,' in *Simulacres et simulations*, Paris: Galilée, 1981.
32  In *Apparition: Holographic Art in Australia*, Sydney: Power Publications, 1995, Rebecca Coyle and Philip Hayward turn to Paula Dawson's subtle artistic experiments with holograms to articulate this distinction: 'while Baudrillard tacitly identifies with verisimilitude as the end-product of holography, Dawson has resisted this drift. Rather, her work develops her central concerns with time, memory, and space' (66).
33  Paula Citron, 'Poles Vaults into New Dimension,' *The Globe and Mail*, 20 September 1996.
34  Lyotard, 'Matière et temps': 54.

# NOW AND THEN

Psychotherapy and the
rehearsal process

*Lisa Baraitser and Simon Bayly*

In response to a call for background material related to rehearsal, we were kindly sent an unpublished text by Tim Etchells from Forced Entertainment, the long-standing Sheffield-based theatre group.[1] Alongside pleasurable meandering over the company's history, it is an attempt at capturing something of the 'mutable logics of play – with its transformations, its power reversals, its illogics, its joys, its potential escapes': a writer/director trying to catch a whisper of the secret of his own methodology.[2]

The text left us wondering if PUR, the company we have co-directed for the last seven years, ever learnt these joys: learnt to 'play' that is. The work of the British psychoanalytic clinician and theorist D. W. Winnicott came to mind, with his assertion that psychoanalysis developed as a 'highly specialized form of playing in the service of communication with oneself and others'.[3] We also wondered what exactly Winnicott was referring to – what that 'highly specialized form' might look or sound like.

Somehow the terms are already becoming overlapped and unclear – psycho-therapy/rehearsal, process/play. What is the difference between rehearsal and play, between rehearsal process and psychotherapeutic process, between what we do with PUR and with other groups, therapeutic and otherwise, which we facilitate on a regular basis? Given that our own working lives are an amalgamation of these two practices, the overlap between the practice of psychotherapy and rehearsal has become an everyday, and so largely unquestioned, experience.

Psychotherapy and rehearsal: already there is something slightly unpleasant, even depressing, in this conjugation. Somehow it heralds the potential co-opting of radical cultural activity under the dreary aegis of encounter group process or paratheatrical pseudo-ritual. Were it psychoanalysis and rehearsal, it might have a different feel, might offer us the hope of something of import arising from the deploy-ment of the complexities of analytic theory in relation to that curiously secretive, relatively unarticulated domain that is rehearsal. Psychoanalysis as a term connotes power, authority, intricacy, elegance; the same could hardly be said for a lay conception of therapy.

And yet, in dealing with practice and process (including therapeutic process), the term psychotherapy seems the most appropriate to denote the eclectic range of activities currently on offer for effecting psychological and behavioural change. It serves to highlight the fact that both psychoanalysis and the psychotherapies, like rehearsal, continue as actual on-going encounters between individuals in small rooms. Currently many more people looking for psychological help will opt for a weekly session with a counsellor or therapist – the chair firmly in its upright position – than a prone encounter with a psychoanalyst five times a week. There is a growing consensus within the psychotherapy field that no one approach is clinically adequate for all patients, and since there are over four hundred types of therapy currently available, no single theory has been able to corner the market on validity or utility. However, a drastically simplified version of psychoanalysis remains a dominant structuring force in not just lay conceptions of self but also in the relation of that self to others, any others. Psychotherapy as a set of pluralistic practices remains haunted by the theoretical weight of its precursor. As Deleuze and Guattari write: 'no-one today can enter an analyst's consulting room without at least being aware that everything has been *played out in advance*'.[4] We might add that today, no-one can enter into any kind of shared reflective activity – from international diplomacy to office meeting – without at least a similar suspicion.

The parallels with psychotherapy are unavoidable in the domain of making performance: the mystique of the 'creative process', the quasi-religious secrets of the rehearsal room, the closed film set for those key intimate scenes, the tantrums and the tears. But what is it that is actually encompassed by the activity of rehearsal?

Within theatre studies, theorising rehearsal remains firmly within the domain of illuminating performance. There are accounts of particular directors and what they do – plenty on Stanislavski, Brecht, Grotowski, Brook – but the analysis of the rehearsal process is usually en route to an uncovering of that director's vision, an understanding of the theatre they are concerned to make. In other words, analysing rehearsal has been seen as necessary in order to develop an understanding of performance.

Obviously, the two are intimately related. Rehearsal is concerned with the notion of preparation, usually the preparation of an event that will eventually be witnessed by an audience. We can distinguish it from a set of activities denoted by the term 'practising'. Practising seems to be about keeping in a constant state of readiness, readiness for an eventual performance, but one that may arrive now, may arrive later or, then again, not at all. Dancers and musicians practise throughout their careers. Rehearsing happens with the event already in sight, in the shadow of the event anticipated, something that happens in the gap between the now and then – some point in the future – with 'then' already visible on the temporal horizon. Whilst it is clearly within the realm of logic to talk of performance that has not been prepared through a process of rehearsal, the notion of rehearsal requires the foreshadow of anticipated performance for it to make any sense at all.

61

Theatricality resonates in the word 'rehearsal', but it has significant meaning for everyday life beyond the performing arts. Rehearsal, both mental and physical, is implicated in a range of activities from preparation for a formal interview to a first date, from a marriage ceremony to the initial meeting between therapist and client. Rehearsal in the context of performance and everyday life might be seen as an attempt to control the first impression and subsequent encounter, to present a coherent image in the face of anxiety about its non-existence. Somehow, by 'going over it in one's mind beforehand', it might be possible to circumvent the awkward silence, the embarrassing noise, the shameful stumble. And yet one of the things offered by the therapeutic encounter is the chance to stumble, to enjoy silence, to dare to make that noise. This form of anxiety, ultimately about the potential failure of signification, seems central to both rehearsal and psychotherapy.

Although rehearsal as a means of generating performance remains a largely untheorised practice, a surprisingly similar working method has arisen from a heterogeneous set of groups making what used to be called avant-garde performance work: companies as diverse as The Wooster Group, Goat Island, (USA); Forced Entertainment; Desperate Optimists and ourselves, PUR (Eire/UK); Baktruppen (Norway); Needcompany (Belgium); and many others besides. Their members tend to stay together for years, working beyond the confines of a particular set of performance dates, creating relationships that either cut across or incorporate those of family, friends, employers, employees and professional colleagues. The place of rehearsal merges into a quasi-home, or in some cases *is* the actual home of members of the group. To the point that these relationships become semi-permanent, they become a way of life that goes against the grain; a site of resistance to a set of cultural practices that gauges most things in terms of outcome: healed person, finished play. In terms of a creative economy, these companies represent a blatant disregard for time and efficiency, so that they come to be seen by some as 'unhealthy' – too introspective, self-reflective, self-absorbed.

There is clearly an echo here of a popular conception of psychotherapy. It shares with these performance companies an antithetical relationship to dominant models for shaping process into product. Perhaps psychotherapy can also be conceptualised as a kind of rehearsal process akin to the process developed by the performance companies mentioned, a process in which a 'performance' is necessarily seen on the horizon (the end point of therapy – the reintegration of a person with the status quo, a functioning, that is, 'performing' individual, a 'healed person') but with the process offering something infinitely more compelling than the performance – a period of time in which everyday life is held in abeyance, identity is deferred, old knots dissolved, and new ideas, emotions, behaviour can be played with. Given that such activities are not readily available or sanctioned by the cultural practices of everyday life in the developed world, the enormous appetite for therapy that has emerged in the last decades is not surprising.

When talking about the performance groups mentioned above, moving from generalities to specifics appears strangely problematic. Somehow rehearsal remains private, something it feels impertinent to ask about, just not anyone else's business –

as if the members of the companies hold an implicit confidentiality within the group. This is compounded by the lack of a critical discourse with which to analyse functional group processes other than the psychotherapeutic, the application of which seems inappropriate or uninterestingly reductive when applied to collaborative art-making. So we are left to draw on our own experiences and add to it snatched conversations with our contemporaries, a rare text in which a company has been prepared to partially break cover,[5] the odd musing we filtered through the Internet.

Some basic principles seem clear. The roles of performers and director have mostly been retained, and the staging of a single text has been decentralised. The rehearsal process appears disarmingly simple: the performers are encouraged to bring in material, which can be anything: a gesture, a textual fragment, a theatre text, a personal confession, a videotape, an object. Nothing is off limits, nothing will be rejected out of hand, everything is forgiven. Then, the performers simply – how else to say it? – free associate with this material. Rules and structures are brought into this unchallenged play, but only as aids to the imagination, to be broken at random and there only to help produce the accidental elisions, trips, and slips that can create meaning. These improvisations are reviewed (often recorded), sifted for meaning, replayed, altered and then finally edited together into a show, an event for public consumption. Often the experience of public performance is itself fed back into the rehearsal process, creating further mutations.

Our purpose here is not to propose some set of family resemblances amongst the working practices of the makers of contemporary live performance. Rather it is simply to note the emergence within progressive performance work of a kind of group process that is essentially loose, open-ended, minimally structured and deliberately untheorised (that is to say, which appears to take on some of the *formal* aspects of a certain type of psychotherapeutic process) and to explore out of this juxtaposition some of the masked space of rehearsal and its function within performance, psychotherapy and everyday life.

For contemporary performance practice, rehearsal can be simply a space, both temporal and geographical (but never, *pace* Peter Brook, empty), in which to play with material. But is this 'play'? Wouldn't 'work' feel more appropriate? Somehow 'playing' fails to do justice to the actual experience of this process. There is an absence of tension, grit or difficulty in the word. Rehearsal – and psychotherapy – have a level of rigour and ardour about them, and appear altogether more radically anxious, insecure and contingent than is suggested by the concept of 'play', full of frustration and repression as much as pleasure and release.

We are not actually in rehearsal at the moment, being somewhat involved with rearranging our activities around Joel, our six-month-old son, and *his* literal involvement with material and play, largely focused around his particular obsession with chewing his thumb and fist, the ears of his toy snails and dogs, even with the little white labels attached to them, in preference to any enjoyment of 'dog' or 'snail' or 'fist' as objects he might identify with and relate to as sharing his world – and with worlds of their own. This, in part, explains the earlier reference to Winnicott, that idiosyncratic British psychoanalyst, whose theoretical work was intimately bound up, in a characteristically British way, with praxis: the observation and treatment of thousands of parents and children. In perhaps his most influential essay, 'Transitional Objects and Transitional Phenomena', Winnicott deals directly with both Joel's current interests and our own.[6]

In his essay, Winnicott maps out a notional period of time between an infant's interest in her own fist and her later attachment to objects such as favourite toys, between her oral eroticism and her eventual ability to relate to true external objects, between her primary creative activity and her projection of what has been introjected. It is in this intermediate area that what he terms transitional objects and phenomena are used. The objects are not part of the infant's body but are also not yet fully part of the object world. While thumb sucking, for example, the infant may take an external object – part of a sheet or blanket – into the mouth along with the fingers. The place of the object is played with – inside, outside, at the border – as is the infant's recognition of the object's 'not-me' qualities. The thing or the phenomenon – corner of blanket, word, tune or mannerism – becomes vitally important as a defence against anxiety, especially for navigating the space between wakefulness and sleep. The object carries on being important. Parents get to know its importance, know not to wash it, not to break the continuity of the infant's experience, know that travelling without it will ruin the holiday. It often has a name: mit-mat, baa, dee.

For Winnicott, from birth the human being is concerned with the problem of the relationship between what is objectively perceived and what is subjectively conceived. Crucially, in what he calls this 'intermediate area of experience', this question (what is or is not 'not-me') is left unformulated. The area remains un-challenged, and a temporary resting place is created, providing relief from what he conceptualises as the strain of keeping inner and outer reality separate and yet interrelated. He describes one of the qualities of the transitional object as 'coming from without from our point of view, but not so from the point of view of the baby. Neither does it come from within; it is not an hallucination'.[7]

This intermediate stage seems to represent a space of 'pre-play', a direct precursor to the play of the small child who is 'lost' in play, and is vital for the initiation of a relationship between the child and the world. Before play is possible, the child needs to experience this unchallenged space where self and object remain crucially unresolved, where the infant does not yet have to make up her mind about what is and is not her. In order that the infant can develop the capacity to relate to objects, she builds a special relationship with her first 'not-me' possession. In his summary of some of the qualities of this special relationship, Winnicott talks of the transitional object seeming to the infant to give 'warmth, or to move, or to have a texture, or to do something that seems to show it has vitality or reality of its own'.[8] Winnicottians argue that the therapist is used in much the same way, that the analytic setting could be seen as a 'transitional space for collaborative exchange'.[9] As Philips argues, up to this point psychoanalysis had been a theory of subjects in some kind of instinctual relation to objects without sufficient notice of the space between them. The space was either pre-empted by the fantasised wish to merge with or annihilate the object, or it had been constituted as real only due to the capacity to mourn the object.

Perhaps this is more like the kind of space that rehearsal wants to occupy. In rehearsal, decisions about subjectivity and objectivity are also temporarily suspended. The performance is not yet formed or fixed, identities can remain fluid, performers can explore versions of themselves, versions whose 'truth value' (that necessary illusion of the sense of 'the real me' as ultimately separate from the sum of what I do and say) is neither asserted nor denied. And in contemporary rehearsal practice, in the groups mentioned earlier, it appears that this is achieved not through a performer's relation to a character or role, nor through a director's relation to a play-text but through the group member's relation to their 'material' – a relation which seems to function much like transitional phenomena. Willem Dafoe, long-term member of the Wooster Group, describes his role in the company's 1984–5 production *LSD . . . Just the High Points*, in just such terms:

> I'm this particular guy who has to go through these particular paces. It's not so much that I'm putting forward my personality, but because of the various actions I have to do, I'm presenting my personality in how I field those actions. That is the acting in it. I'm a guy given a character, a performing persona, and I'm going through these little structures, and how I field them is how I live in this piece.[10]

The material performers work with is taken up not on the basis of its apparent meaningfulness, but without recourse to it needing to mean anything at all. Material is brought in because of its seeming marginality, the interest in it almost born out of boredom with supposedly significant objects, such as concretised themes, whole texts or an overarching political agenda. As Liz Lecompte, director of the Wooster Group, observes:

> When I choose texts, they're in a random way. I feel I could use any text. That was something that started very early with Spalding [Gray]. I could pick anything in this room and make a piece as complete as *L.S.D.* [the 1986 Wooster Group show]. I could take three props here: the printing on the back of that picture, and whatever's in this pile of papers, and make something that would mean as much, no more, no less than what I've constructed in the performance space downstairs.[11]

In the type of performance we are discussing here, these texts are nowadays almost always fragments of *cultural* artefacts, more or less complex. Rather than fire, water or earth, we have the disconnected telephone, a death scene from a third-rate movie, a discarded pantomine horse, a list of fictional bad deeds – objects with symbolic value or texture rather than narrative or discursive meaning. Textual traces left by prior performative events also seem to become 'not-me' possessions: scripts, records, video and audio tapes, transcripts, books, photographs and movie clips are recurrent stage objects in so much contemporary performance, alongside memories, recollected dreams and half-remembered anecdotes. Rehearsal becomes the place where performers worry these artefacts as an animal does its wounded prey, repeatedly subjecting them to violence, love and affection, seeing if they will survive so much attention, hoping they might inform a stronger sense of 'realness'.

This quasi-obsessive worrying finds its corollary in contemporary performance's psychotherapeutic preponderance for the rewind button – the need to review, to replay what has passed and to mine it for some hidden substance. In 1996 whilst on tour in Glasgow, we saw Beckett's *Krapp's Last Tape*, playing in the tiny studio at the Citizens' Theatre – a play we knew well but had not seen performed for a decade. The performance that really engaged our attention was strangely not that of the actor, but of the bulky 1940s reel-to-reel tape deck with which Krapp reviews, edits and rewrites his past and present for some unknown future. Seeing that machine after ten years against a backdrop of American and European performance work, it appeared as a kind of ancient, Ur-recording device, the mother and father of all inscription technologies, somehow uncannily preceding even writing and memory. Its presence brought back the words of Ron Vawter, interviewed by Etchells in 1993:

> I once asked Ron Vawter (Wooster Group) if he ever wished they could deal with new texts instead of (as he described it to me) going back over the tapes of the twentieth century to see what had happened, to see what had gone wrong. He said yes, he could see a time when that might be fun, but for the moment at least there was so much work left to do. There's so much stuff left in the archives.[12]

There was Krapp, literally replaying his own tapes of the twentieth century, looking for what went wrong, to see what happened. Beckett's play suddenly seemed a much more seminal moment in performance history. As Vawter suggests, to do something new might be fun – but therefore possibly frivolous. Examining the archives is somehow the infinitely more urgent and compelling task, the itch that performance just has to scratch.

We were also curious to watch a recent TV drama featuring a psychotherapist (male) who becomes the object of a (female) client's obsession. The therapist's lawyer wife kills the client in a jealous rage when the latter surprises her in an underground car park. She then unsuccessfully defends her husband accused of the murder. The dramatic centre of the piece is a scene in which the wife stumbles on some tapes of sessions between the therapist and his client, a recording of a highly charged, erotic encounter between the two. That she cannot put deeds to the words (are they just talking or touching? – and isn't that talking actually *more* in every way than any physical coupling?) makes the discovery doubly excruciating. There is something deeply voyeuristic about our need to know about what happens between a therapist and their client. What can be more risky than a meeting in which no-one can verify from the outside what happened 'in there'? The fact of tape recordings of sessions existing, available for re-play, locked away in confidential cabinets, only adds to the desire to break open the therapeutic space, increases the forbidden that the encounter holds. For the therapist and client the tape recorder performs a triangulating function, signalling the impossibility of the pre-Oedipal dyad lasting forever, but for the person illicitly listening to the tape, whether innocently stumbled upon or voyeuristically sought out, it sets up the therapeutic encounter as an endlessly replayable primal scene.

Today, Krapp's tape recorder does not seem to stand in a metaphorical way for the activity of memory as it might have done in mid-century, before television, video, answerphone and the mutating networked electronic archive that is the Internet. Indeed, it does not seem like a metaphor for anything: it just 'is' and, being thus, reminds us how the culture of media technology has permanently reshaped our notion of identity, in alliance with psychoanalysis and psychotherapy. Although confined within Beckett's distinctly unerotic existential universe, Krapp's tape recorder seems to open up a previously masked space of transition: a palpable (real) fissure between 'the now' and 'the then' which throws into relief a Heideggerian horizon of time as the fundamental structuring aspect of self, *Dasein*, being. To paraphrase Winnicott's description of transitional phenomena, what Krapp's tape recorder offers up comes from outside our 'now' point of view (but not so from the point of view of 'the then'). But neither does it come from within – it is not an hallucination.

Winnicott's assertion of the 'unchallenged' nature of this transitional space could be read as more of a demand for the acknowledgement of its vital role in mental health than as something structural within the transitional 'stage' of infant development itself. His essay sets out the boundaries of the transitional space in order to defend it – which is to imply that it is also challenged and under threat. Similarly, the idealised, unchallenged play-space of rehearsal – where anything goes – is, of course, equally challenged, subject to demands that cannot be met. Just as the little, chewy ears of the toy snail are irrevocably attached to an oversized, indigestible, implacable body (with which the infant must finally come to terms), so the material of rehearsal, spread out over the cultural field, carries with it the massive and equally implacable body of history, specifically the history of the twentieth – the psychoanalytic – century. In this sense, the rehearsal strategy outlined above could be seen not as the retreat from history, the *polis* and the political as Richard Schechner has suggested, but rather as a confrontation with history *felt* as a set of disjunctive and discontinuous experiences.[13] Indeed, post-Freudian psychoanalysis and post-structuralist theory have fostered this sensibility. Like psychotherapy, rehearsal – as a special meeting of persons – somehow senses its responsibility to gather together this diaspora of meaning and deliver it up for judgement, via performance, to an audience, whilst at the same time finding itself approaching a state of anxious abjection in relation to its material. In this sense, performance becomes simply the bald evidence of the failure of rehearsal to 'do justice' to its own material. As we shall see, this failure to represent – akin to theatre's sense of its diminishing power in the virtual/digital era – is both curse and blessing for performance practice. For, as those who can enjoy contemporary performance testify, there are moments of performance when we manage to believe that justice *is* done. We see it signalled in specific performances to differing degrees.

We recall in the Wooster's *LSD . . . Just the High Points*, Norman Frisch rereading the words of Timothy Leary after a public question and answer session featuring a Vietnam veteran, Earl Sandle, apparently shot and blinded by a Leary follower on LSD. Sandle accuses Leary of direct responsibility for his injuries. After a 'God bless you and goodnight,' Leary falls silent. 'How do you feel?' the chairperson asks. Leary intones helplessly: 'I feel sad. Very, very sad.' We recall someone in Forced Entertainment's *Hidden J*, gibbering hysterically down a phone in a made-up cod-Slavic language at the height of the war in Bosnia. We recall Ron Vawter in *Jack Smith/Roy Cohn*, his own body carrying the visible marks of the AIDS which killed both him and Jack Smith, stopping mid-flow and stepping to the side of the stage to take a drink of water and wait.

These moments share something particular: a kind of reverberating muteness, a rupture in the chain of signification through which the real surfaces almost uninvited. They also share a strong foregrounding of the act of witnessing (trials and interrogations, both historical and pretend, are involved in all of them), in which those on stage are silenced by their own material – just as Leary is silenced by his interlocutor. In *Hidden J*, the staging has the phone-caller hidden behind the curtains of a toy house, whilst the remainder of the cast wait interminably, uncomfortably outside, in silence with the audience. In Vawter's solo piece, his performance (including his initial 'pre-show' address to the audience) is marked by odd silences which issue out of the uncanny self-reflexive intensity which Vawter brought to his previous work with the Wooster Group.

And as an audience, what do we recall with these moments? A simultaneity of pleasurable excitation and anxious dread, unresolved into a manageable feeling? Or is it perhaps that we sense that the performance bears witness to something prior, an event that happened somewhere else, 'in rehearsal', or in everyday life, and that has passed away into representation, into performance? All practitioners can recall the experience of the perfect rehearsal moment that got away, the one that could never be re-achieved either by technical mastery or by 'playing'. These are the moments rehearsal tries to record, replay, frame and represent in a Winnicottian process of 'pre-play', the process of discovering what is and is not under our control. However, in the abrupt shift from rehearsal to performance it seems that these moments are punctured and their significance begins to drain from them. The fact that so many contemporary stages are dressed to appear as rehearsal spaces, eviscerated industrial buildings put to work as auditoria, points to the sense that contemporary performance feels it may be its own worst enemy, in danger of being discounted just as it is produced. Similarly, performers create personas as reluctant 'stands-ins', replacements for the 'real' people who did the 'real' work in rehearsal. Ron Vawter remarks:

> That's just what I think about those days – that I was a stand-in or surrogate acting for both Spalding [Gray, a long-time member who had stopped performing with the Wooster Group] and the audience. With the audience I felt that any one of them could have taken my place, that I just happened to be the person who was standing there. So I felt very connected to the

yearning, the spiritual yearning of the audience. I think audiences have great desires towards the spiritual and all they need is the slightest excuse from the stage to open them up. So I try to find a place between character and in front of the audience which would trigger spiritual or meditative experiences.[14]

The stand-ins just go through the motions, not the emotions. Both sides of the auditorium sense that *rehearsal* is what needs to be shown, *rehearsal* is where the crucial action happens – because that is where worldly material is dealt with in the raw. This is felt as a demand, both from the material and from the audience, a demand that is the very pretext for the activity of rehearsal itself. Etchells writes of the audience:

> What is it about those human persons who . . . 'like to sit in the dark and watch other people do it'? People (like me and maybe you) who pay money to sit down and watch others act things out [. . .] who want to see more pain than anything else. The death scene. The crisis. The agony. The anger. The grief. Done convincingly, done with distance or irony, but done nonetheless [. . .] a desire [. . .] for nakedness, defencelessness. An exposure that does not have a name. Something beyond.[15]

How then to offer this? Etchells continues:

> Isn't that the constant frustration for play? That it isn't real?
> No surprise then that play always dreams of its other. The thing has aspirations.
> Go too far, go too far. More storm. More storm. More storm.[16]

That is one strategy – push the game harder, too hard, until it hurts:

> The chairs routine was already dangerous. It was before we had the rubber floor and the studio floor was lethal once wet. We hadn't even worked out how to do the taping-up properly so sometimes people got taped in such a way that they couldn't protect themselves when falling.[17]

But by the time performance comes, the taping-up is done properly: no-one gets hurt too badly. The 'real' recedes just as it comes into partial view. (But then, how much hurt would there have to be to count as 'real'? Just enough to stop the show, to put an end – permanent or temporary – to the repetitions of performance?) What the audience appears to be demanding is the rehearsal: the sphere of reparation *and* repetition, getting it (the performance) right *and* wrong, now transmuted into the sphere of origination – a private place where the studio floor was really 'lethal', where the therapist and client got involved with the really dangerous stuff. For example, when we recently billed a showing of some work-in-progress as an 'open rehearsal' we were inundated with bookings. After the event, people were disappointed. They wanted an actual rehearsal, not an unfinished piece of work. Think of the pull of seeing a faith healer or an illusionist. They work publicly, the process of cure or transformation is *witnessed*, before your very eyes.

Something of this inadequacy in the face of the audience's demand can also be seen just *after* the conclusion of theatre performances, usually those in small spaces where there is a minimal distance between audience and performance. Once the house lights are up, and both stage and auditorium rejoined, a few spectators step over an invisible line and tentatively finger the scenery, smell the whisky bottle, scan the piece of scrawled-on paper, as if to test their veracity, to see what was really written there. What are they hoping to read, what is the secret they feel might have been withheld?

Contemporary performance and rehearsal are perhaps acutely aware that there is nothing to read, that there is no secret – only a failure to generate one at all. The performers arrive on stage with only the failure, and the accompanying anxiety around it, to offer. They know the audience wants more. If so, what is left to do, to perform? It seems that 'everything being played out in advance' is in fact a necessary structural component of performance, indicative of its supplementary nature to rehearsal. Performance, feeling the demand of the audience that brought it into being, is always gesturing beyond – or perhaps more precisely, behind – itself, and never more so then when it goes for broke in 'playing for real', trying to invoke the secret 'real' of rehearsal and make it present again in public. Thus the 'playing' of rehearsal is foreshadowed and foreclosed by the anticipation of the very event – performance – that legitimises it, in much the same way as the ending of therapy functions for the therapeutic process.

So the audience is always silently present in rehearsal and this creates demands, expectations and judgements. In the making and doing of performance – as in psychotherapy – everyone is still expecting everyone else to deliver. The therapist expects the client eventually to speak; clients expect the therapist to interpret, to describe them to themselves, to help them work out what is going on, to help them feel better; the performers expect the director to facilitate their 'playing'; the director expects the performers to deliver themselves or versions thereof; and the audience expects 'an experience'. Indeed, much of the paraphernalia of rehearsal and the psychotherapeutic processes could be seen as an attempt to keep defusing these demands in an effort to allow something not already played out in advance to take place: the games, relaxation exercises, task-orientated activities of rehearsal, the drawn-out tea-breaks, the struggle through the first three minutes of the therapy session, finding ways to navigate the usual space for mundane small talk, trying to get the session started while being aware that this is always the wrong thing to be doing, to talk for the sake of talking, just to keep talking.

Perhaps it is the impossibility of an unchallenged space that rehearsal constantly plays with, a space where it might be possible to gets some rest from what Winnicott describes as the tension of keeping inner and outer separate. We might more easily recognise this as a current preoccupation with notions of self and subjectivity, the domain of the troubled speaking, traumatised signifying subject. This, after all, is how we would read much of the performance work by the companies mentioned earlier, and is certainly where we would situate our own work with PUR. Just as performance contains within it the real of rehearsal, so rehearsal contains within it the real of a once unchallenged area of experience, the birth-place, as Winnicott saw it, of self and other. If performance can only point to a moment of epiphany that we dream happened in rehearsal, that we are voyeuristically drawn to, given the chance to peek behind the closed rehearsal room door, then rehearsal can only point to a time before play was possible, when we did not have to make up our minds.

All that seems available for performance is 'going through the motions', as 'stand-ins' once more. But this is precisely what generates the significant moment of performance. Maurice Merleau-Ponty writes of the peculiar activity of going to sleep:

> I lie down in bed, on my left side, with my knees drawn up; I close my eyes and breathe slowly, putting my plans out of my mind. But the power of my will or consciousness stops there. As the faithful, in the Dionysian mysteries, invoke the god by miming scenes from his life, I call up the visitation of sleep by imitating the breathing and posture of the sleeper. The god is there when the faithful can no longer distinguish themselves from the part they are playing, when their body and their consciousness cease to bring in, as an obstacle, their particular opacity, and when they are totally fused in the myth. There is a moment when sleep 'comes' settling on this imitation of itself which I have been offering to it, and I succeed in becoming what I was trying to be.[18]

Clients often enter therapy on the very same premise. Anticipating that the talk will be of parents and siblings, failures and anxieties, angers, fears, seductions, frustrations, they must also hope that, by going through the motions, *rehearsing* that is, they might bring on that significant moment, call it insight or the emergence of the authentic, and with it a fuller awareness and appreciation of themselves.

And what becomes of the transitional object?

> Its fate is to be gradually allowed to be decathected, so that in the course of years it becomes not so much forgotten as relegated to limbo. In health the transitional object does not 'go inside' nor does the feeling about it necessarily undergo repression. It is not forgotten and it is not mourned. It loses meaning, and this is because the transitional phenomena have become diffused, have become spread out over the whole cultural field.[19]

This is a highly unusual, decidedly unpsychoanalytic assertion that appears almost disingenuous. A fundamental psychological phenomenon that is not forgotten, not mourned, but just loses meaning, its signification silently leaking away across 'the whole cultural field'. Perhaps this is where performance and rehearsal, conceived of as artistic practices, are perpetually destined to rediscover its trace, as Winnicott suggests:

At this point, my subject widens out into that of play, and of artistic creativity and appreciation, and of religious feeling, and of dreaming, and also of fetishism, lying and stealing, the origin and loss of affectionate feeling, drug addiction, the talisman of obessional rituals, etc.[20]

After such a devastatingly all-encompassing list, it is difficult not to read that last 'etc.' as an ultra-dry Winnicottian joke. His text breaks off abruptly there and then, continuing on a completely different theme, leaving the rest of us behind with that 'etc.', an intimidating expanse of intractable psychological, social and cultural by-products: more material for rehearsal to attempt to reprocess into something intellectually and emotionally digestible, tangible, meaningful.

## Notes

1 This text has recently been published in a revised form as a chapter entitled 'Play On: Process and Collaboration', in Tim Etchells, *Certain Fragments: Contemporary Performance and Forced Entertainment*, London and New York: Routledge, 1999: 50–70. Forced Entertainment is the British company he has directed for ten years and which remains one of the few ensemble-style groups in the UK still renegotiating the boundaries of performance within a distinctively theatrical tradition.

2 Tim Etchells, 'Play On: Collaboration and Process', unpublished manuscript, 1998: 1.

3 Donald Winnicott, *Playing and Reality*, London: Tavistock, 1971: 48.

4 Gilles Deleuze and Félix Guattari, *Anti-Oedipus: Capitalism and Schizophrenia*, trans. R. Hurley, M. Seem and H. Lane, New York: Viking Press, 1984: 308 (emphasis added).

5 David Savran's detailed documentation of the Wooster Group in *Breaking The Rules*, (New York: Theatre Communications Group, 1988), has been an important and influential resource for practitioners and theoreticians alike.

6 Donald Winnicott, 'Transitional Objects and Transitional Phenomena', in *The Maturational Processes and the Facilitating Environment: Studies in the Theory of Emotional Development*, London: Hogarth Press and Institute of Psycho-Analysis, 1951.

7 Winnicott, 'Transitional Objects and Transitional Phenomena': 233.

8 Winnicott, 'Transitional Objects and Transitional Phenomena': 233.

9 Adam Philips, *Winnicott*, London: Fontana Press, 1988: 118.

10 Philip Auslander, 'Task and Vision: Willem Dafoe in *L.S.D.*', *TDR*, 29 (2), 1985: 98.

11 Savran, *Breaking the Rules*: 50.

12 Tim Etchells, 'How to Write Words at the End of a Millennium: Instructions for Ghost Writers', 1996: 2. This paper was presented at the Writing Research Associates, Performance Writing Symposium, Dartington College of Arts, in April 1996, and can be found online at http://www.forced.co.uk/.

13 Richard Schechner, *The End of Humanism*, New York: PAJ Publications, 1982: 14ff.

14 Etchells, *Certain Fragments*: 87.

15 Etchells, 'Play On: Collaboration and Process': 13.

16 Etchells, 'Play On: Collaboration and Process': 17.

17 Etchells, 'Play On: Collaboration and Process': 13.

18 Maurice Merleau-Ponty, *The Phenomenology of Perception*, trans. C. Smith, London: Routledge, 1996: 163–4.

19 Winnicott, 'Transitional Objects and Transitional Phenomena': 233.

20 Winnicott, 'Transitional Objects and Transitional Phenomena': 233.

# Section B

# PARALLEL
# PERFORMANCES

# 5

# VIOLENCE, VENTRILOQUISM AND THE VOCALIC BODY

*Steven Connor*

Ventriloquism is one of the most pervasive metaphors by which issues of identity, ownership and power have been articulated within a culture of performance. It could be said that all performance is broadly ventriloquial, in a double movement whereby the performer gives his or her voice to another, and, in the process, takes the voice of that other into him- or herself. Cultural theorists interested in the ways in which identity can be both sustained and violated in different kinds of verbal performance – in playing the part of another, in borrowing and mixing idioms and intonations – have developed what I have elsewhere called the 'proprietary thematics' of the voice.[1] Psychoanalytic theory, especially of a Lacanian variety, has assisted mightily with this formulation of problems of ownership and identity with respect to language, asking, when I speak, do I, really? With whose words? Whose voice? Ventriloquism has become the master trope for articulating the contemporary concern with the ethics of the voice.

But there is another way of thinking of the meanings of ventriloquism, by means of a somewhat less abstract, and less immediately moralising approach to the voice. I offer in what follows a reading of the contemporary workings of ventriloquism as a specific, which is to say, archaic form of performance, in terms of a Kleinian reading of the primary dynamics of the voice. The widespread use of ventriloquism as metaphor allows the violence and violation that are bound up in the exercise of the voice to be deflected into a judicial register of ownership, possession, property and appropriation. What follows attempts a desublimation of the ventriloquial metaphor, in order to disclose and examine some of the more primary corporeal processes involved in the disembodying and re-embodying of the voice in performance.

## The greatest power of emanation

Guy Rosolato suggests that the infant may experience in the exercise of its voice a sense of sonorous omnipotence, the power to exercise its will through sound which perhaps corresponds to what Freud called the stage of magical thinking, or 'omnipotence of thoughts'. The voice, writes Rosolato, 'is the body's greatest power of emanation'.[2] Initially, the cry produces a generalised vitalisation of the world, in which mass becomes movement, and inertness is subject to excitation:

> The infant takes its measure very early on, like the irradiation of its still largely immobile bodily mass into a much larger space, covering an area which shows itself extending in all directions and overleaping the obstacles to sight. Right from the beginning, the cry is the manifestation of the *excitation* of living matter in pain or pleasure, at once autonomous and reacting to stimulation – an excitation which is life itself.[3]

This apprehension of a generalised vitalisation through the voice gives way to the willed control over vocal sounds. With the fantasy of sonorous omnipotence, another aspect of the voice develops. As well as being the power of emanation, the voice comes to be experienced as something produced. The infant's first cries vitalised and animated the world, surging out of inert objecthood and resisting the relapse into it. The more conscious exercise of control over the voice, and therefore over the world through the voice, begins to form, out of the generalised power of emanation, vocal precipitates, or emissions,

> which are *separated off from the body*, which come from a subterranean work of fabrication, a metabolism, and which, once given out, become objects distinct from the body, and without its qualities of sensitivity, of reaction and excitation, and take on a value which interests the desire of the Other.[4]

At this point in its development, the infant's capacity to produce or project power may exceed its capacity to receive or acknowledge that power as its own. The voices of appeal, threat or raging demand of the child produce a sense of sadistic mastery, which both produces an object of its own, and makes the world temporarily an object. The rage of the infant and the toddler will often manifest itself in a desire to put its will into sound, to force sound into a permanent form; as though the amplitude of a cry would imprint it more firmly and permanently on the world, and give it the quality of manipulability that the child finds lacking. The pleasure in the objectification of sound is perhaps the origin of the sense of sound sculpted into form, by patterning, repetition and synchronic overlay, which provides the pleasure in music. Like the infant's cry, the singing voice manipulates itself into an object. However, once the voice has been separated from the child, it may also be experienced as a Kleinian 'part-object', a part of the body which provokes love or desire (typically the breast, penis or faeces) and therefore becomes split off from the body. For Klein, this separation of the part-object comes about as a result also of ambivalent feelings towards the object, which get affectively polarised: thus the breast which is withdrawn or fails to satisfy also takes on a 'bad' or persecutory form.[5]

The baby is hungry and cries; hunger for young humans is inseparable from crying. No hunger for humans without crying. The cry is the response to the hunger and the means employed to defeat it. The cry is the form of the baby's sonorous omnipotence. The voice is the means – the sole means – that the baby has to escape from so much suffering, and reach and fetch to it the comfort and sustenance (breast, bottle, company) that it needs. Nicolas Abraham and Maria Torok have emphasised this close relationship between need, language and power in the newborn infant, observing that language first arises in the painfully empty mouth. 'The emptiness is first experienced in the forms of cries and sobs, delayed fullness, then as calling, ways of requesting presence, as language.' The executive power of this calling creates a transition 'from a mouth filled with the breast to a mouth filled with words', and then a powerful association between them.[6] The voice is the auditory apparition of the breast, the sound that swells to fill the void opened by the breast's absence. It seems to me that Abraham and Torok do not have good reason to assume that what arises in the empty mouth to substitute for the breast is already 'language'; I would prefer to call it 'voice', meaning by this a raw, quasi-bodily matter from which language will be made. Human beings, I am surmising, can never afterwards give up the belief in the power of the voice to command and countermand space, and to ease suffering.

But the voice is also the voice *of* the infant's suffering and need. When the cry does not bring instant relief, it becomes itself the symbol of unsatisfied desire, even the agency of the frustration of this desire. It is almost as if there arose a 'bad voice', in parallel to Klein's 'bad breast'. But the crying voice is not the breast and cannot provide what the breast can provide. Instead of filling the baby up, it empties it, adding to the need for food an unpleasant and frightening constriction of breath. For the baby, for whom, we may surmise, negation is as difficult to encompass as for the dreamer, the voice is not something other than the breast, which fails to satisfy precisely because it is other than the breast, but is the breast gone bad, the breast that refuses to feed, the breast that screams instead of yielding pleasure. If the cry is the form of the infantile hallucination of the breast, it is a disappointment. The child attempts to feed itself with its voice, but its voice simply crams starvation back down its throat.

Just as the bad breast is the negative version of the good breast, which is both the hypostasis of the bad qualities of the breast and the anxious image of the angry breast's retaliation for the infant's imaginary assaults on it, so the bad voice is both the expression of the infant's rage and the embodiment of the retaliatory rage that the infant fears from the bad breast as a result of its own destructive anger. This is why the bad voice is always directing its angry energies against itself in crying or screaming. The angry voice assaults itself, because it is itself the ugly proof of the hostility that threatens to spoil the transcendent beauty of the good voice. There is no frightening voice – no roar, or scream, or ugly or demanding voice of any kind – that we do not recognise as this bad voice, the voice of rage, and of frustration. This is to say that there is no bad voice – including the ugly and alien voice that we hear in our own voice when it is played back to us – which is not partly our own.

The good voice, on the other hand, is the voice of pleasure and beneficence. When the child is fed, its cry is stifled and then stilled. As the infant feeds, it takes in something good and precious to itself from outside. But, as it feeds, it hears the voice of the one who feeds it. If it takes into itself in a psychological sense the breast that provides the milk which it takes in biologically – Klein's introjection of the good breast – then it also takes in the voice which accompanies the milk which feeds it. Like the introjected image of the 'good breast', of which, perhaps, it is itself the most important and influential form, the good voice becomes an important repository of life and hope and reassurance. This voice is the most important factor in the formation of what Didier Anzieu has called the 'sonorous envelope'.[7] It holds, secures, encloses and supports. The bad voice is the infant's own voice which has been violently estranged from it. The good voice comes initially from the outside, being the voice of another or of many others which the infant hears: but it too can be introjected.

Gradually, the child learns to introject, not just the voice of the 'mother', but also its own voice. But the pleasure it takes in its own voice (and do we not regularly hear and speak of people who are 'in love with the sound of their own voice'?) indicates that something of the value and ideal form of the mother's voice may have been requisitioned for the purposes of the *propria persona*. The child gradually comes to recognise its own voice as the good voice. Thus the bad voice is the voice of the self become other: the good voice is the voice of the other become self. Idealised voices of all kinds derive their power, prestige and capacity to give pleasure from this willingness to hear other voices as one's own.

The exercise of power through and over the voice thus results in the production of vocal objects. But such objects can also suggest a voice which is an active and autonomous presence in the world, and can exercise power on its own account. For the young child, who both relies upon its voice and is so vulnerable to the threat of auditory assault and extinction, a gap may open up between the voice that is spoken and the voice that is heard. The voice, as pure, lyric, unselfconscious I-hood spilling or erupting into the world, suddenly becomes part of that world and recoils upon its originator. Under these conditions, the child may be left depleted and itself vulnerable to the vocal assaults it launches on the world. The exercise of the voice then threatens to make the child part of the objectified world that the exercise of the voice itself creates.

At the same time, the idea of a vocal object, of the voice not as an event but as a thing, also suggests the possibility that it may be manipulated or controlled. It is for this reason that D. W. Winnicott includes the beginnings of control in the baby's voice, in its 'mouthing, accompanied by sounds of "mum-mum", babbling, anal noises, the first musical notes and so on' along with the incorporation of objects such as blankets, bundles of wool or cuddly toys, in the category of what he calls 'transitional phenomena'. These exist between the conditions of 'me' and 'not-me' and assist the passage from oral self-stimulation to a more mature relationship with objects.[8]

The dissociated voice is always closer to the condition of a cry than of an articulate utterance. A cry is not pure sound, but rather pure utterance, which is to say the force of speech without, or in excess of, its recognisable and regularising forms. A cry always seems in excess of the one from whom it issues, and in excess of the semantic content which it may have. In the cry, something else speaks apart from the person from whom it issues. In the cry, and its associated forms, we hear not so much the voice of the feelings, or even of the body, as in certain accounts of hysterical speech, but rather the uttering of utterance itself. The uttering of utterance strikes us as transcendent or frightening largely through its distinction both from subjective origin – it is no longer in the control of the one who emits the utterance – and objective condition – it is more than a mere object. It is an intentionality without subjective intention.

The cry – whether of anger, fear or pain – is the purest form of the compact between the voice and power. Ours has been the century of the mediated or technologically magnified cry, the microphone, megaphone and loudspeaker allowing the generalisation of the aggressive–sadistic use of voice. Amplified voices, like the natural amplification effected by the cry itself, cancel or close up space. Indeed, amplified voices disclose the particular form of the assault upon space constituted by the infant's cry. For when we shout, we tear. We tear apart distance; we disallow distance to the object of our anger, or of our ecstasy. When I shout, I am all voice, you are all voice, the space between us is nothing but a delirium tremens of voice. In shouting, we fall upon our own voices, attempting to claw them apart. At such times, the voice is a malign object, a hot, ulcerous excrescence upon the self that I must at all costs put from me. Why must I put my voice from me, when my voice is the claim and enactment of my power? Because the voice is the means of articulation. The voice is the agent of the articulated body, for it traverses and connects the different parts of me: lungs, trachea, larynx, palate, tongue, lips. It both distinguishes and connects ingestion and utterance. It moves from me to you, and from me to myself, in moving from the mouth to the ear. The shout or the scream obviates all these distinctions; it opens the throat and voids sound, as the stomach, contracting, voids its poisons and surfeits. The cry makes me blind, swallowing up the world of visible distances and distinctions. The crying voice tries to get rid of this burden of voice, which, in extending myself into the world, can only ever hold me at a distance from myself, hold me apart from the world.

For the infant, space, the gap between itself and its satiety, is a wound. The infant does not want interiority, the comfort and safety of the womb. It wants to have done with space, wants to be again where there are no distances or dimensions, no inside or outside. It tries to shape intervals of spacelessness within space. It withdraws into interiority in sleep. Waking, it cries; it demands. Its cries are an attempt to diminish and abolish the space that yawns about it and within it. Shouting is the reassertion of the blind imperative demand of the infant, and of the infant's archaic space, in all its intense intermittence.

But in this, as in all other things, the infant must learn to compromise. Its voice teaches it that its cries go from it, out into the world. Amplification, like the baby's cry, always turns into a matter of reach, and therefore of limit; its transcendence of natural limits always discloses further limits. The abolition of space attempted by a cry always reasserts space. So, if space cannot be consumed in the conflagration of the voice, then it had better be commanded. Voice starts to allow space to be measured and substantiated. From being the antagonist or devourer of space, the voice begins to be its accomplice. Arising in, it begins to gives rise to space. What the scream tears apart, it also holds together. The scream is the guarantee that, after the world has been atomised, it will reassemble and again resemble itself.

The voice confers shape upon the body, and is thereby involved in the process whereby the body itself accomplishes, or shapes its world. It does this through the establishment of what might be called the *vocalic body*.

## The vocalic body

The principle of the vocalic body is simple. Voices are produced by bodies, but can also themselves produce bodies. The vocalic body is the idea – which can take the form of dream, fantasy, ideal, theological doctrine or hallucination – of a surrogate or secondary body, a projection of a new way of having or being a body, formed and sustained out of the autonomous operations of the voice. The history of ventriloquism shows us clearly that human beings in many different cultural settings find the experience of a sourceless sound uncomfortable, and the experience of a sourceless voice intolerable. The history of ventriloquism is to be understood partly in terms of the repertoire of imagings or incarnations it provides for these autonomous vocalic bodies. The 'sound hermeneutic' identified by Rick Altman determines that a disembodied voice must be habited in a plausible body.[9] It may then appear that the voice is subordinate to the body, when in fact the opposite is experientially the case; it is the voice which seems to colour and model its container. When animated by the ventriloquist's voice, the dummy, like the cartoon character given voice, appears to have a much wider range of gestures, facial expressions and tonalities than it does when it is silent. The same is true of any object given a voice; the doll, the glove puppet, the sock draped over the hand, change from being immobile and inert objects to animated speaking bodies. Our assumption that the object is speaking allows its voice to assume that body, in the theatrical or even theological sense, as an actor assumes a role, or as the divinity assumes incarnate form: not just to enter and suffuse it, but to produce it. In bald actuality, it is we who assign voices to objects; phenomenologically, the fact that an unassigned voice must always imply a body means that it will always partly supply it as well.

What kind of thing is a vocalic body? What sorts of vocalic bodies are there? Such bodies are not fixed and finite, nor are they summarisable in the form of a typology, precisely because we are always able to imagine and enact new forms of vocalic body. The leading characteristic of the vocalic body is to be a body-in-invention, an impossible, imaginary body in the course of being found and formed. But it is possible to isolate some of the contours, functions and postures by means of which vocalic bodies come into being. What characterises a vocalic body is not merely the range of actions which a particular voice function enjoins on the body of the one producing the voice, but also the characteristic ways in which the voice seems to precipitate itself as an object, upon which it can then itself give the illusion of acting.

In Didier Anzieu's conception of the sonorous envelope, the vocalic body is formed on the model of a container. It surrounds and supports; it confers physical definition. It may or may not be the case that this construction derives, as Anzieu at certain points seems to claim, from a specific experience of the maternal voice, powerfully associated as it is for the infant with the sensations of being encircled and carried. More important, however, is the post-infantile association of the sonorous envelope with collective experiences of voice, with the knitting together of voices in singing, cheering, conversation and music. Edith Lecourt identifies the experience of the sonorous envelope, not with the mother, but rather with 'the musical quality of the harmony of the group and, in the first case, of the family group, around the baby, for the baby who gives and takes his note amidst a sharing of sounds (noises, musics, words), vibrations and silences: a fusional experience of omnipotence'.[10] The sonorous envelope is the first shape that the voice secretes, and it draws its power from the primary indistinction of auditory and tactile sensations in the baby. In a sense, it is not so much a particular kind of embodied vocal shape as the general possibility or guarantee that sound can confer and take up shape itself.

I have suggested another form of the vocalic body in my discussion of the cry. In the exercise of vocal hostility – rage, aggression, condemnation and so on – the action of the voice upon itself is clearly visible and audible. In these modes, the voice seems to demonstrate its power to inflict harm by attacking itself, taking itself as an object or substance which may be subjected to injuring or exterminating assault. It may enact the envelopment or strangulation of its object; or it may scatter or pulverise its own forms and tonalities. The voice of rage must do this, because it is aimed at transcending its own condition, forming itself as a kind of projectile, a piercing, invading weapon, in order to penetrate, disintegrate and abandon itself. The dimension of elevation is extremely important in anger and vocal assault: we raise our voice; we shout others down. But the angry voice may also be a bringing up and out of what comes from below, or deep within. The characteristic chest voice of anger, attesting, perhaps to an imaginary 'maleness', mimes the existence of a huge, boiling, bottomless reservoir of feeling, which comes both from within and, as it were, below the self, so that it is both contained by, and itself provides a kind of support for that self, and for the voice that may otherwise flame through all supports and restraints, shrivelling shape, space and distance.

The voice of rage therefore presents itself as the antagonist of the sonorous envelope, the denial of the bodying and embodied nature of sound. And yet such a voice is also capable of bracing or armouring itself by its very tonalities; the angry or demanding voice at once destroys and defends itself – in fact, defends itself against itself. Think of the rant of the demagogue as the type of warlike political persuasiveness: the voice cracks with the effort to surpass its own condition, to become an action, achieving a kind of immediate effectivity in the world. Hitler's voice rages at itself, suffocates itself, attacks its own form; yet it also reins and retains the rage it unleashes. Timbre and voice quality are bound in by the percussion and 'attack' of the voice itself. In all of this, we have, to be sure, the gesture and enactment on the body of a certain affective disposition. But the power of the spectacle depends upon something more. It depends upon the production of another, imaginary body, the vocalic body of raging itself. Raging is more than something done to or written over a particular body; it is the desire for, and hallucinated accomplishment of, a new kind of body, a fiercer, hotter, more dissociated, but also more living, urgent, and vital kind of body.

In all instancings and picturings of the vocalic body, the voice secretes a fantasy of a body in its relations to itself, in what it does to the fabric of the very sound it produces. The voice makes itself solid by its self-relation. The most intense and intimate kinds of self-relation result in the voice of seduction. Such a voice seduces by conjuring *itself* up as a precious and fascinating object, or texture, or sensation. This voice is onanistic; it must attend to itself with care, touching itself tenderly and exquisitely at every point. The seductive capacities of voice have been highlighted by technologies of amplification, from the telephone to the microphone. It is said that the crooning style of twentieth-century popular song was discovered by singers and sound engineers in the early days of sound recording, when it was realised that microphones could not cope with the extreme dynamic ranges possessed by singers used to commanding the large space of the concert hall. The crooning voice is seductive because it appears to be at our ear, standing forward and apart from the orchestral background with which it is nevertheless integrated. The crooning voice is full of what Roland Barthes has called the 'grain' of the voice, its individuating accidents of intonation and timbre. The microphone makes audible and expressive a whole range of organic vocal sounds which are edited out in ordinary listening; the liquidity of the saliva, the tiny hissings and shudders of the breath, the clicking of the tongue and teeth, and popping of the lips. Such a voice promises the odours, textures and warmth of another body. These sounds are not merely the signs or reminders of bodies in close proximity to our own; they appear to enact the voice's power to exude other sensory forms. Most of all, perhaps, the imaginary closeness of such voices suggests to us that they could be our own; they are the magical antidote to the grotesque and insufficient effigies of our voice returned to us by the tape recorder. These voices – Frank Sinatra, as it may be, or Billie Holiday, or Placido Domingo, or Tori Amos – are loved because we already know them so well. They sing to us because they seem to be singing to themselves, and thus tempt us to be taken in by the ineffably beautiful air of our own voice. The intensity of self-relation in such a voice is sealed by the use of reverberation which became common in recording in the years following the war. Reverberation attempts to supply to the voice itself something of the solidity and dimension given to a natural voice by the reverberations of its environment. The echoing voice is not a voice in space, it is a voice of space. This voice continuously touches, comes back to itself, marking out a volume in space in the interval between emission and return.

The power of the voice derives from its capacity to charge, to vivify, to relay and amplify energy. But, precisely because of this, the voice can also become deathly; in its decayed or deathly condition, the voice precipitates a peculiarly famished kind of body. We might call this an excremental voice: a voice that is pure discharge, a giving out of mere dead matter, toneless, vacant, absent, sepulchral, inhuman. It seems to demonstrate that it has no connection with the world, or with the one who originates it; it is heterogeneous matter. As opposed to the seductive voice or voice of rage, the excremental voice must aim to have no relation to itself, must aim not to touch itself at any point. It is thus the opposite of the seductive voice. It wants to come apart, not only from its speaker, but from itself. But, as we know, excrement is highly prized; it can be a kind of sacred substance, precisely because it is profane. The very horror which propels the excremental from us creates a bond with it. The disarticulated voice of fatigue or despair finds a kind of consolation in its bleak, emaciated song.

There is also a sublimated form of the vocalic body. Michel Poizat has shown how, in post-Romantic conceptions of song and vocal music, the force of the cry has become embodied in the voice of the soprano, whose soaring, inhuman power becomes both the expression of boundless longing and itself the object of fetishised desire. In the song of the soprano, voice goes beyond utterance into pure uttering; it expresses the passage of the human into the inhuman.[11] If this voice is objectified, this is according to the strange psychoanalytic logic of the fetish, in which a part of the body is violently, obsessively reduced to an object, precisely in order to make up for the fact that it is a dissimulation of or substitute for what is really wanted. The transcendent voice becomes the object of desire precisely through becoming uncapturable. Felicia Miller Frank has suggested that the voice is associated with Edmund Burke's aesthetics of the sublime because it is uncapturable in representation; paradoxically, the transcendent, angelic female voice becomes the very objectification of this refusal to be encompassed in objecthood.[12]

It is for this reason, as Frank has so effectively shown, that the transcendent voice, which 'occupies the space of inhuman otherness opened by the aesthetic of the sublime',[13] also becomes associated with the less-than-human in another sense – with the condition of objectification supplied by mechanical means. But any account of the fortunes of the fantasy of sonorous autonomisation, of the voice given the powers and properties of a separated object or agency, must take account of the remarkable actualisation of this fantasy in the development of technologies which allow the electronic modification, enhancement, storage and administration of the voice. Ours is the first century in which it has been possible to make actual the ideal of the voice of power, the utterance separated from its occasion of enunciation. In one sense, this actualisation of a fantasy has reduced it. The autonomous voice, whether it is the voice of a god, or a spirit, or the more abstract trope of the voice of the spirit, or of nature, derives its power from its ambivalence, from the fact that the voice separated from its source is an object of perception which has gathered to itself the powers of a subject. When it becomes possible to record and replay actual voices at will, the sense of the voice as itself constituting an agentless agency is reduced. From being a source of powerfully mingled pleasure and menace, the technologically autonomised voice becomes a source simply of repeatable pleasure, or of the pleasure of repeatability itself. Once you have the opportunity for playback, the voice from out of the burning bush loses most of its sense of awful portent; it is reduced, perhaps to the ludicrous, scratchy chuffing of the gramophone hidden in the undergrowth in the village pageant described in Virginia Woolf's *Between the Acts*.

## Bloodless surgery

For us, ventriloquism has now become a largely visual phenomenon. Ask anyone to visualise a ventriloquist and the image forms instantly of a single figure, usually male, in colloquy with a single dummy, perched, sometimes on a stand, most typically on the performer's knee.[14] Valentine Vox accounts for the puzzling popularity of radio ventriloquists like Edgar Bergen and Peter Brough in the 1940s and 1950s by suggesting that ventriloquism 'is essentially a vocal, not a visual illusion'.[15] But a vital part of the effect of these radio shows was that the audience knew so well what the dummies were supposed to look like. Charlie MacCarthy and Archie Andrews made frequent appearances in newspapers, comics and magazines outside the radio studio, and, indeed, the radio studio or theatre were often enough portrayed in photographs to be immanent in the listening eye of the audience. We may presume that the scene of radio performance only became invisible, or unvisualisable, very gradually over the century. Charlie MacCarthy featured alongside Edgar Bergen in a number of films, as well. Although the ideal of what I have been calling sonorous autonomisation, of a world of sound functioning separately from and in excess of the visible world, survives for us, it is not carried any more by the art of ventriloquism.

Another reason that it is easy for us to visualise ventriloquism with dummies is the surprising conservatism in the dummy's physical form. Most dummies through the twentieth century have been represented as boys, of an obstreperous or precocious disposition, or puerile men. The choice of the drunken aristocrat for Ray Alan's Lord Charles figure was appropriate not only because tipsy speech makes things technically easier for the ventriloquist (if you try to speak without moving your lips you end up sounding like a half-sloshed hereditary peer anyway), but also because of the well-established infantile associations of the aristocracy. And let's be candid: all non-animal ventriloquists' dummies *have the same face*. This may for a moment sound implausible, especially to the skilled makers of dummies and ventriloquial figures whose livelihood has depended upon the belief in the individuality and infinite variety of their products. But my bet is that you are in fact seeing this face clearly enough as you read this. The dummy's face is garishly coloured, with flushed cheeks and high gloss, bright and fixedly staring eyes, a stiffly jointed jaw and often markedly protrusive chin, cheekbones and nose, topped, almost always, with a mop of rather unruly hair.

The ventriloquist's dummy appears to belong to a different world from that of the technologies which, far from consolidating the body in visible form, have dispersed it into networks, far from giving the voice a face, have multiplied it into interfaces. The dummy seals the arrival of a distinctively modern kind of ventriloquism, in which, as Leigh Eric Schmidt has crisply put it, 'the travails of the soul become the travails of the self'[16]; and yet it no sooner arrives than it begins to be outstripped by a rapidly expanding media society which offers opportunities for multiplying the self far in excess of that offered in slow-moving ventriloquial dramaturgies.[17] Progressively through the twentieth century, ventriloquism has become creepily or even embarrassingly archaic. It is a blockage in the system, a catch in the throat of media technology, the awkward sign of the workings of the works. But its archaism is characteristic of the archaism attaching to the voice itself. In a world which is characterised, not by the autonomisation of sensory channels and their corresponding media, but by their remorseless interchange, the voice is a kind of sluggish impediment to the logic of sensory interchange and conversion.

However, the most striking feature of the dummy, and the identifying feature of the anachronistic hiccup or blockage it represents, is the degree of violence with which it is associated. Threatened or actual violence is a notable feature of the entire history of ventriloquism. It is said that Thomas Britten, a coal merchant, occultist and founder of a fashionable music club in Clerkenwell actually died of fright after a blacksmith-ventriloquist called Samuel Honeyman called to him in the street 'Thomas Britten, prepare to die!'[18] In the early nineteenth century the celebrated French ventriloquist Fitz James performed (invisibly, behind a partition) an auditory rendition of a painful visit to the dentist, a performance which drew together voice and suffering in a particularly telling way, since the extraction of cries and moans from the victim's mouth parallels closely the extraction of their teeth from the same quarter. Perhaps no more powerful association between the exercise of ventriloquism and violent dismemberment can be imagined than the performance recalled by the physicist Neil Arnott:

> A Mr Henderson, of London, about the end of the eighteenth century, used to *kill his calf*, as he called it, to crowded houses every night. After dropping a screen between him and the audience, he caused to issue from behind it, all the sounds, even to a minutest particular, which may be heard while a calf is falling victim in the slaughter-house; – the conversation of the butchers, the struggling and bellowing, and quick breathing of the frightened animal, the whetting of the knife, the plunge, the gush, the agony; and, disgusting as the idea is in itself, the imitation was so true to nature, that thousands eagerly went to witness the art of the mimic.[19]

There seems no limit to the extremity of the violence that can be conjured up by the invisible voice, once freed from appearance or embodiment. There may be a fundamental link between the experiences of rage, hunger and terrified dissolution accompanying the first exercises of the voice and the subsequent powers of the voice. The voice of the needy, protesting infant is both the voice *of* its anguish, and the means at hand to end that anguish, if only by giving it a bodily form apart from the infant. The voice of suffering, the suffering voice, allows suffering to be drawn apart, to be put into another body, the body of the voice. This exercise both contains the suffering and violently prolongs it, since its strategy and effect are to tear the voice out of the body, and to turn the voice on itself. Eventually, if left for too long, a hungry baby will become lost in and for a time inseparable from its own desperation, having surrendered its own body with its once-satisfiable needs to the appalling, ecstatically sundered body constituted and consumed by the conflagration of its own screaming voice. At this point, food cannot satisfy it any more, since the baby is gorging on hunger itself. It can be fed only with another voice, since another voice-body must be fashioned to allow it to be returned to its own body of flesh, which seems, for the time being, so much less real than its incandescent vocalic body.

The threat of violence and dismemberment is therefore intrinsic to the earliest experiences of the voice. It is perhaps only when this pure voice begins to knit together, first into recognisable rhythms, and then into language, that the infant has protection from the danger of extinction in or by its own voice. But, in a sense, this good voice is there from the beginning within the bad voice, since the baby's cries are always powerfully rhythmic, if only because they must continue to be regulated by the breath. In the midst of the danger and pain that it embodies, the voice offers containment; drawn from the baby's own fantasised *membra disjecta*, the voice holds its, and the infant's, shape. The ventriloquial dummy will act in precisely this way, both to focus the threat of violence associated with the voice, and to contain it. Like the baby's dummy, the ventriloquist's dummy can stop the voice. But, because the voice of the dummy will be a thing apart, it can embody the split-off bad voice. With the coming of the dummy, violence will have an object. And the object will speak back, displaying its own powers of violence, preventing and yet also provoking assault, containing and yet conducting violence.

Some of this ambivalence is apparent in what is probably the earliest piece of recorded badinage with a ventriloquial figure, the interchange between the Viennese ventriloquist Baron Mengen and his wooden doll given in a history of ventriloquism by the Abbé Johannes de la Chapelle:

> Miss, I have heard some very unpleasing reports about you. Sir, calumny is always easy. If you pay no heed to the right path, I will return you to it by some very disagreeable routes. Sir, to return is easy when one has never strayed. You are a little coquette, you tease men as much as you can. Sir, when one has only a little beauty, one is exposed to envy and persecution. You are quite the little reasoner. Sir, attack is not always permitted to me; but I have always the right to defend myself. Silence. With these words, he shuts her up again in his pocket. But still the Puppet twists, grumbles and groans. 'See how men are made', she continued. 'Just because they are the stronger, they imagine that Authority is justice. Fie, fie, how villainous it is!'[20]

Certain things about this routine ought to strike us as familiar. The encounter is between a man and a juvenile, a somewhat insubordinate inferior – a young girl in his care, we might suppose. The Baron performed his routines in courtly circles (this one was recorded by two diplomats in the court of Bayreuth in 1757) and the interchange has a sort of frosty politesse that we would not expect from ventriloquial performances in more rustic circumstances. But the use of the puppet also seems to release a distinct sexual frisson, mixed with the threat of violence, that will be one of the most stubbornly recurrent features of dummy ventriloquism. The verbal violence of the dummy is here the warrant for a kind of violence enacted on her, which actualises the threats of punishment issued earlier; the manner of her suppression, which degrades her primly self-possessed speech into muffled grumbles and groans, has (for us) an unmistakable sexual suggestiveness.

Another important aspect of this interchange is the close physical connection between the performer and the dummy. The dummy is held in the hand, or, in the case of the glove puppet, only exists as a posture of the hand. This means that the violence enacted upon the dummy is a violence enacted by the performer upon himself; the audience's half-suspended awareness of the fact that the dummy is in fact a prosthetic part of the performer's own body provides a certain warrant for a violence that might otherwise seem excessive and unpalatable. A favoured illusion for all ventriloquists is the enclosed or stifled voice, as of somebody locked in a cupboard, or a box, or stuck up a chimney, or buried underground. The reason for the popularity of the stifled voice is because it is relatively easy to reproduce its effect in the mouth, by constricting the voice by palate and uvula. I have just said that the thrusting away of the doll into the Baron Mengen's pocket suggests that she is being forced to enact the wantonness of which she is being accused by rendering the Baron some sexual service in there. The Baron's pocket becomes a kind of mouth, in which the phallic puppet is enclosed, even as her own mouth is too full for her to speak. She is eating him, perhaps, but then, he has also in a sense eaten her: when she is out of sight, in his trousers, it becomes more apparent than ever that she is in fact in his mouth.

The disconcerting thing about this exchange is that the violence is enacted upon a female figure. Although late nineteenth-century ventriloquists did use female figures, their use became less and less frequent, until, by the early decades of the twentieth century the figure of the disobedient boy had become almost universal in ventriloquism. Throughout the scenes of ventriloquial interchange offered up in the many 'How to Become a Ventriloquist' books, and especially in those involving versions of the cheeky boy figure, there is an unmistakable undercurrent of violence or threat, as well as an obsession with discipline and punishment, if always masked by comedy. Often, the unavailing struggle of the ventriloquist to subdue the impertinent or precocious youngster will climax in some kind of physical punishment, typically the locking of the dummy away in a chest or box, accompanied by angry cries of protest. The associations of ventriloquism with mutilation survives in the odd recurrence of the idea of surgery in ventriloquial performance. Edgar Bergen had a routine in which he performed an operation on Charlie MacCarthy, and the Lord Chamberlain's Office records the licensing in December 1919 of an entertainment entitled *Ventriloquial Bloodless Surgery* (unfortunately no text survives).[21] Maurice Hurling offers his readers a routine called 'A Visit to the Hairdresser', which is full of sparring between figure and ventriloquist about razors and Sweeney Todd, and ends with the following Beckettian clincher:

V.: You cheeky little beggar . . . if you were MY son, I'd give you poison.
F.: And if you were my FATHER . . . I'D TAKE IT.[22]

Paternity is often an issue in such routines; often the ventriloquist attempts to supply the place of the figure's real father, who is said to be elsewhere. The ventriloquist fathers himself, in a not-quite-bodiless vocal birth, in which the child never in fact leaves the ventriloquist's body (indeed, the ventriloquist is partly inside the body of its figure). Boys were not only to be identified with the child-corpse of the dummy, they were also assumed to be aspirant ventriloquists. From *The Boy's Own Paper* onwards, few comics could do without their stories of ventriloquial capers, or hints for acquiring the discomfiting art.[23] The duality whereby boys are expected to identify both with the dummy and the ventriloquist becomes apparent in the common stunt in which the dummy is made to reveal ventriloquial skills of his own. Edgar Bergen, for example, performed a routine which began with the discovery of Charlie MacCarthy reading a book entitled *Ventriloquism: Its Cause and Prevention*; having poured scorn on Edgar Bergen's capacities, Charlie ended the routine by demonstrating his own skills with the Distant Voice, as he engaged the invisible 'Joe' in the basement in conversation.[24] The inversion of dummy and ventriloquist is combined with the paternity theme in a story by Gerald Kersh. In 'The Extraordinarily Horrible Dummy', published in 1944, a ventriloquist called Ecco is tormented by his dummy Micky, who forces him to practise hour after hour perfecting his art. It emerges that the dummy has been taken over by the spirit of Ecco's violently abusive father, the master ventriloquist, Professor Vox. Where in many such horror stories the ventriloquist is forced to change places with the dummy, here the son is forced by the father-cum-dummy to be a ventriloquist:

> He used to say: 'I'll make a ventriloquist of you if it's the last thing I ever do'. I had to go with him wherever he went, all over the world; and stand in the wings, and watch him; and go home with him at night and practise again – *Bee, Eff, Em, En, Pe, Ve, Doubleyou* – over and over again.[25]

One might suggest that the reason boys became the favoured form of ventriloquial dummy was because they allowed for the exercise of this violence in a way that little girls or animals could not. For little girls and animals are supposed to be helpless and innocent, and we are conventionally outraged when they are hurt. Little boys, those famed repositories of slugs and snails and puppy-dog's tails, are never innocent, or never wholly so. It is always open to the adult to suspect that the little boy is not a proper child at all, but is harbouring adult propensities towards violence and wrongdoing. This then legitimates the exercise of those actual adult propensities for violent punishment on the boy-dummy. One should not perhaps ask what the boy has done to deserve this violence; it seems as though, whenever there is the voice dissevered from the body, there will be violence, and it becomes necessary that there should be a boy to receive and contain it. Since the nineteenth century, the cost of patriarchal ideology for boys has been that they are expected to internalise much higher levels of habitual violence than girls. Typically, it is not enough to silence or restrain the figure: it must, it seems, be annihilated, suffering the kind of 'auditory extinction' spoken of by William Niederland.[26] At the end of the film *Dead of Night*, warders ill-advisedly attempt to draw the ventriloquist Maxwell Frere, who has been imprisoned for the attempted murder of a rival ventriloquist, into speech by bringing him his demonic dummy Hugo (who has, of course, been responsible for the act). On hearing that Hugo intends to take up with his rival, Frere's response is to smash the dummy to pieces.[27] In a more recent replay of the demonic dummy theme, the dummy who has inadvertently been brought to life can only be killed by being pulverised beneath a road-roller, with the accompaniment of a miry stench.[28]

The Jamie Bulger case in Britain in 1993 threw this into striking relief. The nation was shocked by video footage showing two-year-old Jamie being led out of a Liverpool shopping precinct by two ten-year-old boys, who were later found to have battered him to death with bricks and an iron bar. The outpouring of hatred towards the boys who had committed the murder was extraordinary, not least because it seemed to confirm the very thing that was being so massively grieved for, the so-called killing, not just of the child, but of childhood itself. During the trial of the two boys, it was suggested that they had been influenced by videos of the *Child's Play 1, 2 and 3* films, in which a doll called Chucky comes to life and begins to hurt and murder.[29] The dynamics of mimicry and repetition are complex and chilling here. For children to kill a child seemed to be the proof that they are really, like Chucky, changelings, and not real children at all, and therefore have got it coming to them. Demonised by the bottomlessly infantile British popular press, the boys became the legitimate objects of the very violence that they inflicted on their child-victim. The fact that they killed a child who *resembled* the malevolent Chucky much more than they did themselves clinches the bizarre dreamwork that was enacted in media representations of the trial. The dummying of the two boys makes it possible to ensure an absolute separation between the victim and the perpetrators, justifying any repetition of their crime on them. The suggestion that they might have identified with Chucky made it possible for the boys who committed the murder to be turned into the dummy, or impostor-children, and to receive the violence of which there seems to be such an endless reserve for boys.

The forms of ventriloquism which have proliferated in contemporary media culture are of a different kind from this now archaic dummy-ventriloquism. The disembodied voices of airport announcements, automated voicemail and other forms of synthesised speech testify to a truly anaesthetic extraction of the voice from the body, the electronic production of the voice separate from the blood and breath of any actual physiology. It appears, however, that this very analgesia may present itself in the form of an obscure, spreading, impersonal ache. The sound artist Gregory Whitehead, who uses his own voice extensively in his work, has suggested that there may be not only wounding, but the possibility of reparation in the technological severing of the voice from the body.

> The fact is, we cannot find our voice just by using it: we must be willing to cut it out of our throats, put it on the autopsy table, isolate and savor the various quirks and pathologies, then stitch it back together and see what

happens. The voice, then, not as something which is found, but as something which is written. We may have escaped from the judgement of God, but we have not yet escaped from the judgement of the Autopsist – the truth is not in how your voice sounds, but in how it's cut.[30]

Whitehead does here what he does in his work, namely puts back into the disembodied voice a kind of anguish which is in fact missing from contemporary experiences of it. For, far from being dismayed or made anxious by the coming of the technological disembodied voice, we have, it might be said, become prematurely habituated to it. The determination of some cultural historians to find amazement and anxiety and cultural trauma at the coming of the telephone and the phonograph meets with a puzzling lack of evidence. Although there were some at the end of the nineteenth century who were intrigued and amazed by the new invention, in many ways the contemporary reaction to the coming of the telephone seems to have been 'about time, too'. The telephone had been in use only for months before users began wondering irritatedly why the sound quality was so poor, and inventors began thinking of ways to improve it; hearing of Bell's invention, Edison set to work almost straight away on a device that would link the phonograph to it to make a permanent record (the answerphone, which had to wait for a century or so to become actual). In periods like the late nineteenth century, and like our own, in which the technological imagination outruns technological development itself, new inventions have a way of seeming out of date, or used up, on their arrival, like a birthday present with which you have been secretly playing in advance. The rapid naturalisation of the technologically mediated voice does not seem to have resulted in the painful severing of the voice from the subject, for that severing was indeed a bloodless surgery.

And yet there is a loss, of a kind; I mean, the loss *of the loss* of the voice. We have been severed, not from our voices, but from the pain of that severance. What aches most is the numbness; what is strange is the familiarity of the disembodied voice. Technologies of the voice are particularly subject to this estrangement precisely because of the deep-laid associations of the voice with various kinds of corporeal intensity, with suffering, love and pleasure. The desire to recapture this lost estrangement seems to lie not only behind many cultural or philosophical histories of the technologised voice, such as Avital Ronell's *The Telephone Book* and the essays in Douglas Kahn and Gregory Whitehead's *Wireless Imagination*, but also behind the odd ways in which we poke the embers of our astonishment at certain contemporary developments in telephony and phonography.[31] The determination of commentators to be amazed when it first became viable to send voice across the internet a number of years ago, in an otherwise unastonishing reinvention of the telephone (fancy, actually using telephone lines to transmit – voice!), was itself a little amazing. We seem to have missed out on some trauma, some *agon*, the first time that many of our technologies came round. The epoch of their supersession allows for surprising flarings of affect with respect to these 'old' technologies.

## No time like the present

Ventriloquism has had its day. Even when revivals of ventriloquism occur, as in the recent success of David Strassman, it takes a necromantic form. In his performances, Strassman plays both with the magical and the technological prehistory of ventriloquism. His demonic 'Chuck Wood' character is made consciously to refer to the history of mesmerism and possession – his eyes glow and he becomes possessed by an evil spirit at one point, causing him to rotate his head through 360 degrees, like the victim of possession in *The Exorcist*. But this history is a history mediated through twentieth-century media, especially films like *Dead of Night*, *Devil Doll*, *Magic* and *The Exorcist*. Animatronic technology allows Strassman to break the physical link between performer and dummy that has always been so important in ventriloquial performance. The ventriloquist and dummy have a traditional argument about who needs whom most, which leads Strassman to stalk off the stage in a huff, telling Chuck Wood to do the act himself if he thinks he can. After a couple of minutes slumped on his seat, Chuck rolls his eyes, lifts his head and asks 'Is he gone?' But even this is a conscious recall of a scene from *Devil Doll* in which the highlight of the sinister Great Vorelli's show is when his dummy (another Hugo) gets up and walks on his own.[32] The violence which erupts in ventriloquist films allows in what I have elsewhere called the sense of the 'vocalic uncanny',[33] as the corporeal ventriloquism of an earlier period, and in particular an earlier period of 'live' entertainment history, is incorporated within the fundamentally ventriloquial medium of cinema. These films haggle at the sensory wound that seemed to have been neatly sutured by *Singin' in the Rain*. The temporal indeterminacy of these films, which run together the familiar power that the sound film has to separate voice from the body, with dreads and delights of a much more ancient vintage, is intensified in Strassman's anachronistic revival of them in his performances.

In the performance captured in his radio 'play' *To Have Done With the Judgement of God*, Antonin Artaud sought to raise his tortured body into the condition of voice, restoring its undivided wholeness in the fierce enactment of its mutilation by the medium, envisaged as 'a session on the autopsy table in order to remake his anatomy'.[34] Today, the opportunities for the exploration of this ecstatic, arsonous voice-body seem to have dwindled. In a sense, this is because of the fulfilment of Artaud's own prescription for a theatre in which the script-governed voice would lose its pre-eminence, and be set to work alongside other theatrical elements: light, colour, costume, gesture. In the radio performance of Artaud, and in performances which simulate the eyeless exposure of the voice, such as Beckett's *Not I*, or the contorted, abstract sound-ballets of the contemporary deaf performer Aaron Williamson, in which the shouts, groans and crepitations of the performer act out the struggles of an earless voice to establish a relation to itself, the voice is forced to make its own body out of its privation. Trevor Wishart's 'extended vocal technique', in evidence in works such as *Anticredos* and *Vox*, expands the range of voice to include ticks and clicks, groans, whirs and slobbers, both disabling and re-enabling voice for the purposes of a new kind of arduous – and sometimes scandalously infantile – vocal performance.[35]

The technological transformations of the voice effected from the 1960s onwards may seem to press in the same direction of privation. Works from the 1960s such as Karlheinz Stockhausen's *Momente* of 1962 and Luciano Berio's *Sequenza III* cut the voice up into its primal elements in order to make them available for musical rearticulation. The technological disintegration of the voice effected by popular performers like Laurie Anderson, with her use of her 'vocoder' to mutate her voice and mingle it with other sound sources, and by the panoply of effects now routinely available to artists and performers, intensify the ventriloquial rending of the voice from its bodily source by the iterative splitting of the voice *from itself*, pulverising the vocalic body into digital granularity. This privation of the voice is in truth a new kind of sonorous omnipotence. The infant voice spoken of by Rosolato believes that it is everything, and can swallow down the world, but testifies in its suffering that it is not ague-proof. Our present condition is one in which, by contrast, voice is everywhere subject to digital deglutition. When anything and everything can be encoded as voice, and voice can be engineered into any other sonorous output, then there is no more conflict or ambivalence between 'bad voice' and 'good voice'. Voice becomes merely one mode or allotrope of the mobile, multimediary intersensorium, which never ceases unmaking and remaking itself. The stubborn survival, in the work of vocal performers like Phil Minton, Diamanda Galas and Shelley Hirsch, of the impoverished, dismembered voice-body of the ventriloquial sensorium, testifies to a need to keep alive a possibility of being out of date: urging that what we stand to lose, amid all these technological lootings of the voice, is the archaic affluence of its destitution.

## Notes

1 Steven Connor, 'The Ethics of the Voice', in *Critical Ethics: Text, Theory and Responsibility*, ed. Dominic Rainsford and Tim Woods, Basingstoke: Macmillan, 1999: 220–37.

2 Guy Rosolato, 'La Voix: entre corps et langage', *Revue française de psychanalyse*, 38, 1974: 76 (my translation).

3 Rosolato, 'La Voix': 76.

4 Rosolato, 'La Voix': 78.

5 Melanie Klein, 'Some Theoretical Conclusions Regarding the Emotional Life of the Infant', *Envy and Gratitude and Other Works, 1946–1963*, London: Vintage, 1997: 61–93, esp. 61–71.

6 Nicolas Abraham and Maria Torok, 'Mourning *or* Melancholia: Introjection *versus* Incorporation', in *The Shell and the Kernel*, trans. Nicholas T. Rand, Chicago and London: University of Chicago Press, 1994: 127.

7 Didier Anzieu, *The Skin Ego*, trans. Chris Turner, New Haven and London: Yale University Press, 1989: 157–73.

8 D. W. Winnicott, 'Transitional Objects and Transitional Phenomena' (1951), in *Collected Papers: Through Pediatrics to Psycho-Analysis*, London: Tavistock, 1958: 232.

9 Rick Altman, 'Moving Lips: Cinema as Ventriloquism', *Yale French Studies*, 60, 1980: 74.

10 Edith Lecourt, 'The Musical Envelope', in Didier Anzieu, ed. *Psychic Envelopes*, trans. Daphne Briggs, London: Karnac, 1990: 213.

11  Michel Poizat, *The Angel's Cry*, trans. Arthur Denner, Ithaca and London: Cornell University Press, 1992.

12  Felicia Miller Frank, *The Mechanical Song: Women, Voice, and the Artificial in Nineteenth-Century French Narrative*, Stanford: Stanford University Press, 1995: 186–7.

13  Frank, *The Mechanical Song*: 195.

14  I chart the long, uneven process whereby ventriloquism becomes attached to various kinds of dummy in my *Dumbstruck: A Cultural History of Ventriloquism*, Oxford: Oxford University Press, 2000.

15  Valentine Vox, *I Can See Your Lips Moving: The History and Art of Ventriloquism*, North Hollywood, CA: Plato Publishing/Studio City, CA: Players Press, 1993: 133.

16  Leigh Eric Schmidt, 'From Demonic Possession to Magic Show: Ventriloquism, Religion, and the Enlightenment', *Church History*, 67, 1998: 302.

17  I have discussed the ventriloquial dramaturgy of multiple personality disorders in my 'Satan and Sybil: Talk, Possession and Dissociation', in *Talk, Talk, Talk: The Cultural Life of Everyday Conversation*, ed. Shelley Salamensky, New York and London: Routledge, forthcoming.

18  Vox, *I Can See Your Lips Moving*: 41–2.

19  Neil Arnott, *Elements of Physics: Or, Natural Philosophy, General and Medical . . .*, second edition, London: for Thomas and George Underwood, 1827: 591.

20  Jean-Baptiste de la Chapelle, *Le Ventriloque, ou l'engastrimythe*, London: Chez de l'Etanville; Paris: Chez la Veuve Duchesne, 1772: 293–4.

21  British Library L.C. Plays 1919/32.

22  Maurice Hurling, *Ventriloquial Verbosity*, London: Max Andrews, 1946: 51.

23  Frank Richards' *Bunter the Ventriloquist* (London: Cassell, 1961) is a late survival of this tradition.

24  Edgar Bergen, *Ventriloquism Exposed: A Dramatic Composition*, London: Samuel French, 1947.

25  Gerald Kersh, 'The Extraordinarily Horrible Dummy', in *The Horrible Dummy and Other Stories*, London: William Heinemann, 1944: 50.

26  William G. Niederland, 'Early Auditory Experiences, Beating Fantasies, and Primal Scene', *Psychoanalytic Study of the Child*, 13, 1958: 474.

27  *Dead of Night*, dir. Alberto Cavalcanti, Charles Crichton, Basil Dearden, Robert Hamer, Rank (UK), 1945. The film is an anthology of stories, of which the ventriloquist story is directed by Cavalcanti.

28  R. L. Stine, *Night of the Living Dummy*, New York and London: Scholastic, 1993.

29  For reflections on the *Child's Play* films in the context of the Bulger trial, see Blake Morrison, *As If*, London: Granta Books, 1997: 150–4.

30  'Radio Play is No Place: A Conversation Between Jérôme Noetinger and Gregory Whitehead', *TDR*, special issue on 'Experimental Sound and Radio', ed. Allen S. Weiss, 40 (3), 1996: 100.

31  Avital Ronell, *The Telephone Book: Technology – Schizophrenia – Electric Speech*, Lincoln: University of Nebraska Press, 1989; *Wireless Imagination: Sound, Radio, and the Avant-Garde*, ed. Douglas Kahn and Gregory Whitehead, Cambridge, MA and London: MIT Press, 1992.

32  *Devil Doll*, dir. Lindsay Shonteff, Galaworld Productions, 1964.

33  Steven Connor, 'Echo's Bones: Myth, Modernity and the Vocalic Uncanny', in *Myth and the Making of Modernity*, ed. Michael Bell and Peter Poellner, Amsterdam and Atlanta: Rodopi, 1998: 213–35.

34  Antonin Artaud, 'To Have Done With the Judgement of God', trans. Clayton Eshleman, in *Wireless Imagination*: 328.

35  I discuss these and other examples in more detail in my 'The Decomposing Voice of Postmodern Music', in *ELH* (forthcoming).

# 6

# HELLO DOLLY
# WELL HELLO DOLLY
## The double and its theatre

*Rebecca Schneider*

And the Lord God caused a deep sleep to fall upon Adam, and he slept; and he took one of his ribs, and closed up the flesh instead thereof;

And from the rib, which the Lord God had taken from the man, made he a woman, and brought her unto the man.

And Adam said, This is now bone of my bones, and flesh of my flesh.

Genesis, 2: 21–3

The good Lord ordained a time-honored method of creating human life.

US Congressman Vernon Ehlers, Michigan, urging Congress to pass a law making human cloning a federal crime[1]

At this time it is morally unacceptable for anyone in the public or private sector, whether in a research or clinical setting, to attempt to create a child using somatic cell nuclear transfer cloning.

*Report and Recommendations of the*
*National Bioethics Advisory Commission* (NBAC)[2]

The 'this time,' referred to in the Clinton commissioned NBAC report, is now – a now that began immediately after the February 1997 birth of Dolly. 'Dolly' is the sheep cloned from the udder cells of a six-year-old ewe in Edinburgh by a little-known scientist, laboring in a little-known laboratory. Ian Wilmut injected the nucleus from a frozen udder cell into an enucleated egg, called a 'bereft egg,' of another ewe, generating an embryo that was then inserted into a third ewe who brought the embryo to term. The embryo, and resultant lamb, was the exact replica of the embryo and resultant lamb that formed the first Dolly. It was Dolly, again. Or was it? The first Dolly was unnamed and indeed was dead (in fact *eaten*) before the clone Dolly was even ... re-conceived. The clone Dolly was named, instead, for yet a fourth female, the performer Dolly Parton, who 'was also known,' said Wilmut, strangely using the past tense, 'for her mammaries.'[3]

*Figure 6.1* Photograph of Dolly, courtesy of the Roslin Institute, Edinburgh.

Granting that there is an undeniable horror that congeals to the above narrative, this essay is not interested in arguing a 'for' or 'against' regarding the ethics of cloning. On the very day of this writing, 27 May 1999, news has hit the media that Dolly is aging more rapidly than other sheep her age.[4] She is, it now appears, older than she is. Perhaps she is trying to catch up with herself. Clearly, more is unknown than is known, and one would be hard pressed not to side with the NBAC cautious phrasing 'at this time.'

Here, then, I am interested to use the issue of cloning as an invitation to revisit concerns about time and repetition – concerns arguably at the heart of a medium which plays with time, repeatedly: the theater. Though I will discuss cloning and anxiety more than theater proper in the pages below, the analogy of 'the double' to 'the theater' should be read as more than implicit if less than explicit throughout.

## Father mime

*[T]he theater teaches precisely the uselessness of the action which, once done, is not to be done, and the superior use of the state unused by the action and which, restored, produces a purification [. . . .]*

Antonin Artaud, emphasis in original[5]

What can explain [. . . .] how our culture of the copy has come to be so bewildered, even terrified, by figures we shape in our own image?

Hillel Schwartz[6]

'Emphasis in original.' I am interested in probing the fear around cloning to examine the ways in which even as we make restorations (or copies, or doubles, or clones)[7], we simultaneously reenact a rather ancient Western cultural distrust of mimesis. The history of Western theater is packed across the first millennium with antitheatrical sentiment.[8] Though the gesture of reducing such a volume of anxiety to a sentence bears a kind of Artaudian violence, it is possible to argue that this fear concerns the threatening potential of the seeming Second (the double, the theatrical, the rib) to unseat the prerogatives of the First. For Artaud this coming again, this restoration of the 'violence' of gesture without its original use, this twice-behaved behavior, would be 'purifying' – like the repetitions, perhaps, of a cathartic working-through. But, he constantly cautioned, 'there is risk involved.'[9] I have often noted that students seem strangely relieved to find that the man went crazy, as if Artaud's suffering could justify their fear that the risk involved with thinking through the double is precisely too great.

We might think of the 'bewilderment' and 'terror' in the copy (to cite Schwartz again) in the following, perhaps simplistic way. The cultural fear of mimesis is a fear of indiscreet origins – of emphasis gone amok, lost, or appropriated without 'proper' identification. The fear is that the copy will not only tamper with the original, but will author the original – or, perhaps most fearful, that the copy (the rib, the second) will *come to be acknowledged* as author, father, First. Along with concerns about property and the flow of economics that attend 'proper' identification of ownership and lineage, are there less apparent fears that might attend the indiscretions of mimesis? Perhaps one result of a mimesis not properly vilified would be that the seeming first would have to acknowledge its indebtedness to the second – like an ancestor thanking his progeny for his very existence – the second having *made* the first (at least by making the first first, making the origin original). Yes, the doubling begins to be bewildering. Yet it hardly bears mentioning the fundamental threat in such an equation: if seconds or copies or ribs come first then the father as father (or the master as master) is unsettled. When only the mimic originates, scripting an original through articulating a copy, then authenticity is deranged.[10] Looking at it this way, taking more than one rib from Freud and his recombinance in Derrida, we begin to see Originality as a cultural product fraught with anxiety. Originality is umbilically (and anxiously) attached to the idea of a dead or distant patriarch who serves as an anchor thrown backward, etched with words printed as if to appear ancient: 'First Time.'

Through the first second coming of the clone, as through the much earlier 'birth' of psychoanalysis's performative repetition, it is, Derrida writes, 'the very idea of a *first time* which becomes enigmatic' (emphasis in original).[11] The fear of mimesis as 'morally unacceptable' (NBAC) is related to this becoming enigma, or this enigmatic becoming – the cultural fear of a first *explicitly* coming second – a challenge to the 'natural order' of things.

Of course, the fear seems oddly placed – like a reenactment of protest at a commemoration. After all, this echo of anxiety resounds at the backbone of a culture which would seem to be responsible for realizing its own fear in a postmodern age where our technologies increasingly blur the line between representation and 'reality,' or repetition and original. But of course, as will be discussed below, the (seminal) Freudian interjection into the already teeming pool of Western metaphysics was that anxiety is always already a repetition, an echo, a second coming, an always retrocessive trauma.

## At this time, then

> The parodic replication and resignification of heterosexual constructs within non-heterosexual frames not only brings into relief the utterly constructed status of the so-called original, but it shows that heterosexuality only constitutes itself as the original through a convincing act of repetition. The more that 'act' is expropriated, the more the heterosexual claim to originality is exposed as illusory.
>
> Judith Butler[12]

After Dolly, the heat under the beaker of the clone issue was raised significantly – and much of it had to do with the issue of time travel at the heart of clonal regression. Though clones had been created before, they had always been created from embryos – the generation, in essence, of identical twins. Dolly, on the other hand, was a clone generated from an adult – a feat that had been repeatedly declared to be impossible. To clone an adult the genetic material taken from a cell must, as Gina Kolata expressed it in the *New York Times*, 'essentially *go backwards in time*' and enter the state it was in at the moment of conception (emphasis added).[13]

In the US, the hysteria that greeted Dolly's immaculate re-conception was immediate and intense – both pro and con, but mostly con. Thirty hours after the news of Dolly hit the media, New York State legislator John Marchi announced a bill to make human cloning illegal and conservative ministers, rabbis, bishops, and columnists rallied in support.[14] Anticipating the uproar around the clone, a pro-clone action group sprang up composed of members of gay and lesbian communities in New York, calling themselves the Clone Rights United Front.[15] The sympathy that many felt for the project of cloning had not only to do with the interest in repro-duction unmoored from mechanics of sperm and egg, but also with the fear of 'sameness' leveled against homosexuals in a culture which mandated hetero-sexuality as 'properly' originary and normative. 'Clone' had been an appellation adopted by gays to name the hypermasculine camp that had come to signify post-Stonewall gay male style. As Martin Levin succinctly historicized it: 'When the dust of gay liberation had settled, the doors of the closet were opened, and out popped the clone.'[16] Clone style, overt and carefully manipulated signatures of macho affective and behavioral patterns, threateningly outed masculinity as constructed, as masquerade (a category previously reserved for deprecations of femininity), as given to the indiscretions of performativity and mimesis, as imbricated in class politics, and as appropriable. Clones were the signature of post-closet pride until the mid-1980s when the virulence of clonal lifestyle came under panicked attack as the 'cause' of AIDS. At that juncture, clonal fashion was adopted and mainstreamed by interior designers who renamed the style 'high tech.'[17]

There is no question that 'cloning' has long been synonymous with high tech, and high tech has signified masculinity. Mimesis, on the other hand, is no tech – primitivized, feminized, and debased (think of all the deprecations of 'primitives' as 'apers'). That cloning and its penchant for extremes of resemblance became a signature of hypermasculinity, while mimesis or masquerade, and its slippery slope of repetition with difference, has long been feminized, presents an interesting conundrum when one considers that in the space of the hyper the 'pure' is strangely undone. On close inspection it is precisely the heteronormative tenet that femininity and masculinity are fully distinct from each other that is instantly threatened by the clone. One is reminded of E. T. A. Hoffmann's Olympia, the famous Doll of 'The Sandman' – that epitome of femininity who was ultimately a high-tech ruse of masculine wiles (science). That Dolly the sheep should be heralded both high-tech clone *and* christened with a name that connotes a hyperfemininity should remind us of deeper issues surrounding the pleasures and dangers of repetition – the realm Freud aptly named, inspired by Hoffmann if not Olympia herself, the uncanny.

In an essay titled 'Warhol's Clones,' Richard Meyer names Warhol's early 1960s' silkscreen repetitions, such as *Thirteen Most Wanted Men* and *Double Elvis*, as fore-runners of gay clone culture. Meyer points to the doubledness of the clone as the work of acknowledgement. 'When a movie still of Elvis Presley seeks itself through Warholian repetition, it discovers a homoeroticism that its original Hollywood context could not acknowledge.' As Meyer argues, it is by making the copy explicit, again and again beside itself, indeed touching itself, that Warhol 'recovers the *intrinsic* queer appeal of a mass-cultural representation which would otherwise disavow the presence of its (admiring) gay male audience' (emphasis in original).[18] Cloning, in other words, adds emphasis by noting an emphasis already there but not

*Figure 6.2* Andy Warhol, *Double Elvis*, 1963. Synthetic polymer paint and silkscreen on canvas, 82 × 49½ in. (208.3 × 125.7 cm). Andy Warhol Museum, Pittsburgh, Founding Collection, Contribution The Andy Warhol Foundation for the Visual Arts, Inc.

acknowledged, indeed disavowed. The added emphasis of 'emphasis in original' stands beside itself to undo heteronormative disavowal through a double gesture, at once parody *and* the poignancy of exact replication.

Then there is the 'Dolly' who rides the waves of salutation, hailing after hailing, interpellation after interpellation: Hello Dolly Well Hello Dolly. Once is never quite enough.

Think of 'Dolly' who became Barbra Streisand through an adapted Thornton Wilder play which had transmogrified into the Hollywood musical *Hello Dolly!* (1969) after 2844 performances on Broadway (in which Carol Channing became Ginger Rogers, Martha Raye, Betty Grable, Bibi Osterwald, Pearl Bailey, Phyllis Diller, and Ethel Merman before becoming Barbra). Wilder's 'original' play, *The*

*Matchmaker* (1955), was itself already a second go – a rewrite of Wilder's earlier *The Merchant of Yonkers; a farce in four acts* (1939). But *Merchant* was itself recombinant as it was based upon the Johann Nestroy comedy *Einen jux will er sich machen?* (Vienna, 1842) which was in turn based upon *A Day Well Spent; a farce in one act* by John Oxenford (1835).

Writing on images of Jews and women in the films of Barbra Streisand, Felicia Herman gives us the following, linking Streisand to Dolly to Elvis, and to Warhol in one fell swoop:

> America's newest Graceland has just opened. The new shrine, however, is devoted not to Elvis Presley but rather to a figure who, with the exception of her choice of careers, is in many ways Presley's polar opposite. Hello, Gorgeous!, a museum/store centrally located in the predominantly gay Castro district of San Francisco, celebrates the career of Barbra Streisand, the liberal, feminist, Jewish actor/singer/director from New York. The museum's creator, Ken Joachim, says that he felt inspired by the notion that his life, especially his oppression as a gay man, was 'very parallel' to Streisand's . . . Even as Joachim was putting the finishing touches on his museum, Streisand was being feted back in New York in a different way. In an exhibition at the Jewish Museum titled 'Too Jewish?' . . . images of Barbra Streisand were in abundance. In *Four Barbras*, for example, artist Deborah Kass repeatedly silk screened Streisand's profile (with its prominent proboscis) in a parody of Andy Warhol.[19]

We might question Herman's choice of the word 'parody' as to parody Warhol would arguably be to parody parody – but that is perhaps part of the clonal point, where appropriation becomes strangely original. And 'Hello Gorgeous!'? Never mind the confusion in 'museum/store' – the web site calls it a 'shrine to the image, art of Streisand.' The free-floating slashes and commas here make the entire space one where interpellation becomes glossalalia – 'hilariously out of control' – as Joachim described Barbra (and the theatricalities of being 'very, very Jewish'). This from the website:

> Think of it as a kind of Graceland for Jews. There are full-size mannequins of Babs dressed as several of her characters, fake nails with the label 'Just Like Buttah,' magazine covers, postcards and amateur snapshots of her likeness. One of the most festive exhibits is a huge Barbra head, with a bracelet, tiara and necklace made out of light bulbs.[20]

Part of her larger Warhol Project, Deborah Kass's *Four Barbras* (The Jewish Jackie Series) is silkscreen and acrylic on canvas. Multiple Barbras 'substitute' Barbra Streisand for Jackie Kennedy. In Kass's *My Elvis* series, Streisand as Yentl appears as Warhol's *Double Elvis*, a move which Robert Rosenblum sees as 'upping the ante' on Warhol by 'emphasizing a . . . hyphenated minority – Jewish-lesbian.'[21] This 'upped

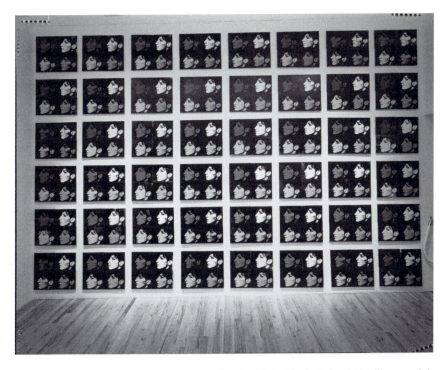

*Figure 6.3* Deborah Kass, *48 Four Barbras* (The Jewish Jackie Series), 1992, silkscreen ink and acrylic on canvas, each 20 × 24 in. Collection of Arthur G. Rosen and the artist.

ante' also arguably occurs at the stroke of the word 'My,' rendering the repetition in the 'personal is political' terms that was foundational to feminism when Warhol was at the height of his fame. If Warhol's Elvis was an 'original clone' as Martin Levin might have it, Kass's pieces are perhaps less clones of Warhol themselves than a 'take' on Warhol's cloning that underscores, *by cloning Barbra*, what Linda Nochlin calls Warhol's 'refusal to engage with ethnicity or sexual preference.'[22] In both cases, Warhol's and Kass's, the clone functions to remark 'emphasis in original' and press acknowledgement of what has otherwise been a subject of refusal.

Though perhaps in a different way than the one Elvis, the *Double Elvis*, the one Barbra, or the *Four Barbras*, Dolly the cloned sheep also raised myriad specters of indiscretion, of something 'out of control.' She threatened naturalized gender identification and heterosexual prerogative and her threat, in its 'hyper' state of repetition, was linked to the improprieties of the theatrical, the theatricalities of the 'very, very' ethnic, and the scary 'queer appeal' of mass cultural representation.[23]

Beside politicians and activists, academics too hit the ground running when ewe Dolly hit the media. As Glenn McGee of the University of Pennsylvania's Center for Bioethics described it, his center and other like constellations all but closed down as 'the faculty moved into "uplink studios" for dozens of interviews with harried, almost frantic journalists.' The faculty found themselves repeatedly answering absurd questions including, wrote McGee, whether 'clones bred for their roles would take over on Wall Street.'[24] If ethicists approached the public's questions as absurd, they also bemoaned a science turned theatrical. Dr Ronald Munson, an ethicist at the University of Missouri told journalist Gina Kolata: 'Here we have this incredible technical accomplishment, and what motivated it? The desire for more sheep milk of a certain type.' It is, he said, 'the theater of the absurd acted out by scientists.'[25]

If all funding for research into the cloning of human beings in the US was halted on the heels of the National Bioethics Advisory Commission report in 1997, nothing slowed the pace of animal cloning. What follows is taken from the *New York Times* on the 1998 cloning of 22 mice, seven of which were clones of clones, and none of which, so far as I know, were named for stars – unless they were all named Dolly.

> 'Wow,' said Dr Barry Zirkin, who is the head of the division of repro-
> ductive biology at Johns Hopkins [. . .] 'This is going to be Dolly multiplied
> by 22' . . . Already, a venture capitalist in Hawaii is setting up a consortium
> of companies and academic scientists to make the cloning of adult animals a
> commercial reality within a few years. But the investor, Laith Reynolds,
> the chief executive officer of Probio America, said, 'We have no interest in
> cloning humans. Besides being the politically correct answer,' he added,
> 'we can't see any business in it.' [26]

In theater and film, the 'business' of cloning is not difficult to see – and it is hardly news. As I write, a performer on Fulton Street outside my New York City apartment has gathered a Saturday crowd by dancing with a life-size female doll. At least from my balcony vantage point, she looks bizarrely real. Their steps are perfectly in sync (her feet, after all, are strapped to his). He places his hands, tied to her hands, on her hips, and together their overtly sex-mimetic gyrations generate business, causing quarters to tinkle into an open bucket at their side. Time travel, too, is a long-standing art of the theater. Around the corner the Shooting Star Theater offers a one-man reenactment bringing Edgar Allen Poe back to life, called *A Touch of Poe*. It is a show that 'took first' at a better-known laboratory in Edinburgh, this one for fringe theater.

Indeed, the South Street Seaport area itself is fast becoming its own double, a self-replica, with facades of the old fish market painted on building walls. Bizarrely, the old market is painted on building walls which *are* the old market, now painted to look like itself in the past – a younger version of its older identity as the fish business is replaced by tours of replicant boats and by newer baited hooks: J. Crew, Godiva Chocolate, and Guess?

One month from this writing, though miles from Fulton Street, thousands will gather at Gettysburg to reenact the Civil War battle of Gettysburg as 'living history' – an event so compelling that area hotels are sold out months in advance. If Munson is right, at least in public sentiment these events are not completely unrelated to

Wilmut's variety of science. Still, 'theater of the absurd' is not the only appellation that might apply, as across the country 'reputable' museums have taken up reenact-ment, or 'living history,' as a viable Zola-esque (which is to say art-scientific) access not to the absurdity of theater, but to 'authentic' understanding. And certainly, at many battle reenactments, the line between 'authentic' and 'virtual' is often hard to read, for the participants if not for the spectators, as versions of trance, 'past-life' experience, and 'channeling' are reportedly common, as are actual wounds.[27]

Of course, battle reenactments are not theater – well not exactly. And neither is cloning – well not exactly. But all share some uncanny properties of repetition – history brought back, again, across the body on stage, or across the body as stage. In biological cloning we see the 'same' body in different stages, and across the proscenium or on the battlefield year after year we see 'different' bodies (different actors playing the same part) on the same stage. The contemporary fear of cloning and its ethics is perhaps not as far from an age-old Western antitheatrical prejudice as it might appear to be in the pages of science sections where the 'reenactment' appears to take place on a stage the size of a single cell. Indeed, as Meyer writes in the context of Warhol, the clone can be taken as 'a directive to abandon the search for an original fantasy object' – like a 'real' Marilyn Monroe or 'real' James Dean or a 'real' Dolly Parton – a directive to take pleasure, and more, in the concatenations of mimesis which instruct that the 'authentic fantasy object' always takes place as a double.[28]

## Re-foundational anxiety

There are already myriad post-Dolly publications that examine the fear surrounding cloning. Most often the focus is on the crisis of reproductive rights – the concerns on the part of liberal feminists that their bodies will be turned into factories for patriarchal replication, on the part of men that the father's function in reproduction will be rendered obsolete, on the part of homophobes that heterosexuality may be outmoded, and on the part of conservative Christians that persons will take the place of God and that children will be 'denied their right to biological parents.'[29] All of these hinge on the place of the father as *original*, in one way or another, and thus they are not unrelated to another fear: the fear of mimesis, or a feminized realm of replication itself, where Origins are fictions, or if not complete fictions then *proton pseudoi*, or 'first lies,'[30] and Foundations are outed as performative re-foundations.[31] This is the fearful potential that the copy will, in the case of clones, *literally* become the original (in fact it is the literalness of the equation that is daunting as the clone is both parent and child). Thus the copy will re-place the original even as it founds an original, backward, as having come first. Such a potential would call for a radical acknowledgment of an insight generally repressed in the name of phallogocentrism, that the original is always already mediated, that is, inscribed backward – a (fictional or secondary) effect of mediation. We might be forced to acknowledge, in other words, that the original *becomes* itself through repetition (disavowed), just as repetition (disavowed) *becomes* the original.

That this is a psychoanalytic insight, mediated by deconstruction, is clear.[32] Well before the historically novel Dolly, Freud was writing his own historical novel aimed at troubling the authentic site of the father as other than a fictional citation, a cover-up on the part of brothers.[33] According to Freud, origins, like the fiction of a fully accessible present, become less actual than active as sedimented sets of performative gestures – actual through repetition – the repeating performance of a protective (or repressive) force – a foundational misrecognition.

The fear of the double is thus not only about the copy *acknowledging* the original as secondary but about the arguably simultaneous potential of the double to theater – to mimicry and parody, to make a mockery of the seeming authentic by passing as 'same.'[34] Let me offer a more mundane example: the questions posed to bioethicist Glenn McGee in 1998 about clones potentially taking over Wall Street reminded me of a freshman at Dartmouth in the mid-1990s who was beside himself with shock after I showed my class the documentary on Harlem Drag Balls, *Paris is Burning*. The boy declared quite innocently, 'This means that anyone on Wall Street might be gay!' Though the rest of the class snickered at his naiveté, it was less the category of 'executive realness' that shocked this young man (of course executives are real) than the fact that the balls rendered the categories both of executive and of real *explicitly* performative (in the ways that the 'real' becomes the affect of felicitous performatives in the Austinian sense[35]). Thus, the student seemed to see like a flash that these categories (executive and real), existing in enactment, were clonal. He was horrified to see that they were capable of transference from what he assumed at Dartmouth was directly inherited from the father (or from the 'fraternal clan' of the Old Boys[36]) to a petri-dish of mimesis in the seemingly not-Dartmouth of the drag ball – and *convincing him*. For this student, 'gay' (or black, it was unclear) equaled mimetic, and mimetic equaled a terrifying dislocation of the world he had been given to trust (or given via trust). That executive realness might be composed of sedimented performative behaviors opened the world to what he perceived as an enormous wound – the degree to which all the world is a stage is the degree to which reproductive trusts and heteronormative ideals might *be* gay, or, in Irigaray's words, 'hom(m)osexual.'[37]

Indeed we ought not to be surprised by this young brother. The fear of the same-which-is-not, or of the different which might pass as the same is, of course, a signature fear of Western phallogocentrism. This is the cave-wound Plato so poetically penned and Irigaray so brilliantly unpacked. The positing through Plato of a true ontological original, a primary Ur-Same Ideal, was simultaneously a positing of the world as crippled by mimesis – the material, bodily world as sadly trapped within a theater. The Ideal is distinguished and debased by its ubiquitous mimics which lend themselves, like shadows, to misrecognition.

But let us, for a moment more, go forward with this regression from the Dartmouth student to the student of Socrates. It will behoove us to recall this foundation in brief. In the theatrical logic of Plato's cave, the replica, the shadow double, is as much the stuff of human material experience as it is a signature of that experience as delusional. According to this logic, we are born into a theater (the cave) where, from birth, we misrecognize shadow-doubles as originals and enter a life-long labor (if we become philosophers) of *remembering* that we have been duped. According to Plato, through that remembering we find access to the truth we had lost. We labor, in other words, *to go back in time*, to recall, to access what we had, through birth, forgotten. We strive for a going back in time that will put us in touch with a more Original Being. It is an ancient road then, which we have been traversing backward as a classical truism: we strive to return to a state prior to our birth in an effort to find, or to have found, or to re-found, the original.

Interestingly, of course, this is not a far cry from Freud's own claims in *Beyond the Pleasure Principle* in which he takes a 'hint' from Plato and argues that the aim of life is to regress to a state prior to its beginning.[38] But for Freud the effort is to return to the peaceful 'Nirvana' state of inanimate matter, or death. The inanimate matter of death, however, is arguably divergent from Plato's notion of Forms, and it is in the replacement of origin by death, the absence (though not the opposite) of origin, that Freud leaves his impression on/in, even as, the 'hint.'[39]

The practice of cloning can be read as a strange translation of Platonic theory into the literal – into the bodies orchestrated through biogenetic engineering. Thus cloning can be read as in keeping with a certain Western logic regarding the promise of knowledge in 'going back in time' to a state before birth. However, the age-old promise of remembering through regression almost immediately calls up age-old fears of the shadow-doubles as well – fears of the Mother-space of the cave, the theater of the masquerading feminine. While the fear of the double bears all the traits which Freud unpacked in the name of the 'uncanny' – (imagine greeting a six-year-old clone of yourself, aging prematurely) – in the case of cloning, and the a-sexual reproduction the practice inaugurates, the fear might more properly be named an anxiety. Anxiety, as Freud made abundantly clear, has its closest ties to sexuality, but finds its 'prototype' not in the bliss of before birth, but in the 'act' of birth itself. Indeed, anxiety itself is a kind of clone, as anxiety, for Freud, is itself always a double, a repetition, of the inaugural shock of separation:

> We believe that in the case of the affect of anxiety we know what the early impression is which it repeats. We believe that it is in the *act of birth* that there comes about the combination of unpleasurable feelings, impulses of discharge and bodily sensations which has become the prototype of the effects of a mortal danger and has ever since been repeated by us as the state of anxiety . . . We shall also recognize it as highly relevant that this first state of anxiety arose out of separation from the mother (emphasis in original).[40]

Whether or not Freud is 'right' to name literal birth – the 'act' of birth – as a primal scene, the 'first state' of anxiety, is not, here, my concern. Elsewhere for Freud literal death in the form of patricide is the generation of a first state of anxiety and repression (of that patricide) results in civilization. The adumbration of anxiety as *modus operandi* of a foundational Western cultural scene is something Freud develops in terms of the generation of 'civilization' from a 'sense of guilt' which is 'at base nothing else but a topographical variety of anxiety.'[41] In all, though Freud is a philosopher whose theories of repetition bear the flavor of their own radical originality (making him The Father of psychoanalysis), it is a flavor which has fundamentally rearranged the palate of philosophy by unsettling phallogocentrism – or making it anxious. As Derrida repeatedly emphasizes, it is not at all insignificant that Freud accomplishes this in a theater of writing which employs overtly theatrical writing. Freud's own 'originality becomes a theater, or becomes itself through the theatrical.'[42]

In any case, perhaps one of the major hints Freud extends from Plato's own (theatrical) writing is the foundational status of misrecognition in the logic of the West as linked to the replica, or the double, which repeats, and defers, an 'original.' Plato, after all, repeats Socrates and *writes* Socrates' distrust of writing (*Phaedrus*). If Socratic distrust of repetition (may we say anxiety about repetition?) generated an *overt* prejudice against theatricality, and compelled a long line of antitheatrical prejudice in the civilization that would come to be known as 'Western,' Freud decided to avoid the overt and follow up on Platonic 'hints.' Freud cited anxiety as productive and turned to repetition as *modus operandi* of the human drive to (re)generate anxiety in an effort to master (backwards) the remains of trauma. For Freud, like Plato (and even like Brecht), the theater of unconscious repetition (the poor blokes in the cave) could be turned toward conscious remembrance. But for Plato true remembrance could only take place through placing theater and repetition (and certainly anything clonal) in a binary opposition to Origin and Ideality. For Freud however (like Brecht), remembrance itself is a theater, enabled *by performance*, not turned away from repetition as debased. In the theater of psychoanalytic transference, the first is always only accessed through reenactment, through *a second time* but, importantly, a second time which constitutes, backward *and* afterward, the first.

## Jacques' fear: to be done with the ritual of patricide

The double, in the case of the clone, is linked resolutely to death of the Empire of the Same as Original. At the same time it inaugurates fantasies that Socrates himself, or ten Socrateses, or a hundred, might be brought back to life (of course, contemporary science cannot yet clone from dead cells). Like a reverse hemlock, or a reverse writing, the phantasmatic magic of cloning is positioned as 'pharmakon' – both remedy and poison.[43] It is, then, a kind of end to death – the death of biological death even as individuals die, and a death of the Origin as singularly back in time. Cloning is an odd unmasking of the delimitation of a temporal marker for 'back in time' as back in time becomes, with the clone, forward in time as well. Loss begins to threaten to be fictive. It may already be too late. In the 1997 words of French President Jacques Chirac, who oddly put his sentence in the past tense, cloning 'undermined the dignity of people by creating a desire to avoid death.'[44]

Now, far be it from me to know exactly what was going on in Chirac's brain. We cannot know which death Chirac intended to signify. He cannot have meant the literal death of individuals, as a clone does not mean that the cloned individual will not die. Perhaps, as I shall attempt to explicate below, he meant, more obliquely, an end to the repetitive death of the station of the father (thus an end to the cult of the father's remains) that haunts and repetitively re-institutes patriarchy. Perhaps he meant that we will be undermined as a people when we awaken the desire to avoid our thrall to dead fathers. When we move on. Let me try and explain.

In the 1970s, Ira Levin's *The Boys From Brazil* focused contemporary fear of the clone on Hitler.[45] In his novel, Dr. Death (Nazi doctor Joseph Mengele) raises clones of Hitler in a replica environment of Hitler's youth. Not only might clones of 'us' take over Wall Street, but we might again witness atrocities (as if only genetic Hitler could become performative Hitler). Two years after Levin's book, in 1978, a scandal erupted around a supposedly nonfiction account of a millionaire named Max who had secretly cloned himself. The book, David Rorvik's *In His Image: The Cloning of a Man*, was on the bestseller nonfiction list in the US and Britain, selling 95,000 copies in hardcover.[46] When the book was unmasked as a fraud, after the matter was taken up in the US Congress, it became a joke – 'the clowning of a man,' in the words of Andre Hellegers of the Institute for the Study of Human Reproduction and Ethics at Georgetown.[47] In the 1990s, concerns about cloning seem to coagulate around sports stars (though one could argue that this fear was as racially motivated as fears around Hitler). After Dolly's birth, George Will took up the example of Michael Jordan to admonish cloning in the name of potential child abuse: 'Suppose a clone of Michael Jordan, age 8, preferred violin to basketball?'[48] Will was apparently worried that the hypothetical young Jordan clone would be tyrannized by 'his cloner' (Jordan himself? Or is Jordan assumed problematically to have no agency in the example?), a parent patently not called father.

In an attempt to assuage fear of the clone, Dave Anderson addressed the issue for 'Sports of the Times' less than a week after Dolly's birth hit the media. Anderson assured his readership that all the hoopla was for naught – it was all hype. In Anderson's logic, we need not fear Michael Jordan because Michael Jordan could never really be cloned. The reason? A biological clone would not be a true Michael because *Michael's clone would never have Jordan's father* – and without a father, one is not one. Jordan is really Jordan's father (which begs the question of whether he is already a clone). But I will let Anderson explain:

> You couldn't just put a clone back in time . . .
>
> Jordan was always close to his late father; a Jordan clone wouldn't even have a biological father. Genetically, a clone would only have a mother, as Dolly the sheep has [this is not true by the way].
>
> A human clone would have a different soul . . .
>
> Without a biological father, would a Ken Griffey Jr. clone grow up as Junior did with his father a big-league outfielder?
>
> Without a biological father, would a Tiger Woods clone grow up as Tiger has with his father nurturing his development as a golfer?
>
> Without a biological father, would a Steffi Graf clone grow up as Steffi has with her father hovering over her every stroke?
>
> Without a biological father, would a Carl Lewis clone grow up as Carl did with his father's devotion to the Olympics?[49]

In Anderson's way of reasoning the 'backward in time' for the clone means nothing without the father. It is 'father time,' then, who saves us from the indiscriminate reproducibility of mother mime. If clones can come to be through time travel, fathers appear to belong only to memory, and it is as both memory and the immemorial that the station of the father can curb the threat of mimesis (a threat with an apparent gender and race ingredient).

Back in time means, here, access to the father. This particular quote is perhaps only surprising for its unapologetic obviousness – and for its errors. Dolly the sheep has the same father as the sheep from which Dolly was cloned – genetically, the mother and the father are the unnamed cloned ewe's even more distant unnamed parents. Suffice to say, the passage shows more about fears for the nominal station of the father than about knowledge of the actual facts of cloning. Though the genetic material was as 'male and female' as any genetic material can claim to be, the repetition of mimesis is feminized as only of the mother.

As sportswriter Anderson would have it, it is precisely the death of the father – the fact that the father will have been dead – that will save us from our fear of, with some irony, the threatening 'sameness' of the mother's difference, her capacity to reproduce, to reproduction, to mimesis. The father, it appears, remains as, precisely, remains (in the sense of something dead). Mimesis, as constituted in Western culture, does not remain. The theater, we like to say, is 'live,' and more often than not that means that our standard approach to theater is that it is given to 'disappear.'[50] The father, as remains, is of the archive – remaining-as-dead to signify originality, and, as Anderson suggests, 'onceness.' A clone will necessarily be fatherless, only of the illegitimate theater of mimesis – the shadowy cave space of the mother – and without access to the archive (the graveyard) of the dead dad. In Anderson's logic, Michael will remain Michael because he will be the only Michael to have known his dad. The Dead Dad, then, survives.

The gendering and racing of this equation, like the equation itself, should be no surprise. As Derrida is careful to plot in *Archive Fever*, the culture of the copy that threatens is also the culture of the archive that redeems. We stockpile remains, the traces of dead authentics, documents of the primary, and shore those ruins *as real* in direct relation to a fear of our own rampant reproductions. In the theater, for example, it is the play text, mummified traces of a dead author, that is given to survive, made available for archive. While the play survives, we are habituated to assuming that the mimetic act reproducing the text is precisely that which slips away, vanishes, refuses to be cataloged, is both reproduction and impossible to ever precisely reproduce. The mimetic act, unlike the remains, the ruin, is not (according to our cultural logic) of the father. Rather, it resides on the threatening side of sameness, a sameness which, passing, will not be acknowledged to remain. *That this is a cultural equation, foreign to those who claim oral storytelling, possession trance, or even embodied ritual practice as history, should go without saying* – but it does not. The mimetic, in Western culture, is inscribed as of the body and is *intended*, by the logic of the archive, to threaten and disappear so that the domain of the archive remains intact.

Accumulating and displaying mummified authentics, in the name of archiving, may appear to be about survival, about salvage and about memorializing, but, as Derrida writes after Freud, the drive has always depended on 'anarchiving' – 'the archive is made possible by the death, aggression, and destruction drive.' Indeed, writes Derrida in *Archive Fever*, 'the theory of psychoanalysis becomes a theory of the archive and not only a theory of memory.'[51] Without the institution of a movement of destruction, Derrida goes on, no archive desire or fever would happen. 'Remains' and the archive are, after all, as much about the institution of a loss that survives as about that which survives as a signature of that which can pass, or passability – in the way that a skeleton, as remains, is a signature of destruction and survival at once. The archive, then, is built on the valorization of regular, necessary loss on display – loss as regulated, maintained, institutionalized, which is to say controlled. Simultaneous signatures of loss and survival, remains dictate Origin as 'Once' (in both senses of the term). The second, always twice of mimesis (think again of Dolly's name), supposedly leaves no remains (at least none acknowledged by the archive) but is given to slip into the subcutaneous, feminized realm of disappearance or repetitive reappearance as masquerade, and so threaten (and refound) the archive.[52] That loss as institution should make an equation that spells the threat and failure of the bodily, the failure of mimesis, to remain, is rife with a 'patriarchal principle,' not to mention a colonialist one.

No one, Derrida notes, has shown better than Freud how the archival drive, which he labels as a 'paternal and patriarchic principle,' is both patriarchal and parricidic. The archival drive

> posited itself to repeat itself and returned to reposit itself only in parricide. It amounts to repressed or suppressed parricide, in the name of the father as dead father. The archontic is at best the takeover of the archive by the brothers. The equality and liberty of brothers. A certain, still vivacious idea of democracy.[53]

Building on Diana Fuss and Lee Edelman, Ann Pellegrini has recently stated this same Freudian insight succinctly, saying 'son fathers parent(s); pre- is heir to post-; and 'proper' gender identification and 'appropriate' object choices are secured backward' – a 'retroaction of objects lost and subjects founded.'[54] If, as Freud claims, this is what we always already do in becoming subjects – if son fathers parent – is *it the glaringly literal translation of that 'ancient symbolic equation' across the body of the clone* that terrifies us?[55]

With his particular version of logic, Dave Anderson assures his sports fans that clones are shams. We should not fear that a clone might 'kill' the station of the father – as he illustrates, the father is already dead, and in that dying, he made his son *one*. It seems rather that the fear of the clone stems from a twist. Does the clone threaten to make the equation of the dead father as necessary, dead father as *repetitive* foundational citation, obsolete? Jordan, by Anderson's way of thinking, is actually constituted as his own dead father. The clone, especially if he *does* play ball (again), might make a mockery of that equation, somehow being Jordan without the requisite access to patricide, to constitution through his father's death. Though Anderson's logic is biologically erroneous, the clone son, being fatherless, could only pass on (pass as?) the mother. And the mother is relegated here to mimesis herself.

The fear of the clone is marked in part by the fear of a future son who will not commit parricide – who will not be able to give the archive its due as he will not be equipped with the requisite production of remains. Will patriarchy fall without parricide as its signature? Anderson's declaration that it would not be enough for Jordan's clone to claim Jordan's dad, already dead, as his own, leads one to suspect that a long-dead dad is no solution. Apparently, one needs fresh parricides for every generation of brothers, placing Barthes' 'Death of the Author' in a long line of attempts to keep the prerogatives of the author resolutely alive. As remains, we can be assured that they will remain. Without killing the father, the father might die.

## Another way to ask the question

How can clones scare us when we are ourselves clones?

We have been telling ourselves since Genesis and Plato that we are ourselves already the very stuff of copies, the meat of inauthenticity, mere inappropriate clones of Original Fathers, or Foundational Ideas. Or, man is 'in his image' but woman, of Adam's rib, is a clone . . . or a recombinant. While postmodernists may claim that the culture of the copy has reached a fevered pitch, that 'pitch' is a habit of Western identity formation as old as our signature fear of father-blind caves. Due to this, the trouble with the double, the *truly* inauthentic, the 'aper,' the actor, or the clown, has always been that in the very 'outness' of its inauthenticity it is more genuine than we. The actor, as a conscious shadow, is closer to the Truth. The actor (to the degree, especially, that she is alienated) makes mimesis apparent. A parent mimesis.

Thus trauma regarding originality is far from original to postmodernism, which may be the latest in a long line of Western (anxiety-driven) compulsions to repeat. The fear of the clone is that one is another – and this fear is arguably habitual, arguably cultural, arguably, even, tiresome. The latest in a long line of concern about seeming disappearance of ideality into corrupted (feminized) mimetic shadow is the current 'trauma' over the so-called 'disappearance of the authentic body' in so-called visual culture. Mark Taylor, in his recent *Hiding*, joins the minions citing TV as the signature screen of a now completely screenal economy, by which screen appearance, screen experience, takes the place of something we vaguely remember as authentic 'real life.'[56] Such a view insists that real life is, today, always already a matter of memory – of being reminded, of traveling only in time lost – a fun-filled world of loss and the compulsion to repeat.

While the newness of screenal culture is debatable (are the TV and the *theatron* entirely distinct?), this relegation of 'mere appearance' to one side of the screen and 'real life' to the side of the screen which disappears is telling in regards to our questions about the clone. If real life is a matter of memory, then the threatening irony of the clone is that it copies our copying too precisely – it 'travels back in time' to become itself. If the clone's very becoming is a matter of literal, cellular (read bodily) time travel, and if 'real life' is that which is disappeared as always in time past in our cultural habituation to the screen, then the clone would, in her becoming, be closer to 'real life' than the cloned. The clone becomes a terrifying and feminized body present as the should-be-lost past – a *living* remain – an oxymoron like an archive of the mother – the father not as dead, but as alive, and born of mimesis.

The problem with the clone is that the old original/copy divide is threatened not simply by wiggy performance artists, cyber-celebrating computer geeks, or word-smithy theorists – but the threat comes from the antiseptic halls of the laboratory with, as Probio America declared, 'commercial reality' just around the corner. The clone is indeed the theater on which the curtain refuses to fall (Michael Jordan's clone will not take off his clone face after his performance to be other than Michael Jordan's clone). We will not go home from this theater because we shall be forced to acknowledge that *in the* theater, as in our rituals, repetitions, and performative occasions, we are home – and that home is real, and now.

And the *really* interesting thing, which is part and parcel of our fear, is that this is not of some untouchable future or some past lost – and it never can be. If what Dr. Lee Silver, a mouse geneticist and reproductive biologist at Princeton, says is true – if 'Absolutely, we're going to have cloning of humans'[57] – then they are among us already, as they become ourselves by traveling back in time. Then we are among them already, as we become themselves, by traveling . . .

## Notes

1 Gregory Pence, *Who's Afraid of Human Cloning?*, Boston: Rowman and Littlefield, 1998: 25.
2 National Bioethics Advisory Commission, *Cloning Human Beings: Report and Recommendations of the National Bioethics Advisory Commission*, Rockville, MD, June 1997: 109.
3 Quoted in Gina Kolata, *Clone: The Road to Dolly and the Path Ahead*, New York: Morrow, 1998: 3.
4 Gina Kolata, 'Cloned Sheep Showing Signs of Old Cells, Report Says,' *New York Times*, 27 May 1999.
5 Antonin Artaud, *The Theater and its Double*, New York: Grove Press, 1958: 82.
6 Hillel Schwartz, *Culture of the Copy*, Cambridge, MA: MIT Press, 1998: 89.
7 See Richard Schechner on theater as 'restored behavior,' also referred to as 'twice-behaved behavior,' in *Between Theater and Anthropology*, Philadelphia, PA: University of Pennsylvania Press, 1985.
8 See Jonas Barish, *The Antitheatrical Prejudice*, Berkeley: University of California Press, 1985.
9 Artaud, *The Theater and its Double*: 89.
10 We might think of this in terms of subject formation, following Judith Butler following Althusser. If subjects are interpellated, the interpellative gesture (a mimetic gesture, such as the waving of a hand and the calling of a name) precedes the subject, though the subject retroactively appears to preexist the hail. Louis Althusser, 'Ideology and Ideological State Apparatuses,' in *Lenin and Philosophy and Other Essays*, London: New Left Books, 1977.
11 Jacques Derrida, 'Freud and the Scene of Writing,' in *Writing and Difference*, translated by Alan Bass, Chicago: University of Chicago Press, 1978: 202.
12 Judith Butler, 'Imitation and Gender Insubordination,' in *Inside/Out: Lesbian Theories, Gay Theories*, edited by Diana Fuss, New York and London: Routledge, 1991: 23.

13  Gina Kolata, 'In Big Advance, Cloning Creates Dozens of Mice,' *New York Times*, 23 July 1998.

14  Pence, *Who's Afraid of Human Cloning?*; Kolata, *Clone*.

15  The name has since changed to Clone Rights Action Center. See www.humancloning. org. The organization no longer overtly declares its allegiance to gay rights. On the genesis and evolution of this group see Lori Andrews, *The Clone Age: Adventures in the New World of Reproductive Technology*, New York: Henry Holt, 1999, specifically the chapter 'The Clone Rangers.' I was also directed in conversation with Randolfe H. Wicker of the Clone Rights Action Center and through Pence (*Who's Afraid of Human Cloning?*) to gaytoday@badpuppy.com for the story 'Clone Rights Advocates Scold Scientists.' Unfortunately, I could not access that site at the time of this writing as Netscape ironically kept denying me access with the message: 'Replace Not a Function.'

16  Martin P. Levin, *Gay Macho: The Life and Death of the Homosexual Clone*, New York: New York University Press, 1998: 7.

17  Levin, *Gay Macho*: 139, 64.

18  Richard Meyer, 'Warhol's Clones,' *Yale Journal of Criticism*, 4 (1), 1994: 79–107, at 96.

19  Felicia Herman, 'The Way She *Really* Is: Images of Jews and Women in the Films of Barbra Streisand,' in *Talking Back: Images of Jewish Women in American Popular Culture*, edited by Joyce Antler, Hanover, NH: Brandeis University Press, 1998: 171.

20  Visit http://www.jewishsf.com/bk960920/etahello.htm. Upon calling the number for the store, retrieved off the web page, one is asked politely to 'Please check the number and dial again.' Worried, I then contacted Felicia Herman who assured me that the shrine had indeed existed and that 'she had been there.' Authenticity was established.

21  Robert Rosenblum, 'Cards of Identity,' in *Deborah Kass: The Warhol Project*, edited by Michael Plante, New Orleans: Newcomb Art Gallery, 1999: 13.

22  Linda Nochlin, 'Portrait of the Artist as an Appropriator,' in *Deborah Kass: The Warhol Project*: 10.

23  For further work on what Meyer calls the 'intrinsic queer appeal of mass-cultural representation' ('Warhol's Clones': 96) in the specific context of musical theater and film, see Stacy Wolf, 'The Queer Pleasures of Mary Martin and Broadway,' *Modern Drama*, 39, 1996: 51–63; and Matthew Tinkcom, 'Working like a Homosexual: Camp, Visual Codes, and the Labor of Gay Subjects in the MGM Freed Unit,' *Cinema Journal*, 35 (2), 1996: 24–42.

24  Glenn McGee, 'Introduction,' in *The Human Cloning Debate*, edited by Glenn McGee, Berkeley, CA: Berkeley Hill Books, 1998: 1–15, esp. 6.

25  Quoted in Kolata, *Clone*: 41.

26  Kolata, 'In Big Advance.'

27  See, for example, Barbara Lane, *Echoes from the Battlefield: First Person Accounts of Civil War Past Lives*: Virginia Beach, VA: A.R.E. Press, 1996. See also Eric Gable and Richard Handler, 'After Authenticity at an American Heritage Site,' *American Anthropologist*, 98 (3), 1996: 568–78.

28  Meyer, 'Warhol's Clones': 97.

29  See Pence, 'Who's Afraid?'; McGee, 'Introduction'; Andrews, *The Clone Age*.

30  Sigmund Freud, *A Project for a Scientific Psychology*, 352–9. See also Jean Laplanche, *New Foundations for Psychoanalysis*, translated by David Macey, Cambridge, MA: Blackwell, 1989: 62.

31  See Luce Irigaray, *Speculum of the Other Woman*, Ithaca, NY: Cornell University Press, 1985. See also Elin Diamond, *Unmaking Mimesis*, New York and London: Routledge, 1998.

32  Of course this also has significant reverberations with historical materialist explorations of mediation and the copy in terms of the production of culture in late capitalism. Perhaps the most often cited in this regard are Walter Benjamin's 'Art in the Age of Mechanical Reproduction' and 'Theses on the Philosophy of History' (See Benjamin, *Illuminations*,

translated by Hannah Arendt, New York: Schocken Books, 1969). The two essays could never be misrecognized as identical, but taken together they press the same issues. For Benjamin, Origin is a bordello, and '*once* upon a time' is a 'whore' ('Theses': 262) – which is to say, a masquerade. That the materialist historian is 'man enough to blast open the continuum of history' ('Theses': 262), will cause us to wince with feminist fatigue, but the critique resonates with psychoanalytic and deconstructionist critiques of originality.

33 Sigmund Freud, *Moses and Monotheism*, translated by Katherine Jones, London: Hogarth Press, 1939. See also *Totem and Taboo*, translated by James Strachey, London: Routledge and Kegan Paul, 1950: 182–92.

34 See Homi Bhabha, 'Of Mimicry and Man: the Ambivalence of Colonial Discourse,' *October*, 28, 1984: 125–33.

35 J. L. Austin, *How To Do Things With Words*, Cambridge, MA: Harvard University Press, 1962. See Andrew Parker and Eve K. Sedgwick, *Performativity and Performance*, New York and London: Routledge, 1995, on the ways in which J. L. Austin replicates antitheatricality even as he enunciates performativity. In a way that should resonate with this essay, Parker and Sedgwick point out the homophobic implications of Austin's antitheatricality.

36 See Freud's postulations in *Totem and Taboo*, on the 'fraternal clan' and its relation to paternal inheritance as one of disavowal.

37 Luce Irigaray, *The Sex Which is Not One*, Ithaca: Cornell University Press, 1985: 171; see also 192–7.

38 Freud takes his 'hint' from the 'poet-philosopher' Plato in Sigmund Freud, *Beyond the Pleasure Principle*, translated by James Strachey, New York: W. W. Norton, 1961: 52.

39 On the 'Freudian Impression' see Jacques Derrida, *Archive Fever*, translated by Eric Prenowitz, Chicago: University of Chicago Press, 1995: 25–31.

40 Sigmund Freud, 'Anxiety,' in *Introductory Lectures on Psychoanalysis*, translated by James Strachey, New York: W. W. Norton, 1966: 392–411. See also Freud's later explication in 'Anxiety and Instinctual Life,' in *New Introductory Lectures on Psychoanalysis*, translated by James Strachey, New York: W. W. Norton, 1965: 72–98.

41 Sigmund Freud, *Civilization and its Discontents*, translated by James Strachey, New York: W. W. Norton, 1961: 92.

42 Jacques Derrida, 'Freud and the Scene of Writing,' in *Writing and Difference*: 229. Derrida's description of Freud's 'scene' of writing, his 'feign[ed] disarmed naivete,' comes close to describing Freud as donning clownface – a performance Derrida refers to in *Archive Fever* (9) as 'vertiginously cunning'. And perhaps here is the moment to note that if Freud clowned himself, in some senses he also had to clone himself. He was the first and the last to psychoanalyze himself as a necessary beginning, after which replication he could replicate himself. As Freud tells would-be psychoanalysts, 'one advances much further if one is analyzed oneself by a practiced analyst and experiences the effects of analysis on one's own self, making use of the opportunity of picking up the subtler technique of the process from one's analyst.' Freud, 'Introduction,' in *Introductory Lectures on Psychoanalysis*: 15–24, esp. 19.

43 See Jacques Derrida, 'Plato's Pharmacy,' in *Disseminations*, translated by Barbara Johnson, Chicago: University of Chicago Press, 1981: 61–171.

44 Quoted in Pence, *Who's Afraid of Human Cloning?*: 1.

45 Ira Levin, *The Boys From Brazil*, New York: Random House, 1976.

46 David Rorvik, *In His Image: The Cloning of a Man*, Philadelphia: Lippincott, 1978.

47 Quoted in Kolata, *Clone*: 104.

48 Quoted in Ronald Bailey, 'The Twin Paradox: What Exactly is Wrong with Cloning People?' in *The Human Cloning Debate*, edited by Glenn McGee, Berkeley, CA: Berkeley Hills Books: 181–8, esp. 185.

49 Dave Anderson, 'Could Jordan be Cloned? Not Exactly,' *New York Times*, 28 February 1997, section B, page 7.

50  See Herb Blau, *Take Up the Bodies: Theater at the Vanishing Point*, Urbana: University of Illinois Press, 1982: 94. See also Peggy Phelan, *Unmarked: The Politics of Performance*, New York and London: Routledge, 1993: 146.

51  Derrida, *Archive Fever*: 190.

52  Repetition and masquerade, inseparable from the death drive, are given to be 'anarchival.' Derrida, *Archive Fever*: 11–12.

53  Derrida, *Archive Fever*: 94.

54  Ann Pellegrini, *Performance Anxieties: Staging Psychoanalysis, Staging Race*, New York and London: Routledge, 1997: 69.

55  See Rebecca Schneider, *The Explicit Body in Performance*, New York and London: Routledge, 1997: 114–17, for a development, following Walter Benjamin, of the fear of literal translation.

56  Mark Taylor, *Hiding*, Chicago: University of Chicago Press, 1997: 201.

57  Quoted in Kolata, 'In Big Advance.'

# 7

# WRITING HOME

## Post-modern melancholia and the uncanny space of living-room theatre

*Ernst Fischer*

As a teenager and budding homosexual I was acutely aware of the disloyalty of my body which, so it seemed to me at the time, with every step, look and utterance betrayed the fearfully kept secret of my difference. Having convinced myself that I left behind me a wake of nudges, winks, whispered accusations and scandalised titters, I began to fear not simply all public spaces but, more particularly, the space behind my back, where rumour found the room to flourish and which thus became by implication private. In order to keep an eye on this *Hinterland* from which I had been expelled, I decided to perform my otherness with thunder and lightning, dressing in loud colours and producing a staccato drumroll by dragging the soles of my wooden sandals across the paved and cobbled streets of the city of my birth. I became quite literally blinding and deafening, dazzling and confusing the all-too-knowing gaze of the onlookers and, so I hoped, reflecting my own uncertainty as a sense of wonder and a need to question appearances. Ever since, the space of performance has seemed to me to be located at the behind, the meeting between spectacle and spectator, an aspect of the 'After life'[1] and the abject.

At about the time of my 'coming out', my identical twin and I began to shun each other's company in public, embarrassed by what we saw in each other's mirror. However, once we had established our separate social circles, I was frequently addressed as my brother by strangers who greeted my explanation of mistaken identities with suspicion and, more than once, with open resentment. In the face of such disbelief, locating myself became an increasingly tenuous task. Sitting in a room or standing in a street, I found myself displaced to a realm of invisibility while my face and body signified an entirely different presence in the eyes of my *vis-à-vis*.

A related sense of dislocation was poignantly illustrated many years ago in a newspaper article concerning the unfamiliarity of many Mediterranean *Gastarbeiter* with the German language. The example I most clearly remember described a Turkish man's frustrated attempts to enter into correspondence with his family in Ankara. Mistaking a temporary traffic sign for the name of his street, the sender gave as his address *Umleitung* (diversion) and thus unwittingly misdirected any response to his letters and postcards into silence.[2]

As a German living in London, as a foreigner estranged from his mother tongue, yet, after 20 years, still with an outsider's view of 'Britishness', as a physical and visual performer who is only reluctantly getting used to theorising about his practice, I too feel lost in language – and although I am merely a first-generation immigrant with no offspring or family, a white Caucasian from a country still widely mistrusted for its recent fascist past, I readily empathise with Homi Bhabha's notion of post-colonial hybridity.[3]

I am then – a cultural hybrid, an 'invisible' double and an extrovert invert – continually on the search for a home in a society that until not so long ago could still with some confidence view itself as singular, linear and straight, and which seems little more homely in all its post-modern fragmentation, fluidity and multiplicity. However, the fact that I can now consider making alliances with other 'others', with cultural entities and individuals that heretofore have guarded the boundaries of their own difference with the jealous zeal of nation states, offers me an (un-)certain amount of hope. Equally promising is the growing number of potential allies who find themselves, often to their surprise and dismay, at an ideological crossroads, from which the formerly so reassuringly linear perspective appears confusingly queer. This loss of certainty and location seems to be much implicated in the increase of what many critical theorists have begun to recognise as a peculiarly post-modern sense of Melancholia.

Martin Jay in 'Apocalypse and the Inability to Mourn',[4] posits the apocalyptic imagination as prototypical for late twentieth-century Western cultures and argues, in concert with Derrida and other post-Marxist thinkers, that Apocalypse can no longer be perceived as a limited event which – as previous scenarios supposed – will be followed by a new Enlightenment, but must be seen as 'a closure without end, an end without end'.[5] In other words, we find (and lose) ourselves perpetually tottering at the edge of a catastrophe that never comes, or that is, rather, continuously in the process of be-coming, and is thus never done with. Jay cites Jean Baudrillard in naming the emotional effect produced by the apocalyptic imagination: 'Melancholy is the fundamental tonality of functional systems, of the present system of simulation, programming and information. Melancholy is the quality inherent in the mode of disappearance of meaning [. . .] And we are all melancholic.'[6]

According to Freud's classic analytical text on 'Mourning and Melancholia'[7] normal mourning follows the loss of a loved person or an abstract surrogate, such as fatherland or liberty. It runs its course when reality demonstrates the objective disappearance of the loved one. This realisation allows the slow and painful with-drawal of the libido cathected to it, which restores the subject's mental equilibrium. Once the work of mourning is completed, Freud claims, 'the ego becomes free and uninhibited again',[8] able to cathect with new love objects. Melancholia, on the other hand, is a pathological condition resulting from the inability to mourn an unidenti-fied – or insufficiently identified – loss. In its post-modern variant this means that the work of mourning can never be completed because the process of losing a loved

object or a cherished idea is itself infinite. The object cannot be demonstrated to be lost and can therefore not be replaced. While the symptoms of melancholia ape many of the characteristics found in normal grief, such as profound dejection and loss of interest in the outside world, it leads, in addition, to 'a lowering of the self-regarding feelings to a degree that finds utterance in self-reproaches and self-revilings and culminates in a delusional expectation of punishment'.[9] Freud also noted the frequent tendency of melancholia to slip into its apparent opposite: manic elation. In 'Group Psychology and the Analysis of the Ego',[10] he admitted that he lacked a fully satisfactory explanation of how these two symptomologies were linked, but argued that they expressed two sides of the same coin. In melancholia the ego was attacked by what he now called the ego-ideal, whereas in mania the two were fused together. In both cases, the working through based on the ego's ability to test reality was now thwarted. The periodic oscillation between the two states, producing the psychotic syndrome of manic-depression, could lead to a perpetual failure to deal with the world in rational terms, meaning, among other things, the inability to acknowledge the separateness of self and other.

Anthony Vidler[11] implicitly links 'Mourning and Melancholia' with another of Freud's canonical texts, namely his essay on 'The Uncanny'.[12] Vidler traces the beginnings of the uncanny to the literature of late Romanticism and particularly to the writings of Edgar Alan Poe and E. T. A. Hoffman, whose short story 'The Sandman' formed the starting point for Freud's own investigation. The favourite motif of these writers, as Vidler points out,

> was precisely the contrast between a secure and homely interior and the fearful invasion of an alien presence; on a psychological level, its play was one of doubling, where the other is, strangely enough, experienced as a replica of the self, all the more fearful because apparently the same.[13]

He goes on to assert that:

> from the 1870s on, the metropolitan uncanny was increasingly conflated with metropolitan illness, a pathological condition that potentially afflicted the inhabitants of all great cities; a condition that had, through force of the environment, escaped the overprotected domain of the short story. The uncanny became identified with all the phobias associated with spatial fear in its various manifestations including agoraphobia and its obverse, claustrophobia.[14]

It hardly requires a leap of the imagination to picture the claustrophobe's response as manic activity – a kicking and scratching and tearing at the boundaries of an enclosing space that threatens its occupant with living entombment, and the agoraphobe's, in contrast, as sullen and fearful withdrawal from a world seemingly without any boundaries at all – a squeezing together of the eyes, a curling into a tight embryonic ball, a cessation of all movement to ward against the danger of dissolution. In other words, the symptoms of the uncanny as spatial disease closely correspond to those of a late twentieth-century, increasingly global, culture with its melancholy fluctuations between preservation and abolition of established ideo-logical categories.

This simultaneous presence and absence of meaningful boundaries lies at the heart of Freud's essay, which concerns itself with the way in which the strange, the queer and inexplicable, the most unhomely and weird of things or places, are ultimately revealed to be not strange at all, but familiar and well known, though – therefore – subject to repression. Deliberately approaching the definition of *unheimlich* by way of its apparent opposite, *heimlich,* Freud exposed the disturbing affiliations between the two by drawing extensively on two nineteenth-century dictionaries: the brothers Grimm's *Deutsches Worterbuch* and Daniel Sanders' *Worterbuch der Deutschen Sprache.* By simply listing page after page of citations, Freud allowed his argument ostensibly to unfold by itself.[15] As a host of examples scrolls past the reader's eye, the homely – initially associated with pastoral landscapes, with house and family as well as with feelings of comfort and quiet contentment, security and freedom from fear – gradually takes on the ominous dimensions of its supposed opposite. Thus the brothers Grimm noted that:

> *From the idea of 'homelike', belonging to the house, the further idea is developed of something withdrawn from the eyes of strangers, something concealed, secret* [. . .] *Heimlich* in a different sense, as withdrawn from knowledge, unconscious [. . . or] that which is obscure [. . .] *The notion of something hidden and dangerous* [. . .] *is still further developed, so that 'heimlich' comes to have the meaning usually ascribed to 'unheimlich'.* Thus: 'At times I feel like a man who walks in the night and believes in ghosts; every corner is heimlich and full of terrors for him.'[16]

What this passage suggests and further etymological research confirms, is that *Heimlichkeit/*secrecy (Lat. *secretus*, p.p. of *se-cernere*)[17] involves an act of separation. However, what also clearly emerges here is its paradoxical opposite, namely that the uncanny, as a characteristic feature, eschews solid boundaries between oppositional terms. In its multidirectional flow between meanings, in its almost imperceptible sliding from the familiar to the strange, from certainty to doubt, secrecy to disclosure and vice versa, it seems to belong instead to a third, inter-binary, space of simultaneous possibilities: a space of disorder between the borderlands of what we profess to know. The involvement of the uncanny in the de/construction of knowledge is signalled by its own interpretative ambiguity, which makes the sensation of 'uncanniness', to cite Vidler, 'an especially difficult feeling to define precisely'.

> Neither absolute terror nor mild anxiety, the uncanny seem[s] easier to describe in terms of what it [is] not, than in any essential sense of its own [. . . It] revel[s] in its nonspecificity, one reinforced by the multiplicity of untranslatable words that serve to indicate its presence in different languages [. . .] Thus the uncanny [may] be sinister, disturbing, suspect, strange; it [may] be characterized better as 'dread' than terror, deriving its force from its very inexplicability, its sense of lurking unease, rather than from any clearly defined source of fear – an uncomfortable sense of haunting rather than a present apparition.[18]

The feeling that the uncanny provokes might best be described then as a sense of *imminence* at the very moment when something invisible is about to take shape or something solid to disappear. It pertains thus to spaces and objects unlocatably suspended in a state of flux, of *not* yet – or any longer – *being* either absent or present but, potentially, being *both and also*, and therefore to performance, whose 'being', to quote Peggy Phelan, 'becomes itself through disappearance',[19] and, I would add, through (re-)appearance in and out of the realm of lived experience.

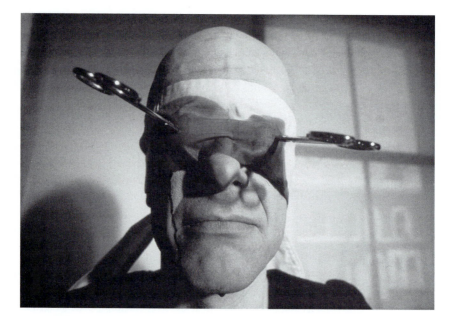

It is my contention, more precisely, that living-room theatre – whose distinguishing characteristics are its suspension between the private and the public, and the simultaneous guise of its architectural space as theatre and as domestic dwelling – has an additional stake in the uncanny. I had initially imagined an oscillating relationship between these two manifestations – the theatrical and the everyday – which exposed the audience member to a tense field of oppositional forces. The concept remained limited for some time to the workings of a quasi-Brechtian *Verfremdungseffekt* resulting from the intrusion of unscheduled (or cleverly arranged) sensory stimulations into the theatrical space from 'outside', that is to say from inside, or belonging to, the sphere of domesticity. The repeated interruption (or extension) of the theatrical event by the various sounds issuing from a residential neighbourhood, or by the intermittent, rattling activity of my old refrigerator, by the smells of cooking wafting through the open window from next door or, for that matter, from the stage-cum-kitchen, by the sight of toothbrushes in the bathroom, of the gas cooker in the auditorium, by the tactile attentions bestowed on members of the audience by my ageing cat, served, I speculated, as a reminder of theatre's rootedness in the unpredictable space of the everyday and of human interaction; the unmistakable presence of theatrical signifiers within the domestic realm, on the other hand, was challenging the notion of 'reality', 'truth' and 'identity' as absolute and unequivocal concepts. Since I have always, however, extensively redecorated my living space between productions, either in response to or as catalyst for a new project/idea, the changes inherent in such a practice began gradually to appear in a more complex pattern. In the slow metamorphosis from domestic dwelling to theatrical scenery (and back again), it now seems to me, no definitive or permanent state is reached; the architectural space rather is held in a constant flux of dis/appearances which are dictated by the contradicting and changing needs of its occupant(s)/performer(s). These changes do not simply occur sequentially, describing a curve between an assumed peak of theatricality – during the performance period – and a corresponding accumulation of domesticity – at the halfway point between productions, let us say, or, maybe more accurately, immediately prior to a concerted programme of alterations designed to house the next show. Instead, a multitude of smaller transformations seem to be at work, all following their own, different and unsynchronised temporalities. Theatre curtains and backdrops may become cushion covers or blinds, or be reincorporated into a later set; wallpaper, paint effects, claddings or screens are applied on top of each other, variously obscuring, revealing and adapting elements of previous designs; objects may double as household utensils and as theatrical props; the staging requirements of a particular performance may introduce semi-permanent additions or modifications to the living space, which, in turn, affect the psychic and physical experience of its occupation. In other words, theatrical and everyday signs and signifiers overlap and co-exist in continuously shifting relationships in the space of living-room theatre which is never exclusively a theatre nor entirely a private space but at the same time – and at all times – *both and also*. Indeed, applied to the territory of domestic performance, the operations of the uncanny expand the apparently dialectic model of a living-room/theatre to include a third, amorphous, space of possibilities and of imminence, resulting in a trialectic spatiality that may be rendered as living-room/living-room theatre/theatre.

The construction of this tripartite model owes much to the writings of self-confessed 'post-modern' geographer Edward W. Soja, particularly his mappings of *Thirdspace* [20] – a term borrowed from the aforementioned Homi Bhabha – which is, by his own admission, 'impossible to describe in less than extra-ordinary language' but is symbolically represented by the Aleph, 'a limitless space of simultaneity and paradox',[21] sited by novelist and essayist Jorge Luis Borges in his short story of the same title:

> Then I saw the Aleph [. . .] And here begins my despair as a writer. All language is a set of symbols whose use among its speakers assumes a shared past. How, then, can I translate into words the limitless Aleph, which my floundering mind can scarcely encompass? [. . .] In that single gigantic instant I saw millions of acts both delightful and awful; not one of them amazed me more than the fact that all of them occupied the same point in space, without overlapping or transparency.[22]

Drawing heavily on Henri Lefebvre's groundbreaking investigation into *The Production of Space*,[23] as well as on the writings of a host of post-colonial cultural anthropologists and, as he calls them, 'spatial feminists', Soja's geography by no means restricts itself to the measurement and phenomenological description of material spaces and territories, but 'encompasses a multiplicity of perspectives that have heretofore been considered by the epistemological referees to be incompatible, uncombinable'.[24] His aim is nothing less than the construction of a spatial ontology that situates the subject in a formative, multi-layered geography of socially created and differentiated nodal regions nesting at many different scales around the mobile personal spaces of the human body, and the more fixed communal locales of human settlements. Moving from a Trialectics of Being that incorporates *spatiality, sociality* and *historicality*, Soja proposes a corresponding spatial model that tempers theory and practice with the *lived experience* of the everyday, and brings together *lived, perceived* (that is, material) and *conceived* (or theoretical) spaces in a complex and fluid inter-relationship without privileging one over the other. However, though Soja's aim is

> to open up our spatial imaginaries to ways of thinking and acting politically that respond to all binarisms, to any attempt to confine thought and political action to only two alternatives, by interjecting an-Other set of choices [. . .], the original binary choice is not dismissed entirely but is subjected to a creative process of restructuring that draws selectively and strategically from the two opposing categories in order to open new alter-natives.[25]

Soja calls this critical strategy 'thirding-as-Othering', which brings us back to the uncanny intermingling of self and other. The perspective, however, has now shifted from the melancholy inability to mourn an on-going and incomplete loss to the opportunity of 'finding more flexible ways of being other than we are while still being ourselves, of becoming open to coalitions and coalescences of radical subjec-tivity, to a multiplicity of communities of resistance'.[26] Soja's view indeed tallies with that of Derrida, who sees in an infinite apocalypse a source of comfort because it forestalls final totalisation. John Leavy Jr. in addition has argued for a decon-structionist strategy that introduces just enough of the apocalyptic to act as a kind of immunisation against its full realisation, thus serving as an apotropaic device akin to circumcision rites and images of genitals or eyes, designed to ward off the threat of castration.[27] Before I return to castration anxiety and the 'evil eye', let me express here my belief that a domestic performance practice, with its peculiarly uncanny mix of the imaginary and the real, can play a similarly multiple role – as *pharmakon*: poison as well as cure – in the critical redefinition of notions such as 'homeliness' and 'be/longing'. As long as the available choices remain reduced to an antagonistic binarism that pits confinement in conventionally sanctioned categories against the social dissolution of a boundless and uncritical pluralism, living-room theatre serves as a heuristic model for the exploration of less exclusive scenarios by providing a safe place for intimate encounters with the ambiguous and the equivocal while simul-taneously exposing the familiar to the play of the imagination. The questioning of dominant – gendered and gendering – perceptions and conceptions of space, implicit in such a practice, renders it paradigmatic for a queer theatre. The historical relationship of homosexuality with performance – as discrete and inclusive alter-native to the previously strictly observed separation between writer, actor and

director – has its roots in *kaloprosopia*, 'the art of personality',[28] espoused by the dandies of late nineteenth-century Paris and most notoriously, perhaps, exemplified in the life and work of Oscar Wilde. The queer and the camp, the art of personality and the private performance practice are uncanny precisely because they conflate the fictional and the everyday, art and life.

Freud has associated this effacement of the boundaries between the literal and the figurative with the 'evil eye' I just referred to, which apparently symbolises the 'omnipotence of thought'[29] in animistic religions and magic, and represents the 'uncanny' female genitalia threatening castration, that is to say, the loss of the penial eye/I and of a phallic and linear perception of the world. The site of this loss was significantly described by Freud as 'the entrance to the former *Heim* of all human beings, to the place where each one of us lived once upon a time and in the beginning'.[30] If Freud's discussion of the uncanny exemplifies the social construction of female gender as signifying home (the sphere of belonging and belongings), we may also detect in it signs of architecture's vital implication in the vision of a gendered reality. Architecture indeed introduces a necessary third term, namely 'house' in addition to 'space' and 'home'. The house – often somewhat prematurely abandoned by feminist and queer theory in search of greater political efficacy – divides space and provides discourse with a proper site. It does not, however, exist separate from language in a pre-theoretical past, nor can it be understood by architectural discourse alone. The house is fiction made concrete, a perspectival grid that shapes and marks the bodies it houses according to the very ideology of visibility in the name of which it is itself constructed. In and through its orthogonal directionality, architecture tames the bewildering limitlessness of space and makes it homely. In

doing so, it puts into place a system of moral and social boundaries that function as their own surveillance mechanism. Judgement of the common good thus becomes a matter of aesthetics: of surface and depth, of public visibility and private effacement, of fitting the mould. It seems pertinent in this connection to recall the already mentioned Latin definition of *Heimlichkeit*/secrecy as an act of separation, and to note that, according to Arnaud Levy, the word originates with the sifting of grain with the purpose to separate the edible from the non-edible, the good from the bad. 'The separation is effected by a hole, an orifice, whose function is to allow something to pass or not pass, depending on the relation of the object's shape and size to the shape and size of the hole.' Hence, this sifting process allegedly constitutes 'a metaphorical representation of the anal function'.[31] The production of *Heimlichkeit* in the sieve of the house is thus achieved through a process of excretion: the separation of the homely from the abject. An illustration of the particular mechanisms involved in such an architectural 'voiding' can be found in Leon Battista Alberti's influential fifteenth-century treatise *On the Art of Building in Ten Books*.[32] Mark Wigley has drawn attention to the 'overt reference' in Alberti's text 'to architecture's complicity in the exercise of patriarchal authority by defining a particular intersection between a spatial order and a system of surveillance which turns on the question of gender'.[33]

Alberti clearly sees the construction of civic society and of a pleasing house as complementary endeavours. The artistry of both hinges on the patriarchal house-holder's successful husbandry of his women. Wedlock and domesticity are explicitly understood as curtailing the unmarried girl's potentially threatening social and sexual mobility. Having entered her husband's estate from 'outside' (from the household of her father), she is immobilised and secreted through confinement in a hierarchically arranged sequence of private spheres. Within this spatial order, the woman is further sub-divided and ultimately effaced as sexual, desiring subject by being put in her proper place among her husband's possessions. She is declared pleasing for knowing her limits which are defined by:

> a number of systems of control – mythological, juridical codes, forms of address, dress codes, writing styles, superstitions, manners, etc. – each of which takes the form of surveillance over a particular space, whether it be the dinner table, the threshold, the church, the fingertips, the bath, the face, the street.[34]

Under such intense scrutiny, the woman seems to disappear. In an exact/ing visual language involving the division of rooms and the appearance and arrangement of furniture in them, she is erased by 'the accuracy of the spacing, the straightness of the row, the regularity of the angles', that are more highly prized than 'the lovely things' they separate.[35] Contained by the proper and therefore beautiful order of objects and spaces, and represented by the gaps between them, the woman is herself attractive only as an Absence, by being content-edly chaste and homely. Her plainness in demeanour and dress matches that of the white and unadorned walls that Alberti prescribes. Both the absent woman and the plain walls are rendered (fixed and plastered over) as smooth, blank surfaces on which the man projects himself. The woman is thus, paradoxically, not only locked up in the architectural grid, and abjected through the holes in the sieve, she becomes those very holes. In the domestication of space as place, its unbroken expanse is punctuated by row upon row of orifices. The art of husbandry in this sense lies in the cultivation of, to use Deleuze and Guattari's term, 'a field of anuses'.[36]

This feminised space of sexuality and desire can of course be entered. In the very distribution of in/activities – to penetrate or to be penetrated – gender is constituted. And yet, the discreet homeliness of the house carries the uncanny threat of diminution. The man, as Alberti warns, has right of access but lingers at his own risk:

> It [. . .] seems somewhat demeaning to me to remain shut up in the house among women when I have manly things to do among men [. . .] Those idle creatures who stay all day among the little females or who keep their mind occupied with little feminine trifles certainly lack a masculine and glorious spirit. They are contemptible in their apparent inclination to play the part of women rather than men.[37]

Gender is here openly acknowledged as performance, a role constituted by the appropriate 'manly'/expansive or 'feminine'/ contracted actions, which, in turn, are an effect of architectural space, of being in the right or wrong place. To sit too long indoors, to be shut up, is to be looked at, which is emasculating and enervating. The confinement of the interior space is transferred in an optical shrinking process onto the occupant, turning him into a tiny inside-out projection of himself: a 'little female' occupied with 'trifles'. The immobilised phallus shrinks and shrivels and wastes away through the sieve's hole, to become a hole itself. In the conflation of shitting and sitting, seat and sight, the man comes face to face with his already accomplished castration: his own blind eye, the site of his excreting orifice through which he may be – retrospectively – entered.

I would like to think that the ever-changing and becomingly flamboyant appearances of living-room theatre invert and mock the architectural drag of the house which, as Wigley points out, is meant to represent – at the same time as it constructs – the uncastrated man:

> classical architectural theory dictates that the building should have the proportions of the body of a man., but the actual body that is being composed, the material being shaped, is a woman. Clothes maketh the man, but they are woman. Man is a cultural construction which emerges from the control of the feminine.[38]

The ensuing masquerade of clothed and (en)closed bodies thinly disguises an array of monsters and ghostly apparitions; chains of metaphors, contaminated by their contiguity, dissolve into a metonymical mess on the carpet. Reappropriating the performative masquerade of spaces thus suggests itself as a particular strategy for the domestic performer and ultimately points towards collaborative ventures between performance artists, architects and interior designers in the construction of un-homely homes that would more appropriately house the fluid and flexible sexualities of post-modern subjects. A related and equally pressing task remains the disruption of the gendering grid, the fouling of the house's orderly withdrawing room(s) through the presence of queer bodies and 'inappropriate', out-sized gestures.

The project of a queer living-room theatre thus is to facilitate and house the return of the abject with all its connotations of death, disease, desire and the 'impure' and 'unclean' functions of the undivided body. The abject's '[dis]respect of borders, positions, rules', upsets the ideological inside/outside dichotomy constructed in the architecture of sexuality, and dislocates the subject into the realm of 'the inbetween, the ambiguous, the composite'.[39] Julia Kristeva links this unstable state – via Borges – to the 'vertiginous and hallucinatory . . . 'object' of literature . . . It is the Aleph' – Soja's model for the Thirdspace of lived experience – 'which appears . . . at the time of its descent . . . into the cellar of the native house, condemned to destruction – by definition [of its transfinitive truth].'

> The Aleph is exorbitant to the extent that, within the narrative, nothing could tap its power other than the narration of *infamy* . . . That is, of rampancy, boundlessness, the unthinkable, the untenable, the unsymbolizable. But what is it? Unless it be the untiring repetition of a drive, which, propelled by an initial loss, does not cease wandering, unsated, deceived, warped, until it finds its only stable object – death.[40]

If we find ourselves here again in the vicinity of the Romantic detective novel, the

fairy tale and the horror story, it seems now that the uncanny was able to escape 'the overprotected domain' of literature precisely because literary structures depend on the suppression of the 'unsymbolizable' and 'the warped'. Lingering a moment longer in the Renaissance house which provides the blueprint for our modern, gendered and oppositional definitions of the private and the public, we notice that indeed two types of privacy were beginning to take shape within its walls: one of the mind and one of the body. There was only one room in this house to which its mistress – like Bluebeard's bride – was denied access, namely the studio or 'thinking room'. Initially a mere writing desk, situated in the patriarch's bedroom, it expanded in time into a separate, adjacent space, literally the space of writing, in which the master of the house composed his memoirs, calculated his accounts and counted and stored his money. By the seventeenth century this room began to be known as the 'closet'. Meanwhile, and to a not inconsiderable degree as a reaction to the outbreak of devastating epidemics such as bubonic plague, cholera, leprosy and syphilis with their wide-ranging social and political implications, physical hygiene was subjected to new and increasingly stringent social controls. While in the early Middle Ages urine and faeces were simply disposed of through a convenient window, staining and corrupting the walls and foundations of buildings and providing a rich breeding ground for the carriers of disease, this practice was gradually modified through the introduction of public latrines and – finally – of private lavatories or privies. The condemnation of female sexuality as disease spread to sexual desire in general but was applied more specifically to sexual perversion, and in particular to 'the love that dare not speak its name'. By the end of the nineteenth century, the installation of the

new water closet was accompanied by the coining of the term 'homosexuality' and the construction of the homosexual as a discrete psychic and sexual subject.

The historical splitting (or doubling) of the closet in and through an anally retentive architecture divided knowledge. Yet, while the language of fiction (of the autobiography and the novel), formulated and preserved in the study, determined the very way reality is perceived, it is now the abject and the 'unspeakable' secret that call into question the old certainties. Indeed, Eve Kosofsky-Sedgwick argues that phrases such as 'to come out' (of the closet) or 'to out somebody' have become so pervasive that they must form the basis of any understanding of the major nodes of thought in twentieth-century Western culture. Sexual orientation more than gender differentiation, she proposes, now informs the social construction of knowledge.[41] The result of such increased self-knowledge, it seems, is melancholia and with it a distrust of language and meaning. 'You will note', lectures Kristeva,

> that, with melancholy persons, meaning appears to be arbitrary, or else it is elaborated with the help of much knowledge and will to mastery, but seems secondary, frozen, somewhat removed from the head and body of the person who is speaking. Or else it is from the very beginning evasive, uncertain, deficient, quasi mutistic: 'one' speaks to you already convinced that the words are wrong and therefore 'one' speaks carelessly, 'one' speaks without believing in it.[42]

Indeed, it seems then that we have not only 'lost our sense of purpose, we have lost the language whereby we can speak of it'.[43] 'One' has become uncanny to 'oneself' as well as to others, for our words no longer correspond to the world. When things were whole, we felt confident that our words could express them. But little by little these things have broken apart, shattered, collapsed into chaos. And yet our words have remained the same. They have not adapted themselves to the new reality. Hence, every time we try to speak of what we see, we speak falsely, distorting the very things we are trying to represent. It's made a mess of everything.[44]

In the search for 'a new language that will at last say what we have to say',[45] the elusiveness of performance offers important clues. The ensuing dialogue is im/properly housed in the 'unwritten'[46] living-room theatre, on the threshold between closet and study, where performer and spectator can face each other blindly and engage in 'the delight of reading' which has always had 'some relation with anality',[47] where they can 'talk' through their backsides and de/construct their own stories without setting their shifting meanings in stone.

## Notes

The illustrations in this chapter show the author in performance.

1 In German, '*After*' is the polite term for anus.
2 The situation seems a perfect illustration of what Derrida calls 'destinerrance', the impossibility of messages ever reaching their destination. See John P. Leavy Jr., 'Destinerrance: The Apotropocalyptics of Translation', in *Deconstruction and Philosophy: The Texts of Jacques Derrida*, ed. J. Sallis, Chicago: Chicago University Press, 1987.
3 See Homi Bhabha, 'The Third Space: Interview with Homi Bhabha', in *Identity, Community, Culture, Difference*, ed. J. Rutherford, London: Lawrence and Wishart, 1990; 'The Other Question: Difference, Discrimination and the Discourse of Colonialism', in *Out There: Marginalization and Contemporary Cultures*, ed. R. Ferguson *et al.*, Cambridge, MA: MIT Press and New York: New Museum of Contemporary Art, 1990; *The Location of Culture*, London and New York: Routledge, 1994.
4 Martin Jay, 'Apocalypse and the Inability to Mourn', in *Rethinking Imagination: Culture and Creativity*, ed. G. Robinson and J. Rundell, London and New York: Routledge, 1994.
5 Jacques Derrida, 'Of an Apocalyptic Tone Recently Adopted in Philosophy', *Semeia*, 23, 1982: 95, quoted in Jay, 'Apocalypse and the Inability to Mourn': 35.
6 Jean Baudrillard, 'Sur le nihilism', in *Simulacres et simulation*, Paris: Galilée, 1981: 234.
7 Sigmund Freud, 'Mourning and Melancholia', in *On Metapsychology: The Penguin Freud Library*, vol. XI, ed. A. Richards, trans. J. Strachey, Harmondsworth: Penguin, 1984.
8 Freud, 'Mourning and Melancholia': 253.
9 Freud, 'Mourning and Melancholia': 252.
10 Sigmund Freud, 'Group Psychology and the Analysis of the Ego', in *Civilization, Society and Religion: The Penguin Freud Library*, vol. XII, ed. A. Dickson, trans. L. Strachey, Harmondsworth: Penguin, 1985.
11 Anthony Vidler, *The Architectural Uncanny: Essays in the Modern Unhomely*, Cambridge, MA and London: MIT Press, 1992.
12 Sigmund Freud, 'The Uncanny', in *Art and Literature: The Penguin Freud Library*, vol. XIV, ed. A. Dickson, trans. J. Strachey, Harmondsworth: Penguin, 1985.
13 Vidler, *The Architectural Uncanny*: 3.
14 Vidler, *The Architectural Uncanny*: 6.
15 As Vidler points out, 'Freud's lengthy display of dictionary research [. . .] was of course

staged – his argument [. . .] carefully constructed to an already determined end' (*The Architectural Uncanny*: 230).

16  Jacob and Wilhelm Grimm, *Deutsches Worterbuch*, 16 vols., Leipzig: S. Hirzel, 1854–1954, vol. 4, book 2: 874.

17  Walter W. Skeat, *The Concise Dictionary of English Etymology*, Ware, UK: Wordsworth Editions, 1992.

18  Vidler, *The Architectural Uncanny*: 22.

19  Peggy Phelan, *Unmarked: The Politics of Performance*, London and New York: Routledge, 1993: 146.

20  Edward W. Soja, *Thirdspace: Journeys to Los Angeles and Other Real-and-Imagined Places*, Cambridge, MA and Oxford, UK: Blackwell, 1996.

21  Edward W. Soja, *Postmodern Geographies: The Reassertion of Space in Critical Social Theory*, London and New York: Verso, 1989: 2.

22  J. L. Borges, 'The Aleph', in *The Aleph and Other Stories: 1933–1969*, New York: Bantam Books, 1971, quoted in Soja, *Postmodern Geographies*: 2.

23  Henri Lefebvre, *The Production Of Space*, trans. D. Nicholson-Smith, Cambridge, MA and Oxford, UK: Blackwell, 1991.

24  Soja, *Thirdspace*: 5.

25  Soja, *Thirdspace*: 5.

26  Soja, *Thirdspace*: 117.

27  John P. Leavy Jr., 'Destinerrance: The Apotropocalyptics of Translation', *Deconstruction and Philosophy: The Texts of Jacques Derrida*, ed. J. Sallis, Chicago and London: University of Chicago Press, 1987.

28  The term was coined by Josephin Peladan in his treatise on *L'Art idealiste et mystique* (1894) and is quoted in Frantisek Deak, *Symbolist Theatre: The Formation of an Avant-Garde*, Baltimore and London: Johns Hopkins University Press, 1993: 248–63.

29  Freud, 'The Uncanny': 362.

30  Freud, 'The Uncanny': 368.

31  Arnaud Levy, 'Evaluation etymologique et semantique du mot "secret"', *Nouvelle revue de psychanalyse*, 14, 1976: 117–30, quoted in Gerard Vincent, 'The Secrets of History and the Riddle of Identity', in *A History of Private Life*, vol. 5, ed. A. Prost and G. Vincent, Cambridge, MA and London: Belknap Press/Harvard University Press, 1991.

32  Leon Battista Alberti, *On the Art of Building in Ten Books*, trans. J. Rykwert, N. Leach and R. Tavernor, Cambridge, MA: MIT Press, 1988.

33  Mark Wigley, 'Untitled: The Housing of Gender', in *Sexuality and Space*, ed. Beatriz Colomina, Princeton: Princeton Architectural Press, 1992: 332.

34  Wigley, 'Untitled: The Housing of Gender': 338.

35  Xenophon, 'Oecenomicus', trans. H. G. Dakyns as 'The Economist', in *The Works of Xenophon*, vol. 3, London: Macmillan, 1897: 229, quoted in Wigley, 'Untitled: The Housing of Gender': 341.

36  Gilles Deleuze and Felix Guattari, *A Thousand Plateaus*, London: Athlone Press, 1988: 32.

37  Leon Battista Alberti, *Della Famiglia*, trans. R. Neu Watkins as *The Family in Renaissance Florence*, Columbia: University of South Carolina Press, 1969, book III: 207.

38  Alberti, *Della Famiglia*, book III: 357.

39  Julia Kristeva, *Powers of Horror: An Essay on Abjection*, New York: Columbia University Press, 1982: 4.

40  Kristeva, *Powers of Horror*: 23.

41  Eve Kosofsky-Sedgwick, *Epistemology of the Closet*, Harmondsworth: Penguin, 1994.

42  Julia Kristeva, *Black Sun: Depression and Melancholia*, New York: Columbia University Press, 1989: 43.

43  Paul Auster, *The New York Trilogy*, London and Boston: Faber and Faber, 1987: 7.

44  Auster, *The New York Trilogy*: 77.

45 Auster, *The New York Trilogy*: 7.
46 See Alan Read, *Theatre and Everyday Life: An Ethics of Performance*, London and New York:
Routledge, 1993: 2, 15. The term refers to non-text-based theatre, to theatre that eludes
the notice of critics and reviewers, and to the critical neglect of the roles of performers and
audiences in the production of theatre: 'In this [last] sense the majority of those making
theatre are considered [. . .] to be speechless, until orality has become literacy'.
47 Roland Barthes, 'On Reading', *From Science to Literature*, in *A Roland Barthes Reader*, ed. S.
Sontag, London and New York: Vintage, 1993: 39.

# 8

# THE WRITER'S BLOCK

## Performance, play and the responsibilities of analysis

### Joe Kelleher

'The interpretation of the game then became obvious.'

Sigmund Freud[1]

## Obvious horizons: flying/limping

In *The Interpretation of Dreams*, Freud classifies dreams of flying among the 'typical dreams' that recall the games of childhood – being rushed across the room in the 'outstretched arms' of an 'uncle' – games which 'though innocent in themselves, give rise to sexual feelings'. Except that 'in the dreams they leave out the hands which held them up, so they float or fall unsupported', and it may be that 'the pleasurable feelings attached to these experiences are transformed into anxiety'.[2] 'The information provided by psycho-analyses'[3] appears to restore the supporting arms of a responsible adult, to underwrite childish pleasure with at least a *rhetorical* guarantee, but does so at the level of a speculative writing that may find itself infected by the same anxiety that it seeks to negotiate and even conquer. After all an utterance is less substantial than an embrace, if I am falling. Is it not? And as for what guarantees the analytic utterance, whether we think of that as the analysis of a performance or the *performance* of an analytic reading: who or what authors the horizons of our analytic speculations? The word of Freud the Father? And what hands hold us up to see?

My concern in the present essay is with responsibilities we might incur when we speculate analytically upon performance: more precisely, when our analysis reifies the movement of signifiers (in the way we might observe, through a lens and at a distance, the movement of small particles and remark a pattern) and purports to recognise its object – a piece of play, or movement, or behaviour, or writing – 'as' performance. A key instance in the psychoanalytic canon of texts and occasions would be the *fort/da*, where Freud accounts for his infant grandson's game of discarding and retrieving a toy over the horizon of a cot, as a compensatory performance (a 'staging [of] the disappearance and return of the objects within his reach'[4]) that negotiates anxiety with regard to the child's mother's absence. As I shall seek to remember in this essay, Freud's analysis there seems no less infected by anxiety (or at least, melancholic ambivalence) than the child's play that comes into view on the near (perhaps too near) horizon of the analysis's identification of its object.

My intention is to consider one or two texts of Freudian metapsychology alongside an attempt at reading a recent piece of mainstream British theatre, with a view to raising questions about what we might term analytic proxemics. That is, I wish to address some of the specific and not so specific *distances* across which analyses and performances may face each other, scoping each other's horizons, seducing each other perhaps, and not least learning to take care (not least, of each other). I would seek to invoke hereby modes of writing that infect these distances and invade these horizons. In particular I am interested in how analytic care might experience a tension between embracing its object and at the same time maintaining a proper distance. This 'ethical' tension may appear to give rise to the production of a writerly performance that is at the same time disinterested and all-consuming, a writing that performs like a virus; perhaps thereby performing its own 'ethical' agenda: provoking and blocking the analysis that would seek to make sense of it, that would seek to reduce the *performance* to an *object* of understanding.[5]

The occasion for this essay is an experience I had as an audience member at a theatrical event in London in October 1997. The event was a staging of the production by Out of Joint and the Royal Court Theatre of Caryl Churchill's double bill of plays *Blue Heart*. Watching these two scenes that measure out vertiginous distances in cross-generational dialogues, I felt myself (I would say now) suspended across the theatre space in the avuncular arms of 'theory', but somehow aware that those arms would not support me if I fell. Put simply, what struck me on that occasion was that my response to what I saw and heard performed sought to express itself in psychoanalytic terms. Either the drama and its staging were 'obviously' articulating processes and structures that could only be best described as 'psychoanalytic'; or else my own interpellation into this or that discourse of psychoanalytic theory had brought me to only be able to articulate my responses in such terms. The situation was unsettling, however. That is to say, the more obvious (in the sense of being irrefutably evident) my reading appeared to me to be, the more obvious in that *other* sense (the sense of a naivety that misses the mark of a greater critical interest) it also appeared. I was approaching the horizon of my interpretation either too quickly or too slowly, but either way with insufficient care. But what was being missed? And what, then, would be the 'care' proper to the speculations of such a performance analysis? – if, that is, the answer to that question is anything other than the traditional scholarly rigours of research and argumentation.

At the close of *Beyond the Pleasure Principle* Freud cites a poet: 'what we cannot reach flying we must reach limping . . . The Book tells us it is no sin to limp'.[6] The citation stands to authorise a delay and underwrite a risk: Freud's delay in coming up with 'answers', and his risky speculations made in the interim. It also, though, sounds an injunction: the injunction to take proper care with respect to whatever horizons we find ourselves launched against. As such, the scientist leans on the poet to make his excuses and depart, but in the same gesture seems to take up, to entertain, a burden of responsibility. In short, the citational gesture is ambivalent. Freud's concern here seems to be somewhere between a sober and responsible patience ('We must be patient and await fresh methods and occasions of research'), and on the other hand a hint of uncertainty ('We must be ready, too, to abandon a path that we have followed for a time, if it seems to be leading to no good end') that, literally, has something about it of abandonment, if only an abandonment to the interminability of the pursuit.[7] It is as if analysis itself must sustain an ethics of performance, operating in the delay between the leap and the look, in the distance between risk and rigour.

As suggested, the object of Freud's concern, as long as we are dealing with metaphors of approach, is a horizon of sorts, the horizon of an analysis or interpretation, where the object of the analysis would come into view with some clarity, as an object of care and understanding. However, some of the horizons glanced at in Freud's text – the war's end that occasions the subsequent fatal illness of a daughter, among others; or the horizon of a curtained cot where a child's toy is given to disappear, reappear, disappear *ad nauseam* – are measured by tricky distances. The analysis that would attempt such distances, attempt them so as to account for what is *performed* across such distances, would want to take care. It would seek – with something like an ethnographic nicety – to go carefully, to keep its distance to an extent, if only to avoid infecting and being infected; to avoid disturbing the performance there when and where it is playing itself out. At the same time, analysis may be impatient. It may take risks, for example in the gesture of second guessing, of 'reading ahead', of speculating upon the horizon in advance of any approach. In its own performance analysis may be caught between a responsibility towards its object, a selfless care to support the object in its 'alterity', and an inclination nevertheless to get better acquainted, to make an investment and draw the object (the 'other' performance) into the horizon of a *self* understanding. At stake here are the responsibilities of analysis *per se*.

## Caryl Churchill: other analyses

Caryl Churchill's work as a playwright has long been concerned with the responsibilities of analysis. In part, this concern might be contextualised within prominent traditions of late twentieth-century British theatre where feminist and social realist agendas have been pursued in the service of critique of societal practices and hegemonic structures. Churchill's work, however, has always brought more to the stage than the transparent efficacy of a critical agenda. Within works such as *Vinegar Tom* (1976) which explores the violent scapegoating diagnoses of seventeenth-century witch-hunting, or *Softcops* (1978/1984) which borrows from Foucault to illustrate processes whereby voices and agents of opposition are depoliticised through the diagnosis of criminality, she has continued to confront audiences with the problematic of analysis itself.

Something of the problematic is brought out in Elin Diamond's comment on 'a double strain in Churchill's work':

> on the one hand, a commitment to the apparatus of representation (actor as sign of character; character as sign of a recognizable human fiction) in order to say something *about* human oppression and pain . . . on the other hand, a consistent though less obvious attention to the powers of theatrical illusion, to modalities within representation that subvert the 'aboutness' we normally call the work's 'content'.[8]

Along the way analysis enacts heartbreaking allegories of writing. Diamond notes the scene in Churchill's *Fen* where 'unable to "write" her body in the sense of figuring its desires, Val can only mark her chest with a pen indicating where her lover should stab her'.[9] However, as Diamond goes on to point out, even as the obviousness of an allegory appears, the *perspective* from which it appears – 'the vanishing point in perspectival space that corresponds to the spectator's view . . . a position that in psychoanalysis, as in Western philosophy, is gendered male', that consolidates the seer of the horizon into the position of a 'knower' – is challenged by 'a different way of seeing, a different order', a countermining analysis. That is, rather than returning to the spectator-analyst's perspective as a victimised body that must 'represent itself as dead', to be restored by a (psycho)analytic writing or reparation of the return of the repressed (and the oppressed); rather what reappears – immediately '*through the door on the other side of the stage*' – is 'a consciousness' that, in what Diamond identifies as the 'death-space' of Churchill's drama, 'instantiates a new theatre space'.[10] As Val says immediately, here in the room, to the lover who has stabbed her and put her body in the wardrobe, 'It's dark. I can see through you. No, you're better now'.[11] What I am trying to suggest here, with the aid of Diamond's argument, are ways in which the analytic perspective (the spectator-critic's perspective, for instance) is met by an *other* analysis immanent in the drama itself. In this meeting, even as they appear, the horizons of analysis become speculative – a conjectural risk and investment in securities, whereby (to return to the metaphor offered earlier) supporting arms and voices are both too material and too *im*material to hold up the bodies they would keep from falling. Whether those bodies are bodies of writing or the body of a loved one, or even the performing body subjected – voluntarily or otherwise – to an analysis of its 'symptoms', they may resist the embrace: not so much in the form of a refusal, although that also happens, but in the performance of an other embrace that (we might suggest) speaks of love in an 'other' tongue. It may be that the embrace of analysis, and the analysis of an embrace, grab at empty air; but in so doing, they grab at love. And, as far as risk, responsibility and investment go, that might be the first and last word on the (psycho)analytic horizon.

### *Blue Heart . . .*

But where would we find, where might we 'look for' the analytic 'horizon'? A colour-coded scene, and a scene unseen – blue; heart. The proper name of this play, if it is 'a' play, sounds or looks like a metaphor. It seems to speak of a melancholy interiority, in the terms of an old-fashioned topology wherein the heart would be the seat of the

135

emotions; and sad songs of loss and desire, in the face of the brutalities of the external world, will be performed with all the authenticity of something that comes 'from the heart'. According to the lights of particular linguistic adaptations of the Freudian psychic processes of condensation and displacement into the structures of metaphor and metonymy (an adaptation made much of in later psychoanalytic theory),[12] the title is indeed a metaphoric condensation: of the two short plays *Heart's Desire* and *Blue Kettle* that make up this double bill. But thereby, already, this body of writing is a split subject with maybe little heart (these are dramas of cruelty, as we shall see), and hardly any sort of interiority either. Rather, any approach to an anterior or interior or even exterior heart's desire is deferred and displaced onto the opaque surfaces of writing and theatrical illusion. And an infected illusion at that.

*Heart's Desire*: the older members of a family prepare for their grown-up daughter's first return home; she is flying back from Australia. They repeatedly work towards the end of the conversation when the father will greet the daughter's entrance with the line 'You are my heart's desire'; but every time their performance is interrupted – a slip in the lines, an improper effusion ('I'm telling you. I have this terrible urge to eat myself'), or instead of the daughter the appearance of what was not to be expected: men with guns who slaughter them all, a horde of small children who rush round the room and out again, a ten foot tall bird. 'She's taking her time', says father (it was always his first line). Father would embrace her – with something more unavowable, we are given to suspect, than the affection proper to the paternal relationship – but she does not come in to land. Or rather, she does arrive two-thirds of the way through the play ('Mummy. Daddy. How wonderful to be home'), but that in its ideality is an interruption as unlikely as the others. And so they have to start again. And again. But, as far as the characters are concerned, the interruptions seem to be erased from memory each time. It is as if the stage were a screen, perpetually crashing, perpetually rebooted, unremembering, but harbouring something.

*Blue Kettle*: a 40-year-old man is collecting mothers (while his own mother is in a geriatric ward, becoming lost to a journey on which no-one can accompany her), passing himself off to various older women as the lost child they gave away to adoption. These 'mothers' meet him with the proper kindness and consideration. But increasingly their speech, the speech of all the characters, is infected by apparently arbitrary signifiers, 'blue' and 'kettle.' The infection becomes critical, until at curtain down we are left with little more than an apparent gibberish ('MRS PLANT T b k k k k l? / DEREK B. K.'), but at the level of the drama again the infection goes unremarked. 'Real conversation' is obviously still continuing, but a veil has already been drawn.

If we do not simply credit these strangenesses, these seemingly viral eruptions, to the motivated actions of 'characters' in an authored 'fiction' that represents a psychic as well as a social 'reality', we should say the writing has run away with itself, pursuing its own unavowable agenda. It appears that something other than the drama is being performed here, in such a way that it is not immediately obvious whether the drama is the occasion for these appearances or the other way around.

The melancholia of the blue heart, it appears, is no soft touch. Or worse, there may not be any heart of the matter after all.

## ... The melancholia of analysis

For the Freud of the 1915 paper 'Mourning and Melancholia', the melancholic is figured as the site of love's impossibility. According to the Freudian schema the three preconditions of melancholia are 'loss of the object, ambivalence, and regression of libido into the ego'.[13] Love abandons (or feels itself abandoned by) its object, takes flight instead into the ego – the 'self', and experiences (as self-reproach, but also at times as an eager and exultant mania) the ambivalences of love and hate at an 'internal' psychic level: that is, in a conflict between the ego and the ego's critical agency, the latter of which Freud here equates with 'the agency commonly called "conscience"'.[14]

The *Blue Heart* dramas seem to invite a mapping of such a schema. Certainly there is, as in Freud, something *like* mourning at stake but something more ambivalent. Simply put, neither the daughter nor the mother are dead, altogether 'lost'. 'The object has not perhaps actually died', but rather 'has been lost as an object of love'.[15] Further, the obscurities of motivation in the dramas accord with Freud's characterisation of the melancholic as one who 'knows *whom* he has lost but not *what* he has lost in him'.[16] We could go further, noting the ambivalences of affection and cruelty played out in the plays both on substitute others and on the self; and noting particularly how the desire of the prominent male characters, the father of the first play and the son of the second, is dramatised as a *self*-defeating pursuit of the embrace of the other, a pursuit that returns repeatedly to *self*-love and *its* impossibility – or at least its mangled articulation.

However, what concerns me here is not so much the efficacy of a particular reading, but – to the extent that melancholia is figured as a process of critical reading that, in aiming to address itself to something outside itself produces instead (and in spite of itself) a performance of *self*-consciousness – a question of how to 'read' a melancholic performance as such. What, in such a reading, is being read? Or, to what extent is such a reading itself a performance? Which, to gather up again the question of analytic *responsibility*, may be as much as to ask, where does conscience draw the line?

Judith Butler has argued recently, with regard to the Freudian melancholia, that the separation between self and self (ego and the critical agency of conscience, which Freud will later develop as super-ego), identified in the melancholic turn from exterior object to psychic internality, is itself instantiated in that turn. Put simply 'the turn from the object to the ego produces the ego'.[17] That is to say psychic internality is itself a turn – a trope, a metaphor. Melancholia is not so much an effect of a psychic structure, as the 'tropological' condition of the psychic structure's appearance at the level of representation. In this peculiar figure of melancholia that appears as the impossible condition of its own appearance (Butler writes, in relation to melancholia's 'unavowable loss', of 'a withdrawal or retraction from speech that makes speech possible'[18]), is a higher level of ambivalence: an ambivalence with regard to the availability of an other's melancholia to representation (or analysis) at all, except as the site of the performance of an 'other' melancholia which analysis must fail to grasp without having already 'withdrawn' into 'itself'. It may be that, even as melancholia appears in view in all its evident obviousness, it defeats the efficacy of analysis to get a grip on its condition. Rather (let us suggest) like a program virus built into the production of tropes, like the viral signifiers that infect the *mise-en-scène* and dialogue of *Blue Heart*, along with the subsequent critical analysis that attempts to account for these eruptions as symptoms of some sort of textual 'condition', the analysis of melancholia becomes itself the site of production of the melancholia *of* critical analysis.[19]

Freud's comments on melancholia had long been characterised by a certain melancholy uncertainty.[20] But even when the comments achieve a greater conviction, as for example in the 1923 *The Ego and the Id*, what remains is a psychic ambivalence situated between the horizons of a protective but also critical agency (here characterised as the super-ego) and a demand for love. In this later narrative, the melancholic ('internal') fear of death is put down to the ego's feeling itself hated rather than loved by the super-ego – the super-ego fulfilling 'the same function of protecting and saving that was fulfilled in earlier days by the father and later by Providence or Destiny'. When the ego finds itself in danger, 'it feels itself deserted by all protecting forces and lets itself die', a situation analogous to 'the first great anxiety-state of birth and the infantile anxiety of longing – the anxiety due to separation from the protecting mother'.[21]

However, these sorts of anxieties could be the occasion for a renunciation (as in the *fort/da* game, 'that is, the renunciation of instinctual satisfaction' in 'allowing his mother to go away without protesting') that is to be recuperated as a 'great cultural achievement', the infant's entry into symbolic activity. And, if we briefly follow through some of the arguments of later psychoanalytic theory, we may get a glimpse into the scope of melancholia's ambivalent contribution to the staging and articulation of a form of *social* responsibility. As Lacan will put the case, this moment 'in which desire becomes human is also that in which the child is born into Language'.[22] At the same time, as Lacan is not slow to point out, this achievement cannot be separated from a sort of living towards death, or at least a 'sepulture', or even at the most extreme a suicide that 'leaves forever present in the memory of men this symbolic act of his being-for-death'.[23] All of which is offered briefly to suggest, here, some of the ambivalences of loss and gain (experiences of familial loss and the ambivalent gain of symbolic compensation, for instance) that the performance of the melancholic analysis might implicate us in. As Lacan states:

> Of all the undertakings which have been put forward in this century, that of the psychoanalyst is perhaps the loftiest, because the undertaking of the psychoanalyst acts in our time as a mediator between the man of care and the subject of absolute Knowledge.[24]

Nothing melancholic about that, it seems. However, it is at this point that Lacan insists on the dialectic between melancholic solitude and something like social responsibility.[25] Or at least, the 'realisation' of solitude in a performance ('be it in the vital ambiguity of immediate desire or in the full assumption of his being-for-death') that, in its engagement of others within the horizon of its desire, binds itself to a social concern. For Lacan

> the question of the termination of analysis is that of the moment when the satisfaction of the subject finds a way to come to realization in the satisfaction of everyone – that is, of all those whom this satisfaction associates with itself in a human undertaking.[26]

How, let us ask, according to the horizons of care (care for the others, care for the self) and the articulation of analytic knowledge, does such a responsibility undertake to speak? What speaks it? What does it speak of? And how is its speaking to be heard? What hubris of that Lacanian mediation 'in our time', or in the societal 'binding' of psychic life identified by Butler, must be guarded against (guarded perhaps by the Freudian uncertainty, a choice of limping over flying)? Within the scope of our present concerns – writing for and of theatrical performance – what sort of ambivalences might interrupt or infect our scriptings? And, in the ambivalent 'overcoming' of these invasions – which is as much as a binding of them, after all, to the voice of another subject – how do we reconcile a critical conscience with what appears to appear, the body of performance marked by all sorts of wounds,[27] all sorts of infections, as if for our consumption and satisfaction?

So we turn to listen again to Churchill's dramas. The peculiar interruptive or infective devices of each of the plays, these viral signifiers of 'performance' that have invaded these otherwise very 'straight' dramas, these seem to speak to us *like* symptoms of psychic repressions. The interruptions of *Heart's Desire* seem like the metonymic displacements that betray unconscious desire, a motivated forgetting or deferral of an anxious horizon (the daughter's arrival), displaced onto associative images. For instance, a friend at the theatre took that ten foot tall bird for an ostrich but I found myself insisting it had to be something like an emu – another flightless bird but surely an antipodean species, a non-speaking messenger conjured across the impossible but specific distance of the daughter's disappearance from 'down under'. It seems obvious. As for the apparently arbitrary signifiers that infect the dialogues of *Blue Kettle*, here surely was metaphoric condensation at work, especially in the compression of the words into their constituent phonemes (or more precisely, the phonemes of their *letters*) towards the play's end: these same signifiers standing throughout – as according to the mechanism of condensation 'which allows a single unconscious idea to express the content of several chains of association'[28] – for a whole complex of crossed messages, demands and deceptions.

However, it still seems less than obvious what is effected by such a schema, other than a peculiarly academic satisfaction. I have been trying to suggest throughout this essay that there are ways in which, even as the body of writing-and-performance appears to lay itself bare to our speculations, another analysis appears (akin to what Diamond characterises as the 'death-space' of Churchill's earlier dramas): a 'new theatre space' where bodies and voices otherwise written into disappearance by the relative certainties of a patriarchal perspective appear to confound that perspective's articulation. It may be that, through the metonymic interruptions whereby the arrival of a daughter fails to be re-delivered to the family scene, or the metaphoric infections that seem to say something of the failure to return to the instinctual satisfactions of the singular body of the 'real' mother, the dramas are staging their own resistances to (psycho)analysis.[29]

As such the real drama, so to speak, at the scene of writerly performance would be something like the melancholic condition of a 'writer's block', and the overcoming of such a block through a giving voice to some sort of 'other' agency, an extra-authorial agency that underwrites the life of the performance while appearing to speak towards the death of the ostensible stage drama.[30] In the simplest terms, I am thinking, for example, of how the invasion of signifiers in *Blue Kettle* overrides the motivated speeches and actions of the ego-centred characters of the play, and operates like what we might today recognise as a 'computer virus'. This invasion shuts down the production of discourse, invading it with the production of 'alien' characters, like a disease programmed into the technology of the writing itself, while the dramatic writing attempts to perform its humane analysis of inter-generational distances – and cross these distances with a loving embrace. Like the germ cells examined in Freud's *Beyond*, whose 'performance . . . work[s] against the death of the living substance and succeed[s] in winning for it what we can only regard as potential immortality, though that may mean no more than a lengthening of the road to death',[31] even the performance of an embrace will be shot through with ambivalence.

## Beyond play

'Beyond the pleasure principle': the phrase sounds like a motto for the would-be sober agendas of analytic care and theoretical knowledge pursued in the research and pedagogic practices of academic theatre studies. Like the poet Keats, tolled back by melancholia from the melodious singing of the nightingale to his 'sole self' and the self's uncertainty in the face of a music that has always already fled, the theatre academic is as often as not concerned with overcoming the disappearing body of performance by recuperating the flight of pleasure into the vertigo of speculative, self-situating theory.[32]

In the *Beyond*, Freud makes his own brief return to theatre studies, suggesting how deliberate theatrical imitations, aimed at audiences, engage precisely in a dialectic of pleasure and unpleasure that may one day have its yield in theoretical analysis, 'a subject to be recollected and worked over in the mind', preferably 'by some system of aesthetics with an economic approach to its subject-matter'.[33] However, he states here that such cases 'are of no use for *our* purposes', to the very extent that they operate within the 'presuppose[d]' horizons of 'the dominance of the pleasure principle'. He makes this qualification, moreover, at the conclusion of the very chapter that elaborates his speculations upon the infant's game of *fort/da*, a chapter that makes much play of an observed scene of performance – of sorts – that Freud does not hesitate to refer to in terms of theatrical metaphors, as having a 'first act' and a 'second act', as a 'staging': the infant's compensation for his mother's disappearance 'by himself staging the disappearance and return of the objects within his reach'.[34]

The scene of the *fort/da* is the scene of a domestic space. Freud is in Hamburg, September 1915, visiting his daughter Sophie and her family. The infant is Sophie's son Ernst. The observers of the scene, therefore – a scene, we presume, which is not performed *for* their benefit – are the child's mother and grandfather, who together agree to hear that which is not, strictly speaking, said. With regard to the child's 'long drawn out "o-o-o-o" . . . his mother and the writer of the present account were agreed in thinking that this was not a mere interjection but represented the German word "fort" ["gone"]'.[35] From this follows the famous interpretation of the child's symbolic compensation for his mother's disappearance. And from this (or apparently from this) – through accounts of the 'acting out' of reproductions of repressed material in the scene of the psychoanalytic transference,[36] and the observation 'in the lives of some normal people' of 'the impression . . . of being pursued by a malignant fate or possessed by some "daemonic" power'[37] – follows the identification of that 'compulsion to repeat which over-rides the pleasure principle',[38] the entropy of the '*conservative* nature of living substance',[39] which arrives at the famous and formidable theory of the inextricability of the life-preserving instincts with the so-called 'death drive'.[40]

That, in short, is the path of the analysis. But what of the steering between care and abandonment that such a journey might demand? Freud to Ferenczi, 31 March 1919:

> I am writing the essay 'Beyond the Pleasure Principle' and, as in all instances, I am hoping for your understanding, which has not abandoned me in any situation. In it I am saying many things that are quite unclear, out of which the reader has to make the right thing. Sometimes one can't do otherwise. But I hope you will find something interesting in it. Unfortunately, it is not the same thing as an exchange of ideas face to face.[41]

But what is the right thing? And what is lost (and gained) in the absence of that face to face? The account of the infant's performance of the *fort/da* game, for instance, does *not* lead, argumentatively speaking, to the elaboration of the death drive theory. Freud is eager, on more than one occasion, to insist on the 'other ways' (such as pleasurable imitation of elders, or the mastering of unpleasurable experiences) by which the emergence of the compulsion to repeat may be interpreted in children's play.[42] It is only readers, through an interpretive step of their own, who can read the child's play as a being-for-death. Nothing of the sort is spoken by the mother or grandfather. Meanwhile, the text appears to be continually warning of the traps of an interpretive performance. Along with 'the interpretation . . . then became obvious',[43] and 'we are therefore left in no doubt',[44] and 'it is obvious that all their play is influenced by', all with regard to the infant's game, we are given 'we shall find courage to assume',[45] and 'enough is left unexplained',[46] and 'what follows is speculation, often far-fetched speculation',[47] with regard to the theory of the death-drive.

Speculation opens a gap, between the analysis of a performance (or play analysed *as* performance) and the performance of an analysis, a gap into which one might fall, flying – without realising that supporting arms have been taken away. In the event, the demand for the returning embrace ('You are my heart's desire'), or the sustaining guarantee of the 'face to face' (if that solves *anything*, 'Do you remember me?' 'Yes I have blue a blue mental kettle of you with a lot of black hair'), walks a fine line: between the temptation of the *pathetic* melancholy of a felt emotional bond, and an *overcoming* melancholy that binds – ambivalently – a sociality to itself in the service of a proper care of others.

A question may appear to frame itself as 'which others?' Are, for instance, Churchill's domestic scenes and Freud's domestic scene the 'same' scene – to the extent that they 'are' domestic: of the home: from the heart(h)? It is not always mentioned that Freud, in this text, leaves the identification of the particular scene of the *fort/da* to scholarly detective work. We need to refer to a 1919 footnote to *The Interpretation of Dreams* (596n) to ascertain the Freud family triad of grandfather/father, daughter/mother and son/grandson. Any pathos to be derived from such recognition is thereby written out of this later text. However, an occasion for pathos (which is often mentioned) – a pathos of Freud's 'own' writing, as it were – is given at a certain remove (which is to say crossed out, refused by Freud) in a *Beyond* footnote (286n) that informs readers that the child's mother has subsequently died and that now 'that she was really "gone" ("o-o-o") [only three vocables this time], the little boy showed no signs of grief'. Sophie Halberstadt, Sigmund and Martha's 'Sunday child', died in the influenza epidemic that followed immediately on the conclusion of the First World War.[48] To Pfister, 27 January 1920:

> Although we had been worried about her for a couple of days, we had nevertheless been hopeful; it is so difficult to judge from a distance; we were not able to travel at once, as we had intended, after the first alarming news; there was no train, not even for an emergency. The undisguised brutality of our time is weighing heavily upon us. Tomorrow she is to be cremated, our poor Sunday child![49]

I am not concerned here with rehearsing 'the most crushing psychobiographical style' of a relating of Sophie's death to the Freudian text.[50] Nor will it do, I suppose, to map one text onto the other, to tease out – through the figures of different viruses prevalent in Freud's time and our own – the disappeared mother/daughter of Freud's text in the company of the returning daughter and departing mother of Churchill's text; although, as Freud allowed, analysis may be inclined to pursue such operations. 'I certainly would have stressed the connection between the death of the daughter and the Concepts of the *Jenseits* in any analytic study on someone else. Yet it is still wrong . . . *Probability is not always the truth*'.[51]

It is difficult to judge at a distance, even when (especially when) the judgement appears most obvious, although distance has marked the space of the psychoanalytic judgement – and the theatrical effect. The ethics of psychoanalysis, presumably, are concerned with resisting an emotional tie (such as that experienced in transference love) for the sake of sustaining the distance of a contingent analysis – with an eventual view to taking proper care. At stake is the *responsibility* of analysis. That is a responsibility to the legitimacy of an interpretation (for example, an interpretation legitimised by the titular name of the (grand)father: 'Freud'); but also to legitimising the alienated signifiers that appear as the 'issue' of an other's (even illegitimate, resistant) desire. The embrace of love in psychoanalysis (as Freud explained to Jung in 1906, it 'is essentially a cure through love'[52]) is not the same thing as a face-to-face loving embrace.[53] There is a distance between the two, but the male protagonists of these plays of Churchill's attempt to betray this distance. Distance, then, reasserts itself – against the collapsing of a game and an analysis – as a performance writing that embraces play as a deathly effect: a virus-like writing that attempts to divest itself of death 'by repeated attempts to enter the symbolic, only to be caught all over again'.[54] There is, as Elizabeth Wright has argued, 'no ethical consolation to be had', but *that* after all may be the issue of a psychoanalytic – and theatrical – ethic. Analytic writing reifies the performance immanent in play. It can do no other; but the play – even as it passes – remains to resist analytic certainties, which is why the analysis has to take care, it has to limp. The Book (Freud's book?) tells us it is no sin to limp. You would have to believe it.

## Notes

1 Sigmund Freud, *Beyond the Pleasure Principle* [1920], trans. James Strachey, in Angela Richards, ed. *On Metapsychology, The Penguin Freud Library*, vol. XI, London: Penguin, 1991: 285.

2 Sigmund Freud, *The Interpretation of Dreams* [1900], trans. James Strachey, *Pelican Freud Library*, vol. IV, Harmondsworth: Penguin, 1976: 516–17.

3 Freud, *Interpretation of Dreams*: 516.

4 Freud, *Beyond the Pleasure Principle*: 285.

5 In this age of the word-processor, where slips may no longer be credited simply to the parapraxes of tongue or pen, the virus may be built into the technology of writing itself. Of course Freud explores parapraxes throughout the *Psychopathology of Everyday Life* (Sigmund Freud, *The Psychopathology of Everyday Life* [1901], trans. Alan Tyson, *Pelican Freud Library*, vol. V, Harmondsworth: Penguin, 1975. But see also Jonathan Goldberg, 'On the One Hand . . .', in John Bender and David E. Wellbery, eds, *The Ends of Rhetoric: History, Theory, Practice*, Stanford: Stanford University Press, 1990: 77–99 for interesting commentary on how Freud fails to get to grips with parapraxes of *writing*, even in his chapter (Chapter 6) on that subject. Goldberg goes on to consider the future of a psychoanalytic graphology when texts are produced by means of the word-processor rather than the 'phallic' pen, 'when it is no longer the flow of liquid onto the page that produces traces' (Goldberg, 'On the One Hand': 99). It may also be worth reminding

ourselves that although computer viruses may appear 'like' the symptoms of a techno-logical unconscious, they are usually the effects of altogether more deliberate, more 'conscious' performances.

6 Freud, *Beyond the Pleasure Principle*: 338. 'Was man nicht erfliegen kann, muss man erhinken. /. . ./ Die Schrift sagt, es ist keine Sünde zu hinken'. Freud is quoting the last lines of Rückert's 'Die beiden Gulden', a version of one of the *Maqâmat* of al-Hariri.

7 For more on the Freudian certainty and uncertainty, as underwritten by doubt and resistance, see Jacques Lacan, *The Four Fundamentals of Psycho-Analysis*, ed. Jacques-Alain Miller, trans. Alan Sheridan, London: Penguin, 1994: esp. 34–9.

8 Elin Diamond, *Unmaking Mimesis: Essays on Feminism and Theater*, London and New York: Routledge, 1997: 83–4.

9 Diamond, *Unmaking Mimesis*: 93. 'VAL. Look. I marked the place with a biro. That's where the knife has to go in. I can't do it myself' (Caryl Churchill, *Plays: Two*, London: Methuen, 1990: 186).

10 Diamond, *Unmaking Mimesis*: 93.

11 Churchill, *Plays: Two*: 187.

12 For brevity's sake let me recite Mikkel Borch-Jacobsen's concise account of these theoretical developments. Borch-Jacobsen's narrative is also useful, with its asides on audacity, vagueness, temerity, and perilous leaps, in helping us to recall the rhetoricality of these sometimes monolithic theoretic constructions:

> Benveniste, in a rather vague and prudent manner, outlined a comparison between the oneiric processes described by Freud and the stylistic figures of speech: meta-phor, metonymy, synecdoche, but also euphemism, allusion, antiphrasis, litotes, ellipsis, and so on. [Roman] Jakobson, more precisely (or more audaciously), proposed assimilating displacement and condensation to metonymy, identifi-cation and symbolism to metaphor – these two rhetorical figures being themselves reduced, by a perilous leap, to the two properly linguistic operations of syntag-matic combination and paradigmatic selection. Lacan, extending the hypothesis of Jakobson, with no less temerity suggested identifying condensation and symptom with metaphor, displacement and desire with metonymy, thus promoting a linguistic interpretation of the unconscious.

> Mikkel Borch-Jacobsen, *The Emotional Tie: Psychoanalysis, Mimesis, and Affect*, Stanford: Stanford University Press, 1992: 64. See also Emile Benveniste, 'Remarques sur la fonction du langage dans la découverte freudienne', in his *Eléments de linguistique générale*, Paris: Gallimard, 1966: 75–87; Roman Jakobson, 'Two Aspects of Language and two Types of Aphasic Disturbances', in Roman Jakobson and Morris Halle, *Fundamentals of Language*, Gravenhage: Mouton, 1956: 55–82; Roman Jakobson, 'Linguistics and Poetics', in Thomas A. Sebeok, ed. *Style in Language*, New York and London: John Wiley, and MIT, 1960: 370–5; and Jacques Lacan, 'The Agency of the Letter in the Unconscious or Reason since Freud', in Jacques Lacan, *Ecrits: A Selection*, trans. Alan Sheridan, London: Tavistock, 1977: 146–78.

13 Sigmund Freud, 'Mourning and Melancholia' [1917], trans. James Strachey, in Angela Richards, ed. *On Metapsychology, The Penguin Freud Library*, vol. XI, London: Penguin, 1991: 245–68 (267).

14 Freud, 'Mourning and Melancholia': 256.

15 Freud, 'Mourning and Melancholia': 253.

16 Freud, 'Mourning and Melancholia': 254.

17 Judith Butler, *The Psychic Life of Power: Theories in Subjection*, Stanford: Stanford University Press, 1997: 168.

18 Butler, *The Psychic Life of Power*: 170.

19 It may be worth quoting a short passage of Butler's text in full:

Melancholia does not name a psychic process that might be recounted through an adequate explanatory scheme. It tends to confound any explanation of psychic processes that we might be inclined to offer. And the reason it confounds any such effort is that it makes clear that our ability to refer to the psyche through tropes of internality are themselves effects of a melancholic condition.

(Butler, *The Psychic Life of Power*: 171)

20 The opening paragraph of 'Mourning and Melancholia', while noting the obviousness of 'such impressions as are open to every observer', notes at the same time the fluctuating definitions of the condition in descriptive psychiatry, the '[un]certainty' of grouping together its forms 'into a single unity', and the 'small number of cases whose psychogenic nature was indisputable'. These opening sentences, then, refrain 'from the outset' to any 'claim to general validity for our conclusions', and turn instead to a self-consolation ('we shall console ourselves by reflecting') with regard to the possibility that 'we could hardly discover anything that was not typical, if not of a whole class of disorders, at least of a small group of them' (Freud, 'Mourning and Melancholia': 251).

21 Sigmund Freud, *The Ego and the Id* [1923], trans. James Strachey, in *The Penguin Freud Library*, vol. XI: 350–407 (400).

22 Jacques Lacan, *Speech and Language in Psychoanalysis*, trans. Anthony Wilden, Baltimore and London: Johns Hopkins University Press, 1981: 83. It is also worth noting that at this moment in his text Lacan is about to speak explicitly of the *fort/da*, or *Fort! Da!* as he transcribes it.

23 Lacan, *Speech and Language*: 84.

24 Lacan, *Speech and Language*: 85.

25 See again Judith Butler: 'melancholy offers potential insight into how the boundaries of the social are instituted and maintained, not only at the expense of psychic life, but through binding psychic life into forms of melancholic ambivalence' (Butler, *The Psychic Life of Power*: 167–8).

26 Lacan, *Speech and Language*: 85.

27 'The conflict within the ego, which melancholia substitutes for the struggle over the object, must act like a painful wound which calls for an extraordinarily high anticathexis' (Freud, 'Mourning and Melancholia': 267).

28 David Macey, 'Introduction' to Jacques Lacan, *The Four Fundamental Concepts of Psycho-Analysis*, ed. Jacques-Alain Miller, trans. Alan Sheridan, London: Penguin, 1994: vii–xxxiii (xxviii).

29 In *Blue Kettle* the economic – in the most mundane sense – may be at issue as much as instinctual satisfaction. The question is not obscured, but it is left ambiguous. 'ENID: Is it a contrick or is it a hangup? DEREK: It's a contrick. Which would you rather? It's a contrick. ENID: It's not which I'd rather. DEREK: You've got hangups yourself' (Churchill, *Blue Heart*: 61).

30 For an account that, in an early chapter, fulsomely draws together the several but scattered psychoanalytic sources on writer's block, see Zachary Leader's book-length study (Zachary Leader, *Writer's Block*, Baltimore and London: Johns Hopkins University Press, 1991).

31 Freud, *Beyond the Pleasure Principle*: 312–13.

32 We might characterise the *Beyond* as both dodgy and dodgily seductive. Gay speaks of an 'avalanche of papers' (Peter Gay, *Freud: A Life for Our Time*, London: Papermac, 1995: 767) that has followed upon Freud's identification of the aggressive drives. The avalanche was not slow in beginning. Gay also cites a 1921 letter of Freud's to Eitington: 'For the *Beyond* . . . I have been punished enough; it is very popular, brings me masses of letters and encomiums. I must have made something very stupid there' (Gay, *Freud*: 403).

33 Freud, *Beyond the Pleasure Principle*: 287. See also the earlier (but posthumously published)

Sigmund Freud, 'Psychopathic Characters on the Stage' [1905–6], trans. James Strachey, in Albert Dickson, ed., *Art and Literature*, *Penguin Freud Library*, vol. XIV, London: Penguin, 1990: 119–27. For a concise and recent reading of this paper see Elizabeth Wright, 'Psychoanalysis and the Theatrical: Analysing Performance', in Patrick Campbell, ed., *Analysing Performance: A Critical Reader*, Manchester: Manchester University Press, 1996: 175–90 (175–6).

34  Freud, *Beyond the Pleasure Principle*: 284, 285.

35  Freud, *Beyond the Pleasure Principle*: 284.

36  Freud, *Beyond the Pleasure Principle*: 288–9.

37  Freud, *Beyond the Pleasure Principle*: 292.

38  Freud, *Beyond the Pleasure Principle*: 293.

39  Freud, *Beyond the Pleasure Principle*: 309.

40  Freud, *Beyond the Pleasure Principle*: 311–12.

41  Sigmund Freud and Sándor Ferenczi, *The Correspondence of Sigmund Freud and Sándor Ferenczi*, vol. 2: *1914–1919*, trans. Peter T. Hoffer, ed. Ernst Falzeder and Eva Brabant, London and Cambridge, MA: Belknap Press of Harvard University Press, 1996: 341.

42  Freud, *Beyond the Pleasure Principle*: 293.

43  Freud, *Beyond the Pleasure Principle*: 285.

44  Freud, *Beyond the Pleasure Principle*: 286.

45  Freud, *Beyond the Pleasure Principle*: 293.

46  Freud, *Beyond the Pleasure Principle*: 294.

47  Freud, *Beyond the Pleasure Principle*: 295.

48  See Gay, *Freud: A Life for Our Time*: 391–3.

49  Sigmund Freud, *Letters of Sigmund Freud 1873–1939*, trans. Tania and James Stern, ed. Ernst L. Freud, London: Hogarth Press, 1961: 333.

50  The phrase is Derrida's, from his long essay on Freud and the *Beyond*, 'To Speculate – on "Freud"', in Jacques Derrida, *The Post Card: From Socrates to Freud and Beyond*, trans. Alan Bass, Chicago and London: University of Chicago Press, 1987: 327. Derrida does, however, pursue this same material at length – and Freud's own rejection of such closures of reading in this instance. Derrida seems to be arguing that it is neither proper to pursue the materials for the sake of a psychobiographical prurience, but *nor* is it helpful to discount consideration of the life events for the sake of an unimpugned 'science'. See 327–37.

51  Ernest Jones, *The Life and Work of Sigmund Freud*, vol. 3, New York: Basic Books, 1957: 41, cited in Derrida, *The Post Card*: 328–9; Freud's emphasis.

52  Gay, *Freud*: 301. See also Freud to Jung, 6 December 1906: 'Essentially, one might say, the cure is effected by love. And actually transference provides the most cogent, indeed, the only unassailable proof that neuroses are determined by the individual's love life.' (Sigmund Freud and C. G. Jung, *The Freud/Jung Letters: The Correspondence between Sigmund Freud and C. G. Jung*, ed. William McGuire, trans. Ralph Manheim and R. F. C. Hull, Harmondsworth: Penguin, 1991: 50).

53  For a key text on the ethics of psychoanalysis see Jacques Lacan, *The Ethics of Psychoanalysis 1959–1960. The Seminar of Jacques Lacan*, trans. Dennis Porter, ed. Jacques-Alain Miller, London: Tavistock/Routledge, 1992. Lacan's focus there, as here, is on a theatricalised relation between a parent and 'child' (Antigone and Creon), the failed temporality of a father's embrace, across distance, and the unimpugnability of desire.

54  Wright, 'Psychoanalysis and the Theatrical': 179.

# 9

# THE PLACEBO OF PERFORMANCE

## Psychoanalysis in its place

### *Alan Read*

Performance and psychoanalysis are offspring of the same ancestor: the placebo effect. Despite transgressive signs to the contrary, both in their own ways seek to please, to be acceptable, and both are characterised by their psychological rather than their physiological effects. The relationship between the two was first consummated on a fine evening in 1889 when Sigmund Freud took a night off from the 'Congress in Hypnotism' he was attending in Paris to see a performance artist. Since that fateful evening the two have been artificially sundered to protect the scientific legitimacy of psychoanalysis in its flight from its origins in hypnotic performance. Seeking medical authority and the status of treatment, psychoanalysis might be reminded of its debt to a performance tradition. If, since Chaucer, to 'play at the school of Placebo' has meant to flatter with servility, the task here is to contest the intellectual sycophancy shown to psychoanalysis by practices in search of a spurious theoretical rigour, to reassert a prior place for performance in the psychoanalytic turn.[1]

The senses in which psychoanalysis was in its earliest manifestations already and always performance might illustrate ways in which the 'and' in psychoanalysis and performance can operate more critically.[2] In an age of Prozac and the resurgence of a pharmaceutical mind field, Jacques Lacan has become the midwife of psychoanalysis *beyond* the impulse of treatment and cure, beyond the pale imitation of medical integrity. His project returns us to its origins, located closer to the hypnotist Carl Hansen than to Hippocrates. As Adrian Dannatt says: 'Just as painting exploded in entirely unprecedented, unimaginable directions when photography took on the burden of realism, so psychoanalysis will revolutionize itself in the wake of its freedom from the "cure".'[3] But the return, while hastened by Lacan, has always been inherent in Freud's formulation of the field he invented. Like all good revolutions this promises to be as much a reprise as an advance and it is the degree of the return, measurable as the uncanny refrain of stage hypnotism within the talking cure, that will remind us once again of the inherent interdisciplinarity of these practices.

## Installation

Such thoughts come to mind amidst a temporary installation by the French-born artist Sophie Calle at 20 Maresfield Gardens in Hampstead, London, Freud's last home and work place, and now preserved as the Freud Museum. Here Sophie Calle has followed in a tradition of other artists including Susan Hiller and Cornelia Parker by installing her work between the folds of the museum's artefacts. Calle's project, *Appointment*, takes the form of a sequence of thirty short text pieces interspersed with related objects, some of which draw upon the Freud archive itself (Freud's overcoat, wedding ring, etc.) and some constructed scenarios introducing new but equally mundane objects to the collection. As a spectator you are never secure that the identities being discussed in the small texts are Calle or someone autobiographically close to her, whether it is the six-year-old who took to stripping in the elevator on the way to her grandparents' sixth-floor apartment, or the 27-year-old stripper whose blonde wig is torn off by a colleague in a fight. Some of the sequences are sombre; others are apparently lighter, but with a touch of foreboding (see Figure 9.1).

The joke is a good one (as is the Freudian slip) within this specific setting – for this is a site-specific performance, albeit a staging of the absent aura of the analysand. Memories and characterisations from a related past accumulate in this building and permeate its already redolent ether with inscriptions of its myriad consultations.

My interest in this installation is the attention it draws to the performative qualities inherent in the architectural cradle of psychoanalysis. This would be by no means the first time Calle has provided such a hermeneutic bridge between disciplines. Indeed, Peggy Phelan rounds off the opening of her celebrated essay, 'The Ontology of Performance', in her collection *Unmarked*, with a rhetorical ploy recruiting Sophie Calle from the 'other arts' to verify the draw of performance, the problematic of reproducibility: 'Calle demonstrates the performative quality of all seeing'.[4] But Calle, though a very interesting artist, is not a recruit who can bring credence to special claims made for performance's ontology, from beyond performance's own boundaries, as she is at odds with the very categories of artist that Phelan herself identifies. She is clearly not a painter or even a 'photographer' (although she

---

I was thirty, and my father thought I had bad breath. He made an appointment for me with a doctor whom I assumed was a general practitioner. Except that the man I found myself facing was a psychoanalyst. Given the hostility my father always manifested towards this profession, my surprise was total. My first words were: 'There must have been a mistake, my father is convinced I have bad breath and he sent me to a generalist.' 'Do you always do what your father tells you to do?' replied the man. I became his patient.

---

*Figure 9.1* Sophie Calle, Text from *Appointment*, The Freud Museum, London, 1999.

uses photographs in her work these are only ever the record of deeper performative strata). She is a time-based artist working principally with durational projects of simulation and surveillance, which implicitly places her within a performance tradition quite distinct from object-based work that can be physically assessed in space and time. And she is a performer whose very stock-in-trade is the kind of reproducibility that Phelan is questioning on behalf of performance. 'The performative quality of all seeing' is in fact a problem in the phenomenology of perception which has very distinct historical traces that are all about reproduction as well as representation. It is these reproducibles that makes Calle's installations so engaging and it is on this ground that some historical questions of the relations between psychoanalysis and performance might be worked through.

The perception of any space is always structured by this historical accretion, but for Phelan 'performative seeing' suggests perception differs on each and every occasion, that it is new every time. The naiveté here is that this new irreducible, irreproducible moment might for Phelan elude the circulating energies of the exchange of capital, retaining its potential for oppositional politics. Nothing could be further from the truth in this re-constructed second site of psychoanalysis, Freud's London consulting room, a mimesis of his original Viennese study, where all transactions are in the end ones of capital, where money is at the heart of the matter. This is not so much a world of free association as one of fee association.

## Circulation

There are a number of circulations at work in this place that make the question of the return of reproduction inevitable and playful, and that do nothing it seems to me to impoverish the status of what might have occurred here as performance and indeed enhances the sense of that activity and its history. Let us keep in mind Calle's work but look beyond the specificity of this installation towards some of its terms of reference within an historical context: that is, the specific cultural history of the emergence of psychoanalysis itself from within this site of performance. In the process of so doing, it might become possible to notice the reproducibles stacking up alongside the representations without disarming for a moment the power of the multiple performances within this history.

From the outset it is worth recalling the complexity of the professional's role at the end of the nineteenth century, when the distinctions between physician, surgeon, charlatan, dentist, barber and performer might have appeared less determined than they are now. The terms on which professional alignments were organised on one or other side of a disciplinary divide do much to situate contemporary practices, and their conditions of relating in ways that, Bruno Latour suggests, might never have been separated.[5] In this context I am interested in Bertha Pappenheim's (Anna O.'s) little-quoted likening of the talking cure to 'chimney sweeping'. Setting aside banal Freudian associations, one may wish to draw from the phrase an attractive sense of historical location coupled with domestic science: an image of architectural purgation brought about by the character who in local lore delivered good fortune and a dose of theatricality to the hearth. As in Herman Melville's short story 'I and My Chimney', narration is set off by proximity to the chimney, the 'centre' of the home both in its structure and function. For Melville's unreconstructed narrator the chimney has the added benefit of listening, for 'it did not like his wife "talk back"'.[6] At 20 Maresfield Gardens the hearth, which has heard it all, is mute for other, more mundane, reasons.

The first thing one notices on entering Freud's study is not so much the couch, for that has disappeared under a woven rug, which in turn has been temporarily covered by a white wedding/night dress and elegiac textual accompaniment left there by Sophie Calle, but the way the arrangement of the couch and the analyst's chair at its head rest against what would appear to be a chimney breast. On easing back the tapestry that drapes the hearth, it becomes apparent that the fireplace has been blocked in. The chimney still rises to the roof from this point, and is clearly visible from outside the house, but it is no longer open. At the head and foot of the couch are radiators. The museum caretaker tells me that Freud's architect son Ernst had, on arrival at the house in 1938, fitted a diesel-fired central-heating system that was 'revolutionary' for its time. The expiratory systems of hearth, fire and draught have here been replaced by an internal system of circulating waters, a new age of comfort and technological rationality. It had not always been that way. Above the couch and proud of the chimney breast hangs an image of a performance masquerading as diagnosis that points to a history of psychoanalysis prior to this centralising moment, when whispering eddies of the interdisciplinary were still at play.

The theatricality of the talking cure, its performative origins in mystic speech, the confessional apparatus, possession and exorcism, have long been noted by commentators seeking to disturb the originary myth of Freudian analysis. Indeed the very origins of the term 'talking cure' itself, in 'Anna O.'s' notorious formulation of the 1880s, has located the beginnings of Freudian orthodoxy within a lattice of verbal conceits, some would say lies, constructed by Freud in retrospect around the treatment and so called 'cure' of Bertha Pappenheim by the physician Josef Breuer. Much of this commentary, for understandable reasons, seeks to depose the overwhelming and suffocating authority of the Freudian 'beginning' for a heterodox and less manicured but more appealing complexity of continuities from earlier and ongoing concerns. The recovery of an early Freud, just prior to the revisionism of *Studies on Hysteria* (1895) is therefore the recovery of psychoanalysis within the province of hypnotism, magnetism and somnambulism: in other words from within a performance tradition. And lying, masquerading and malingering play an inevitable and overtly performative role within that tradition.

The trajectory of the talking cure from Freud's couch to the confessional platform of the day-time television of Oprah Winfrey, Vanessa Feltz *et al.* (with all their recent admissions of fake characterisations and simulated scenarios) is a distinct paradigm of durational performance – albeit punctuated by the regime of the 50-minute hour and of generic site-specific domestic performance that if temporarily unleashed from its mitigation 'as treatment' might reveal a legacy of unexpected delinquencies from within the heart of the analyst's domain. In this performance legacy, the long-

*Figure 9.2* Freud's study. Photograph Nick Bagguley. Copyright Freud Museum, London.

derided 'innocents' of analysis, contained and constrained by Freud's rhetoric – Anna O., the Rat Man and the Wolf Man – become the self-possessed forebears of Eleanora Duse, Antonin Artaud and Josef Beuys. Whether the placebo of performance 'did them good' is not my question, rather, are we willing to acknowledge the place of performance within psychoanalysis?

These borrowings from the regime of signs associated with performance do nothing to destabilise the efficacy of the cure itself – Prozac is doing that – nor do they intimate that the 'mad business is show business'[7]; rather, in the interests of interdisciplinarity, they once more seek for performance in the face of disciplinary disempowerment, redress. For if, as Michel de Certeau says, psychoanalysis 'moves forward over lands that are not its own . . . it becomes a "novel" within the foreign field of erudition', and further 'it is a fragile discourse because its postulate is the non-place of its place', then the terms of its endearment in an economy of circulating energies and beliefs usurp the very grounds for performance which it occupies and empties.[8] While de Certeau concludes that psychoanalysis can only be a 'fantasy', the reality of that fantasy for performance is a lost opportunity. For it was at the precise historical juncture when the belief in theatre that had been purloined by spirituality might have been returned with interest on the announcement of the death of God, that the birth of the talking cure displaced performance from its potential second renaissance. By implication, Adrian Dannatt believes it is not too late:

> Psychoanalysis guards a unique space that does not exist elsewhere in social relations, neither in the closest friendship nor the psychic's parlor, and it is in this defiantly indescribable zone that its continued importance lies, as a laboratory to explore the unthinkable.[9]

But if this unique space sounds precisely like a zone contested and fought for in the cycle of theatre avant-gardes of the twentieth century, from the site-specific constructivism of the 1920s to the intimate autobiographical live art of the 1990s, how has this coalescence come about?

## Location

Let us leap to an end which inevitably is also a beginning in order find out. By spring 1938 the complex conditions necessitating Freud's departure from Vienna and the Nazi threat had been realised. On arrival in London, Freud took up residence in temporary accommodation secured by his architect son, Ernst. In June 1938, referring to this house in Elsworthy Road, Hampstead, Freud said: 'It is difficult for us to live vertically instead of horizontally'.[10] In the latter part of this configuration, Freud was referring to the single-storey accommodation that his family had occupied at Bergasse 19 in Vienna and in which Freud had conducted his analysis and writing for 47 years. This architectural location is already the subject of a detailed study by Diana Fuss and Joel Sanders who, through a topographical and semiotic analysis, read the photographic record of Freud's home made during the rise of Nazism in Vienna by Edmund Engelman.[11] While Sanders and Fuss make incisive headway with this 2D record of this originary location, moving between the 'porous boundary' of photographic space and the fixed dimensional volumes of architectural space, they do not pursue the telling theatricality of these settings, or what might be described as a *fourth* dimension of performance. While Freud's premises in Vienna are now empty, simply adorned with the simulacrum of the photographs of what was once there, the Freud house in London is a more replete, uncanny mimesis of that original site of psychoanalysis.[12]

As Ernest Jones records in *Sigmund Freud: Life and Work*, Bergasse 19 was not Freud's first office. Freud had originally occupied premises in a newly built block on the site of the Ringtheater in Vienna which had burnt down in 1881 with the loss of 600 lives.[13] Freud and his fiancée, Martha, reputedly had tickets for the fateful night, 8 December, but had spent the evening elsewhere. Part of the rental proceeds from these apartments went to recompense those children who had been orphaned by the disaster. Setting aside the extraordinary poetic neatness of psychoanalysis's birth in a block which came to be called the *Suhnhaus*, the 'House of Atonement', there are more directly performance-related associations to be drawn out. It was after all at the Ringtheater in the early 1880s that mesmero-hypnotic fever had gripped Vienna and

Freud himself had first recognised the power of hypnotic suggestion through the stage practice of Carl Hansen. In his 'Autobiographical Study', Freud writes about his concern for the efficacy of treatment, his loss of faith in electrotherapy and yet his confirmed interest in hypnotism:

> With hypnotism the case was better. While I was still a student I attended a public exhibition given by Hansen the 'magnetist', and had noticed that one of the subjects experimented upon had become deathly pale at the onset of cataleptic rigidity and had remained so for as long as the condition lasted. This firmly convinced me of the genuineness of the phenomenon of hypnosis.[14]

Why this condition convinced Freud where it left others sceptical he does not elaborate, but he does note that 'professors of psychiatry' continued to declare hypnotism to be fraudulent and dangerous. Freud had seen hypnotism used in Paris as a method of 'producing symptoms in patients and then removing them again'; the Nancy school had used suggestion and hypnosis to great effect and Freud notes how it became his 'principal instrument of work' in the early days. He locates the need for this approach topographically; working in a large town in private medical practice, Freud comments on the 'crowds of neurotics' who hurried with their troubles unsolved from one physician to the next. But apart from this utilitarian purpose Freud notes something more salient for my performative argument: 'there was something positively seductive in working with hypnotism. For the first time there was a sense of having overcome one's helplessness; and it as highly flattering to enjoy the reputation of being a miracle-worker.'[15] This Ur-showmanship remains with Freud even when the strategies of hypnosis are replaced by free association. Freud acknowledged this debt in retaining, like some cod-certification, the image of Charcot conducting hypnotic master-classes above his couch. As Freud said:

> Hypnotism endows the physician with an authority such as was probably never possessed by the priest or the miracle man, since it concentrates the subject's whole interest upon the figure of the physician; it does away with the autocratic power of the patient's mind which, as we have seen, interferes so conspicuously with the influence of the mind over the body, such as is normally to be observed only as an effect of the most powerful emotions.[16]

Freud comments that it was not until later that he discovered the drawbacks of the procedure, a procedure that was in effect the recognition of the power of the mind over the body – the placebo effect.

## Elaboration

While one might concur with the political reclamation of complex identities for 'Anna O.' from Freudian misinterpretation, there are stultifyingly sensitive reservations to her own claims that she 'performed' her symptoms. The analogy between deconstructing this one case through performative strategies and the general statement that there are no symptoms, just performed constructions, is admittedly all too close to the nineteenth century's obsession with identifying the difference between authentic patient and malingerer. This rhetoric comes down to us today in the industrial West as the surveillance and monitoring of people with disabilities so as to expose the performance of their injuries and infirmities. While this panoptical scepticism is a gross perpetuation of injustice (there are and have always been real illnesses most of which at one time or another have been grouped under the catch-all 'hysteria'), it does not deny the centrality of the relationship between authenticity and mimesis in the talking cure. Bertha Pappenheim did after all explicitly tell Breuer that the whole 'business had been simulated', and repeated the assertion of invention on more than one occasion.[17]

If one root of the talking cure as performance is within the hypnotic tradition's tension between simulation and sincerity, another resides in the origins of the authentic sufferer/malingerer debate that arose on each occasion of a nineteenth-century train wreck.[18] Freud himself had drawn on the copious documentation of early analyses of trauma that followed railway crashes from the 1860s to the 1880s. The brutal escalation of 'commotion' suffered by those in railway disasters had long been known to give rise to symptoms that prevailed after and distant from the crash, and which were originally diagnosed as having their cause in the physical compression of the spinal chord. Given there was no visible means of proving this diagnosis, insurance companies faced with descriptions of tears, panic attacks and fear were left to adjudicate between the authentic sufferer and the malingerer.

By the end of the 1880s the concept of 'railway spine' had been replaced by that of 'traumatic neurosis'. Between John Erichsen's work 'On Railway and other Injuries of the Nervous System' (1866) and Herbert Page's 'Injuries of the Spine and Spinal Chord without Apparent Mechanical Lesion and Nervous Shock' (1883), the psychological theory of accident traumatisation became the dominant discourse expressing a condition which had been variously described as: 'fright neurosis', 'hysterical neurosis', 'libidinal neurosis' and, during World War One, 'war neurosis'. Freud soon abstracted trauma into a psychological function within the framework of sexual causation of neuroses, but the trace of the judicio-legal framework of the insurance industry, offsetting the credits payable to genuine sufferers against the debits to be reclaimed from malingerers, provided the prevailing economy within which the diagnosis of trauma was to proceed. It was at root a symptomatology predicated on the economy of performance.

This debate between authenticity and simulation extends deeper still, to the rationale of the psychoanalytic act itself. As John Forrester says, 'The context for the elaboration of an ad-hoc but sophisticated epistemology of lying by psychoanalysis is to be found in the medical practices of the late nineteenth century.'[19] In Forrester's reading there is no moral implication to this lying but an opportunity to examine the trust that underlies the institution of truth saying, the distinctive connection between truth and lies that operates through psychoanalysis. He traces a history of hysteria leading doctors on a wild-goose chase from Sydenham's definitions as early as 1681 where 'organic disease of the nervous system is mimicked', to Falret's observation of 1866 that 'The life of the hysteric is one perpetual lie.'[20] He outlines a range of concomitant professional strategies, from physiological attempts by doctors to outwit this deception, giving rise to the lie detector, to the collusion of the doctor with the patient, 'playing the same game' as Forrester puts it, and deceiving the patient through the use of hypnosis.

Hypnosis may have been the stage on which pains and symptoms could be suggested away, but also it was intended 'as a sure physiological technique for the duplication and reproduction of hysterical symptoms, as in Charcot's work, which met the reproducibility requirement of science by using the theatrical techniques of rehearsal and staging'.[21] It is the idiosyncratic place of reality in the psychoanalytic scene that encourages the patient to surrender the relationship between speech and sense, and it is the reality principle that announces the impossibility of the patient not conforming to rhetorical structures:

> This dialectic of lying, deception, and truth was played out between doctor and patient in a malign form in hysterical malingering, in a more benign form with hypnotism, both against the background of a search for an ultimate truth of the disease.[22]

In the context of a discussion of performance we might side-step the implicit moral question associated with the axis between malingering and authenticity, between reality and simulation, and reflect on the terms of this debate and on how in the fields of psychoanalysis and performance there was a simultaneous preparation for acts which were neither real nor simulated but, to use Mikkel Borch-Jacobsen's term, were 'surreal'. As Jacobsen says:

> Bertha, playing her role (her second 'personality') on the stage of hysteria, was also watching from the wings, as spectator of her own theatricality. The paradox of the trace (of hysteria) is nothing other than the 'paradox of acting', as Diderot put it, which is why Bertha concluded that 'the whole business has been simulated'.[23]

## Simulation

From the hypnotic domain, let us compare these claims with a document of 1891 by a Dr Foveau de Courmelles who, at the heart of a work on hypnotism, poses questions about the significance of simulation. Courmelles begins by defining simulation in judgemental terms as a word 'applied equally to persons who "feign" in order to deceive others, or who are themselves labouring under self deception'.[24] He is at pains to prove the possibility of feigned effects on the part of 'nervously affected subjects' in order to sustain an argument about the reality principle that all somnambulists maintain, keeping them safe from the two key dangers of external suggestion: criminal acts and submissive complicity with rape. These twin figures were the recurring threat to stage hypnotism in the nineteenth century and return in almost all dialogues about its safety and moral rectitude.

A Dr Gerard is recruited by Courmelles to give an extreme account of the neurotic's motives:

> A woman suffering from neurosis has no will-power, but something replaces that absent faculty; she is a liar in every comprehension of the word . . . Every hysterical subject craves for a pedestal, whether it is a velvet cushion, the foot-lights of a theatre, or even the prisoner's dock.[25]

Courmelles is more reserved in his judgements. In the interest of justice, he is concerned to detect simulation in hypnosis, to counter what he describes as the medical man's tendency to see in every case 'lunatics rather than criminals'. The deeper search is to distinguish between consciousness and unconsciousness, the voluntary and involuntary: 'Someone has said that it required great ability to play the fool, and that is by no means paradoxical; but criminals have often enough intelligence to play such a part.'[26]

There was an 'artificial vocabulary' of gestures in catalepsy which Courmelles aligns with the habituations of restored behaviour: 'We must always make allowance for training, and recollect that story of Montaigne, about a woman, who, having accustomed herself to carry a calf from its birth, carried it when it became a bullock!'[27] The society of simulators were sharing their techniques like the best theatre workshops. They had become 'addicted to simulation . . . encouraging each other in simulation, rehearsing amongst themselves, or even before the medical students of the establishment, the experiments to which they had been subjected; and going through their different contortions and attitudes to exercise themselves in them', until the dues of training could be paid back with the hagiography of the theatre artist: 'in the present day has not the designation of an "hypnotical subject", become almost a social position? To be fed, paid, admired, exhibited in public, run after, and all the rest of it?'[28]

Freud's colleague and mentor Bernheim had admitted that his 'great therapeutic successes by means of suggestion were only achieved in his hospital practice and not with his private patients'.[29] The invitation to performance within the setting of the hospital, as distinct to the invitation to therapy within the dialogue of the consulting-room, is reinforced by the image on the chimney-breast at 20 Maresfield Gardens. Freud understood well the performative allure of hypnotism and directly alludes to its sublation in the talking cure by marking its genealogy directly above the couch from which he practised.

Here was, and still is (thanks to the care of Anna Freud and the family maid Paula Fichtl), a lithograph by Eugène Pirodon of Charcot lecturing/performing for an audience of students at the Salpétrière, entitled *Une leçon du docteur Charcot à la Salpétrière*. It is an image of a painting by Andre Brouillet exhibited first in the Salon of 1887, then to great acclaim in the Exposition Universelle Internationale of 1889. The

*Figure 9.3* Eugène Pirodon, lithograph, *Une leçon du docteur Charcot à la Salpêtrière*, from the painting *Une leçon clinique à la Salpêtrière*, by P. A. Brouillet, 1887. Copyright Freud Museum, London.

print is, in its own right, an uncanny restoration of the painting, miniaturised and greyscaled. It shows Charcot with his patient Blanche Wittman who is in the familiar and weekly process, 'the Tuesday saga', of being demonstrated as a hysteric in hypnosis to doctors at the Salpêtrière Hospital.

Charcot opened his clinics on hysteria and hypnotism not only to physicians but also to the non-medical public. As Axel Munthe, an English physician, noted in his record of the Latin quarter and the Salpêtrière at the time of Charcot: 'The huge amphitheatre was filled to the last place with a multicoloured audience drawn from tout Paris, authors, journalists, leading actors and actresses, fashionable demi-mondaines, all full of morbid curiosity to witness the startling phenomenon of hypnotism.'[30]

With his literary colleague from this audience, Guy de Maupassant, Munthe had travelled to the Nancy clinic under Bernheim and was convinced of the fakery of what he described as 'the stage performances of the Salpêtrière', a 'muddle of truth and cheating'. Among the 'true' somnambulists there were 'frauds, knowing quite well what they were expected to do, delighted to perform their various tricks in public, cheating both doctors and audiences with the amazing cunning of the hysteriques'.[31] Munthe's purple prose has to be placed in the context of his own banishment by Charcot from the Salpétrière for attempting to 'liberate' under hypnotic suggestion a young woman who he believed would recover if returned to her family in Normandy.

Nevertheless, their contemporary witness to a scene that Munthe described as 'the Tuesday gala performance', a scene that Freud was very familiar with and chose to situate as a window to the origins of his own work on, and above, the couch, is in performance terms of great interest. Worthy of actors undertaking Grotowski's transformational exercises, Charcot's *grande hystérie*: 'would crawl on all fours on the floor, barking furiously when told she was a dog, flap her arms as if trying to fly when turned into a pigeon, lift her skirts with a shriek of terror when a glove was thrown at her feet with a suggestion of being a snake'.[32] Munthe likens the whole affair to a 'suggestion en masse', and there appeared in the newspapers of the day denunciations of these public demonstrations of hypnotism as spectacles unworthy of the traditions of the Salpétrière. But from the perspective of performance, it is clear that this was *all* these events were – the iconography clearly indicates their performative nature and the image that Freud chose to oversee his couch is a further exaggeration of this theatrical tradition. This, of course, is not to deny the efficacious placebo effects these operations might have wrought on their subjects.

## Innovation

In his only overt writing on theatre, the essay 'Psychopathic Characters on the Stage', Freud takes the Aristotelian line on the purpose of drama: 'the prime factor is unquestionably the process of getting rid of one's emotions by "blowing off steam"'.[33] Character and 'acting' are presumed to be central to the performer–audience relationship in which 'someone other than himself . . . is acting and suffering on the stage'. It is, after all, Freud notes, 'only a game, which can threaten no damage to his personal security'.[34] Freud's economy of theatre expects that suffering should not be caused to the audience, that drama should know how to compensate its spectators and that 'Modern writers have . . . often failed to obey this rule'. But here, as Adorno would remind us, lies Freud's symptomatic distancing of the contemporary in the reassuring embrace of the canonical.[35]

However, the modernity of Freud's own practice, the degree to which the talking cure was already and had always been to some degree a game, played equally knowingly by analysand and analyst, has an echo in his real interest in performance. From the 1880s to the 1930s in Vienna, Freud had time for only one contemporary stage artist, and she had little to do with the Shakespearean canon he espoused in his writing. Yvette Guilbert was a celebrated singer whose annual performances in Vienna were typical of her chameleon, hybrid style, a style that has more to do with a legacy of solo performance artists working across sexuality and gender today than with any dramatic tradition whose effects were to 'blow off steam'. She sang in a vast variety of personae, prostitutes and schoolgirls providing the most obvious of many axes of identity morphing. And she was to visit Freud's house at Maresfield Gardens shortly before his death.

*Figure 9.4* Photograph of Yvette Guilbert, dedicated to Freud. Copyright Freud Museum, London.

Her signed photograph nestles in the library shelves behind Freud's desk as another reminder of a repression of a contemporary counter-tradition in the formation of psychoanalysis. Guilbert's work explored a new realism within the conventions of the 'Chat Noir' singer and had an unusual preference for representing the low life of the city. The description of *diseuse* does not convey the formal experiment of her work combining songs with intellectually demanding lectures honouring figures such as Baudelaire and Verlaine. Guilbert was loved by Eleanora Duse who recognised the advanced physicality of her gestural range. Freud was an ardent 'Guilbertian', his interest dating to 1889, the precise moment of his fascination with hypnosis:

> That year, while he had been attending a Congress on Hypnotism in Paris, he had yielded one evening to a friend's urgings to go to hear a new caf'- conc' singer – 'for relaxation'. Instead of relaxation, however, he had experienced that night a deep excitement that he never forgot.[36]

From this point on, Freud describes a clear rupture in the formation of his field, from the 'cathartic' method, the discharge of symptoms through the hypnotic procedure, and 'psycho-analysis proper': 'So I abandoned hypnotism, only retaining my practice of requiring the patient to lie upon a sofa while I sat behind him, seeing him, but not seen myself.'[37] From this juncture Freud describes himself as 'set free' from hypnotism and begins almost immediately to denigrate hypnosis's screening from view the true interplay of forces that would provide him with his theory of 'repression', the repressed impulses of the unconscious and their conversion into symptoms. By 1900, hypnotic states had become 'that unfortunate idea that had been forced on me' and in 1901 that 'superfluous and misleading idea'.[38] Here the task of analysis changed dramatically from a process of abreacting affects which had 'got onto wrong lines', to uncovering repressions and replacing them with acts of judgement. The juncture is recognised by Freud in a change of name: 'I showed my recognition of the new situation by no longer calling my method of investigation and treatment catharsis but psycho-analysis'.[39] This is the date from which the psychoanalysis that is performance has to become the psychoanalysis that might have relations with performance.[40]

The reminder and remainder of the hypnotic history of this space of consultation was retained by Freud directly above the couch. The detail to the upper left edge of the Charcot image is a drawing based on the work of Paul Richer whose illustrations of the 'contortion' stage of hysterical attack were well known in their day. If ever there was a 'compulsion to repeat', that uncanny performance is played out here. Blanche is 'striking attitudes', no less potent than Lady Hamilton's classical poses or the *poses plastiques* that followed them in nineteenth-century acting styles, constructing for the attentive onlookers a 'typical hysterical attack'. This image, as Forbes Morlock has conclusively shown, is, in its own turn, an uncanny replication of a photograph, which, for the purposes of securing a clear exposure, would have required a still pose of 20 minutes duration.[41] Charcot described himself as a photographer fixing through clinical descriptions his observations while the multiple refrains at work here deny any definitive fixing of source and influence. Where in this scene is the 'original' disturbance, and where is its repetition and refraction through the conventions of photographic portraiture and hypnotic staging? The fixing gaze is that of a male audience while the 'Napoleon of the Neuroses' and his faithful aide Babinski stand by. While Babinski appears to gaze into Blanche's cleavage, a nurse's hands reach out to redeem her for the stretcher. Any 'ontology of performance' is destabilised by this show, counter-show and representation within reproduction.

The *poses plastiques*, which gave rise in the nineteenth century to the first exhibitions of 'nude statuary', body-stockinged performers posing for audiences, were not so far from the disarray of Blanche Wittman. Freud's daughter, Mathilde, said of the lithograph:

> It held a strange attraction for me in my childhood and I often asked my father what was wrong with the patient. The answer I always got was that she was 'too tightly laced', with a moral of the foolishness of being so. The

look he would give the picture made me feel then even as a very young child that it evoked happy or important memories in him and was dear to his heart.[42]

One might extend Forbes Morlock's penetrating analysis of the image of Charcot to the consulting room itself. There is a move from the visibility and demonstration of practice to the absence of seeing in the talking cure and therapy; the reproduction of the hypnotic scene or the location is replaced by acts of memory and remembering. Here the performance of the talking cure moves beyond reproduction to a paratheatrical state where the surreality of simulation through multiple 'fictions' is, as Hélène Cixous says in her reading of the uncanny, 'neither real nor fictitious, "fiction" is a secretion of death, an anticipation of non-representation, a doll, a hybrid body composed of language and silence that, in the movement which turns it and which it turns, invents doubles, and death.'[43] This consulting room which is neither 'real' nor 'fictitious' evokes the deadly double of the uncanny. The performative allusions of Sophie Calle serve to remind us of the haunting theatrical illusions in the place of psychoanalysis.

## Restoration

In *Civilisation and its Discontents*, Freud had summoned a fabulous representation of Rome in which incompatible places would coincide:

> in which nothing that has come into existence will have passed away and all earlier phases of development contrive to exist alongside the latest one. If we want to represent historical sequence in spatial terms we can only do it by juxtaposition in space.[44]

This has often been read as the rendition of the psychoanalytic act itself, but more prosaically it provides a means of reading the uncanny accretions of this speech-site with its lineaments in stage hypnosis, solo cross-gendered performance and durational live art acts. Here, in Freud's last year, text and site become one. With reference to Freud's final edit of his last work *Moses and Monotheism*, Michel de Certeau constructs a symmetry of textual and biographical space:

> In *Moses and Monotheism* the old man Freud has become will gather all of his essential theses around the idea of repression which had been '. . . the true point of departure for our extended study of psychopathology'. In sum he entirely recomposes *the* place that he had made for himself – psychoanalysis . . . But when he collects all of the furniture around him that proves the establishment of his own place, the other returns in the inevitability of an effacement; that is of filiation and of death. When Freud makes his inventory of acquired goods, he is really packing his bags.[45]

According to Freud's diary, his son Ernst had:

> transformed the house into a ruin in order to restore it anew in a more
> suitable state for us. He is building in a lift making two rooms into one or
> the other way round. Sheer sorcery translated into architectural terms.[46]

The sorcery of the uncanny had begun earlier with the building of the house itself.
Designed by the architect Albert G. Hastilow in 1920, it was already a reflection of an
earlier more sedate architectural period that Ernst described, not wholly accurately,
as neo-Georgian. So the façade of the house is already a recovery from an order of
the past in a play of associations that writes large the accretions of the images in the
study:

> The apparently irreconcilable demands for the absolute negation of the
> past and full 'restoration' of the past here meet in their inevitable reliance
> on a language of architectural forms that seem, on the surface at least, to
> echo already used-up motifs *en abime*.[47]

The ruin that Ernst mimics, one of the earliest acts of gentrified 'knocking through'
in North London, is itself a palimpsest of Freud's previous locations, simultaneously
reproduced and rendered in this final resting place. It is this very specific reproduction that makes a visit to 20 Maresfield Gardens such an uncanny encounter.

The fireplace in the study might be bricked in, discreetly veiled by a tapestry, but
delinquent draughts eddy around the couch. The chimney acts as a conduit that
blows both ways. It might let out the mutterings of the analysand like an amplifier to
the ether of other voices on air, but it also draws down unwelcome house guests to
the hearth of a discipline in disarray. The uncanny reminds us this is no simple
haunting but the revisiting of powers that have long been thought dead: 'at any
moment what seemed on the surface homely and comforting, secure and clear of
superstition might be re-appropriated by something that should have remained
secret, but that nevertheless, through some chink in the shutters of progress, had
returned'.[48]

The compulsion to repeat, through representation and reproduction, is not only
at the root of mimetic behaviour, of restored behaviour and of the twice performed
of performance, it is also inherent within the very setting in which those acts take
place, at the heart of the psychoanalytic tradition. In Freud's consulting-room it is the
restoration to their rightful place of a myriad antiquaries, books, masks and images
that construct a setting in which he might 'pack his bags'. He describes the
composition of *Moses and Monotheism* within this setting in recalcitrantly conventional
theatrical terms. Close to death, on the publication of this final work, in 1939 Freud
noted in his diary: 'Quite a worthy exit'.[49] In the Latin rite Freud's departure would
have been accompanied by vespers, an office for the dead, or in the ecclesiastical
word originally given to such soulful songs, a 'placebo', a pleasing performance of
passing.

# Notes

I am indebted to Mikkel Borch-Jacobsen, John Forrester, Sonu Shamdasani, Joel Sanders and Diana Fuss who gave talks related to these themes at the Institute of Contemporary Arts in London while I was Director of Talks there between 1994 and 1997, and to Patrick Campbell and Adrian Kear for their scrupulous editing of this essay.

1 See *The Oxford English Dictionary*, second edition, Oxford: Clarendon Press, 1989: 942.
2 The 'theatre' of Freud from Oedipus to Hamlet is already well known and poetically underpins both the authenticity of his operations and the field of practices these works have generated. The pre-eminent place afforded Shakespeare in Freud's study attests to his position in a canonical pantheon alongside the complete works of Goethe. Yet the prominence of Shakespeare here and in Freud's only titled writing on the theatre, 'Psychopathic Characters on the Stage', should not obscure a more engaging and multifarious dialogue between psychoanalysis and performance in his work and work-place.
3 Adrian Dannatt, 'Psychoanalysis?' in *lacanian ink*, no. 12, 1997: 43.
4 See Peggy Phelan, 'The Ontology of Performance: Representation Without Reproduction', in *Unmarked: The Politics of Performance*, London and New York: Routledge, 1993: 146–7.
5 See Bruno Latour, *We Have Never Been Modern*, trans. C. Porter, London: Harvester Wheatsheaf, 1993.
6 See Anthony Vidler, *The Architectural Uncanny*, Cambridge, MA: MIT Press, 1992: 42.
7 See Mikkel Borch-Jacobsen, *Remembering Anna O*, trans. Kirby Olson, London: Routledge, 1996: 89.
8 See Michel de Certeau, 'The Fiction of History: The Writing of Moses and Monotheism', in *The Writing of History*, trans. T. Conley, New York: Columbia University Press, 1988: 322.
9 Dannatt, 'Psychoanalysis?': 42.
10 *The Diary of Sigmund Freud, 1929–1939*, trans. M. Molnar, Freud Museum (London), London: Hogarth Press, 1997: 239.
11 Diana Fuss and Joel Sanders, 'Bergasse 19', in *Stud: Architectures of Masculinity*, ed. J. Sanders, Princeton: Princeton University Press, 1996: 112–39.
12 I am interested in such places as part of a wider project on the locations of locution, the speech sites of the metropolis that have shaped modes of communication at certain historical moments. See Alan Read, 'Speech Sites', in *Architecturally Speaking: Practices of Art, Architecture and the Everyday*, ed. A. Read, London: Routledge, 2000.
13 Ernest Jones, *Sigmund Freud, The Life and Work*, vol. 1: *The Young Freud, 1856–1900*, London: Hogarth Press, 1953. See 'Combustion', in Alan Read, *Theatre and Everyday Life*, London: Routledge, 1993, for an account of the historiographical significance of theatre fires.
14 Sigmund Freud, 'An Autobiographical Study', in *The Standard Edition of the Complete Works of Sigmund Freud [SE]*, vol. XX, ed. J. Strachey, London: Hogarth Press, 1959: 16.
15 Freud, 'An Autobiographical Study': 17.
16 Sigmund Freud, 'Psychical Treatment' [1890], *SE*, vol. VII: 298, quoted in John Forrester, *Dispatches from the Freud Wars*, Cambridge, MA: Harvard University Press, 1997: 75–6.
17 See Borch-Jacobsen, *Remembering Anna O*.
18 See Borch-Jacobsen, *Remembering Anna O*.
19 John Forrester, *Truth Games*, Cambridge, MA: Harvard University Press, 1997: 67.
20 Forrester, *Truth Games*: 68.
21 Forrester, *Truth Games*: 69.
22 Forrester, *Truth Games*: 74.

23 Borch-Jacobsen, *Remembering Anna O*: 89. It is not surprising that Jacobsen places Bertha in an overtly theatrical setting of her day, with its panoply of stage, wings and spectation. As George Taylor has shown in *Players and Performances in the Victorian Theatre* (Manchester: Manchester University Press, 1991), the theatre of 'feeling' and 'passions' of the early Victorian period, with its techniques of sudden perception such as 'the start' and 'the recoil' of surprise, were, from Garrick onwards, well-known theatrical motifs. Diderot's *Paradox of Acting*, maintained that 'sensibility was not necessary for an actor imitating emotion – the secret was to maintain a cool head in order to be able to give the impression of a warm heart'. But there was a continuing fascination with the dialogue between truth and artifice. Edmund Kean's technique of 'making points', the striking of distinct attitudes to signal new passions, was resented by figures such as Leigh Hunt who described them as 'trickery'. As George Taylor says in summing up the mid-Victorian period, the actors of the period 'relied on an artificial vocabulary of grimaces, gestures and tones of voice which playgoers had learnt to recognise'. While theatre, through the work of the Kembles in Britain, developed the beginnings of a notion of a psychological through-line to characterisation, the latter part of the century still saw handbooks of acting producing detailed instructions of how the passions might best be portrayed. But the 'staging' of the hysteric harked back to an earlier period such as Edward Mayhew's manual of 1840, *Stage Effect*, where he wrote:

> To theatrical minds the word 'situation' suggests some starting point in a play likely to command applause, where the action is wrought to a climax, where the actors strike 'attitudes' and form what they call a 'picture' during the exhibition of which a pause takes place.

24 Foveau de Courmelles, *Hypnotism*, London: Routledge, 1891: 151.
25 Dr J. Gerard, quoted by Courmelles, *Hypnotism*: 152.
26 Courmelles, *Hypnotism*: 157.
27 Courmelles, *Hypnotism*: 158.
28 Courmelles, *Hypnotism*: 159.
29 Freud, 'An Autobiographical Study': 18.
30 Axel Munthe, *The Story of San Michele*, London: John Murray, 1936: 224.
31 Munthe, *The Story of San Michele*: 228.
32 Munthe, *The Story of San Michele*: 229.
33 Sigmund Freud, 'Psychopathic Characters on the Stage', *SE*, vol.VII: 305.
34 Freud, 'Psychopathic Characters on the Stage': 306.
35 'The familiarity of estrangement in modern art, Adorno concluded, as opposed to the distance of the apparently familiar "classic" artwork, was a result of the very "repression" of modern art's effects.' See Vidler, *The Architectural Uncanny*: 9, for an extended discussion of this question.
36 Bettina Knapp, *That Was Yvette*, New York: Holt, Rinehart, 1904: 313–14.
37 Freud, 'An Autobiographical Study': 28.
38 Jones, *Sigmund Freud, The Life and Work*, vol. 1: 301.
39 Freud, 'An Autobiographical Study': 30.
40 The remainder of hypnosis returns one more time, for all time and conclusively for Jacques Derrida in 'Telepathie', writing in the first person as Freud, in Freud's writing:

> I've never given up hypnosis. I've simply transferred one mode of injunction to another: one might say that I've become a writer and have poured all my powers and hypnogogic desires into the writing, into the rhetoric, into the staging and into the composition of texts.
>
> (*Cahiers Confrontation*, 10, autumn 1983: 219)

41 I am indebted in the analysis of the Charcot image to an unpublished paper presented by Forbes Morlock to an MFA seminar at Sheffield Hallam University, England, on 10 May

1994, 'The Very Picture of the Primal Scene: Une leçon du docteur Charcot à la Salpétrière', and provided for me from the archive of the Freud Museum, London.

42  Jones, *Sigmund Freud, The Life and Work*, vol. 1: 230–1.

43  Hélène Cixous, 'Fiction and Its Phantoms: A Reading of Freud's *Das Unheimliche* (The "Uncanny")', *New Literary History*, VII (3), spring 1976: 548.

44  For a reading of this see de Certeau, *The Writing of History*: 312.

45  de Certeau, *The Writing of History*: 329.

46  *The Diary of Sigmund Freud*: 255.

47  See Anthony Vidler, *The Architectural Uncanny*: 13.

48  Anthony Vidler, *The Architectural Uncanny*: 27.

49  *The Diary of Sigmund Freud*: 255.

Section C

# HISTORY, MEMORY, TRAUMA

# 10

# FREUD, FUTURISM, AND POLLY DICK

*Elin Diamond*

On what was known as Black Friday, 18 November 1910, 500 women from the militant Women's Suffrage Political Union, hearing that suffrage was once again shelved for the future parliamentary session, attempted to rush past police.

'Everything is in movement,' wrote Umberto Boccioni in 1910, 'everything rushes forward, everything is in constant swift change.'[1]

'Following 1907,' Sigmund Freud wrote in 'On the History of the Psycho-Analytic Movement (1914), 'when the schools of Vienna and Zurich were united, psychoanalysis made an extraordinary surge forward of which the momentum is felt even today.'[2]

In the years before WWI, while militant suffragettes were smashing store windows and chaining themselves to city railings, Freud and the Italian Futurists worked toward reconceptualizing their epistemological fields. The dynamic violation of bodily integrity promoted by technophilic Futurists found a corresponding echo in Freud's metapsychological papers. Freud described a human organism pulsing with transgressive drives, held in check by a mental apparatus that he called 'a device for mastering excitations.'[3] Indeed Freud's language in 'On the History of the Psycho-Analytic Movement' bears a striking resemblance to that of certain contemporary artistic and political radicals. In 1911, Boccioni wrote to his friend Gino Severini about the manifestos he had co-written and signed – the 'Manifesto of the Futurist Painters' (January 1910) and the 'Technical Manifesto of Futurist Painters' (April 1910). The first, an imitation of F. T. Marinetti's 'First Futurist Manifesto,' promised to smash 'cult of the past, all things old, academic pedantry'; to bear 'bravely and proudly' the banner of 'madness' with which 'they' try to dismiss innovators.[4] In the second Boccioni and his co-signers railed against secessionists and independents. 'Dear Gino,' he wrote to Severini, 'I . . . ask you secretly for your judgment of who can sign our manifesto; we have full confidence in your judgment. But I must warn you that the signers must be young men absolutely convinced of what the manifesto asserts. Adherence must be complete without mental reservations.'[5]

A briefer version of this essay appeared in *Theatre Research International*, 24 (3): 264–7.

'I must now mention two secessions which have taken place among the adherents.'[6] Freud's reference was not, of course, to Arnoldo Bonzagni and Romolo Romani, signers of the first Futurist painters' manifesto, but to Alfred Adler and Carl Jung who, he claimed, distorted the theoretical bases of psychoanalysis (repression, transference, the unconscious, and the sexual etiology of neuroses). Adler was guilty of 'twisting' the disagreeable facts of analysis, of 'petty outbursts of malice,' and of 'an uncontrolled craving for priority.'[7] Of Jung, the man Freud trusted to lead the movement from Zurich, Freud wrote, 'I had not an inkling at that time that I had lighted upon a person who was incapable of tolerating the authority of another . . . and whose energies were relentlessly devoted to the furtherance of his own interests.'[8] Such men were little more than 'adventurers and profiteers [who] are always to be found on both sides in times of war.'[9] In *The Great Scourge and How to End It* (1913), Christabel Pankhurst, whose own movement was fiercely divided, echoed Freud's metaphors: '[War must be waged] not only on all anti-suffrage forces, but on all neutral and non-active sources.'[10]

To read 'On the History of the Psycho-Analytic Movement' as a modernist manifesto is to understand better Freud's attacks on a hostile public ('my work is called "eccentric," "extreme," or "very peculiar"') and a tone that oscillates between victimization and self-aggrandizement.[11] At the end of the piece, Freud's contentious 'I' arrives where most manifestos begin: with a fearless and courageous 'we' – those who labour selflessly in the 'depths.' Like the Futurist manifestos, Freud's is a rhetorical performance aimed at separating ignorant naysayers from those tirelessly in pursuit of revolutionary truth.

Formed in the crucible of this angry rhetoric is what I would like to call a 'modernist body' – a figure closely related to F. T. Marinetti's *fisicofollia* or 'mad body,' which exalted 'authority of instinct' as opposed to private feelings and emotions.[12] Both Freud and the Futurists posit at about the same time a body whose internal eruptions (Freud) and plastic permeability (Boccioni) complete the destruction of the ideal of human rationality begun by Nietzsche in the final years of the nineteenth century. This distinctively modernist body is also performative: deviating from the controls of the ego's rational intention, a body whose meanings are constituted only by its acts.[13] As Freud liked to personify his concepts, comparing the ego's repressive tactics toward unconscious wishes to the bourgeois homeowner turning out the stranger in the hall, I propose a performative counterpart to his description of the turbulence of human instinctual life: the acts of militant suffragism. In making this connection I follow Janet Lyon's excellent work on pre-war suffragettes and Futurists. In 'realigning' the discourses of the avant-garde militant suffragism, she argues that 'the rhetoric and tactics of the militant women's movement were enfolded into the foundations of English modernism, and [. . .] conversely, the closely watched public activities of Futurists and Vorticists in England helped produce the public identity of militant suffrage movement.'[14]

Lyon further argues that militant suffragettes made literal the violent exhortations of Futurist manifestos. Between 1905 and 1914, the Pankhursts and the Women's Social and Political Union incited actual riots: the WSPU's militant speech acts took as their referents the bodies of WSPU members, Lyon argues, insofar as they aimed to incite physical rebellions as tangible evidence of widespread and incessant civil disobedience. While Futurism's founder F. T. Marinetti called on his adherents to 'destroy the museum, libraries, academies of every kind,' it was a WSPU adherent, the artist Mary Richardson, alias Polly Dick, who went to the National Gallery on 10 March 1913 and took an axe to one of the British nation's art treasures, Velasquez' *Rokeby Venus*.[15] This action resulted, Lyon reminds us, in the very closing of the museums that the Futurists had been urging. At her arrest Richardson's words on the dock were uncompromising: 'I have tried to destroy the picture of the most beautiful woman in mythological history as a protest against the Government destroying Mrs Pankhurst, who is the most beautiful character in modern history.'[16]

Richardson's action, Lyon argues, was an attack upon representation, a political and aesthetic act that validated the suffragette slogan: 'Deeds, not words.' The hortatory excess of the Futurists had no referent in their actual behavior, Lyon argues, while the suffragettes put militant rhetoric into practice, committed the deeds to which the words referred.

Rather than take issue with this judgment, I want to expand its frame of reference, working not just through the Futurists but through Freud's metapsychology and Jacques Lacan's concept of the imaginary. The relationship of body to language, body to agency is precisely at issue in Freud's metapsychological papers. For Freud the instinct or drive was a border concept: a certain 'quantity of excitation' crossed the 'frontier between the mental and the somatic' and entered the mind via an 'instinctual representative' or idea.[17] That crossing was never direct, and certainly not empirical or evidential. The instinct attached itself to an idea and was only knowable through the idea. What is important to the modernist conception of the body is Freud's sense that the psychic apparatus was rooted in, and continually assaulted by, 'an incessant and unavoidable afflux of stimulation' – what Richard Boothby calls the 'substratum of somatic impulses and energies.'[18] Indeed I want to argue that the intentionality implied by the suffrage slogan 'Deeds, not words' is challenged by Freud's model of the psychic apparatus under assault. The turbulent body in Freudian discourse, the *fisicofollia* or 'mad body' of Futurist discourse, helps us situate and decode the embodied acts of suffrage militancy, and sharpen our sense of pre-war politics and performance. On her side, Mary Richardson does not simply embody the masculine magisterial discourse circulating around her. Her discursive framing of her 'mad' act presciently enunciates the limits of the modernist body.

'Gesture,' wrote Boccioni in 1910 will no longer be a single moment within the universal dynamism brought to a sudden stop . . . [but rather] *dynamic sensation* given permanent form.'[19] Such dynamism was achieved by a feature of the body's perceptual machinery: 'Because images persist on the retina, things in movement multiply, change form, follow one another like vibrations within the space they traverse.'[20] In *Instincts and Their Vicissitudes* (1915) Freud emphasizes the constant internal motor activity of human drives or instincts, while stressing their dynamism and variability: 'Every instinct is a piece of activity' whose 'very essence' is 'pressure.'[21] Pressure, the quantitative economic component of Freud's system, is a 'demand made upon the mind for work.'[22] While the source of instincts is somatic and unspecifiable, the aim of the instincts is clearer: to resolve internal tensions through objects that vary according to the vicissitudes of the subject's own history. Freud represents the instinct's constant, changing dynamism as 'successive eruptions of lava.'[23] After the original eruption, 'the next wave would be modified from the outset' – turned, for example, from active to passive – 'and with this new characteristic, [would] be added to the earlier wave.'[24] Freud claims that the accumulation of waves with their modifications or vicissitudes will 'present the picture of a definite development.'[25] Boccioni's 'vibration' metaphor similarly rests on pulsing repetitive movement, change of form, and accumulation. For Freud's internal biological system, Boccioni offers the artwork's 'given space' and asks us to imagine a horse whose image on the human retina is of accumulative movement: 'a horse in swift course does not have four legs: it has twenty.'[26]

In both Freud and Boccioni, it is difficult to keep dynamism separate from another conceptual intersection: simultaneity. Elaborating the lava image, Freud reminds us that an instinct turned passive (being looked at, for example) can exist beside one that is active (looking), in a state of unresolvable ambivalence. Eventually the active–passive oscillation will 'coalesce' with the 'antithesis masculine–feminine.'[27] But until that happens there is functional 'plasticity' and 'simultaneity' of action. Moreover, Freud's metapsychological papers describe the psychical apparatus as a 'topography' that separates the conscious system from that of the unconscious. The 'topographical point of view' produces 'the possibility that an idea may exist simultaneously in two places in the mental apparatus – indeed, that if it is not inhibited . . . it regularly advances from the one position to the other, possibly without losing its first location.'[28]

The Futurist object, Boccioni argued, must exhibit simultaneously the subject's states *and* its setting in a single canvas. With his fellow Futurist painters he placed the viewer 'at the center of the picture.' This meant understanding the artwork not only as 'dynamic sensation' but as an externalization of the topography of the viewer's mind. In the co-written 'The Exhibitors to the Public' (1912), Boccioni asserts that the painting becomes the synthesis of *what one remembers* and of *what one sees*. '[One] must render the invisible which stirs and lives beyond intervening obstacles . . . and not merely the small square of life artificially compressed, as it were, by the wings of a stage.'[29] In practical terms this suggests, in a painting, an interpenetration of lines and forms, which would draw the viewer toward the picture's center.[30] However, a more arresting example of simultaneity is Boccioni's *Fusion of a Head and a Window* in which a sculpted grotesque head, with braided (real) hair is jammed off-kilter into a window frame with real panes of glass above it. Neither in nor out of the frame, fixed only in its unfixedness, Boccioni's 'head' is a synecdoche of the modernist body.

Freudian and Futurist discourse and practice undermine all pretenses to a psychic apparatus, an ego, in control of its boundaries or distinct from its surround. For Boccioni, body and environment interpenetrate: 'our bodies enter the very sofas we sit on and the sofas themselves enter into us, in the same way as the passing tram enters into houses which in their turn hurl themselves on the tram and become one with it.'[31] In his 10 April manifesto, anticipating Marinetti's praise of *fisicofollia* in 1913, Boccioni asked, 'Who can still believe bodies are opaque [given] our heightened and multiplied sensibilities?'[32] The Freudian body of the meta-psychological papers also loses its apparent integrity and singularity. Its regulative mental apparatus contends constantly with disturbing pressures and excitations from internal drives, as well as external stimuli. Even libido, the sexual drive, which, when conscious, feels most like an expression of uniqueness, is in fact a mechanical urge joined to the same urge in others.

> On the one view, the individual is the principal thing, sexuality is one of its activities and sexual satisfaction one of its needs; while on the other view the individual is a temporary and transient appendage to the quasi-immortal germ-plasm, which is entrusted to him by the process of generation.[33]

For Freud the drive-riven body suggests no individuality. For Boccioni, it has no credible borders: 'How often have we not seen upon the cheek of the person with whom we are talking the horse which passes at the end of the street.'[34] If Boccioni emphatically left behind his perspectivalist training in favor of dynamic rupture, Freud in the metapsychological papers turned from the imagery of *Studies on Hysteria*, in which, vicariously digging along with Schliemann, he overturned layer upon layer of resistance in order to release the strangulated affect and thus the symptom. The futuristic spatiality of the metapsychological papers is striking.

As a movement in the streets of London, with hundreds of thousands of women of all classes marching side by side, with the WSPU committing acts of random violence, the *fisicofollia* discourse of drives, flows, aims, pressures, and of a psyche disarticulated from its body, seems entirely apposite. Indeed Boccioni himself accompanied the suffragettes in their window-smashing demonstration during the first Futurist exhibition at London's Sackville Gallery in 1912. Yet when Lyon claims that 'Suffragettes commit deeds. Vorticists and Futurists are all talk'; when she says the 'WSPU's militant speech acts took as their referents the bodies of WSPU members,' she denies the aggressive disarticulation of the modernist body, a body as politically meaningful to women as to men.[35] To posit the suffragette's body as a referent for a speech act is to enclose woman in the net of her own symptoms and to assume a transparent model of signification.

And yet, Lyon's gendered dualism (he talks; she acts) is itself symptomatic of the *Zeitgeist*. Despite their dynamism, their plasticity, their *fisicofollia*, Freudian and Futurist models are infected with a fundamental dualism. In Freud, libidinal instincts are inconceivable without ego-preserving instincts, and the plasticity of the drives, simultaneously flipping from active to passive, is soon settled teleologically by the dead hand of gender. The drives 'coalesce' Freud says – rigidify we might say – with the antithesis masculine/active–feminine/passive. Gender, says Freud, 'meets us as a biological fact,' although he adds the caveat of the speculative researcher: 'it is by no means so invariably complete and exclusive as we are inclined to assume.'[36]

Boccioni's theological metaphysics also tames his plastic penetrating and penetrated *fisicofollia*. Liberating himself from objective fact he arrives at a notion of spiritual expression. For all the compelling materiality of his canvasses and sculpture he was seeking a new finite 'symbol of our conception of the infinite.'[37]

As is well known, the suffragettes, too, were susceptible to transcendent idealizations. In their struggle to imagine the unimaginable, various suffragettes in WSPU parades took turns dressing as Joan of Arc, mounted on a white horse in full armor. Christabel Pankhurst referred to the martyred Joan as 'our patron saint.'[38] The younger Pankhurst had been thrust into prison with the rest as an 'unsexed shrieking sister.' She was the paradigm of both female militancy and its persecution. Wrote Christabel, 'the day of visions and celestial voices is not yet past, and there are women in England this moment who are ready to pay the extreme penalty for the faith that is in them!'[39]

A fuller picture of the modernist body discourse is now required: not only do we have the notion of internal body excitations; we have a dematerializing discourse: the modernist body is not only riven by internal excitation, but driven by fantasy, by imaginary heroes, saints, and, more vaguely, the infinite.

Let us return to Polly Dick and her deadpan statement in the dock: 'I have tried to destroy the picture of the most beautiful woman in mythological history as a protest against the Government destroying Mrs Pankhurst, who is the most beautiful character in modern history.'

To speak, in carefully balanced syntax, of Mrs Pankhurst as a contemporary 'character' on a par with a painted image is to recall Freud's mediation of the 'psychical' or 'ideational' representative in the psycho-somatic apparatus. It is through the idea or instinctual representative that the drives reach consciousness. Richardson may be illuminating what Lacan, reading Freud's theory of narcissism and the libidinal drives, calls the 'imaginary' register of psychic life. An infant's pleasurable attachment to her or his mirror image is, as Lacan puts it, a fixation on a 'salutary imago,' an 'ideal of unity' which contrasts acutely with its own infantile lack of motor coordination. The perceived/imagined *Gestalt* unity in the mirror phase becomes a permanent element of an individual's psychic life.[40] As Richard Boothby puts it, the mirror phase 'marks the point at which the impulse-life of the human being is decisively tipped into the register of symbols.'[41] But Boothby goes a step further: he links Freud's 'instinctual representative' to the Lacanian imago:

> In the mirror phase the primitive formations of the libido are thought to come into being in and through the recognition of a perceptual *Gestalt*. The imago might thus be taken to be the most fundamental form of instinctual representative.[42]

Having invoked the imago as the fundamental form of the instinctual representative, Boothby suggests 'that the Impulse could perhaps emanate from fantasy.'[43] As Laplanche and Pontalis put it: 'The origin of fantasy cannot be isolated from the origin of the drive itself.'[44]

174

What Mary Richardson's act *and* her discursive act in the dock reveal is the destructive intimacy of image and drive. We can appreciate her carefully worded explanation in the dock as a demonstration of a drive utterly in the grip of the imaginary. Kobena Mercer has suggested that 'militancy offers a set of signs that lend ideological coherence to intersecting and evolving marginal group identities.'[45] Richardson mutilates a sign (the *Rokeby Venus*) to traffic in other signs. That is, her militant suffragism was an attempt to gain access to, and to shape, the metropolitan public sphere. Toward this end, the modernist body had to be sacrificed – transformed into an efficient instrumental body in the service of politics.

What Polly Dick shows us most of all, however, is that to instrumentalize the drive-riven body is not to produce a predictable political trajectory. Desire of the image, identification with the image, are impulses whose aim is clear, but whose source remains as unknowable in a political woman as it is in the most influential of medical myth-makers, or in an avant-garde movement soon to be associated with Fascism.

## Notes

1  Ester Coen, *Umberto Boccioni*, New York: Harry N. Adams, Inc., 1998: xxii.
2  Sigmund Freud, 'On the History of the Psycho-Analytic Movement', *The Standard Edition of the Complete Psychological Works [SE]*, vol. xiv, trans. J. Strachey, London: Hogarth Press, 1957: 30.
3  Sigmund Freud, 'On the History of the Psycho-Analytic Movement': 85.
4  Cited in *Futurist Manifestos*, ed. Umbro Apollonio, trans. R. Brain, R. W. Flint, J. C. Higgitt and C. Tisdall, New York: Viking Press, 1970: 26.
5  Coen, *Umberto Boccioni*: xxi–xxii.
6  Freud, *SE*, 'On the History of the Psycho-Analytic Movement', vol. xiv: 48.
7  Freud, *SE*, 'On the History of the Psycho-Analytic Movement', vol. xiv: 51.
8  Freud, *SE*, 'On the History of the Psycho-Analytic Movement', vol. xiv: 43.
9  Freud, *SE*, 'On the History of the Psycho-Analytic Movement', vol. xiv: 38–9.
10  Cited in Lisa Tickner, *The Spectacle of Women: Imagery of the Suffrage Campaign, 1907–1914*, Chicago: University of Chicago Press, 1988: 9.
11  Freud, *SE*, 'On the History of the Psycho-Analytic Movement', vol. xiv: 23.
12  Cited in Apollonio, ed. *Futurist Manifestos*: 129.
13  The notion of a modernist performative body takes up J. L. Austin's concept of the performative, as a kind of speech that acts or enacts that to which it refers. It was Shoshana Felman, however, who insisted on the performative speech act's relation to a speaking body. As Judith Butler phrases it, it is this body that subverts the intention of the speech act: 'the body becomes a sign of unknowingness precisely because its actions are never fully consciously directed or volitional.' (Judith Butler, *Excitable Speech: A Politics of the Performative*, New York and London: Routledge, 1998: 10.)
14  Janet Lyon, 'Militant Discourse, Strange Bedfellows: Suffragettes and Vorticists Before the War,' *Differences*, 4 (2), 1992: 101–2.
15  Apollonio, *Futurist Manifestos*: 22.
16  Lyon, 'Militant Discourse': 121; Tickner, *The Spectacle of Women*: 134.
17  As many have remarked, James Strachey's translation of Freud's *Trieb* as 'instinct' is probably misleading. Lacan was most vocal, insisting that the Freudian *Trieb* has nothing to do with 'pre-wired' patterns of stimulus-response that one associates with the instinctual life of animals. *Trieb* is better translated as 'drive,' which in Freud's usage

signals much more variation between impulse and object of satisfaction. As Boothby puts it, 'It belongs to the essential nature of *Trieb* to be errant, shifting, deviant – in a word, perverse.' (Richard Boothby, *Death and Desire: Psychoanalytic Theory in Lacan's Return to Freud*, London and New York: Routledge, 1991: 30.)

18 Boothby, *Death and Desire*: 27.
19 Coen, *Umberto Boccioni*: xxii.
20 Coen, *Umberto Boccioni*: xxii.
21 Freud, *SE*, 'Instincts and Their Vicissitudes', vol. xiv: 122.
22 Freud, *SE*, 'Instincts and Their Vicissitudes', vol. xiv: 122.
23 Freud, *SE*, 'Instincts and Their Vicissitudes', vol. xiv: 131.
24 Freud, *SE*, 'Instincts and Their Vicissitudes', vol. xiv: 131.
25 Freud, *SE*, 'Instincts and Their Vicissitudes', vol. xiv: 131.
26 Coen, *Umberto Boccioni*: xxii.
27 Freud, *SE*, vol. xiv: 134.
28 Freud, *SE*, 'The Unconscious', vol. xiv: 175.
29 Apollonio, *Futurist Manifestos*: 47.
30 Futurist paintings whose surface dynamism draws in the spectator are Boccioni's *The City Rises* (1910) and Carlo Carra's *Funeral of the Anarchist Galli* (1911–12).
31 Coen, *Umberto Boccioni*: xxii.
32 Apollonio, *Futurist Manifestos*: 28.
33 Freud, *SE*, 'Instincts and Their Vicissitudes', vol. xiv: 125.
34 Apollonio, *Futurist Manifestos*, 28.
35 See Lyon, 'Militant Discourse': 121.
36 Freud, *SE*, 'Instincts and Their Vicissitudes', vol. xiv: 134.
37 Coen, *Umberto Boccioni*: 1.
38 Cited in Lyon, 'Militant Discourse': 124.
39 Lyon, 'Militant Discourse': 124.
40 Jacques Lacan, *Ecrits*, trans. A. Sheridan, New York: W. W. Norton, 1977: 18–19.
41 Boothby, *Death and Desire*: 28.
42 Boothby, *Death and Desire*: 27–8.
43 Boothby, *Death and Desire*: 28.
44 Boothby, *Death and Desire*: 28.
45 Cited in Lyon, 'Militant Discourse': 109.

# 11

# (LAUGHTER)[1]

## Ann Pellegrini

Naturally for the convenience and clarity of my little theoretical
theatre I have had to present things in the form of a sequence, with a
before and an after, and thus in the form of a temporal succession.
There are individuals walking along. Somewhere (usually behind
them) the hail rings out: 'Hey, you there!' One individual (nine times
out of ten it is the right one) turns round, believing/suspecting/
knowing that it is for him, i.e. recognizing that 'it really is he' who is
meant by the hailing. But in reality these things happen without any
succession. The existence of ideology and the hailing or interpellation of individuals as subjects are one and the same thing.

Louis Althusser

I thought I'd start this story at the beginning. But now I've decided
that's too late.

Holly Hughes

More than two-thirds of the way through his essay on 'Ideology and Ideological
State Apparatuses,' Louis Althusser arrives at what has become, in the three decades
subsequent to its publication, the most cited feature of his argument, his theory of
interpellation.[2] He is trying to account for the relation of the individuated subject to
the liberal state. It is not enough, Althusser suggests, to offer a theory of a wholly
repressive state, which bends individuals and groups to its will. In order to account
for the reproduction of the conditions of production, conditions that prominently
include exploitation and inequality, Althusser needs also to explain how and why it
is that subjects freely consent to their own ongoing subordination and exploitation,
indeed, how and why they come to misrecognize this submission as freedom. For, if
the story of state power is only a monotonous tale of overt domination, subordination, naysaying, how are we to make sense of the disquieting fact that the
subordinated come to identify with – find themselves in – the very conditions
that hold them in check? What secures the ongoing investment or 'passionate
attachment,' to use Judith Butler's term,[3] of the dominated to their conditions of
subjection?

177

It is at this juncture, between prohibition/regulation and production/normalization, that Althusser introduces interpellation and with it 'the subject.' Under the italicized subheading, '*Ideology Interpellates Individuals as Subjects*,'[4] he advances a conception of subject-formation that scarcely comforts. Reaching out through a plurality of sites (e.g., family, school, media, religion, law), ideology interpellates – 'hails' – individuals as subjects, fitting them to the needs of the liberal state and its on-going structures of inequality. To be a subject is to be subjected to and in some sense for dominative ideology (in Althusser's language, 'the ideology of "the ruling class"').[5] There seems no way to opt out of ideology without losing claim to 'being' at all. Althusser: 'Ideology has always-already interpellated individuals as subjects.'[6] Thus the paradox of subjection: the ideology that constrains the subject also launches him or her into being.

To come at this from the other direction: the conditions of the individual's emergence as a subject are the very conditions that bind him or her to the law. Individuals are preappointed as subjects – and before their arrival on the scene. For example, parents anticipate their child's future, and in highly gendered terms, even before that subject-to-be is born. Forms of family ideology shape and are shaped by highly specific forms of gendered ideology, and both participate in, are generative for, the normalizing structure of constraint and pre-appointment that is subjection.[7] What is the ritualized cry, 'It's a boy!' or, 'It's a girl!' but a command performance that declares interpellation is already underway?

Underlying Althusser's account of interpellation, and the violences that sustain it, are some familiar psychoanalytic notions, of misrecognition, repression, the unconscious, generative prohibitions. The famous scene of interpellation – 'Hey, you there!' – with its stress on the subject called out, called into being, by language, recalls Freud after Lacan. If Althusser ultimately leaves these psychoanalytic points of contact 'on one side,'[8] he yet provides a suggestive account of 'the subject' as itself a point of contact, a go-between of sorts, forged at the juncture of prohibition and production, individual and state, the psychic and the social.

Might performance offer a potential site of rejoinder, helping not just to illumine relations between the psychic and the social but, perhaps, even to remake them? Certainly, Althusser makes the turn into subjectivity a highly theatrical one. In his own initial presentation of interpellation, he figures subject formation as a kind of street theatre: 'There are individuals walking along. Somewhere (usually behind them) the hail rings out: "Hey, you there!" One individual (nine times out of ten it is the right one) turns round, believing/suspecting/knowing that it is for him, i.e. recognizing that "it really is he" who is meant by the hailing.'[9]

It is here, in this 'little theoretical theatre,' that we encounter the possibility of resisting interpellations. However, this brief glimmer of resistance, admitted in the *sotto voce* of the parenthetical – 'One individual (nine times out of ten it is the right one) turns round' – closes down in the next breath. Althusser writes, 'Experience shows that the practical telecommunication of hailings is such that they *hardly ever* miss their man: verbal call or whistle, the one hailed *always* recognizes that it is really him who is being hailed.'[10] Which is it: hailing 'hardly ever' misses, or hailing 'always' hits its mark? The fate of the tenth individual – the one who either did not turn when he should have or turned round when she was not the one being called – hangs on this difference.

In what follows, I want to pursue this difference and to do so specifically in relation to performances, on stage and off. In the admittedly schematic and frankly polemical scenes to follow, I stage my own theatrical turn, asking whether and how a collective space of performance might offer resources for doing subjection otherwise. I offer this series of ruminations as an opening gambit in what will become a far larger project on the matter of 'excess' and 'excessive' performance.

## Scene one: Smile!

If gender is among the founding interpellations of the subject, it also bears repeating. The call to gender – the injunction to do it so seamlessly as to 'be' it – is made not just once, but across a lifetime. Thus, the initiating call – 'It's a girl!'– is repeated in varying contexts, with valences of threat and approval, sometimes both at once. The social rituals of recognition (and of gendering as a form of recognition) take multiple forms: from the 'sir' or 'madam' at the check-out line to the decision 'Ladies' or 'Gents,' a decision most make so easily and automatically that the 'choice' between one door and the next does not appear as one at all. It is 'nature.' It is a 'primary obviousness' that the subject 'cannot *fail to recognize.*'[11]

Crucially, gender is also an obviousness that the subject cannot fail to be recognizable *to* without becoming liable to sanction, even unto death. As in: 'Are you a woman or a man, a lady or a gent?' Only in the breach does the bathroom as a site of intense regulation and production – through which door do you pass, 'as' which door can you pass? – do its policing work, its violence, with an open hand.[12] But I have in mind here another kind of street theatre, less overtly violent perhaps, namely, the verbal calls and whistles that perform gender in everyday life. To wit: 'Hey, baby, smile!' Sometimes subjection is a laughing matter, but for whom?

In *Jokes and their Relation to the Unconscious* (1905),[13] Freud stages the joke-work and – I will argue – heterosexual gender too as a kind of triangulated theatre. He does so by way of explaining a particular class of jokes, 'tendentious jokes,' jokes with a purpose. Perhaps it is better to say jokes with a double aim, for all jokes would seem to have at least this purpose: making the hearer laugh. Freud expends considerable effort distinguishing between jokes that are ends in and of themselves, serving no particular aim, and jokes that do serve other aims (that is, aims other than, or in addition to, making the hearer laugh). Freud introduces this distinction in the service of exploring the gap between the one who tells the joke and the one(s) who listen. As he says, 'only jokes that have a purpose run the risk of meeting with people who do not want to listen to them.'[14] Arguably, the success or happiness of the tendentious joke depends upon closing this gap. Under what circumstances can this gap be closed? Under what circumstances does the gap open to sight?

'Tendentious' jokes make possible 'the satisfaction of an instinct (whether lustful or hostile) in the face of an obstacle that stands in the way. They circumvent this obstacle and in that way draw pleasure from a source which the obstacle had made inaccessible.'[15] Elsewhere in the same chapter on the purpose of jokes, Freud says that, 'the joke *will evade restrictions and open sources of pleasure that have become inaccessible.*'[16]

Who or what is this obstacle to the happiness of a joke? And is the pleasure the joke accesses, by doing an end-run round this obstacle, a pleasure equally open to all? In other words: what happens when the joke is on you?

Freud imagines the following three-person scenario, what I am designating (*pace* Amy Robinson's analysis of the triangulated theatre of passing) as the triangulated theatre of the joke-work. Focusing on a subcategory of tendentious jokes, namely, obscene or dirty jokes, Freud proposes that smut is initially directed at someone in whom one has a sexual interest, and the expectation (hope) is that upon hearing it the one addressed will, first, become aware of the teller's sexual excitement and, second, become sexually excited in turn.[17] Evidently, in this interchange, there is no such thing as no interest; even signs of embarrassment or shame are only reactions against the excitement and, thus, in a roundabout way, admission of it.

Additionally, not just any one is addressed by the dirty joke. Freud explicitly identifies its heterosexual charge when he says that 'smut is thus originally directed [by men] towards women and may be equated with attempts at seduction.'[18] If the woman does not immediately yield to the man's sexually exciting speech, the sexually exciting speech ceases to be a pretext to sexual action and becomes an aim in itself in the form of smut. (Does it stretch the imagination to suggest that in such a circumstance sexually exciting speech stops hiding behind its official pretext – the pretext that it is only speech and not act – and reveals itself as a form of sexual action? If so, then we might here espy one way – surely a gendered and sexualized way – in which word and deed are not so easily distinguished.)

Barred pleasure in one place, the sexual speech changes course; it will seek its pleasure in the responses of the woman addressed. These responses may well include agitation and upset, but this is no bar to the man's pleasure. Freud observes that the sexual aggressiveness of the man's verbal ripostes will alter in character in the face of the woman's objections; the comments will become 'positively hostile and cruel,' summoning all the sadistic components of the sexual instinct on their behalf.[19]

Faced with the woman's resistance, the ideal circumstance (but 'ideal' for whom?) is one in which another man happens on the scene. Freud again: 'Through the first person's smutty speech the woman is exposed before the third, who, as listener, has now been bribed by the effortless satisfaction of his own libido.'[20] The second man (the third party) laughs *with* the first man and *at* the woman. In this three-person scene, there are two subjects, both men, and one object, woman. Woman-as-object is the social exchange of men. As will become clear, she is so taken for granted as man's object of desire as to be dispensable.

I want to stop for a moment on Freud's analysis of obscene jokes and the paradox that woman should be at the same time object of and obstacle to man's pleasure. Freud sees through her rebuff, making it evidence for her unconscious resistance to (hetero)sexuality:

The obstacle standing in the way is in reality nothing other than women's incapacity to tolerate undisguised sexuality, an incapacity correspondingly increased with a rise in the educational and social level. The woman who is thought of as having been present in the initial situation is afterwards retained as though she were still present, or in her absence her influence still has an intimidating effect on the men.[21]

There are, needless to say, obvious limitations to this diagnosis, which takes hetero-sexuality so for granted that it can thereby pathologize a woman's refusal of a man's come-on. Yet, Freud unintentionally 'outs' the regulatory psychic and social work performed by the dirty joke; the dirty joke functions, at least in part, as an inter-pellating call into place.

Even when the object of the joke is absent, a trace of her remains. In the three-way street theatre just described, the teller addressed his smut to the woman, seeking to seduce her thereby. If and when she failed to respond to his sexual jests, he calls on the third person, another man, as his ally. The woman may not succumb to his seductions and yield to his pleasure, but this other man will laugh with him and at her. What if we are in the company of men alone? How, in Freud's estimation, does the obscene joke do its work? The woman is bypassed, and the male onlooker is transformed in the telling into the addressee of the joke. Importantly, if the second man takes the place of the woman, he does not thereby become the object of the teller's seduction-cum-derision. This homosocial scene, between men, is made safe for heterosexuality by conjuring the figure of the woman. Though absent she is implied; her trace is an alibi of masculine and heterosexual innocence, just boys being boys.

We can, then, take the expression 'a side-splitting joke' in this other way: as a matter of taking sides. Freud suggests that jokes allow us 'to exploit something ridiculous in our enemy which we could not, on account of obstacles in the way [such as rules of civil social interaction], bring forward openly or consciously.'[22] But the stress here is less on what the teller of the joke cannot bring forth openly or consciously, than on what his audience cannot admit in the open. (Freud's jokesters are always male except, of course, when they are not – e.g., the 'riddle' of femi-ninity.) Jokes are veiled propaganda, in which the third person, the audience of the joke, is enlisted on 'my' side (the first-person teller) and against some second person, who is the butt of the joke. The third person collaborates with the teller by laughing at the joke.

What are the conditions of this collaboration? That is, what allows the felicitous meeting of the teller's joke and the audience's laughter? What gets in its way? A joke's failure is not always a technical one. Sometimes the joke misses its mark, laughter, because it is missing its target. By target, I do not here mean the object of the joke, the 'enemy' the teller seeks to expose in the joke. Rather, target here refers to the joke's neutral third party. According to Freud, the teller requires an audience predisposed to 'get' the joke. And getting the joke does not come down to the technical virtuosity of the teller. Openness to the joke, and to the laughing lifting of prohibitions it solicits, requires some sympathy between the teller and his listener or listeners. This sympathy might be as simple as the listener's good cheer; a listener in a particularly serious or sober mood does not make a good audience.[23] (Of course, there are exceptions to this too – as I will suggest in the next section.) At minimum the listener must be in a neutral mood; the best situation is the listener who brings good cheer and meets the joke halfway.

However, even where this ideal condition apparently applies – I am about to tell my joke, and I am in a room filled with people out for a good time – my joke may produce a result contrary to my expectations. For what if I am playing to the wrong room? What if my idea of a good time does not conform to yours? In such a case my joke may be greeted not by embarrassed but by outraged silence. Freud presents the unhappy situation in which the implied or actual object of a teller's obscene joke is the 'highly respected relative' of the person to whom he is telling the joke. (As in: 'Your mother . . . oh, I'm sorry, I did not mean *your* mother.')

In other words, the context in which a joke is told can trump the technical virtuosity of the joke, though it can trump in both directions. Two more of Freud's unhappy examples:

> before a gathering of priests and ministers no one would venture to produce [Heinrich] Heine's comparison of catholic and protestant clerics to retail tradesmen and employees of a wholesale business; and an audience composed of my opponent's devoted friends would receive my most successful pieces of joking invective against him not as jokes but as invective, and would meet them with indignation and not pleasure.[24]

Yet, to counter with an example of my own, learned from Freud: in the company of men, remarks containing little of humor may produce rainbows of laughter. One man's rainbow is another's, a woman's, rainstorm?

### Scene two: Oyez, oyez, oyez!

On 25 June 1998, the Supreme Court of the United States rendered its decision in the case of the *National Endowment for the Arts et al.* versus *Finley et al.* By an eight to one majority, the Court upheld the constitutionality of a 'decency and respect' clause regulating government funding for the arts. The National Foundation on the Arts and Humanities Act, as amended by Congress in 1990, required the National Endowment for the Arts to evaluate grant applications for 'artistic excellence' and now also for 'decency': 'artistic excellence and artistic merit are the criteria by which applications are judged, taking into consideration general standards of decency and respect for the diverse beliefs and values of the American public'.[25] This clause was inserted by the US Congress into 1990 legislation reauthorizing – vesting with government authority and funding – the National Endowment for the Arts (NEA).

The backdrop for the amended statute was the highly politicized controversies over NEA support of allegedly 'offensive' and 'pornographic' art. Congressional opponents focused their wrath on two awards in particular, both made in 1989: a grant to the Institute of Contemporary Art at the University of Pennsylvania for a retrospective of Robert Mapplethorpe's photography; and a grant to Andres Serrano, which was routed through the Southeast Center for Contemporary Art (an NEA recipient). Mapplethorpe's work was decried as homoerotic pornography; Serrano was denounced for his now-notorious 'Piss Christ,' a photograph of a crucifix immersed in urine. The 1990 decency and respect clause was framed as a bipartisan compromise worked out between those who would defund and dissolve the NEA altogether in the face of its assault on American 'values' and those who wished to preserve it, but wanted to do so without appearing to be defending 'indecency.'

At about the same time as Congress was heatedly and very publicly debating the future of government funding for the arts, John Frohnmayer, then chair of the NEA, rescinded the grants of four performance artists: Karen Finley, John Fleck, Holly Hughes, and Tim Miller. They just went too far. The four artists, who came to be called 'the NEA Four,' variously addressed questions of gender and sexuality in their performance work. The four sued. They sought reinstatement of their grants, and they also challenged the constitutionality of the newly passed decency and respect clause. The case that came before the Supreme Court in 1998, nearly a decade after North Carolina Senator Jesse Helms had taken to the floor of the US Congress to denounce Robert Mapplethorpe and Andres Serrano, concerned only the constitutionality of the decency and respect clause. This is because, as the case was winding its way through the courts, Finley, Fleck, Hughes, and Miller settled the first part of their lawsuit out of court. In 1993, under pressure of legal action, the NEA restored their initial grants and paid them some additional monetary damages.

In the Supreme Court's June 1998 ruling, the Court's majority held that the decency requirement was advisory only – 'merely hortatory,' in the words of Justice Sandra Day O'Connor, who authored the majority opinion – and thus did not constitute unconstitutional viewpoint discrimination.[26] However, the decency and respect clause would be unconstitutional, the Court held, if the NEA actually applied it in a way that suppressed 'disfavored viewpoints.' Not to worry, though: as the amended statute was currently being implemented, the Court reasoned, there was no imminent danger to free speech. As interpreted by the NEA and as parsed by the Court's majority, 'this rather innocuous amendment' (as it was called by Solicitor General Seth P. Waxman, the lawyer who represented the government's point of view in oral arguments of the case) did not really mean what it said.

Yet, it is difficult to imagine how this distinction between considering standards of decency and applying them works in practice except as an incentive to would-be grant recipients to bring themselves into line with community standards *before* they apply. To threaten censure is to enforce it – indeed, to enforce it all the more effectively once burden and proof alike are shifted from the government's side (law in its repressive/censorious form) to the grant applicants', who are henceforth called to self-censorship (law in its disciplinary/productive form).[27] However, the happy news for the constitution and its citizenry is that as long as the would-be subjects of state funding do not cross the line between favored and disfavored speech, the NEA need not cross the line between lawfully considering and un-constitutionally applying the standards of decency and respect. To put a sharper point on the matter: as long as grant applicants do not cross the line between decency and indecency, respect and non-conformity, the statute would not have to mean what it seemed to say.

This difference – between saying and meaning, between, perhaps, word and deed – flashed into view at several instances during the oral arguments, which were held on 31 March 1998. In an exchange cut by laughter, the justices pressed the government's lawyer:

> General Waxman: Well, if you're talking about – if we're talking about whether Congress can say, okay, the NEA is going to apply the following standards but it's not going to fund Robert Mapplethorpe, that raises many different constitutional concerns that don't have – in other words, going to single out one particular person, at that point may violate – it would have to be scrutinized under, for example, the Due Process Clause as to whether there is a rational basis –

> Associate Justice Kennedy: Well, is it constitutionally principled for the Government to do this by a wink, wink, nudge, nudge –

> (Laughter.)

> Associate Justice Kennedy: – approach, which is what you're suggesting was done here.[28]

The laughter fixes me, captures me in its parenthetical embrace. The 'wink, wink, nudge, nudge' is the light touch of the state, as it disavows its own power.

Powerfully forgetting the originating context for the case before them, the Court wrote off – laughed off? – worries of censorship as abstractions only. In a bitter irony, the fact that the four artists who initially brought the lawsuit had eventually received their grants (but only after they had fought for them) led to the astonishing assertion by the Court that the four had suffered no injury. In this parsimonious accounting, injury comes with a dollar sign or it is no injury at all. No injury, no cause for alarm, just a 'rather innocuous amendment.' Lawyer David Cole and the artists on whose behalf he was speaking were looking for trouble that had not happened yet. The Court could thus uphold a statute whose manifest aim appears to be conformity to standards of decency, yet claim, and even sincerely believe, it was doing so in the interest of both free speech and 'respect for the diverse beliefs and values of the American public.'

The American identity imagined and re-produced by such a ruling is an Americanness whose diversity is kept safely within bounds. The likes of 'Karen Finley and the three homosexuals' (as Holly Hughes has wincingly quipped, cutting to the heart of the problem) exceed the compass of the 'American public.' Their challenges to commonly agreed upon (but by whom?) standards of decency can be absorbed by the state only by jettisoning Mapplethorpe, Serrano, Finley, *et al.* from the meaning of America. Cast outside the magic circle of 'we the people,' their unassimilable difference functions as constitutive outside, the state's and the liberal subject's excessive remainder. What is this but identity's disavowed dependence on differences internal to it?

## Scene three: Repeat after me:
## Holly Hughes' *Preaching to the Perverted*

That individuals must continuously be called back into line, into alignment with disciplinary norms, suggests not the fulsome success of interpellation into identity but the ever threatening possibility of failure. In her own extension of Althusser's theory of interpellation, Judith Butler suggests the ambivalent course of name-calling. Though called one thing, I may become another; or I may become that name, but do it – that name, that identity – in ways counter to the terms first given me, first given *as* me.[29] Butler calls this 'the traumatic and productive iterability of power,'[30] by which the 'I' can come to resignify the interpellation that has constituted identity as a kind of injury.

In her 1998/9 performance piece, *Preaching to the Perverted*, first presented in a workshop version at New York City's Dixon Place in the summer of 1998, Holly Hughes returned to her own traumatic encounter with disciplinary power. In the piece, Hughes stages – better: re-stages – the oral arguments presented to the nine justices of the Supreme Court in March 1998; she also performs the majority opinion that upheld the decency standards. Importantly, and importantly unlike the Court, she does not bracket the larger political and social context 'behind' the *National Endowment for the Arts et al.* v. *Karen Finley et al.* Hughes explicitly foregrounds the case's cultural surround, pronouncing a litany of the abjected:

Museum Director Dennis Barrie, arrested in Cincinnati for . . .
2 Live Crew arrested in Florida . . .
Jock Sturges arrested in San Francisco,
Annie Sprinkle . . .
Carlos Guiterrez Solana . . .
2 Live Crew, 2 Live Crew, 2 Live Crew,
Helms orders audits of NEA recipients . . .
Watermelon Woman . . .
Urban Bush Woman . . .
Today in San Diego!
Today in Atlanta!
Today in San Antonio!
Audre Lorde, Marlon Riggs!
Today in normal, Illinois, David Wojnarowicz!

> Heather Has Two Mommies, Heather Has Two Mommies, Heather
> has . . .
> 2 Live Crew, 2 Live Crew, 2 Live Crew, 2 Live Crew![31]

In an act of re-naming, Hughes calls upon her audience to remember – re-call – with her. If this renewed naming does not undo the injuries of racism, homophobia, sexism that she and the other artists she names have variously endured, it yet refuses to let those earlier namings be the end of the story nor even its absolute origin.

Suggestively, although Hughes provides the social context behind the case, she refuses to pose this 'behind' as unmediated origin, as a pure moment 'before.' 'I thought I'd start this story at the beginning. But now I've decided that's too late.' We begin, then, *in medias res*, already in hot water, unable ever to recover a moment before – before subjection, perhaps?

The medium of performance allows Hughes to get at, and help her audience glimpse, the ritual performances of the state. She conjures something of the mechanisms whereby American national identity is performatively instated. One of those apparatuses is 'Justice.' At times, she will make a joke of state justice's performative dimension, as when she calls the Supreme Court 'a long running hit.' In an hilarious sequence, tinged with rage, Hughes recalls waiting in line – but was it the right one?, she worries – to get into the hearing. She had that rare commodity, a ticket to the big show.

The 'Supremes,' as she calls them more than once, are 'a situation comedy. A stable of regulars face a zany new set of problems everyday.' The joke has a ring of truth; the Supreme Court hearing is a spectacular show, with its ticketed audience commanded to silence. Hughes sets the scene, projecting her audience backwards to March 1998 and into the place she once sat:

> When all the visitors are seated
> One of the secret service men greets us with this:
> 'ok, here's the deal.
> You respect us
> We'll respect you.'
>  . . . .
> The warm-up act concludes with yet another reminder
> That *there is absolutely no talking in the US Supreme Court!*
> (emphasis in original; ellipsis added)

To be sure, silence is usually the worst enemy of the comedic performance. But, as the government transcript of the 1998 Supreme Court hearing suggests, with its parenthetical '(Laughter),' state justice had provided its own laugh track.

The 'warm-up act,' as she calls it, enjoins the Supreme Court's audience to silence, calling them to bear mute witness to the operations of justice. The silence constitutes and confirms its audience not just as mute witnesses to their own silencing but as willing participants in it. 'We, the people' are the ones who sit and silently watch the actual hearing unfold as well as the larger and national audience implied by the law, namely, 'the American public.'

By contrast, *Preaching to the Perverted* helps to imagine another position for the audience, and its solo performer, to occupy. The command to speechlessness that had once silenced Hughes can do so no longer. In re-living the demand – *Silence in the court!* – she breaks it, bringing sound to silence with her words, her body movement, and with the laughter of her audience. The audience plays the part Hughes once played, when she was an audience member at the hearing of 'her' case. This requires imaginatively identifying with her abjection, but with a crucial difference. The audience of her performance is not asked to make the same forced choice that had been presented to her: between social death and, what may amount to the same thing, forms of national belonging that depend upon the marking out and exclusion of a range of 'excessive' others, whose 'differences' scandalize the contract of Americanness, resisting absorption into the one of 'us.'

Hughes out-performs the state, and in this double sense: she brings out the performative dimension of subjection to and for national belonging; and her embodied acts before an audience call up a different sort of public: one in which subjection might be lived out differently. In the space opened by her performance, those who have been defined as outside the nation's bounds – its extra-national subjects – may come together to form and inhabit a counter-public.

In this regard, then, *Preaching to the Perverted* draws its audience into a project of collective 'disidentification,' a term I am borrowing from José Esteban Muñoz. In *Disidentifications: Queers of Color and the Performance of Politics*, he advances a conception of disidentification that borrows at once from psychoanalysis and Marxism. By disidentification he means strategies of resistance undertaken by the oppressed that work 'on and against dominant ideology.' It is a 'third mode,' which refuses the either/or of identification with/assimilation to dominant norms or a counter-identification/reversal that is determined by what it would resist. Instead, as he writes, disidentification 'is a strategy that tries to transform a cultural logic from within, always laboring to enact permanent structural change while at the same time valuing the importance of local or everyday struggles of resistance.'[32] From 'inside' ideology, then, the 'disidentificatory subject' works to transform the conditions of her or his own pre-appointment as subject.[33]

One of the things Muñoz is trying to theorize is how and under what circumstances misrecognition might be politicized, in what ways getting – doing – interpellation 'wrong' might offer unanticipated resources for reconfiguring self and community. Disidentification, he cautions, is not a simple matter of 'pick[ing] and choos[ing] what one takes out of an identification.' In place of the wishful fantasy of setting outside or somehow leaving behind all that has shamed and injured, there is the possibility, painful and necessary, of reworking those 'politically dubious or shameful components' of identity, investing them with new life.[34]

Muñoz proposes performance as a rich site for just such collective reimaginings and remakings. *Preaching to the Perverted* seems to me an especially powerful instance of this performed and performative renewal in which injury – perhaps identity *as* injury – is not so much left behind as it is worked on and through.

As Ann Cvetkovich has suggested,[35] the trauma of identity that Hughes relives and works through is both collective and individual. By resituating personal trauma within a national frame, Hughes lays bare its political dimensions. Not only this, but identity 'itself' is revealed as a kind of trauma. Hughes connects the trauma of national identity to family and gender–racial formation. She makes this individual–state link by intercutting her public stories – the censorship of 'indecent' art, the Supreme Court hearing, the American romanticization of childhood and related demonization of homosexuality – with reminiscences of Michigan summers when she was a girl and her passion for the American flag her family raised at their cabin. In this retelling, her younger self's passionate attachment to the family flag provides a way to negotiate the demands still being made of Hughes. Her flag – 'Not all flags. Just ours' – does not symbolize her attachment to the abstraction Americanness, but comes to constitute a way for her to make some sort of peace with her own whiteness or, rather, with all that is done in its name,

> To me, she was a thing,
> the most beautiful thing we owned.
> The red was completely without orange,
> the kind of red Michigan tomatoes can only dream of.
> The blue was the fearless eye of the lake after she woke up from winter,
> And the white was
> nothing to be ashamed of.

This whiteness and its shaming return later in *Preaching to the Perverted*, when Hughes leads her audience on a guided tour of the Supreme Court building – a tour she did not get to have during her own 1998 visit to the nation's capital. She had to do it for herself. Reading from her imaginary guide to the architectural splendor of the Supreme Court, she tells us that the depression-era workers who built the Court ran out of materials. They needed to come up with something 'that would stay/Cold and white no matter what,'

> So instead of using marble the builders used bricks of ice cream.
> . . . .
> The ice cream used in the construction of the Supreme Court
> Is a type commonly referred to as 'vanilla'
> But there is nothing vanilla about it,
> there is no flavor to this ice cream
> It is merely white.
> (ellipsis added)

Reveries on the bricks of vanilla ice cream take her home again, to 'Kiwanis club father–daughter banquets / In Saginaw, Michigan' where the food 'plops' onto paper plates, ice cream right next to the Salisbury steak. 'The ice cream was cold and hard and white and so was I,' Hughes recounts. Bricks of ice cream, bricks of state, building blocks of subjection: the individual is linked to the state through family formations of race, class, gender.

But these links are not the all of it. *Preaching to the Perverted* enacts the possibility of turning another way, reworking the ties that bind 'the subject' – to identity, to the state, to race and sex – as 'truth'. Who or what are the 'Perverted' of her title? A popular and colloquial reference to 'perversions' of justice does not seem out of place, though it is Hughes, and not the nine Supreme Court justices, who must bear the weight of this justice perverted.

The term perversion also recalls Freud's discussion of the sexual perversions in *Three Essays on the Theory of Sexuality*.[36] There, perversion appears as a turning away from the expected course, a turning away that serves to define the normal. Finally, this notion of turning away also recalls Althusser's 'little theoretical theatre,' and that tenth man, the one whom the 'practical telecommunication of hailings' has somehow missed or at least has not hit in the entirety. The hail rings out: '"Hey, you there!" One individual (nine times out of ten it is the right one) turns round.'[37] What if the tenth man, the one who turns the wrong way or at the wrong time, is a woman, Holly Hughes? In the space of her embodied performance, laughter re-turns us to the fresh work of renewing and remaking a social world.

## Notes

1  This writing has been profoundly shaped through conversations (collaborations in the best possible sense) with Janet Jakobsen, Linda Schlossberg, and José Esteban Muñoz. I am particularly grateful to José for inviting me to take part in a roundtable discussion on performance at the October 1999 meeting of the American Studies Association. Conversations with José and with the other members of that roundtable – Ann Cvetkovich, Jason King, Carmelita Tropicana (Alina Troyano), and Holly Hughes – reverberate throughout this essay. Thanks, lots of them, also to Patrick Campbell and Adrian Kear for including me in this volume. Finally, I want to mark my debt to the students at Barnard College and New York University with whom I re-read Althusser's 'Ideology and Ideological State Apparatuses' during fall 1999. This essay is my extended thank you note to my students, from whom I learned, and continue to learn, so much.

2  Written January–April 1969, 'Ideology and Ideological State Apparatuses' was first published in *La Pensée*, in 1970. It subsequently appeared in a collection of Althusser's essays, *Lenin and Philosophy and Other Essays*, trans. B. Brewster, New York: Monthly Review Press, 1971: 127–86. All citations to his essay are from this 1971 volume.

3  Judith Butler, *The Psychic Life of Power*, Stanford, CA: Stanford University Press, 1997: 102. I am pursuing lines of flight opened up by Butler's psychoanalytically informed return to Althusser and Foucault and by José Esteban Muñoz's *Disidentifications: Queers of Color and the Performance of Politics*, Minneapolis, MN: University of Minnesota Press, 1999.

4  Althusser, 'Ideology and Ideological State Apparatuses': 170.

5  Althusser, 'Ideology': 146.

6  Althusser, 'Ideology': 175.

7  Althusser, 'Ideology': 176.

8  Althusser, 'Ideology': 176. Of course, I am myself setting to one side some of the

limitations of Althusser's conception of the liberal state (which he imagines as a police state with highly centralized forms of power) as well as his ultimately underdeveloped picture of subjectivity and resistance. Mark Poster is helpful on these issues. He notes that the modern state works through multiple and decentered sites, which thus multiply not simply locations within which power operates, but also locations for resistance. If power is dispersed, so too are the potential locations – and forms – of resistance. Relatedly, to the extent that Althusser refers to 'the subject,' its particular function and form, as reproducing relations of production, he makes subjection a functionalist matter: reproducing class relations and with them exploitative relations of production. Class, for Althusser, is the first and last determination of 'the subject.' He thus allows little room for the complex processes of differentiation, both social and psychic, through and in which 'the subject' is only ever a provisional unity. These limitations, and they are not insignificant, do not block the resources Althusser does offer for trying to think between the psychic and the social. Althusser, then, must serve as point of departure, not first and last word. See Mark Poster, *Foucault, Marxism and History: Mode of Production versus Mode of Information*, Cambridge: Polity Press, 1984.

9  Althusser, 'Ideology': 174–5.
10 Althusser, 'Ideology': 174, emphasis added.
11 Althusser, 'Ideology': 171–2.
12 See Judith Halberstam's discussion of 'the bathroom problem,' in *Female Masculinity*, Durham, NC: Duke University Press, 1998: 20–9.
13 Sigmund Freud, *Jokes and their Relation to the Unconscious* (1905), in *The Standard Edition of the Complete Psychological Works of Sigmund Freud*, vol. VIII, ed. and trans. J. Strachey, London: Hogarth Press, 1955.
14 Freud, *Jokes and their Relation to the Unconscious*: 90.
15 Freud, *Jokes and their Relation to the Unconscious*: 101.
16 Freud, *Jokes and their Relation to the Unconscious*: 103, emphasis in original.
17 Freud, *Jokes and their Relation to the Unconscious*: 97.
18 Freud, *Jokes and their Relation to the Unconscious*: 97.
19 Freud, *Jokes and their Relation to the Unconscious*: 99.
20 Freud, *Jokes and their Relation to the Unconscious*: 100.
21 Freud, *Jokes and their Relation to the Unconscious*: 101.
22 Freud, *Jokes and their Relation to the Unconscious*: 103.
23 Freud, *Jokes and their Relation to the Unconscious*: 145.
24 Freud, *Jokes and their Relation to the Unconscious*: 145.
25 Section 954(d)(1) of the amended National Foundation on the Arts and Humanities Act. Qtd. in Justice Antonin Scalia's concurring opinion. Available at http://www.csulb.edu/~jvancamp/doc28.html. This website also provides the full text of the Court's majority opinion, written by Justice Sandra Day O'Connor, and Justice David Souter's lone dissent. Scalia (concurring) and Souter (dissenting) at least understood that, against the government's own claims to the contrary, the clause *did* make decency and respect criteria for awarding NEA grants. Where Scalia and Souter disagreed, and profoundly, though, was on the issue of the clause's constitutionality.
26 http://www.csulb.edu/~jvancamp/doc28.html.
27 In fact, this was precisely the worry of David Cole, the lawyer representing the artists. As he told the Court:

> We – I represent the National Association of Artists' Organizations [which joined Finley, Fleck, Hughes, and Miller as respondents], which represents 500 arts institutions and individuals who have regularly applied for, are denied funding by the NEA. What the – the claim is that the application of such open-ended criteria to an applicant creates a chill which . . . and you can't sit back and let that chill affect artists' speech in the meantime.

Unofficial transcript of the oral arguments in *National Endowment for the Arts et al.* v. *Karen Finley et al.* (31 March 1998). Available at http://www.csulb.edu/~jvancamp/doc26/html.

28 Unofficial transcript, http://www.csulb.edu/~jvancamp/doc26/html.

29 Butler, *The Psychic Life of Power*: 83–105.

30 Butler, *The Psychic Life of Power*: 104.

31 Holly Hughes, 'Preaching to the Perverted,' unpublished manuscript, 1998/9. Unless otherwise noted, I am reproducing the line breaks, punctuation, and capitalization preferences of Hughes' script. I am extremely grateful to her for letting me quote from it.

32 Muñoz, *Disidentifications*: 11–12.

33 Muñoz, *Disidentifications*: 12.

34 Muñoz, *Disidentifications*: 12.

35 Ann Cvetkovich, 'Performances of Crossing – A Roundtable,' American Studies Association annual meeting, Montreal, Canada (October 1999).

36 Sigmund Freud, *Three Essays on the Theory of Sexuality* (1905), in *The Standard Edition of the Complete Psychological Works of Sigmund Freud*, vol. VII, ed. and trans. J. Strachey, London: Hogarth Press, 1955.

37 Althusser, 'Ideology': 174–5.

# 12

# SPEAK WHITENESS

## Staging 'race', performing responsibility

*Adrian Kear*

. . . it is to works of art that has fallen the burden of wordlessly
asserting what is barred to politics.

Theodor Adorno[1]

## Introduction

This essay presents an initial, provisional attempt to outline some of the complex,
contradictory currents in the cultural dynamics of 'multi-racist Britain' at their point
of intersection with contemporary British performance practice. It tentatively seeks
to engage with the specific temporalities and geographies that mark its subject out as
'a little local difficulty' – to resituate a favourite colonialist trope – without shying
away from more 'global' issues. In particular, it is concerned to pursue the links
connecting white racial fantasies and racist identities with psychoanalytic conceptions of subjectivity. Following the groundbreaking work of Frantz Fanon in *Black
Skin, White Masks*, the essay argues that the historical conjunction of colonial relations
of power and psychoanalysis's theorisation of unconscious desire invests the latter
with particular importance in the analysis of the psychic and social identifications
produced within this racialised 'regime of representation'.[2] At the same time, it
attempts to suggest that as these formations are historicised – or are in the process of
being historicised – alternate frameworks for understanding and undertaking inter-
subjective relations are called for. By tracing the interplay of dominant, residual and
emergent discursive currents in a precise historical event cum 'moment', the paper
endeavours to sketch an image of this process *in process*. It is in this temporal territory
that it seeks to situate the work of performance: as an economy in which fantasies
circulate, histories exchange and ethics revaluate. Though the claims it makes and
the tone it takes may be politically 'risky', the essay stems from a commitment to try
to speak from within the belly of the beast, against disavowal, and through the logic
of responsibility. It addresses itself primarily, therefore, to the place I'm compelled to
acknowledge as 'home'.

## Locality and responsibility

Sitting late at night at my desk, staring out of the window, I'm confronted by an image drawn from the London streets below. Adjacent to 'Sussex House' opposite and its Victorian oak tree, sits a bus-stop remarkable only for its ubiquity. A gentle glow emanates from it unerringly, offering low-key lighting for my projective fantasy. I'm aware as time passes that this simple, everyday image reverberates with a daunting spectrality. Geographical proximity and temporal indeterminacy combine to produce a moment of hauntological complexity: the bus-stop scene framed here is linked inexorably to another more famous one happening just half a mile down the road from me. A young Black man named Stephen Lawrence is being stabbed to death repeatedly, whilst his attackers – young white men, like me – are allowed to get off with their crime scot-free. We know the story all too well already; know of its indictment of an embittered, institutionally racist society.[3] There's little to suggest the past tense could be deployed more appropriately, little to indicate that this racist violence isn't a constant, continuous obscenity. So looking out on the bus stop in front of me, I'm compelled to consider how it interpellates me. Though distant, I'm present nonetheless – anticipated, included as a silent witness.

As I write/read this scene, I'm disturbed by my encounter with it as an *aesthetic* phenomenon, whose 'principle of stylization . . . alone does an injustice to the victims'.[4] This recognition is itself sufficient to produce a 'terrifying shudder' along the lines that Adorno characterised – 'shudder' as a physiological 'premonition of subjectivity' produced by 'a sense of being touched by the other'.[5] Distance collapses as the psychic dynamics of the spectatorial relation become literalised in a physical sensation, reproducing ideology at the level of the *experience* of the body. I'm reminded instantly of the shockingly material power of psychic performativity, of its ineluctable incorporation of fantasy into the body's very corporeality. 'The eroticism you feel is on your skin. The violence you feel is in your skin.'[6] Of course, this realisation is itself a repetition – or a retrospective admission – of the deferred effects of what Fanon provocatively termed 'epidermalization': the inscription of 'race' upon the surface tissue of the skin which then serves to stand in for and seemingly guarantee its presumed ontological primacy. Such split temporality reveals the scene to be implicated in what might be called a primal fantasy of *racially constituted subjectivity*. Its seductiveness resides not in its representation of an event but in its reflection on an event – an event which, despite being irreducibly real, in this version becomes 'a retroactive fiction, retroactively anticipatory', so that it belongs, without doubt, 'to the realm of *Fantasy*'.[7] This fantasy bus-stop scene must therefore be seen as both the product of a mode of perception produced by the structuring framework of unconscious racism *and* as a reminder of its basic logic of operation. It conflates perceptual reality with subjective fantasy in a way that offers the spectacle as a more or less 'enigmatic' message directed towards sustaining the unconscious circulation of ideology.[8] Moreover, the real event to which it so presumptuously refers might itself be seen as a tragic, traumatically literal restaging of racism's own 'primal scene'. This is not to deny the historicity of the event but rather to insist upon it: to see the murder of Stephen Lawrence not merely as a symptom of racist pathology but as a testament to its continuing material history – a history replayed across countless 'other scenes'[9] linked through temporal and spatial contiguity – the specificity of which may none the less be grasped historically. The 'significance' of the Stephen Lawrence event, I will argue, rests not so much in its confirmation of a 'universal' structure underlying white colonial fantasies but rather in the way their acting out 'flashes up at a moment of danger'[10] in the emergence of a distinctively post-colonial society.

The 'premonition' accompanying my experience of a 'terrifying shudder' is perhaps something akin to what might be an ontological recognition of the fact of my white skin. In Fanon's own highly personalised formulation of colonialism's multiplicity of primal scenes, a parallel encounter evidences its performativity: 'Look, a Negro! . . . Mama, see the Negro! I'm frightened!' a white boy proclaims in his proximity. From this moment, for Fanon, 'assailed at various points, the corporeal schema crumbled, its place taken by a racial epidermal schema'.[11] As he feels the material force of the racist performative on and within the reality of his skin, 'the evanescent other, hostile but not opaque, transparent, not there, disappeared'.[12] In the same instant that Fanon uncovers 'the fact of blackness',[13] he recognises the key ideological strategy of the very 'whiteness that burns me'.[14] Homi Bhabha's analysis of the structure of this image has further suggested that as 'the white man's eyes break up the Black man's body' in an act of 'epistemic violence', 'its own frame of reference is transgressed, its field of vision disturbed'.[15] I shudder to think that this is the logic structuring the bus-stop scene, my aimless gaze complicit in the cutting to pieces of a young black body, fragmenting its autonomy, acting – to further appropriate Fanon – as 'an amputation, an excision, a haemorrhage' that spatters 'my whole body with black blood'.[16] And yet through such sensate experience, the incorporation of affect, I know that the materialisation of the body is precisely what's at stake in this imagery. The repetition of such racialised primal scenes without doubt plays a key role in 'the succession of phantasies' through which, Lacan argues, the illusion of bodily totality is sustained by a projective imaginary morphology, literalised as the boundary limit of the skin.[17] For Fanon, the experience of 'epidermalization' is coextensive with the 'black' man's corporeal fragmentation and ontological negation – a violent return to the status of a 'body in pieces'[18] – whilst its designation for me, as a 'white' man, is the total reduplication of a discursively totalising identity. Accordingly, 'blackness' for Fanon is the mark attributed to the signifier assigned the task of embodying racial difference within the colonial regime of representation, whilst 'whiteness' remains unmarked, the silent centre of cultural hegemony. Diana Fuss summarises his position accordingly:

> Claiming for itself the exalted position of transcendental signifier, 'white' is never a 'not-black'. As a self-identical, self-reproducing term, white draws its ideological power from its proclaimed transparency, from its own self-elevation over the very category of 'race'. 'White' operates as its own other, freed from dependency upon the sign 'Black' for its symbolic constitution.

In contrast, 'Black' functions, within a racist discourse, always diacritically, as the negative term in a Hegelian dialectic continuously incorporated and negated.[19]

However, to assert that 'white operates as its own other' would seem to forget Bhabha's rejoinder that the epistemic violence of scopic splitting destabilises the very subjectivity it otherwise appears to ground. Whilst 'white' may 'operate as its own other' to the extent that the colonial 'black' mirrors its topography and 'mimics' its perspicacity, the disruptive effect of disturbing its 'field of vision' might be characterised more properly as the disjunctive resituating of 'white' *as* other, producing the disorienting experience of 'whiteness' as 'otherness'. This, then, is how I'd want to characterise the bodily affect of the spectatorial relation described above: 'shudder' is the phenomenological experience of oneself as other. The bus-stop fantasy scene simultaneously confirms and disturbs my 'whiteness'; it plays out a repetitious Self–Other bifurcation and yet is generative of a different register of apprehension. It speaks my whiteness back to me, not as some infinitely expanding Hegelian totality but as a limited, historically specific discourse of 'identity'.

The terms of this account so far may appear to be coterminous with the by now familiar calls for an ontological 'decentring' of whiteness that often end up being coextensive with its epistemological re-centring. Whiteness as 'identity' is displaced only to re-emerge with post-modern bells on, reasserting its dominance by 'out-othering the Other'. What remains in place is the logic of 'whiteness' itself – the differential dialectics of otherness in which the Other is figured merely as negation in order to serve the end of Self perpetuation. In this sublative schema, 'whiteness' does not merely designate a specific identity position but rather nominates the very process of identity production authorised by colonial power relations. The silent signifier in the colonial episteme, 'whiteness' retrospectively comes to stand for and name its ideological determinacy. The psychoanalytic account of the way the 'fiction' of the bodily subject is sustained through the theatrical illusion of 'The Mirror Stage' takes place within the playing space of this specifically political visual economy. As Lacan revealingly puts it, 'the imaginary structuration of the ego forms around the specular image of the body itself, of the image of the Other'.[20] Embedded as it is within the racialised logic of the 'epidermal schema', psychoanalysis in effect articulates a decidedly historical conception of the primacy of inter-subjective fantasy. As both constitutive of and constituted by the materiality of 'whiteness', psychoanalytic discourse might be seen not so much as the engendering of a precipitous experience of the *jouissance* of 'relativity' but as a means of staging a necessary return to the question of 'responsibility'.

## Tragedy, history and futurity

'The other man's death calls me into question', writes Levinas in 'Ethics as First Philosophy', 'as if, by my possible future indifference, I had become the accomplice of the death to which the other . . . is exposed.' 'The Other becomes my neighbour', he continues, 'precisely through the way the face summons me, calls for me . . . and in so doing recalls my responsibility, and calls me into question'.[21] For Levinas, the 'face' denotes the other in their absolute alterity, incommensurable with and irreducible to the idea of the Other in the dialectic of self-identity. 'The Other is others', he insists repeatedly, and the 'face-to-face' relation cannot be subsumed into totality; rather it concretely produces the injunction of inter-subjective responsibility.[22]

The violent death of Stephen Lawrence just half a mile down the road appears to me to be an event that brings us face to face with the recognition of such historical responsibility. Even the set for the scene replayed outside my window would appear to act as a reminder of its necessity, with the brick wall dividing bus-stop from oak tree revealing a crack, an S-shaped fissure that seems to be screaming something silently. The injunction it enunciates is also written on this young man's face as its image circulates in the media's spectral economy. Its silent stillness acts as a reminder of his dignity, that non-recuperable aspect of alterity that articulates the subject's absolute singularity.[23] And yet the name Stephen Lawrence is simultaneously subject to the play of political performativity, being made to force more and more 'meaning' discursively. Stephen Lawrence carries a particularly heavy 'burden of representation' – embodying both the sign of 'race' in his black male body and the history of its marking by violent racism, plus the implicit coextensiveness of this with the policy and practice of the state apparatus. This, in effect, was what the public inquiry into the criminally incompetent police investigation of his murder became about – moving the problem of racism from fringe to mainstream, margin to centre, and in the process offering a damning indictment of both institutional racism and racism as an institution. The opposite strategy had been apparent in the extraordinarily pre-emptive headline run by the *Daily Mail* (Britain's most dangerously apologist right-wing paper) directly naming the five suspects as 'MURDERERS!' (14 February 1997). The splitting here was an attempt to limit racism to the preserve of a 'tiny minority of white thugs' rather than generally right-thinking society. However, the inquiry offered a comprehensive litany of testimony that indicted racism as a societal responsibility, drawing together our criminal complicity. Stephen Lawrence has come to name this configuration too, acting as his own witness in prosecuting a persecutory 'whiteness'. This was particularly evident in the way *The Colour of Justice* (The Brix, London 1999), a documentary drama drawn from the inquiry proceedings, invoked his name to perform the *capitonnage* of racism's discursive domain.[24] In Britain, 'Stephen Lawrence' is now coterminous with the endemic racism of the state – and social – apparatus. At the same time, his parents, Neville and Doreen, have been at pains to retain their son's dignity throughout their quest to do justice to and in his memory, reminding us of his individuality despite this metaphorical substitution and metonymical displacement. Their loss was without doubt a personal catastrophe, and the logic of trial and testimony at the core of the case further suggests a deep affinity with the spectatorial dynamics of tragedy.

The Stephen Lawrence Inquiry seemed to focus attention in Britain on the otherwise muted politics of 'race' and nation. Although no one was on trial, it was clear that institutional racism was. The courtroom drama in effect globalised the 'scene' of Stephen's murder, and produced a worldwide audience of 'witnesses' to the event. It found a body of evidence sufficient to indict socially sanctioned racist violence but not, apparently, to convict its direct perpetrators. In Fanonian terms, the Inquiry seemed to bespeak the perpetual 'state of emergency in which we live', but at the same time it gave rise to the impression that, this 'state of emergency is also always a state of *emergence*'.[25] As a complex performative event, the inquiry appeared to deploy something of the 'clarifying optics' that Benjamin locates in the unconscious mechanisms of modernity, freeze-framing and enlarging a snapshot of historicity in a way that 'does not simply render more precise what in any case was visible' but rather 'reveals entirely new structural formations of the subject'.[26] The inquiry seemed to generate more than its report could recuperate, producing the sense of a shifting, emergent episteme. Of course, as Bhabha suggests, emergence and emergency function simultaneously; resistance and recuperation dance their ideological two-step synchronically as well as diacritically.

In order to suggest how this performance was worked through the inquiry, I'd like to turn to Walter Benjamin's framework for understanding representational tragedy.[27] Tragedy, Benjamin argues, is 'based on the idea of sacrifice' – a sacrifice made by the victim/hero that is at once 'first' and 'final'. It is 'final' to the extent that it satiates some ancient principle, but it is 'first' in that the sacrifice also inaugurates a 'representative action, in which new aspects of the life of the nation become manifest'.[28] Importantly, the tragic hero/victim's sacrifice is made silently; 'silence', says Benjamin, is the 'one language that is completely proper to him'.[29] Silence for Benjamin articulates the immanence of resistance: 'the tragic devised itself the artistic form of the drama precisely so as to be able to present silence'.[30] In contrasting 'image and speech',[31] tragedy creates a distance between the tragic situation and the words used to describe it; but embedded in the hero's silence 'is the unarticulated necessity of defiance' and the secret topology of an 'unknown' 'word enclosed within it'.[32] The tragic hero's silent sacrifice translates this immanence into materiality, and 'the community learns reverence and gratitude for the word with which his death endowed it'.[33] Rather than function as a form of 'trial' aimed at the judgment of the victim/hero, tragedy is thereby transformed into a 'hearing' about the society in which 'the latter appears as a witness' against its atavistic violence.[34] And on 'isolated occasions', Benjamin says, 'the hero's word' can be heard to 'break through' as 'a cry of protest'[35] such that the spectator, Benjamin concludes, 'is summoned . . . by the tragedy itself'.[36]

The conjunction of Benjaminian aesthetics and Levinasian ethics would seem to suggest, therefore, a way of reading the social significance of the Stephen Lawrence tragedy as public inquiry. The image of Stephen Lawrence is a 'face' that 'summons me, calls for me . . . and in so doing recalls my responsibility, and calls me into question'. Its defiant silence – the silence of the 'without response'[37] – contains within it a word that articulates both this as an historical actuality and temporalises it with the promise of future possibility. The word I think the face of Stephen Lawrence points to, signifies enigmatically, is the very word that remained silent within the inquiry – 'whiteness'. The tragic death of Stephen Lawrence brings me face to face with responsibility for the violence of whiteness as episteme; he names it retrospectively. Looking on, I find myself back with Fanon, 'no longer aware of my body in the third person but in a triple person . . . responsible for my body, my race, my ancestors',[38] experiencing the limit of skin. At the same time, however, the temporality of the face-to-face encounter seems to move across past and future possibility simultaneously. At the moment of marking 'whiteness' historically, the testimony offered by the murdered body retains a dignity that cannot be sublated dialectically and suggests an emergent, alternate framework of 'alterity'. The situation of the face-to-face, here created through the spectatorial dynamics of tragedy, enables 'the encroachment of the present on the future' in a way that conjures the presence of what Levinas calls 'infinity' within the hard, historical actuality of inter-subjective responsibility.[39] Put more directly, Stephen Lawrence appears as a witness to and against an otherwise silent whiteness in a way that holds out the possibility of his being its 'first' as well as purely 'final sacrifice' – the prospect of whiteness being temporalised historically.

## Theatre and temporality

In her foreword to Tim Etchells' recent book, *Certain Fragments: Contemporary Performance and Forced Entertainment*, Peggy Phelan pauses to consider what theatre 'can add to the force of witnessing itself'.[40] The documentary drama *The Colour of Justice*, with its restaging of key moments of the Stephen Lawrence Inquiry, offers a model of theatrical testimony that works through a persuasive literality, resuscitating the power of representation as dissemination and mobilisation. Its essential logic of repetition serves as an insistent reminder of the event's materiality, bringing the audience face to face with the fact of history. At the same time, however, such representation is always already at a remove from the event, working through a distance and temporal delay that enables its significance to be grasped primarily retrospectively. As such it parallels closely the psychoanalytic conception of deferred action – the 'afterwardsness' that accounts for the performativity of the primal scene[41] – as well as articulating something akin to the 'latency' of historicity. But as psychoanalysis's encounter with the temporality of performance has also shown, the significance of the historical event is not purely present in itself but rather resides in its translation of an 'enigmatic message' across differentially experienced moments in time. This unevenness disrupts the teleology of a purely representational economy, and gives the lie to 'the peculiar temporal structure, the belatedness, of historical experience' in which 'the traumatic event . . . is fully evident only in connection with another place, and in another time'.[42] The theatre, as Benjamin suggests, offers just such a space of retroactive supplementarity. Perhaps what it 'adds to the force of witnessing itself' is an unwitting testimony to a belated experience, a bearing witness to a 'truth' that might nonetheless continue to elude it. Indeed, Phelan's question arises directly from consideration of Forced Entertainment's 'alternative' theatre work, and in particular from their attempt to produce an audience of 'witnesses' rather than simple 'spectators'. Across 15 years of experimental practice, their non-representational performances have sought to enjoin the audience to them as performers, to entrust us with the responsibility for events born from the sheer nakedness of their theatrical expression. For Etchells and Forced Entertainment, 'to witness an event is to be present at it in some fundamentally ethical way, to feel the weight of things and one's own place in them, even if that place is simply, for the moment, as an onlooker'.[43] Such participation positions the audience as implicated in the performance, and insinuates 'every gesture of the other' as 'a sign addressed to me'.[44] The very 'liveness' of the theatre event, however fragile that may be, situates the observer within a network of an entrusted responsibility. The audience comes face to face with the performer's irreplaceability, comes to recognise their irreducibly human dignity. Theatre's inescapable materiality, the visceral presence of the live performer, necessarily disturbs the solipsistic fantasy of a purely projected imaginary. 'The artwork that turns us into witnesses', Etchells explains, 'leaves us, above all, unable to stop thinking, talking and reporting what we've seen. We're left, like the people in Brecht's poem who've witnessed an accident, still stood on the street corner discussing what has happened, borne on by our responsibility to events'.[45] The performatively produced witness, in other words, further produces important testimony as to what they've witnessed, simultaneously reflecting and formulating its scale, scope and significance. We come to care about it.

Certainly this was my experience after watching Forced Entertainment's *Speak Bitterness* at the Purcell Rooms in London last spring, a few weeks after the publication of the McPherson Report on the Stephen Lawrence Inquiry (1999). The show, a revival of their 1995 production, was, ostensibly, a textual form of taking responsibility for the crimes, failings and banalities of the twentieth century. It adopted the confessional register of a collective 'we', which seemed to interpellate the audience in its act of performing responsibility, to include us in its acknowledgement of our complicity. 'We' were anticipated in every twist and turn of the allusive, associative textuality. The bare stage, front-on performance quality and a constant open white light on those watching meant that, as Etchells claims, 'the two-way nature of every line was emphasised – something spoken, something heard – eye contact made and then broken again, eye contact offered, rejected, then offered again – a series of complex negotiations . . . about who's done what or who is implicated in what'.[46] The work engaged the audience in a dialogical encounter with shared histories and anticipatory fantasies:

> We sent death threats by fax machine and kept a list on a computer of the people we were going to kill. We put the bop in the bop shee wop. We loved each other too much. We held each other's hands. We spat in the beer when no one was looking. We're guilty of murder, arson, and theft. We crashed the space ship on purpose. We got drunk too often, we nobbled horses, we made each other bleed.[47]

The constant shifts of tone simply served to bring its address more directly home. And whilst its topics ranged widely, its topicality was, for me, clearly available to see. The performance seemed to be offering testimony of/against the 'whiteness' that the performers themselves could be seen to embody retrospectively. Their 'confessions' provided the discourse that seemed to enunciate the silent word that then in effect 'marked' the company and included the audience in its temporality. The past tense of this register appeared to mark out 'whiteness' as a continuing historicity, at the same time as deferring its acknowledgement directly. Whilst 'whiteness' remains unnamed within the body of the text, it begins to be felt as a visceral affect. Across the duration of the show, we recognise it in the shudder at confessions that are not our own but which we come to own, or own up to. 'Whiteness', so to speak, in this way seems to creep beneath the skin at the very moment when we witness its temporalising.

## Notes

1  Theodor Adorno 'On Commitment', in *The Essential Frankfurt School Reader*, ed. A. Arato and E. Gebhardt, New York: Continuum, 1982: 318.

2  The phrase 'regime of representation' is drawn from Stuart Hall's body of work on the subject. For an example of his conceptual deployment of it, see Stuart Hall, 'Old and New Ethnicities', in *Culture, Globalization and the World System*, ed. A. King, Minneapolis: Minnesota University Press, 1997.

3  The extraordinary complexity and importance of the Stephen Lawrence case is impossible to account for fully here. For a precise chronology of events and the full text of the McPherson Report into the Stephen Lawrence Inquiry go to http://www.guardianunlimited.co.uk/lawrence and for a range of perspectives on their significance see *Sociological Research Online*, 4 (1) (http://www.socresonline.org.uk/4/1/contents.html).

4  Adorno, 'On Commitment': 313.

5  Theodor Adorno, *Aesthetic Theory*, ed. G. Adorno and R. Tiedeman, trans. C. Lenhardt, London: Routledge, 1984: 455.

6  Alphonso Lingis, 'Schizoanalysis of Race', in C. Lane, ed., *The Psychoanalysis of Race*, New York: Columbia University Press, 1998: 188.

7  J.-B. Pontalis, quoted in Timothy Murray, *Drama Trauma: Specters of Race and Sexuality in Performance, Video and Art*, London and New York: Routledge, 1997: 10.

8  Jean Laplanche, 'Seduction, Persecution, Revelation', in *Essays on Otherness*, ed. J. Fletcher, London and New York: Routledge, 1999: 170–1.

9  The concept of the 'other scene' is the structuring principle of André Green's analysis of the similarities between psychoanalysis and performance:

> My constant concern will be to show the double articulation of the theatrical phantasy: that of the scene, which takes places on the stage, and is given ostensible significance for the spectator; and that of the other scene that takes place – although everything is said aloud and intelligibly and takes place in full view – unknown to the spectator, by means of this chain-like mode and its unconscious logic.
>
> (André Green, *The Tragic Effect: The Oedipus Conflict in Tragedy*, trans. A. Sheridan, Cambridge: Cambridge University Press, 1979: 28–9)

10  Walter Benjamin, 'Theses on the Philosophy of History', in *Illuminations*, ed. H. Arendt, trans. H. Zohn, New York: Schocken Books, 1969: 255.

11 Frantz Fanon, *Black Skin, White Masks*, trans. C. L. Markmann, London: Pluto Press, 1986: 112.
12 Fanon, *Black Skin, White Masks*: 112.
13 Fanon, *Black Skin, White Masks*: 109–40.
14 Fanon, *Black Skin, White Masks*: 114.
15 Homi K. Bhabha, 'Remembering Fanon', foreword to Fanon, *Black Skin, White Masks*: xii.
16 Fanon, *Black Skin, White Masks*: 112.
17 Jacques Lacan, *Ecrits: A Selection*, trans. A. Sheridan, London: Routledge, 1977: 4.
18 Jacques Lacan, *The Ego in Freud's Theory and in the Technique of Psychoanalysis: The Seminar of Jacques Lacan*, book II, ed. J.-A. Miller, New York: Norton, 1988: 54.
19 Diana Fuss, *Identification Papers*, London and New York: Routledge, 1995: 143–4.
20 Lacan, *The Ego in Freud's Theory and in the Technique of Psychoanalysis*: 95.
21 Emmanuel Levinas, 'Ethics as First Philosophy', in *The Levinas Reader*, ed. Seán Hand, Oxford: Blackwell, 1989: 83.
22 Emmanuel Levinas, *Totality and Infinity: An Essay on Exteriority*, trans. A. Lingis, Pittsburgh: Duquesne University Press, 1969: 80, 202.
23 In this context, it is worth noting with Alphonso Lingis that 'for Kant, dignity is the unexchangeable value, the term that is an end without being at the same time a means for something further.' He insists that, contra Žižek and Lacan:

> it is the fantasy space in another that commands our respect. The fundamental fantasy of another is that which we cannot share. Bound intrinsically to the sensual impulses of his or her body, this fantasy fills in a gap in the meaning-system of the environment in an utterly singular way.
> (Alphonso Lingis, 'Fantasy Space', http://www.focusing.org/lingis.html, 1997: 7)

24 According to Lacan, the deployment of the proper name as 'the point of convergence that enables everything that happens in this discourse to be situated retroactively and prospectively' is a key strategy in the performative 'quilting' (*capitonnage*) or stabilisation of ideological meaning. For details of this concept, see Jacques Lacan, *The Psychoses: The Seminar of Jacques Lacan*, book III, ed. J.-A. Miller, trans. D. Porter, London: Routledge, 1993: 268, and Slavoj Žižek, *The Sublime Object of Ideology*, London: Verso, 1989: 101–3. For a more fully developed example of the significance of this process see Adrian Kear, 'Diana Between Two Deaths: Spectral Ethics and the Time of Mourning', in *Mourning Diana: Nation, Culture and the Performance of Grief*, ed. A. Kear and D. L. Steinberg, London and New York: Routledge, 1999: 169–86.
25 Bhabha, 'Remembering Fanon': xi.
26 Walter Benjamin, quoted in Homi K. Bhabha, 'Day by Day . . . with Frantz Fanon', in *The Fact of Blackness: Frantz Fanon and Visual Representation*, ed. A. Read, Seattle: Bay Press, 1996: 192.
27 Walter Benjamin, *The Origin of the German Tragic Drama*, trans. J. Osborne, London: Verso, 1985: 102–20.
28 Benjamin, *The Origin of the German Tragic Drama*: 106–7.
29 Benjamin, *Origin*: 108.
30 Benjamin, *Origin*: 108.
31 Benjamin, *Origin*: 108.
32 Benjamin, *Origin*: 115.
33 Benjamin, *Origin*: 109.
34 Benjamin, *Origin*: 109.
35 Benjamin, *Origin*: 116.
36 Benjamin, *Origin*: 119.
37 The experience of the 'without response' is, for Levinas, the survivor's experience of the other's death:

> Death is, in beings, the disappearance of the expressive movements that made them appear as living – movements that are always *responses*. Death will touch above all this autonomy or expressivity of movements that goes so far as to cover someone's face. Death is the *without-response*.

Emmanuel Levinas, quoted in Jacques Derrida, *Adieu to Emmanuel Levinas*, trans. P.-A. Brault and M. Naas, Stanford: Stanford University Press, 1999: 130.

38 Fanon, *Black Skin, White Masks*: 112.
39 Emmanuel Levinas, *Time and the Other*, trans. R. Cohen, Pittsburgh: Duquesne University Press, 1987: 79.
40 Peggy Phelan, 'Performing Questions, Producing Witnesses', Foreword to Tim Etchells, *Certain Fragments: Contemporary Performance and Forced Entertainment*, London and New York: Routledge, 1999: 13.
41 Jean Laplanche, 'Notes on Afterwardsness', in *Essays on Otherness*, ed. J. Fletcher, London and New York: Routledge, 1999: 260–5.
42 Cathy Caruth, ed., *Trauma: Explorations in Memory*, Baltimore and London: Johns Hopkins University Press, 1995: 8.
43 Tim Etchells, *Certain Fragments: Contemporary Performance and Forced Entertainment*, London and New York: Routledge, 1999: 17.
44 Levinas, quoted in Derrida, *Adieu to Emmanuel Levinas*: 7.
45 Etchells, *Certain Fragments*: 18.
46 Etchells, *Certain Fragments*: 18.
47 *Speak Bitterness*, in Etchells, *Certain Fragments*: 181.

# 13

# THE UPSILON PROJECT

## A post-tragic testimonial

*Gregory L. Ulmer*

### The emerAgency

The emerAgency is a virtual organization. At its literal moment of conception the emerAgency consisted of a neon sign, or, rather, a representation of a neon sign made in Photoshop and posted on the world wide web (www.elf.ufl.edu). In this story the emerAgency will have come to life as a consulting practice, staffed by student volunteers (from all levels of schooling), demonstrating the workings of the emergent apparatus of electracy (electracy is to digital technology what literacy is to print). The reality of this organization is created at the point of reception.

Part of the difficulty of this name is its descent into calligraphy: its shape – with the A rising above the small letters – creates a silhouette that is part drawing. A passage from Walter Benjamin, composed in the 1930s, is one of the motivations for the name of the project.

Theses On The Philosophy of History

VIII

> The tradition of the oppressed teaches us that the 'state of emergency' in which we live is not the exception but the rule. We must attain to a conception of history that is in keeping with this insight. Then we shall clearly realize that it is our task to bring about a real state of emergency, and this will improve our position in the struggle against Fascism. One reason why Fascism has a chance is that in the name of progress its opponents treat it as a historical norm. The current amazement that the things we are experiencing are 'still' possible in the twentieth century is not philosophical. This amazement is not the beginning of knowledge – unless it is the knowledge that the view of history which gives rise to it is untenable.[1]

Are we still amazed that the things we are experiencing are still possible in the twenty-first century? The choice of name for the consulting organization suggests an affirmative answer to such questions. Some of the purposes of our practice are suggested at once in this portmanteau word; figuring out what we are about involves extracting the terms condensed in this name ('we' refers to anyone who decides to be an emerAgent). The very nature of our name indicates an important feature of method – analytical and creative exploration of language. A first reading might be: we are an 'agency' ('an organization that provides some service') that addresses contemporary conditions within this frame of 'the state of emergency.' This word 'agency,' unfortunately, is not at all stable. The 'A' inserted into 'emergency' is a heraldic device whose associations remain to be unpacked as the project evolves. The consulting methods of emerAgents derive from the practices gathered together by this 'A.' A short list of practices evoked by the 'A' includes: Brecht's Alienation effect; Derrida's 'differAnce'; Lacan's 'Autre' or other (big and little 'a'); Cixous's ladder of writing (an open step ladder viewed in profile resembles an 'A'). Other terms included in the pormanteau with important potential for guiding the method are: emergence, merge, urgency, urge.

Walter Benjamin also explained why the sign has to be neon.

One-Way Street

This Space For Rent

Fools lament the decay of criticism. For its day is long past. Criticism is a matter of correct distancing. It was at home in a world where perspectives and prospects counted and where it was still possible to take a standpoint. Now things press too closely on human society. The unclouded, innocent eye has become a lie, perhaps the whole naive mode of expression sheer incompetence. Today the most real, the mercantile gaze into the heart of things is the advertisement. It abolishes the space where contemplation moved and all but hits us between the eyes with things as a car, growing to gigantic proportions, careens at us out of a film screen. And just as the film does not present furniture and facades in completed forms for critical inspection, their insistent, jerky nearness alone being sensational, the genuine advertisement hurtles things at us with the tempo of a good film . . . What, in the end, makes advertisements so superior to criticism? Not what the moving red neon sign says – but the fiery pool reflecting it in the asphalt.[2]

In emerAgent consulting it is not that the neon effect replaces critical reason, but that reason and neon merge in a hybrid modality: not reasoning but reasoneon.

## The subject of knowledge

I was reminded of the aura of the neon effect by this evocation in Benjamin, and in part by its further elaboration in the writings of the psychoanalyst Jacques Lacan. Lacan was one of those French theorists present at the conference, held at Johns Hopkins University in 1967 (the year I entered graduate school), that is said to mark the beginning of the poststructuralist movement in America.

When I prepared this little talk for you, it was early in the morning. I could see Baltimore through the window and it was a very interesting moment because it was not quite daylight and a neon sign indicated to me every minute the change of time, and naturally there was heavy traffic, and I remarked to myself that exactly all that I could see, except for some trees in the distance, was the result of thoughts, actively thinking thoughts, where the function played by the subjects was not completely obvious. In any case the so-called 'Dasein', as a definition of the subject, was there in this rather intermittent or fading spectator. The best image to sum up the unconscious is Baltimore in the early morning.[3]

A commentator has explained the fit between the material and the theoretical information, between the neon tube and the concept of the subject in Lacanian psychoanalysis.

In his L-schema Lacan represented the unconscious as a four-sided relation in which the flow from the Other to the Subject is modulated by the ego-other relation. He used the image of a triode vacuum tube to clarify this movement: the flow of electrons from cathode (o) to anode (s) is modulated by the third electrode (e-o, the imaginary relation) which can either interrupt the current or amplify it depending on its charge. As with any electrical circuit, the current will flow only when the circuit is closed, and in alternating current, a system of feedback is set up such that the flow in one direction reverses the charge and thus automatically opens the circuit, inducing it to flow in the opposite direction. Moreover, if the tube is filled with a gas such as neon, it will light up only when the flow of the electric current is interrupted and forced to move back onto itself. The point of his little electronic parable, is that the interruption of the flow, transference as resistance, is necessary for the lighting up, transference as the relation to the Other.[4]

'Transference' refers to any experience from the past reactivated in the present relationship between analyst and analysand during psychoanalytic treatment. Lacan observed that as soon as there is a subject who is supposed to know (the Other), there is transference. My love of knowledge, according to this theory, has something to do with my identifications with the figures of authority for me, beginning with my parents and displaced thereafter as my life experience moved away from the family into other institutions, including the institution of the street and its premises (the Bar, Tavern, Honky Tonk). French theory rather than neon signs attract me now (and both are examples of the 'other' or 'objet a' – 'a' abbreviating the French word for other, 'autre'). Or rather, what I have learned from theory is that my attraction to it has something in common with the attraction of a neon sign and the world that it evokes. One purpose of the emerAgency is to introduce the neon effect into problem solving as the basis for a new consultancy.

## The personal sacred

One of the first actions taken by the newly formed virtual consultancy known as the emerAgency was to invite proposals for the creation of a new dimension of memorial – an electronic monumentality – with responsibility for revising and registering the borders and boundary areas of American National Identity. The question is: what is inside, and what is outside (of anything)? The purpose is a recalibration of this kind of distinction at every level of being, beginning with logical, psychological, ethical, and political categories. Mourning is as important to national as to individual identity, with the me-morial constituting a specifically electronic monumentality, creating a circuit, like that of the triode tube, between the private and public dimensions. A basic analogy guiding the project is the figure of a symptom as a 'monument' marking the site of a repressed trauma. The superego too has been characterized as an internal monument. An image of how an individual identity comes into formation around certain paradigmatic experiences may be found in the way tourist sites are created through a process of 'site sacralization'.[5] A me-morial is to the information highway what a tourist attraction is to the interstate highway system.

The notion of 'sign' guiding the discourse of the me-morial comes from Lacan's modification of Saussure's discussion of signifier-signified. A sign means not by reference to 'reality,' but by a relationship between its parts – a material element (sound or letter) and a concept. Saussure illustrated the relationship with the word 'tree' and a drawing of a tree, separated by a horizontal line. Lacan replaced Saussure's example with his own – a pair of words ('ladies' 'gentlemen') above, and a pair of doors below (above and below separated by a line or bar), while noting that the public life of Western Man, like that of the great majority of primitive communities, 'is subjected to the laws of urinary segregation'.[6] The illustration includes a 'hypericon' (a paradigmatic anecdote condensing in an image or scene the essence of a theory),[7] based on 'a memory of childhood.' The anecdote is well known, concerning a little boy and girl seated opposite one another looking out the window of a train as it arrived at a station. 'Look', says the brother, 'we're at Ladies!'; 'Idiot!' replies his sister, 'Can't you see we're at Gentlemen.'[8] 'For these children, Ladies and Gentlemen will be henceforth two countries towards which each of their souls will strive on divergent wings, and between which a truce will be the more impossible since they are actually the same country and neither can compromise on its own superiority without detracting from the glory of the other.'[9] The 'A' of 'emerAgency' diagrams these 'divergent wings.'

The basic unit of the Symbolic order in Lacan's theory is not the sign, we might say, but the emblem, given that his counterexample has the tripartite structure of the genre known as 'emblem' (slogan + picture + commentary). The emblem embodies the abstractive power of writing in a specific social rule and place – the bathroom. While, in principle, any such place may supply the materials of the sign, the bathroom is the prototype and will serve as the category guiding this theorization of the Upsilon Project. Michel Leiris identified the bathroom as a primary site of the sacred in modernity. In the secularized conditions of modernity, it was easier to understand the sacred at a personal level ('those objects, places, or occasions that awake in me that mixture of fear and attachment, that ambiguous attitude caused by the approach of something simultaneously attractive and dangerous, prestigious and outcast').[10] To locate the sacred in one's own experience, Leiris looked to memories of childhood, the earlier the better. His family home was organized by a sacred polarity on a right–left axis of parental bedroom and the bathroom. The bathroom served not only its designated function but also doubled as a secret clubhouse where he and his brother collaborated on the composition of fantastic narratives.

> There was something more or less forbidden in what we were doing, which, moreover, brought us scoldings when we stayed shut up in there too long. As if in a 'men's house' of some island in Oceania – the place where the initiates gather and where from mouth to mouth and from generation to generation, secrets and myths are passed on, we endlessly elaborated our mythology in this room, our clubhouse, and never tired of seeking answers to the various sexual riddles that obsessed us. Seated on the throne like an initiate of higher rank was my brother; I, the youngest, sat on an ordinary chamber pot that served as the neophyte's stool. The flushing mechanism and the hole were, in themselves, mysterious things, and even actually dangerous.[11]

Such humble, elemental experiences are overlooked by conventional consultants following the rules of sufficient reason. In a time of emergency, however, which Leiris shared with Benjamin (they both participated in the College of Sociology conference held in Paris just before the beginning of World War II), a moment when the repressed sacred seemed to have erupted once again directly into political life, it was necessary to take a more inclusive approach to experience, in order to figure out what was going wrong. Ludwig Wittgenstein provides still further insight into the sign-toilet, showing how the personal sacred supplies the guiding pattern for the creative process, which is to say that the creative process relies on opening a conduction line between purely private and fully public regions of memory. '[Wittgenstein] told Reeve a childhood memory,' Ray Monk states in his definitive autobiography of the philosopher,

> which obviously had a great significance for him. In the lavatory of his home, he said, some plaster had fallen from the wall, and he always saw this pattern as a duck, but it frightened him: it had the appearance for him of those monsters that Bosch painted in his *Temptations of St Anthony*.[12]

Monk does not relate this memory to the famous double figure, the duck-rabbit, that Wittgenstein appropriated from *Gestalt* psychology, which had appropriated it from a popular humor magazine, and that has become one of the prototypes of a metapicture.[13]

## The safety patrol

The relevance of Lacan's sign-emblem to electronic monumentality presented itself to me through the circumstances of my own encounter with this hypericonic emblem. The context was the fifth-grade trip to Washington, DC, for which I was one of the chaperones, accompanying my son. The trip was a reward for those students who had served in the safety patrol during the year. Such trips have become part of an annual ritual at schools all over the country, whose official purpose is that of a pilgrimage to the shrines of American democracy, inculcating in the younger generation a connection with the monuments representing the founding beliefs of the nation. The unofficial or actual experience of the trip itself is somewhat different from the ideal. Our group took the train from Gainesville, Florida, to the nation's capital, a long, overnight ride. It soon became clear that our destination was a matter of symbolic importance only, relevant to the educators and the institution of schooling, but of no importance to the children. Their focus was never on the monuments or any part of the object of the tour, and always on their interactions with each other.

The children paid almost no heed to the adults (only when forced to) and instead acted out a sorting and resorting process that was at once biological and metaphysical. Lacan observed that 'the rails in this story materialize the bar in the Saussurian algorithm.'[14] In my scene the bar was materialized not only by the train tracks but by the belt that the safety patrol wore while performing their duties before and after school – the belt, colored day-glow orange, that included a diagonal strap crossing from the front to the back of the waist band. This diagonal belt emblazoned the bar or slash, the division, split, separation productive of meaning in language as such, sorting tenor and vehicle in figuration, metaphor and metonymy, and representing the repressing operation of the unconscious that permitted the sliding of the signified under the signifier through displacement and condensation.

Two behaviors dominated the social interactions manifesting the filtering of the signifier into the signified that was part of Lacan's emblem. Within each sex a cruel, pitiless (from the standpoint of an adult) sorting took place between those 'included' and those 'excluded,' those considered 'cool' and those judged to be 'nerds' ('dorks'). Adult interventions in this polarizing were futile, since any rearrangements imposed at the official level dissolved as soon as supervision relaxed. Across the sexes, meanwhile, an opposite behavior developed, concentrated around the rather large bathroom with which each car of the train was equipped. There was only one bathroom in the car. Small mixed groups of boys and girls continually attempted to slip into the bathroom together and lock the door. Further symmetry was created by the fact that the boys and girls trying to get into the same bathroom belonged to their respective 'in' groups.

Indeed, a willingness to transgress the official codes played a part in determining the coolness of a person. My duty became that of sitting in the seat next to the bathroom to enforce the rule of urinary segregation, a problem expressive of the human body that combines multiple functions in one organ.

## The Me-morial

The creation of an online virtual commemorative practice aims to support the public–private circuit of mourning by taking into account the various embodiments of the 'bar' line in the hypericon of 'sign.' A me-morial is peripheral to an existing monument (or memorial) in the computer sense of the term (an extra device, added on to the basic computer hardware, to give new functionality to the machine). The purpose of the peripheral is to open to further thought the relation between private and public experience, individual and collective actions, events, behaviors. The premise of an existing memorial is that the loss it commemorates is recognized as a sacrifice on behalf of a public, collective value. The prototypical memorial is a war monument such as the Vietnam Wall. The more than 58,000 lives lost in that war were not wasted, the memorial proclaims, but represent a sacrifice made for a value, something in which the community believes and for which it is willing to pay with the blood of its members. The value may be stated abstractly – 'freedom,' for example – but it is understood that certain actions and behaviors in daily life embody and perform the belief. A monument condenses an inferential sequence, in other words, moving in either direction along a chain of reasoning that might be spelled out as follows: behavior, belief, value, cost-benefit, sacrifice, public recognition, memorialization. Within the apparatus of literacy it has been difficult to sustain an awareness of this entire sequence. Indeed, the point that usually is forgotten is the specific behaviors bought by the sacrifice. A me-morial patches this break in the chain.

I say that the Vietnam Wall is the prototype for our moment, since its history includes an extensive public conflict and controversy regarding the value of that war. Ultimately this debate has confirmed the traditional view that lives lost in battle are sacrifices on behalf of the nation, even if it is decided at some point that the nation made a mistake in the action of the war. The purpose of the peripheral memorial is to make a case for losses of life (or other kinds of loss) whose public, collective relevance as 'sacrifice' is not yet recognized. The most spectacular success of this sort of promotion from private-individual to public-collective, from waste to sacrifice, is that of the AIDS Quilt.[15] The display of the Quilt on the Mall in Washington, DC, exemplifies the peripheral tactic of a me-morial (the Mall being part of one of the heaviest concentrations of monuments and memorials in the world). The AIDS Quilt is instructive in other respects, having to do with the activist politics associated with the process of the shift of category (waste to sacrifice). The relevance of the Lacanian emblem to this project is clarified by this goal of value alchemy, transforming waste into worth (the circuit gold-shit).

For its part, the emerAgency also proposed its own prototype, which remains at a conceptual stage for now, which is not to say that a me-morial always needs to be built or materially embodied to fulfill its categorical mission. I have in mind the proposal for a kiosk to be added to the Vietnam Wall, with a computer printout keeping track of traffic deaths as they occurred throughout the year.[16] The number killed in Vietnam has come to serve as a kind of benchmark or unit of measure indicating when a collection of individual losses mutates into a significant group loss. The number of lives lost in traffic deaths annually approaches the total loss of the war over a number of years. Still, traffic deaths are not recognized as a public, collective sacrifice in the monumental sense. Part of the me-morial project is to inquire into this question of why some losses are recognized as sacrifices on behalf of the community while other, often much greater losses, are not granted collective status, so that their cumulative totals never register in the record of group identity as a price paid for the maintenance of a certain lifeworld.

## ATH/ate

The hypothesis of the me-morial project is that commemoration must be rethought in electrate terms (within the apparatus of electracy) and that, within electracy, monumentality could become a primary site of self-knowledge both individual and collective. The mystery or question about the worthiness of a loss for memorialization is informed by the problem of the status of tragedy in a post-literate society. Basing its consultancy on the knowledge of grammatology, the emerAgency method is reasoning by analogy: what tragedy was to the ancient Greeks as a form guiding them through the transition from orality to literacy, the me-morial is to postmodern America, guiding us through the transition from literacy to electracy. The consistent question joining the different apparatuses is: why do things go wrong? why do we make mistakes despite our best efforts to assure desired and intended outcomes of our actions? The ultimate collective response to this question in orality is religion, and in literacy is science. Electracy has not been around long enough to have produced its ultimate response, but it is working on one.

To apply our analogy, then, tragedy as a form is an oral-literate hybrid – performed as part of a religious ritual festival (such rituals being the central institutionalized mnemonic practice of orality), while employing the new technology of writing (the plays are scripted) and introducing innovations, such as the individual actors apart from the chorus, made possible by the new order of memory. Commentators have shown that literacy in general and tragedy in particular were important factors in the transformation of Greek collective identity from a group of allied tribes to a city-state.[17] Individuals were beginning to experience themselves precisely as autonomous beings with a clearly defined inner experience apart from the external and outwardly directed relations with tribe and the gods in nature. Within this process the tragedies addressed the problematic of error in a pre-conceptual way, since categorization by concept was still to be invented, or had yet to be codified by Plato and made accessible or learnable by means of the practice of method introduced in Plato's Academy and refined in Aristotle's Lyceum.

The aspect of tragedy of most interest in our context is (in Greek) 'ATH' (or 'ate' in lower case) which means 'blindness' or 'foolishness' in an individual, and 'calamity' or 'disaster' in a collectivity.[18] The effect of literacy just beginning to be felt and explored as Greece assimilated alphabetic writing was a new power of abstraction that made it possible to analyze and compare actions and statements, making visible certain patterns that were unintelligible and unnoticed using oral means. The proto-conceptualist, Socrates, for example, used literate reasoning (even if he did not write) to call attention to someone such as Euthyphro the contradictions in his reasoning, while examining the consequences of this insight for guiding the possible actions one might take. Tragedy in its preconceptual style dramatized foolish mistakes, actions without knowledge or understanding (blindness) and their consequences for the community (the prototype being *Oedipus Rex* by Sophocles). The specific feature of tragedy known as ATH has to do with the hero losing control, being overwhelmed temporarily by a passion, taken or possessed from without, and producing an action that might be trivial in itself, but that had catastrophic consequences not only for the hero but for the community as a whole. Examples in our own time would be: Mike Tyson biting the ear of Evander Holyfield (he 'ate' his ear); Bill Clinton and Monica Lewinsky (again the macaronic pun on 'ate' may be heard).

A premise of the me-morial is that ATH continues to be a factor in our own time, even if theater and the genre of tragedy are no longer adequate expressions of it. It is important at a fundamental level of survival to formulate a new way to notice and attend to ATH in electracy. The Greeks invented theater to focus public attention on disaster, and the experience of the audience at these performances is given major credit for the creation of the polis as city-state and for the formation of individual identity as citizen and self. Similar credit is given to the novel in the formation of the modern nation-state, including its representation of disaster, which is quite different from that of classical tragedy. Our analogy suggests that a form and practice (institution) will emerge within electracy that will do for the new apparatus what theater and literature did within literacy. The internet me-morial is an experimental search for this new practice.

### Kindertotenlieder

A first step in the design of a me-morial is to select an 'abject' loss that the community acknowledges is a problem but that it has not accepted as a sacrifice on behalf of a belief. The use of 'abject' here no doubt is related to Julia Kristeva's sense of the term, although I will not elaborate on this point for now, except to say that the me-morial does address abjection in national identity, having to do with a lack of fit, a certain disparity between the two sides of what is compared in an 'identity' condition. The association with our guiding emblem may also be apparent.

> While the body ego, formed at the time of the mirror stage, signifies a unified, phantasmatic gestalt of a newly formed subject's body, the stability of this image is continually threatened from within by traces of abjection, such as corporeal wastes (excrement, urine, blood, breast milk, vomit, pus, and spit) that are jettisoned or leaked from the body. These traces of abjection represent both 'me' and 'not me,' referring back to the child's 'physiological natal prematuration' and the traumatic and liminal separation of self and other. Furthermore, the ideal bodily imago is also

threatened from without, in a 'society of control' which disperses bodies into desiring machines and part-objects. Observing the early modern workplace, Georg Lukacs noted that, 'the fragmentation of the object of production necessarily entails the fragmentation of its subject.' This slicing and portioning of the body finds its corollary in abjection.[19]

A premise of the me-morial is that the affect of abjection is felt collectively as well as individually. John Caputo describes the feeling in his account of a poetics of obligation, in which something shocks me, some event or condition has a hold on me.[20] He suggests a starting point not with the best but with the worst of our world, such as the case of a child dying of AIDS. The example resonates with the mission of the 'safety patrol'.

> There is no *principium* or standard of Good behind the child or beyond the child, watching over the child and making the child safe. The child is not safe. The child is a disaster. There is no sure principle that is implicitly at work that renders possible the recognition of the disaster that besets the child. We cannot begin at the beginning, with a *principium*, but only where we are, with the child. We can only begin by responding to the child, who is a disaster, by coming under the singularity of the claim she makes upon us, and by making damaged lives our business. That is where we are.[21]

The emerAgency takes up just such disasters as this, whose modality is that of 'impossibility,' according to Caputo, since they are 'without why.' A me-morial then exists in the same modality as the poetry of Paul Celan:

> The poem happens not as a meaning-giving event but as an event of commemoration, as a way of keeping a record, of recording the date of a disaster. The poem is a re-cording, *im Herzen*, in the heart, of a disaster. It does not bestow beauty on the event (aesthetics), or sense (theology) . . . Divested of both *Kehre* and *Resultat* the poem simply re-cords the event, writes it down – or lets the disaster do the writing – as a gesture of mourning and commemoration . . . There is no suggestion that we can put a stop to it, only that we can watch out for it or provide an idiom for its record.[22]

Paul Celan, of course, wrote about Auschwitz. Caputo in several books has established an abject domain joining the obscenity of even attempting to give reasons why the Holocaust took place (imposing the order 'Here There Is No Why' that Claude Lanzmann took as the title of a manifesto for his SHOAH project),[23] with the ethics of the Mystic Rose of Angelus Silesius and Meister Eckhard ('the rose is without why; it blooms because it blooms. It cares not for itself; asks not if it is seen').[24] The connection between these domains is Heidegger.

## *Warumverbot*

As an example for this call for proposals, let us consider a me-morial for abused children. The purpose of the commemoration is to witness and testify regarding the event of this abuse, to shift it from the private, individual status of one-at-a-time, each case in isolation, to a cumulative public status of sacrifice on behalf of a value in which we believe as a nation. What could this value be, such that it is sustained in the face of such a high cost? The abuse is the behavior we want to forget and that in fact is impossible to remember, or at least impossible to place in the chain or put on the rails of the tracks leading from event to principle (the emblematic shot of SHOAH – the train tracks leading into Auschwitz). Not every child is abused, anymore than is every soldier killed in action. It only takes a certain number annually needed to pay the price so that we may have our way of life. The me-morial simply re-cords this commitment and makes it visible, even monumentally evident. I take up Caputo's suggestion, follow his lead, since the occasion that holds me and obliges me is the story of one Bradley McGee (the event reported in the local newspaper), a toddler killed by a father whose toilet training method was to hold the two-year-old by his feet and plunge him head first into the porcelain bowl of the commode.

Now here is the point of the consultancy. The community does not recognize Bradley's death as a sacrifice, that is, as necessary to the way of life we currently embrace as a civilization. As this death and similar ones are reported day after day in the paper, leaders, pundits, spokespersons, sermonize against the disaster, even putting public money behind the call to eliminate such events. These leaders lack an idiom that would help them and us grasp what is happening (ATH), and so they hire empirical consultants whose commitment to the principle of sufficient reason prevent them from taking into account the unconscious. Slavoj Žižek referred to such circumstances as 'the sublime object of ideology,' noting this need to treat as exceptions and anomalies those matters that were in fact essential qualities of the way of life.[25] The intractability of the 'problem' would make more sense to empiricist consultants if they could grasp the link between abuse and the foundational value of 'family' (to give one name to it). We lack what Fredric Jameson called a 'cognitive map' that would graph the passage connecting individual experience with collective historical structure. In short, we need a cartography of ATH, tracing the paths joining blindness and calamity.

## The upsilon astronauts

As Caputo observed, on good authority, the best monument is a name and a date (JFK, 22 November 1963).[26] The rule of a me-morial is that the peripheral for abused children must be attached to an extant memorial for acknowledged sacrifice. In this case the peripheral is attached to the 'Space Mirror,' the Astronauts' memorial at Kennedy Space Center. There are fourteen names engraved in the black granite,

42.5 feet high and 50 feet wide, polished to a reflective finish, mounted on

213

a platform that rotates and tilts. As the Earth turns, so does the slab, keeping its back to the sun; the names of the astronauts are carved through the stone so that the letters glow with sunlight, floating in a dark field of reflected sky and clouds.[27]

The peripheral or add-on feature, juxtaposing the death of Bradley McGee with that of Virgil 'Gus' Grissom and the other heroes, consists of an electronic panel substituted for just one of the 93 granite panels of the memorial (the 93 panels provide a troubling amount of room for future names, Adler points out). The panel is activated only during a total eclipse of the sun, and flashes (one name each second) as many names of children who died from abuse as may fit into the duration of the eclipse while the heroes' names are invisible.

In his magazine article about the 'Space Mirror,' Jerry Adler commented:

> it is hard to imagine improving on the spontaneous memorial that appeared in the sky when the space shuttle *Challenger* blew up in January 1986: the immense twisted Y of the contrails formed by the solid rocket boosters as they diverged, a graphic depiction of vast power gone berserk. Hanging for hours in the clear, still air over the Atlantic Ocean, it was seen by millions and inspired one of them, a Florida architect named Alan Helman, with the idea of a permanent memorial.[28]

That the Challenger wrote a Y in the sky when it exploded is of considerable importance in the context of the poststructural expertise that the emerAgency consultancy has to offer. Nearly every description of a disaster or a foolishness (ATH), whether coming from victims, witnesses, or commentators, poses the question, 'why?' But as the context of Auschwitz for Celan's poetry would indicate, the kinds of problems we are addressing fall into the category of being 'without why'.[29] Conventional consulting only takes up those problems considered to be within the domain of 'sufficient reason,' subject to rational solution. The challenge of Auschwitz, of course, is that it represents rationalist consulting gone mad. The 'final solution' to 'the Jewish problem,' arrived at using all the formal procedures of a European state, was genocide. From such a catastrophe the Real (the ultimate limit) may be inferred (in the manner of the sublime).

The Mirror Peripheral takes the Challenger Y as an idiom with which to re-cord this condition. The idiom works as a map linking together a series of disparate items on the basis of the letter and shape 'Y' (the 'A' unfolded). This Y supplements the 'why' that citizens cannot help but ask in the face of disaster, to mark the dimension of blindness, foolishness, that goes unnoticed amidst the overwhelming calamity. A confirmation of this link between Bradley McGee and Gus Grissom was the appearance of the Y in the details of several stories of children's deaths reported while this proposal was in preparation. In one story, Sabrina Aisenberg, aged five months, was snatched from her home in the middle of the night while the parents and two older children slept. 'Sabrina has an identifying birthmark: a little red 'y' on the back under the right shoulder' (*Gainesville Sun*, 11 January 1998). In the previous year, a middle-school student named Troy Silcox committed suicide. In the article describing the memorials spontaneously offered by friends and acquaintances, the name of Troy's mother was listed as 'Rose Weihe (pronounced like the letter 'Y')' (*Gainesville Sun*, 25 February 1997). The Mystic Rose has a Weihe, but not a why.

In the idiom of our peripheral, the Y traced by the *Challenger* explosion, the 'y' in the name, and the birthmark of the missing or dead children, the 'why' posed rhetorically in the wake of every disaster (for example, the 'WHY' on the cover of *Newsweek*, 3 May 1999, special issue on the 'massacre in Colorado') are juxtaposed with the Pythagorean 'Y.' We may wonder about what such an echo means for the future of the Wye River accord and the prospects for peace between Israel and the Palestinians.

> In classical times the philosophers who called themselves Pythagoreans had come to illustrate the 'parting of the ways,' or choice, by means of the Greek letter upsilon, the equivalent of the capital Y of the Latin alphabet. The letter Y can be interpreted as a path that divides, and the image is even better if one arm of the Y is made wide and the other narrow. The one is the 'broad path' of Vice, comfortable, easy, and without problems but leading toward materialism and perdition. The other is the 'narrow path' of Virtue, steep, laborious, thorny, dangerous but at the same time morally the 'right path.' In European decorative art, ornamentation, and allegorical embellishment of the 16th and 17th centuries the letter Y is also sometimes seen. As a rule it symbolizes the difficult choice between virtue and vice, between evil and good, between the easy and the right path. By extension the Y can stand for the freedom of the will and man's responsibility for his own life.[30]

## Agency of the letter

In his thorough reading of Lacan's 'Agency' article, Gilbert Chaitin shows that Lacan's revision of Saussure's hypericon of the sign as 'tree' included not only an anagram ('arbre' = 'barre', the slash of emptiness, the nothing that opens the place that makes possible the human subject), but also the Y. To make his point about the chain in which the 'tree' was but one link, Lacan ran through most if not all the meanings associated with 'tree' culturally and historically: 'Used to stand for the notion of branching, the tree was schematized in the letter Y as the sign of the diverging paths of vice and virtue in a tradition which traced its origin, perhaps mistakenly, to the Pythagoreans.'[31] The mapping of the links between experience and structure consists of letters composed at the scale of this Y or upsilon. The memorials trace the operations of these letters, that 'produce meaning effects in the collective beyond intent, without understanding, without individual consciousness.'[32] In the prosthesis of electracy this discourse becomes legible, available for reading and writing.

It turns out that 'agency' is caught up within a translation detour passing through 'insistence' and 'instance' to the Greek 'enstasis.' Chaitin explains the origin of 'enstasis' as a dialectical procedure in Aristotle's logic by which one adduces a counter-example to refute a claim of universality for a rule. The letter in the unconscious moves Lacan to add a modality to the modalities of the proposition available in logical practice, extending the necessary and the possible to an exception that is an exemption from the rule altogether. Chaitin proposes a new translation of the title – 'the exception of the letter.'[33] The 'agency' in emerAgency is caught up in this play of modalities as well, as part of the shift from the metaphysics of literacy to electracy and a different order of categorization altogether. For us the title might become: 'the virtuality of the letter.' The me-morial probes this new zone by opening the Y within each why.

## Notes

1  Walter Benjamin, *Illuminations*, ed. H. Arendt, trans. H. Zohn, New York: Schocken Books, 1969: 257.
2  Walter Benjamin, *Reflections*, trans. E. Jephcott, New York: Schocken Books, 1978: 85–6.
3  Jacques Lacan, 'Of Structure as an Inmixing of an Otherness Prerequisite to Any Subject Whatever,' in *The Structuralist Controversy: The Languages of Criticism and the Sciences of Man*, ed. Richard Macksey and Eugenio Donato, Baltimore: Johns Hopkins University Press, 1970.
4  Gilbert D. Chaitin, *Rhetoric and Culture in Lacan*, Cambridge: Cambridge University Press, 1996: 163.
5  See Dean MacCannell, *The Tourist: A New Theory of the Leisure Class*, New York: Schocken Books, 1976.
6  Jacques Lacan, 'The Agency of the Letter in the Unconscious or Reason since Freud,' in *Ecrits: A Selection*, trans. Alan Sheridan, New York: Norton, 1977: 151.
7  See W. J. T. Mitchell, *Picture Theory*, Chicago, Chicago University Press, 1994.
8  Lacan, 'The Agency of the Letter': 152.
9  Lacan, 'The Agency of the Letter': 152.
10  Michel Leiris, 'The Sacred in Everyday Life,' in *The College of Sociology, 1937–39*, ed. D. Hollier, Minneapolis: University of Minnesota Press, 1988: 24.
11  Leiris, 'The Sacred in Everyday Life': 26.
12  Ray Monk, *Ludwig Wittgenstein: The Duty of Genius*, New York: Free Press, 1990: 451.
13  See Mitchell, *Picture Theory*.
14  Lacan, 'The Agency of the Letter': 152.
15  See Marita Sturken, *Tangled Memories: The Vietnam War, the AIDS Epidemic, and the Politics of Remembering*, Berkeley: University of California Press, 1997.
16  See Gregory L. Ulmer, 'Sacrificing Music: Electronic Monumentality,' *Semiotexte/Architecture*, 1992: 34–41.
17  See Karen Hermassi, *Polity and Theater in Historical Perspective*, Berkeley: University of California Press, 1977.
18  Richard E. Doyle, *'ATH': Its Use and Meaning*, New York: Fordham, 1984.
19  Simon Taylor, 'The Phobic Object: Abjection in Contemporary Art,' in *Abject Art: Repulsion and Desire in American Art*, New York: Whitney Museum, 1993: 60.
20  John D. Caputo, *Against Ethics: Contributions to a Poetics of Obligation with Constant Reference to Deconstruction*, Bloomington: Indiana University Press, 1993: 30.
21  Caputo, *Against Ethics*: 21.

22  Caputo, *Against Ethics*: 183.
23  Dominick LaCapra, *History and Memory After Auschwitz*, Ithaca: Cornell University Press, 1998: 100.
24  John D. Caputo, *The Mystical Element in Heidegger's Thought*, New York: Oberlin Printing, 1978: 9.
25  See Slavoj Žižek, *The Sublime Object of Ideology*, London: Verso, 1989.
26  Caputo, *Against Ethics*: 72.
27  Jerry Adler, 'Putting Names in the Sky,' *Newsweek*, 13 May 1991.
28  Adler, 'Putting Names in the Sky.'
29  Caputo, *Against Ethics*: 29.
30  Sven Tito Achen, *Symbols Around Us*, New York: Van Nostrand, 1978: 221.
31  Chaitin, *Rhetoric and Culture in Lacan*: 18.
32  Chaitin, *Rhetoric and Culture in Lacan*: 120.
33  Chaitin, *Rhetoric and Culture in Lacan*: 145.

# 14

# STAGING SOCIAL MEMORY
## Yuyachkani

*Diana Taylor*

'In Quechua, the expressions 'I am thinking,' 'I am remembering,' 'I am your thought' are translated by just one word: Yuyachkani,' the noted Peruvian commentator Hugo Salazar del Alcazar wrote in one of his many pieces on the Yuyachkani theater group.[1] The term 'Yuyachkani' signals embodied knowledge and memory, and blurs the line between thinking subjects and the subjects of thought. The reciprocity and mutual constructedness that links the 'I' and the 'you' is not a shared or negotiated identity politics – 'I' am not 'you,' nor claiming to *be* you or act *for* you. 'I' and 'you' are a product of each other's experiences and memories, of historical trauma, of enacted space, of sociopolitical crisis. But what is 'embodied' knowledge/memory, and how is it transmitted? And how does it differ from the 'archival,' usually thought of as a permanent and tangible resource of materials available over time for revision and reinterpretation? What is at stake in differentiating between these systems of organized thought, especially perhaps when thinking about trauma?

The transitive notion of embodied memory encapsulated in 'Yuyachkani' – the 'I am remembering/I am your thought' – entails a relational, non-individualistic understanding of subjectivity. Coya, the indigenous survivor, recounts a vision of annihilation that is and is not her own. The 'I' who remembers is simultaneously active and passive (thinking subject/subject of thought). Yuyachkani, a collective theater group, sees itself implicated – both as product and as producer – in various modes of cultural transmission in an ethnically mixed and complex country. For the past 25 years, the group has participated in at least three interconnected survival struggles – that of Peru, plagued by centuries of civil conflict; that of the diverse performance practices that have been obscured (and at times 'disappeared') in a racially divided, though multiethnic, Peruvian culture; and that of Yuyachkani itself, made up of nine artists who for decades have worked together in the face of political, personal, and economic crisis. In adopting the Quechua name, the predominantly 'white' Spanish-speaking group signals its cultural engagement with indigenous and mestizo populations and with complex, transcultured (Andean–Spanish) ways of knowing, thinking, remembering. Yuyachkani attempts to make visible a multi-

218

lingual, multiethnic praxis and epistemology in a country that pits nationality against ethnicity, literacy against orality, the archive against the repertoire of embodied knowledge. In Peru, the urban turns its back on the rural, and languages (Spanish, Quechua, and Aymara) serve more to differentiate between groups and silence voices than to enable communication. Yuyachkani, by its very name, introduces itself as a product of a history of ethnic coexistence. Its self-naming is a performative declarative announcing its belief that social memory links and implicates communities in the transitive mode of subject formation.

There is a continuum of ways of storing and transmitting memory that spans from the 'archival' to the 'embodied,' or what I will call a 'repertoire' of embodied thought/memory, with all sorts of mediated and mixed modes in between.

'Archival' memory maintains a material core – records, documents, archeological remains, bones – that are resistant to change. The archive preserves Freud's 'permanent memory-trace,' the inscribed piece of paper for those who distrust their memories and want to 'supplement and guarantee its working by making a note in writing.'[2] What changes, over time, is its value, relevance, meaning, how it gets interpreted, even embodied. Bones might remain the same while their story may change – depending on the paleontologist or forensic anthropologist who examines them. *Hamlet* might be performed in multiple ways, while the unchanging text assures a stable signifier. In so far as it constitutes a materiality that endures, the archive exceeds the 'live.'

The repertoire, on the other hand, stores 'embodied' memory – performances, gestures, orature, movement, dance, singing and, I would argue, traumatic flash-backs, repeats, and hallucinations – in short, all those acts usually thought of as ephemeral, non-reproducible knowledge. Unlike archival knowledge and memory, the *thing* does not remain the same. Dances change over time, even though generations of dancers (or even individual dancers) swear they are always the same. Visceral traumatic aftershocks may replay the anxiety associated with the live event without being the event itself. But even though the embodiment changes, the meaning might very well remain the same. Traditional dances, for example, might communicate stable meaning and relevance even with modified moves. However, there is a long tradition, which in the Americas dates back to the conquest, of thinking of embodied knowledge as that which disappears because it cannot be contained or recuperated through the archive. Part of the colonizing project consisted in discrediting autochthonous ways of preserving and communicating historical understanding. As a result, the very existence/presence of these popu-lations has come under question. The *Huarochirí Manuscript*, written in Quechua at the end of the sixteenth century by Friar Francisco de Avila, sets the tone: 'If the ancestors of the people called Indians had known writing in early times, then the lives they lived would not have faded from view until now.' The very 'lives they lived' fade into 'absence' when writing alone functions as archival evidence, as proof of presence. Certainly it is true that individual instances of performances disappear, and can never be 'captured' or transmitted through the archive. A video of a performance is not a performance, though it often comes to replace the performance as a *thing* (a film, a documentary) in itself. Embodied memory, because it is 'live' and uncapturable, exceeds the archive. But that does not mean that performance – as ritualized, formalized, or reiterative behavior – disappears. Multiple forms of embodied acts are always present, though in a constant state of again-ness. They reconstitute themselves – transmitting communal memories, histories, and values from one group/generation to the next. Embodied and performed acts, though they belongs to the repertoire, in themselves record and transmit knowledge through physical movement.

In-between and overlapping systems of knowledge and memory constitute a vast spectrum that might combine the workings of the 'permanent' and the 'ephemeral' in various different ways. The media help shape and circulate knowledges and memories that we internalize as our own. Innumerable practices in the most literate societies still require both an archival and embodied dimension – weddings need both the performative utterance of 'I do' and the signed contract. The legality of a court decision lies in the combination of the live trial and the recorded outcome. Claims are performative as well as legal. We have only to think of Columbus planting the Spanish flag in the 'New World' or Neil Armstrong planting the US flag on the moon. While non- and semi-literate societies have long validated the legitimacy of the performed act (the Mexica married by literally tying the knot between the robes of the bride and groom), the emotional force of the act continues to carry power in literate societies. Same-sex marriages in the US, for example, rely on the performative utterance to bring about the social recognition of a very real union that is not legally recognized as 'contractual.' We transmit events, thoughts, and remembrances not only through our literary writings and documented histories but also through our bodily acts and performances. The techniques of storing, transmitting, and decoding these materials differ, of course, as do the possibilities of access.

Focusing on Yuyachkani's political performance practices, this paper teases apart several interconnected questions central to performance studies, Latin American studies, and psychoanalysis: what is at risk politically in thinking about embodied knowledge and performance as that which disappears? Does trauma, whose very nature 'precludes its registration,' leave no trace because 'a record has yet to be made'?[3] Whose memories 'disappear' if only archival knowledge is valorized and granted permanence? Should we simply expand our notion of the archive to house the mnemonic and gestural practices and specialized knowledges transmitted 'live'? Or is there an advantage to thinking about a 'repertoire' of knowledges performed through dance, theater, song, ritual, witnessing, healing practices, and the many other forms of repeatable behaviors that build on past materials while allowing for the new as something that cannot be understood in terms of the archive? Perhaps the inability to analyze embodied memory as distinct from (though not necessarily oppositional to) archival knowledge has resulted in the eclipse of the former.

Thinking about the interconnections between atrocity, embodied knowledge, and subjectivity proves urgent for the many Latin American populations that have experienced centuries of social trauma. The universalist approaches to memory and trauma that privilege 'the subject' fail to do justice to the accumulative and collective nature of the trauma suffered by illiterate and literate communities and transmitted through embodied performances. For the past 500 years, both writing and embodied performance have often worked together to layer the historical memories that constitute community. Local scribes in the Andes have been keeping written records in Quechua and Spanish since the sixteenth century. Even so, historical and genealogical information has been, and continues to be, performed and transmitted through performed 'memory paths,' as anthropologist Thomas Abercrombie puts it, that access ancestral stories, hearsay, and eye-witness accounts.[4] And as the percentage of literate persons in the Andes has actually *decreased* since the sixteenth century, the need to recognize cultural transmission through embodied knowledge becomes even more pressing. The archive and the repertoire have always been important sources of information, both exceeding the limitations of the other, even in the most literate societies. The relationship is certainly not a straightforward binary – with the written and archival constituting hegemonic power and the repertoire providing the anti-hegemonic challenge. The modes of storing and transmitting knowledge are many and mixed, and embodied performances have often contributed to the maintenance of a repressive social order. We need only look to the broad range of political practices in the Americas exercised on human bodies from pre-conquest human sacrifices, to Inquisitorial burnings at the stake, to the branding of slaves, to contemporary acts of state-sponsored torture and 'disappearances.'

Even though the relationship between the 'archive' and the 'repertoire' is not by definition antagonistic or oppositional, written documents have repeatedly announced the disappearance of the performance practices involved in mnemonic transmission. Writing has served as a strategy for repudiating and foreclosing the very embodiedness it claimed to describe. Friar Avila was not alone in prematurely claiming the demise of practices, and peoples, that he could neither understand nor control. Yet, there was no doubt in the minds of any of the early evangelists that performance practices efficaciously transmitted collective memories, values, and belief systems. Fray Bernardino de Sahagún's sixteenth-century opus, *Florentine Codex*, states that he needed to write down all the indigenous practices in order better to eradicate them: 'it is needful to know how they practiced them in the time of their idolatry, for, through [our] lack of knowledge of this, they perform many idolatrous things in our presence without our understanding it.'[5] An ethnographic approach to the subject matter offered a strategy for handling dangerous practices. It allowed for a simultaneous preservation and disappearance – the accounts preserved 'diabolic' habits as forever alien and unassimilateable, even as they transmitted a deep disgust for behaviors condemned to erasure.[6] 'Preservation' functioned as a call to erasure. A studied, scholarly distancing functioned as affect of repudiation. Yet, even after 50 years of compiling the massive materials on Mexica practices, Sahagún suspected that they had not completely disappeared. The Devil, he concluded, hates transparency, and takes advantage of songs and dances and other practices of indigenous people as 'hiding places in order to perform his works [. . .] Said songs contain so much guile that they say anything and proclaim that which he commands.

But only those he addresses understands them.'[7] The colonist's claim to access met with the diabolic opaqueness of performance. 'And [these songs] are sung to him without its being understood what they are about, other than by those who are natives and versed in this language [. . .] without being understood by others.'[8] Shared performance and linguistic practices, this statement suggested, not only transmitted cultural memory, they constituted the community itself. The spiritual conquest, these friars feared, was at best tentative. The Devil awaits the

> return to the dominion he has held [. . .] And for that time it is good that we have weapons on hand to meet him with. And to this end not only that which is written in this third Book but also that which is written in the first, second, fourth and fifth Books will serve.[9]

Clearly Father Avila and Sahagún and others were ambivalent about preserving information about certain kinds of ritualized behaviors through writing. They want to make available information about these practices in order to stamp them out – that is, put an end to idolatry. Conversely, they want to 'preserve' information about performance practices that would be lost without writing – a preview to 'salvage' ethnography. These early colonial writings are all about erasure – either claiming that these practices are disappearing, or trying to accomplish the disappearance they invoke. Ironically, they reveal a deep admiration for the peoples and cultures targeted for destruction: what Sahagún refers to more than once as 'the degree of perfection of this Mexican people.'[10] And these writings have become invaluable resources as archival data on practices since extinguished. During Sahagún's lifetime, in fact, the Office of the Holy Inquisition decreed that the books were dangerous indeed. Instead of serving as 'weapons' against idolatry, as Sahagún had claimed, they in fact preserved what they attempted to eradicate. The prohibition was outright:

> with great care and diligence you take measures to get these books without there remaining originals or copies of them [. . .] you will be advised not to permit anyone, for any reason, in any language, to write concerning the superstitions and way of life these Indians had.'[11]

Yet for all the ambivalence and prohibitions, these sixteenth-century writers begrudgingly observed something again and again: these practices were not disappearing. They continued to communicate meanings that their nervous observers did not understand.

Again, let me stress that this repudiation of practices under examination cannot be limited to archival documentation. As Barbara Kirshenblatt-Gimblett makes clear in *Destination Culture*, exhibitions, model villages, and other forms of 'live' display often do the same.[12] We need not polarize the relationship between these different kinds of knowledge to acknowledge that they have often proved antagonistic in the struggle for cultural survival or supremacy.

The writing = memory/knowledge equation, central to Western epistemology, continues to bring about the disappearance of embodied knowledge that it so frequently announces. Freud's 'A Note Upon the "Mystic Writing-Pad"' bypasses the historically situated human body in his theorizations on memory. By using the admittedly imperfect analogy of the 'mystic writing pad,' Freud attempts to approximate the 'unlimited receptive capacity and a retention of permanent traces' which he sees as fundamental properties of 'the perceptual apparatus of the mind.'[13] A modern computer, of course, serves as a better analogy, though it too fails to generate memories and its exterior body – a see-through shell in the new Macintosh models – serves only to protect and highlight the marvelous internal apparatus. Neither the mystic writing pad nor the computer allow for a body. So, too, Freud's analogy limits itself to the external writing mechanism and the pure disembodied psychic apparatus that 'has an unlimited receptive capacity for new perceptions and nevertheless lays down permanent – even though not unalterable – memory-traces on them.'[14] The psyche can only be imagined as a writing surface, the permanent trace only as an act of writing. Writing, instead of reinforcing memory, or providing an analogy, becomes memory itself: 'I have only to bear in mind the place where this "memory" has been deposited and I can then "reproduce" it at any time I like, with the certainty that it will have remained unaltered.'[15] Derrida, in 'Freud and the Scene of Writing,' refers to the 'metaphor of writing which haunts European discourse' without expanding towards the idea of a repertoire of embodied knowledge.[16] Even when he points to areas for further research, he calls for a 'history of writing'[17] without noting what that history might disappear in its very coming to light. When he states that 'writing is unthinkable without repression,' the repression that comes to my mind is that history of colonial repudiation through documentation that dates back to Friar Avila. For Derrida, those repressions are 'the deletions, blanks, and disguises' of and within writing itself – surely an act of writing that stages its own history of erasure and foreclosure.

Yuyachkani's work has drawn on Peru's archive and repertoire not only to address the country's many populations but to elucidate the multiply constituted history. Some dance, sing, speak, or otherwise perform historical memory, while others access other versions through literary and historical texts, maps, records, statistics, and other kinds of archival documents. Nonetheless, contradictions abound. How can a group, made up predominantly (but certainly not exclusively) of urban, white/mestizo, middle-class, Spanish-speaking professional theater people think/dance/remember the racial, ethnic, and cultural complexities and divides of the country without minimizing the schisms or mis-representing those who they are not? Who exactly is thinking whose thought? Thought and remembrance, as the name 'Yuyachkani' makes clear, are inseparable from the 'I' and 'you' who think them. As a group made up predominantly of Limeños, does Yuyachkani have access to the memories of the Andean communities? Can it celebrate their fiestas or perform their rituals? Can Yuyachkani tell their story of accumulative social trauma? How to avoid charges of cultural impersonation and 'appropriation?'

One obvious response to this danger of cultural trespassing that threatens practitioners lies in simply turning one's back on the rural indigenous and mestizo populations and tacitly accepting that 'performance' is a European practice carried out by and for white urban audiences in the Americas. The indigenous and mestizo practices, one can argue, belong to a self-contained, parallel circuit of cultural (and economic) transmission – oral, mythic, calendar-based fiestas, rituals, and festivities. 'Theater' practitioners, then, might decide to stick to European repertoires and archives. There are all sorts of staging, lighting, and acting traditions, methods and theories of professional training to choose from. By sticking to this pool, practitioners might either want to distance themselves from the 'non-educated' elements of the population, or signal their fear of appropriating artistic languages that are not their own. Why not do Brecht, still the most honored theater practitioner in Latin America and – ironically – the world's greatest borrower? After 500 years of colonialism, many Latin Americans, especially those from middle-class, urban backgrounds and education, are far more familiar with 'first world' cultural materials that are readily available through the media and publishing circuits than those 'non-reproducible' performances from their own countries. Some acts of 'appropriation' are safer, and potentially less offensive, than others. Class, racial, and linguistic affinities often supersede bonds that grow out of geographical and national interconnectedness.

If, conversely, one acknowledges that indigenous and rural mestizo populations also have deep performance traditions that make up part of the rich repertoires of the Latin American countries, then how do artists from all ethnic backgrounds approach their multiethnic, transculturated traditions? Can they draw from these diverse cultural backgrounds with the same ease with which contemporary European practitioners draw from their recent and distant past? Is this, or any, 'borrowing' unburdened by the political, historical, or aesthetic baggage of 'value' attached to 'style?' Do *criollo* (European Americans) or mestizo performances that include indigenous elements in their work risk turning them into exotic, folkloric add-ons? Performing 'Indian' often reveals some kind of romantic notion of authenticity in festivals, pageants, and national spectacles.[18] It is not difficult to see the dangers of separating performance practices from the people who perform them and from the ideological framework that gave rise to them. How can a theater group such as Yuyachkani dream of avoiding all the representational pitfalls?

Thinking about how performance participates in and across these networks of social memory might allow us to consider cultural participation more broadly. While *criollo*, middle-class Peruvians share innumerable artistic traditions with Europeans, they also clearly participate in the reality of Peru's social, racial, linguistic, and political cacophony. The very categories – 'criollo' and 'Indian' – are a product of that conflict, not its reason for being. 'Indians' were invented, not discovered. 'The people called Indians' are a product of naming. It is through this performative invocation by the colonist that 'Indians' enter the world stage. Their lives, 'faded from view,' become suddenly visible as something else. Performance becomes itself, paradoxically, both through disappearance and re-appearance. Again, it is simplistic to think of 'performance' as somehow embodied and liberating, in opposition to a hegemonic, archival non-performative. The archive, like the repertoire, is full of verbal performances – some that disappear, some that evoke, some that invent their object of inquiry. The naming of the 'people called Indians' both conjured up and disappeared a people. While claiming to give life to a 'fading' population, the naming was an attempt at annihilation – verbally performing the leveling and non-differentiation that the conquest aspired to militarily. The Incas, the Mexica, the Mayans and innumerable other groups suddenly become 'Indians.' The label 'Indian' also erroneously connotes an uncomplicated homogeneity that belies the reality of extensive racial and cultural mixing both before and after the conquest. The manuscript invokes the past of the 'people called Indians,' firm in its belief that social memory is preserved through writing and history and not through orality and embodiment. Their story was the Europeans' to tell, to preserve, to fit into their biblically informed narrative of universal History. Were the 'natives' from India? Were they the lost tribes of Israel? Or even migrant Moors? The same 'scenario of discovery' created the 'white' conquerors – themselves a mixed grouping who came to the Americas only to find the ghosts of their enemies – Jews and Moors – there to haunt them. The conquest in Spanish America continued the re-conquista against the Jews and the Moors back home – a performative resuscitation in the face of very real racial and ethnic diversity. Converted Jews (conversos) and free and enslaved Africans swelled the ranks of newcomers to the American shores. The 'criollo' colonizers proved a mixed group indeed. These antagonistic positions have been polarized and cemented into the social imaginary as biological 'fact.' This way of thinking of lineage and tradition would certainly insist on keeping the various circuits of memory and transmission separate – to each their own. But there is a competing Imaginary – that of the nation state, conjured into being in Latin America during the nineteenth century. National identity, theoretically, supersedes regional or ethnic difference. This model assumes that 'Peruvians' (for example), are a product of, and participants in, mutually constituting historical and cultural processes such as those I have just outlined. However, the national imaginary is shaped not only by what it chooses to remember, but also by what it chooses to forget, as Renan observed over one hundred years ago.[19] 'Perú es un país desmemorizado' (Peru is a de-memorized country) Teresa Ralli, an actor of Yuyachkani told me, and the 'de' captures the violent refusal at the heart of a country that does not recognize or understand the realities of its many parts.[20] Peruvians participate by forgetting, not just by remembering. Therefore it is not a question of *if*, but rather how, they participate.

'Yuyachkani' is a product of complicated national, ethnic, linguistic, cultural memory and thought. Actors Teresa Ralli, Rebeca Ralli, Ana Correa, Débora Correa, Augusto Casafranca, Julian Vargas, Amiel Cayo, the director Miguel Rubio, and the technical director Fidel Melquiades (most of whom have been in the group since it started in 1971) have worked together close to 30 years, a momentous achievement, given the severe economic and political hardships they have faced. Only a few other Latin American collectives – i. e., La Candelaria and TEC from

Colombia – boast similar accomplishments. Yuyachkani makes visible a series of survival struggles culminating in the recent atrocities associated with *Sendero luminoso* (Shining Path) that left some 30,000 people dead and 80,000 homeless. Perhaps as daring, however, Yuyachkani has insistently re-membered Peru as one, complex, racially, ethnically, and culturally diverse country.

The white, Westernized Lima, built with its back to the Andean highlands affords Yuyachkani one of the spaces to stage this re-membering for urban audiences. They perform throughout the city, staging 'public acts' on streets, in schools, on the steps of the national cathedral, in orphanages, cemeteries, jails, and government buildings. This city-wide staging follows the tradition practiced in indigenous and mestizo festivals and fiestas – everyone participates in the procession and festivities by following the actors from place to place, by talking, discussing, celebrating, and being part of the community-wide event. Through the physical performance itself, Yuyachkani invites Limeños to follow the lead of their rural *compatriotas* (compatriots) in recognizing themselves as part of a broader national community.

Yuyachkani also stages street performances in non-theatrical spaces throughout the country. Their *pasacalles* (literally 'through the streets') follow in the indigenous and mestizo custom of theatrical street processions. Recognizable characters from traditional popular culture – musicians, masked figures on stilts, characters from *comparsas* (the bands and dancers) that make up the large-scale fiestas such as Candelaria and Virgen del Carmen, parade through the streets inviting bystanders to join in. These parades, like most indigenous and mestizo performances, end in a fiesta. The *pasacalles* simultaneously affirm the validity and dynamism of these performance practices, and open the arena for intercultural conversation. Drawing from Western models (Brecht's political theater) and Boal's 'theater of the oppressed' as well as Quechan and Aymaran legends, music, songs, dances, and popular fiestas, Yuyachkani's work asks spectators to take seriously the coexistence of these diverse ethnic, linguistic, and cultural groups/traditions. These performances broaden the experience of those who agree to physically follow these actors through all the different spaces. These routes become the new 'memory paths' that allow participants to recognize and bear witness to Peru's history of extermination and resistance, alienation and tenacity, betrayal and remembrance.

When Yuyachkani began working in the early 1970s, the members of the group saw themselves as politically 'committed' popular theater practitioners. Popular theater in the late 1960s and early 1970s, with its *by* the people *for* the people ethos, challenged the systems that placed 'Theater' with a capital 'T' and 'Culture' with a capital 'C' in lofty, aesthetic realms, beyond the reach of working-class people and racially marginalized communities. Nonetheless, popular theater at times presented an oversimplified and programmatic view of conflict and resolution. In Latin America, popular theater sprung up in the wake of the Cuban revolution, animated by Marxist solutions to class/labor struggles. Progressive, at times militant, university students and intellectuals instructed the disenfranchised about how to improve their economic lot or lead a more productive life. Because Marxism privileged class, anti-capitalist, and anti-imperialist struggles to the expense of racial, ethnic, and gender conflict, its implementation by popular theater groups in Latin America ran the risk of reducing deep-seeded cultural differences to class difference. In Peru, and other countries with large indigenous and mestizo communities, the 'proletariat' in fact consisted of indigenous and mestizo groups who lived on the margins of a capitalist society for various reasons – including linguistic, epistemic, and religious differences not reducible (though bound into) economic disenfranchisement. A call for solidarity organized around anti-capitalism allowed for rampant, unthinking trespassing on cultural, ethnic, and linguistic domains. Furthermore, the 'popular,' as understood by some of its activists, became entangled with fantasies of a simple, pure world existing somewhere beyond the grips of capitalism and imperialism.

These problems plagued the initial endeavors of Yuyachkani. The marginalized groups they were addressing in their own country had their own languages, expressive culture, and performance codes that the group knew nothing about. Miguel Rubio recalls their first play, *Puño de Cobre* (1971), staged for miners during a particularly violent strike. The actors, dressed in jeans and T-shirts, played a variety of roles and characters. After the performance, one miner commented: 'Compañeros, that's a nice play. Too bad you forgot your costumes.'[21] 'Much later,' Rubio continues,

> we understood why the miners thought what they did. We had forgotten something much more important than costumes. What they wanted to tell us was that we were forgetting the audience that we were addressing. We were not taking their artistic traditions into consideration. Not only that, we didn't know them!'

Aware that they did not know Peru, or its complex traditions, they committed to remembering this dismembered entity they had believed they knew. Their theater no longer became 'about them' but about envisioning a more complex heterogeneity. They added members from rural communities to their group; the actors learned Quechua; they trained in indigenous and mestizo performance practices that included singing, playing instruments, dancing, movement, and many other forms of popular expression. They expanded the notion of theater to include the popular fiesta that emphasized participation, thus blurring the distinction between actor and spectator. Performance, for Yuyachkani as for other popular theater groups, provided an arena for learning – but here it was Yuyachkani learning 'our first huaylars, pasacalle, and huayno dance steps [;] between beers and warm food, we started to feel and maybe to understand the complexity of the Andean spirit.'[22]

Since those beginnings, Yuyachkani has continued to train in various linguistic and performance traditions to offer a deeper vision of what it means to 'be' Peruvian, one that reflects the temporal, geographical, historical, and ethnic complexity of that articulation. There are many tenses involved in 'to be,' and various ways of situating the 'pre-' and 'post-' (either in terms of 'conquest' or 'modern') depending on who is doing the telling. For Yuyachkani, performance includes the layering, contemporaneousness, and juxtaposition of the diverse traditions, images, languages, and histories found in the country. Poised between a violent past that is never over and a future that seems hopelessly pre-scripted, their performances represent images and scenarios that live and circulate in a variety of systems and forms – from the media, Western theatrical repertoire, children's stories, silent movies, to indigenous myths, songs, and dance performances.

Two of Yuyachkani's best-known pieces, *Contraelviento* (1989) and *Adios Ayacucho* (1990), combine moments from Peru's remote and recent past to reflect on the transmission of traumatic social experience. Developed and performed during the conflict between the military and *Sendero luminoso*, these works specifically engage with the questions I posed earlier – how does the repertoire store and transmit social memory? Whose memories/traumas disappear if we privilege the archive over the repertoire of embodied experience/knowledge? *Contraelviento*, one of Yuyachkani's largest and most spectacular pieces, reenacts the testimony of an *indígena* survivor of a massacre in which peasants were forced off a cliff to their deaths. The performance stages one more traumatic repeat – Coya, in a trance, revisits the scene of devastation. Her body shudders as she reexperiences the intrusive image. An entire community has been annihilated by armed forces. Is that vision an unsolicited reapparition of a traumatic event situated firmly in the past? Is it a witnessing of an atrocious episode in the here and now? Is it the here, now, and always of a violent history of the exploitation and extermination of indigenous peoples? Is it a vision of a future catastrophe? The body responds to and communicates a violent occurrence that may be hard to locate temporally or spatially. Coya's sister and father listen to her testimony. They all understand that a furiously approaching storm will scatter them. Huaco, raging against the violence she sees coming, joins the guerrillas, fighting fire with fire. Papai stays firm to his commitment to find the seeds of life by practicing ancient, invocational rituals. Coya runs to the courts, hoping to find redress through the justice system. The judges – farcical, aged, bent figures with oversize hats who perform a vaudeville version of the pre-conquest comic dance of 'los viejitos' and speak broken English – pretend not to understand her. Her language, represented as flute music, needs to be translated by Peru's famous sell-out character, the Felipillo, translator to the conquerors. 'This woman says that she comes from far away to tell us that her ancestors have told her that the Caporal is killing them . . . She says too that everyone's life is in great danger and that the seeds of life are being destroyed.' The judges dismiss her with a good beating – 'if that woman can't speak, it's because she has something to hide.' This scene elucidates several points in my argument: the courts, an 'archival,' document-producing system that in Latin America serves the interests of the powerful, cannot encompass or 'understand' pleas from the poor. (Official documents, records, and figures relating to genocidal practices hardly ever make it into the national archives.) Institutionalized circuits of memory and transmission keep the Europeanized sectors of the population walled off from the rural mestizo and indigenous populations. Expressions of trauma might just as well be delivered in a foreign tongue.

*Contraelviento* was performed at the peak of militarized conflict in Peru. 'Disappearances' and mass murder had become common political practice in Latin America during the 1970s and 1980s. How, Yuyachkani asked itself, can theater compete with or elucidate the theatricality of political violence? Miguel Rubio sums up the challenge: 'Nothing that you create on stage can be compared with what is happening in this country.'[23] Furthermore, the heightened spectacularity of political terrorism, as I argue elsewhere, forces potential witnesses to look away.[24] It blinds the very spectators that theater calls on 'to see.' What role do artists have when, as Adorno asks, genocide is part of our cultural heritage?[25]

In the most lyrical of forms, *Contraelviento* succeeds in posing the most urgent questions. How can indigenous and mestizo communities address genocidal policies and practices that are often not acknowledged by the national or international community? How can atrocity be 'remembered' and 'thought' when there are no external witnesses, or no recourse to the archive? What is the relationship between the theatrical representation of trauma and the traumatic 'repeat'? Whose memories disappear when scholars and activists fail to recognize the traces left by embodied knowledge?

*Adios Ayacucho* takes the question of witnessing further – the dismembered victim of torture and 'disappearance' is forced to act as sole witness to his own victimization. As the play begins, the members of the audience sees a ramp displaying a suit of clothing and candles laid out in a funerary ritual. Only as their eyes become accustomed to the dim light can they discern movement within a large black plastic bag behind the display. Little by little, a nameless, almost voiceless figure reconstitutes himself and breaks out of the bag. As he tells his story, his voice becomes strong. He was tortured. His tormented body was cut into bits and discarded, in a garbage bag, by the side of the road. In this crime without an external witness, and with no survivors, no one but he himself can demand that justice be served. No documents, photos, or gravestones attest to his annihilation. Only his bones, shoved in plastic, serve as archival 'proof' of an event that left no other material evidence. Only through performance can 'disappearance' be rendered visible. Here, then, we have the sociohistorical challenge to the psychoanalytic formulation that 'performance becomes itself through disappearance': disappearance, as Latin American activists and artists know full well, becomes itself through performance.[26]

Yet while no external witnesses exist in *Adios Ayacucho*, the play affirms the vital role of what Dori Laub calls the 'the witness from inside' or 'the witness to oneself.'[27] This witness from inside, though impossible according to Laub in the context of the Holocaust that 'made unthinkable the very notion that a witness could exist,'[28] because it allowed for no 'outside,' no 'other,' is nonetheless posited as the only hope for justice in the Andean context. The victim reconstitutes himself by finding his scattered body parts. Little by little, he reclaims his human form. Finally he finds his face, finally he finds his voice that will proclaim the violence done to him and his community. He not only voices his denunciation, over and over again, but he determines to take a letter to the President of the Republic, outlining the violence he has suffered. This letter, finally, will make it into the archive, a testimony that even the President might acknowledge of the erasure of mestizo and indigenous populations. This haunting image from *Adios Ayacucho* suggests the way in which Yuyachkani layers its approach to representing violence. The clothes laid out in memory of the dead re-presents the missing body of the victim of disappearance, even as it echoes an ancient burial practice. These practices are alive; other bodies will perform them just as the man fits himself back into the waiting clothes. Andean performance practices, this shows, are not dead things, fading from view. Nor do they function in a parallel universe. These traditions continue to allow for immediate responses to current political problems. Every response to political violence carries with it a history of responses, conjured up from a vast range of embodied and archival memories. For Yuyachkani, performance is not about going back, but about keeping alive. Its mode of transmission is the repeat, the reiteration, the yet again of the twice-behaved behavior that Richard Schechner defines as 'performance.'[29] The violence of the past has not 'disappeared.' It has reappeared in the violent response against the miners' strike (1971), the massacre of Soccos (1986), in the displacement of local populations caught between *Sendero* and government forces, on the empty streets of Lima in the 1980s and early 1990s, torn and made strange by the violence. The remembering was always past, present, and seemingly future. As Rebeca Ralli puts it, their work represents the struggle for survival of the Peruvian people even as it represents their own struggle to survive both as individuals and as a group. 'We put up with so much just to be able to live, just to be able to create.'[30]

Yuyachkani's performances make visible a history of cumulative trauma, an unmarked and unacknowledged history of violent conflict. As in *Adios Ayacucho*, the attempts at communicating an event that no one cares to acknowledge need to be repeated again and again. Part of the reiteration stems from the traumatic nature of the injury. Cathy Caruth argues that the obsessive repeats occur because 'the event is not assimilated or experienced fully at the time, but only belatedly, in its repeated *possession* of the one who experiences it. To be traumatized is precisely to be possessed by an image or event.'[31] The same, Caruth's proposes, occurs with historical understanding: 'For history to be a history of trauma means that it is referential precisely to the extent that it is not fully perceived as it occurs.'[32] Trauma produces dislocation, a rupture between the experience and the possibility of understanding it. But trauma, as Caruth's notes, 'opens up and challenges us to a new kind of listening, the witnessing, precisely, of *impossibility.*'[33] For members of traumatized communities, such as the Andean ones Yuyachkani engages, past violence blends into the current crisis. The trauma of the persecuted and deracinated indigenous and mestizo populations is a 'symptom of history,' as Caruth puts it: 'The traumatized, we might say, carry an impossible history within them, or they become themselves the symptom of a history that they cannot entirely possess.'[34] As in *Adios Ayacucho*, trauma becomes transmittable, understandable, through performance – through the reexperienced shudder, the retelling, the repeat.

The retelling and reenactment, however, pose problems of legitimacy. While the performances capture the ongoing nature of the violence against indigenous peoples, it complicates a historical accounting. What is time without progression? What is space without demarcation? What happens to a people's concept of history when markers are few, or known only through a performative repeat?

Most writing on atrocity insists on fixing the time and place of the traumatic wounding. Situating the event in a temporal and spatial frame establishes that vital 'outside' that Laub refers to – the space in which witnessing can take place. The telling of atrocity tends to unfold as narrative, setting the stage to enable the act of bearing witness, however retroactively, even to events that had no witnesses.[35] The traumatic *re*call is performative – i.e. a *living through*, 'repossessing one's life story through giving testimony [which] is itself a form of action, of change, which one has to actually pass through.'[36] Each attempt at communication is also a repeat, as the person who survived the trauma tries to transmit it to another person outside the experience – the one who bears witness and accepts the burden of performative contagion. Like performance, the recounting involves bracketing, framing, setting up the scene. 'Listen to this,' says the victim, the narrator, the testimonial writer. 'Look at this,' say the survivors who return to the place, the *lieu de mémoire*,[37] or the photographers, playwrights and film makers who need us to recognize something with our mind's eye, if not first-hand with the eye itself. In trauma, the past is replayed in the present – both as a symptom of distress (as in flashbacks), and as part of the healing process (reclaiming the experience).

The undifferentiated, reiterative nature of Peru's traumatic history folds seamlessly with the Andean paradigm of memory (summed up in the Inkarrí cycle), which defies the fixity of a before and after:

> Inkarrí's dismembered body (whose severed head has been taken, variously, to Cusco, Lima or Spain) is coming together again, underground [....] The lower world, region of chaos and fertility, becomes the source of the future, an extension of the belief that the dead return to present time and space during the growth season.'[38]

Faced with the consciously deployed strategy of colonial dis-memberment, the myths offer the promise of re-membering. 'Perú es un país desmemorizado,' as Teresa Ralli put it. Who can say, after 500 years of ongoing conquest and colonization, where the memory of trauma is situated, whether trauma affects 'the subject' or the entire collectively, if it is experienced belatedly or continually embodied, whether it resides in the archive or only in the repertoire, and how it passes from generation to generation? We only know from myths and stories that Peru's indigenous populations see themselves as the product of conquest and violence. Violence is not an event but a worldview and way of life.

Yuyachkani, it seems to me, intervenes in this problematic in two fundamental ways – one having to do with the transmission, the other with the role and function of witnessing.

In regard to the first: Yuyachkani understands the importance of performance as a means of re-membering and transmitting social memory. Its use of ethnically diverse performance traditions is neither decorative nor citational – that is, Yuyachkani does not incorporate them as add-ons to complement or 'authenticate' its own project. The group's commitment to enter into conversation with rural populations has led them to learn the languages, the music, and the performance modes of these communities. Rather than attempt to restore specific behaviors, i.e. recreating museum pieces that somehow dislocate and replicate an 'original,' they follow the traditional usage of reactivating ancient practices to address current problems or challenges. Moreover, Yuyachkani does not participate in the reproduction and commodification of 'popular' culture. Their texts do not circulate. Other actors or companies do not perform their plays. The only way one can access their work is by participating in it – on the streets as bystander caught up in the action, in Casa Yuyachkani as spectator and discussant, or in the many workshops open to students from around the world. New, younger members are joining the group and they, too, are Yuyachkani. They will not act 'like' Yuyachkani, but 'be' Yuyachkani, adopting and adapting the character of the group itself. Their performances, just like the performances they draw from, are inseparable from them as people. The 'I' who thinks and remembers is the product of these collective pre- and post-colonial performances.

Furthermore, unlike groups that appropriate the performance practices of others, Yuyachkani's work does not separate the performances from their original audiences but, rather, tries to expand the audiences. The productions are not about 'them' – the indigenous and mestizo 'others' – but about all the different communities that share a territorial space defined by pre-conquest groups, colonialism, and nationalism. Yuyachkani attempts to make their urban audiences culturally competent to recognize the multiple ways of being 'Peruvian.' In addressing Lima audiences, however, Yuyachkani feels it has to start 'from zero.'[39] The country's theatrical memory, much like its historical, cultural, and political memory, has been deracinated. These performances remind urban audiences of the populations they have forgotten. Storing and transmitting these traditions prove essential, because when they disappear, certain kinds of knowledges, issues, and populations disappear with them. These traditions – the street procession, fiestas, songs, masked characters – bring together *criollo*, mestizo, Afro-Peruvian, and indigenous expressive elements, each vital to the deeply complicated historical, ethnic, and racial configuration of the actual political situation. Performance provides the 'memory path,' the space of reiteration that allows people to replay the ancient struggles for recognition and power that continue to make themselves felt in contemporary Peru.

This brings us to a second point: looking at performance as a retainer of social memory engages history without necessarily being a 'symptom of history' – that is, the performances enter into dialogue with a history of trauma without themselves being traumatic. These are carefully crafted works that create a critical distance for 'claiming' experience and enabling, as opposed to 'collapsing,' witnessing.[40] This performance event has an 'outside,' which is what, according to Laub, allows for witnessing. Yuyachkani, as its name indicates, hinges on the notion of interconnectedness – the 'I' who thinks/remembers is inextricable from the 'you' whose thought 'I' am. The 'I'/'you' of Yuyachkani promises to be a witness, a guarantor of the link between the 'I' and the 'you,' the 'inside' and the 'outside.' Yuyachkani becomes the belated witnesses to the ongoing, unacknowledged drama of atrocity, and asks their audience to do the same. For this reason, no doubt, Yuyachkani was awarded the highest national honor for Human Rights in 1999. The group's practice points to a radically different conclusion than the one Adorno arrived at in 'On Commitment.' Representation, for Yuyachkani, does not further contribute to the desecration of the victims, turning their pain into our viewing pleasure.[41] Rather, without representation, viewers would not recognize their role in the ongoing history of oppression which, directly or indirectly, implicates them. Who, *Adios Ayachuco* asks, will take on the responsibility of witnessing? The witness, like Boal's 'spect-actor' accepts the dangers and responsibilities of seeing and of acting on what one has seen. And witnessing is transferable – the theater, like the testimony, like the photograph, film or report, can make witnesses of others. The (eye) witness sustains both the archive and the repertoire. So rather than think of performance primarily as the ephemeral, as that which disappears, Yuyachkani insists on creating a community of witnesses by and through performance.

These understandings of the political and historical importance of performance counter the performance as pathology model that assumes in theory, at least, that the need for repetition disappears when the wounding is healed. Treatments for post-traumatic stress disorder try to minimize the anxiety and depression that are triggered by flashbacks.[42] A successful outcome, in the best of all possible worlds, would mean the end of the performative repeat. At the same time, Yuyachkani counters the performance-as-disappearance of colonialism, that pushes autochtho-nous practices into the oblivion of the ephemeral, the unscripted, the uncontrollable. For many of these communities, on the contrary, when performance ends, so does the shared understanding of social life and collective memory. Performances such as these fiestas, testimony, and theatrical productions warn us not to dismiss the 'I' who remembers, who thinks, who is a product of collective thought. They teach communities not to look away. As the name Yuyachkani suggests, attention to the interconnectedness between thinking subjects and subjects of thought would allow for a broader understanding of historical trauma, communal memory, and collective subjectivity.

This piece, of course, is destined for the archive.

## Notes

1 Hugo Salazar del Alcazar, 'Los músicos ambulantes.' *La escena latinoamericana*, no. 2, August 1989: 23. This essay, created in conversation with photographs taken by Miguel Villafañe, is dedicated to Hugo's memory.
2 Sigmund Freud, 'A Note Upon the "Mystic Writing Pad",' *The Standard Edition of the Complete Psychological Works of Sigmund Freud*, London: Hogarth Press, vol. XIX, 227.
3 Cathy Caruth, quoting Dori Laub, in the Introduction to her edited collection, *Trauma: Explorations in Memory*, Baltimore: Johns Hopkins University Press, 1995: 6.
4 Thomas A. Abercrombie, *Pathways of Memory and Power: Ethnography and History Among an Andean People*, Madison: University of Wisconsin Press, 1998: 6.

5  Bernardino de Sahagún, *Florentine Codex*, ed. and trans. Arthur J. O. Anderson and Charles E. Dibble, Santa Fe, NM: School of American Research and University of Utah, 1982: 45.

6  See Steven Mullaney's *The Place of the Stage*, Ann Arbor: University of Michigan Press, 1988, for an analysis of 'the spectacle of strangeness' and the politics of repudiation (particularly Ch. 3, 'The Rehearsal of Cultures').

7  Sahagún, *Florentine Codex*: 58.

8  Sahagún, *Florentine Codex*: 58.

9  Sahagún, *Florentine Codex*: 59.

10  Sahagún, *Florentine Codex*: 47.

11  Sahagún, *Florentine Codex*: 36–7.

12  Barbara Kirshenblatt-Gimblett, *Destination Culture: Tourism, Museums, and Heritage*, Berkeley: University of California Press, 1998: 162.

13  Freud, 'A Note Upon the "Mystic Writing-Pad"': 229.

14  Freud, 'A Note Upon the "Mystic Writing-Pad"': 228.

15  Freud, 'A Note Upon the "Mystic Writing-Pad"': 227.

16  Jacques Derrida, 'Freud and the Scene of Writing,' in *Writing and Difference*, trans. Alan Bass, Chicago: University of Chicago Press, 1978.

17  Derrida, 'Freud and the Scene of Writing': 214.

18  See, for example, the essays in the issue 'Performance, Identity, and Historical Consciousness in the Andes,' ed. Mark Rogers, of *Journal of Latin American Anthropology*, 3 (2), 1998, especially the essay by Mark Rogers, 'Spectacular Bodies: Folklorization and the Politics of Identity in Ecudadorian Beauty Pageants.'

19  Ernest Renan, 'What is a Nation?' in Homi Bhabha, ed., *Nation and Narration*, London: Routledge, 1990: 11.

20  Personal interview, Paucartambo, Peru, July 1999.

21  Miguel Rubio, 'Encuentro con el Hombre Andino,' *Grupo Cultural Yuyachkani, Allpa Rayku: Una experencia de teatro popular*, Lima: Edición del 'Grupo Cultural Yuyachkani' y Escuelas Campesinas de la CCP, second edition, 1985: 9.

22  Cited in Brenda Luz Cotto-Escalera, 'Grupo Cultural Yuyachkani: Group Work and Collective Creation in Contemporary Latin American Theatre,' unpublished dissertation, University of Texas, Austin, 1995: 116.

23  Cited in Cotto, 'Grupo Cultural Yuyachkani': 156.

24  Diana Taylor, *Disappearing Acts: Spectacles of Gender and Nationalism in Argentina's 'Dirty War'*, Durham: Duke University Press, 1997.

25  Theodor Adorno, 'Commitment,' in *Aesthetics and Politics* (ed. E. Bloch *et al.*), London: Verso, 1977: 189.

26  Peggy Phelan, in *Unmarked: The Politics of Performance* (London and New York: Routledge, 1993) offers a psychoanalytic analysis of the 'ontology of performance' proposing that 'Performance's being, like the ontology of subjectivity proposed here, becomes itself through disappearance' (147). As I argue elsewhere (in 'Downloading Grief: Minority Populations Mourn Diana,' in *Mourning Diana: Nation, Culture and the Performance of Grief*, ed. Adrian Kear and Deborah Lynn Steinberg, London and New York: Routledge, 1999), I come to the appearance/disappearance quality of performance from a different, though related, angle.

27  Dori Laub, 'Truth and Testimony: The Process and the Struggle,' in Caruth, *Trauma: Explorations in Memory*: 66.

28  Laub, 'Truth and Testimony': 66.

29  Richard Schechner, *Between Theater and Anthropology*, Philadelphia: University of Pennsylvania Press, 1985.

30  Interview, Rebeca Ralli, Casa Yuyachkani, June 1996.

31  Caruth, *Trauma: Explorations in Memory*: 4–5.

32  Caruth, *Trauma*: 8.
33  Caruth, *Trauma*: 10.
34  Caruth, *Trauma*: 5.
35  Shosana Felman and Dori Laub, *Testimony: Crisis of Witnessing in Literature, Psychoanalysis, and History*, New York: Routledge, 1992: 85.
36  Laub, 'Truth and Testimony': 70.
37  Pierre Nora, *Les lieux de mémoire*, Paris: Gallimard, 1984. Quoted in Dominick LaCapra, *History and Memory After Auschwitz*, New York: Cornell University Press, 1998: 10.
38  William Rowe and Vivian Schelling, *Memory and Modernity: Popular Culture in Latin America*, London: Verso, 1991: 55.
39  Rubio, *Allpa Rayku*, also quoted in Cotto, 'Grupo Cultural Yuyachkani': 115.
40  See Cathy Caruth's *Unclaimed Experience*, Baltimore: Johns Hopkins University Press, 1997, and Dori Laub's notion of the 'collapse of witnessing' in 'Truth and Testimony': 65.
41  Adorno, 'On Commitment.'
42  I want to thank Rebecca Schneider for this observation and for the several conversations we have had over the years on the concept of the 'archive.'

# INDEX